University of London Historical Studies

XVIII

UNIVERSITY OF LONDON HISTORICAL STUDIES

I. HUGH TINKER. *The Foundations of Local Self-Government in India, Pakistan and Burma.* 1954

II. AVROM SALTMAN. *Theobald, Archbishop of Canterbury.* 1956

III. R. F. LESLIE. *Polish Politics and the Revolution of November 1830.* 1956

IV. W. N. MEDLICOTT. *Bismarck, Gladstone, and the Concert of Europe.* 1956

V. JOHN LYNCH. *Spanish Colonial Administration, 1782–1810: The Intendant System in the Viceroyalty of the Rio de la Plata.* 1958

VI. F. H. W. SHEPPARD. *Local Government in St. Marylebone, 1688–1835.* 1958

VII. R. L. GREAVES. *Persia and the Defence of India, 1884–1892.* 1959

VIII. M. J. SYDENHAM. *The Girondins.* 1961

IX. MARGARET HOWELL. *Regalian Right in Medieval England.* 1962

X. N. M. SUTHERLAND. *The French Secretaries of State in the Age of Catherine de Medici.* 1962

XI. GWYN A. WILLIAMS. *Medieval London: from Commune to Capital.* 1963

XII. CHARLES DUGGAN. *Twelfth-century Decretal Collections and their Importance in English History.* 1963

XIII. R. F. LESLIE. *Reform and Insurrection in Russian Poland, 1856–65.* 1963

XIV. J. A. S. GRENVILLE. *Lord Salisbury and Foreign Policy.* 1964

XV. P. W. J. RILEY. *The English Ministers and Scotland, 1707–27.* 1964

XVI. J. F. BOSHER. *The Single Duty Project: A Study of the Movement for a French Customs Union in the Eighteenth Century.* 1964

XVII. JOAN MCDONALD. *Rousseau and the French Revolution, 1762–1791.* 1965

XVIII. IAN H. NISH. *The Anglo-Japanese Alliance: The Diplomacy of Two Island Empires, 1894–1907.* 1966

THE ANGLO-JAPANESE ALLIANCE

This volume is published with the help of a grant from the late Miss Isobel Thornley's Bequest to the University of London

THE ANGLO-JAPANESE ALLIANCE

The Diplomacy of Two
Island Empires
1894-1907

by

IAN H. NISH

UNIVERSITY OF LONDON
THE ATHLONE PRESS

Published by
THE ATHLONE PRESS
UNIVERSITY OF LONDON
at 2 Gower Street London WC1
Distributed by Constable & Co Ltd
12 Orange Street London WC2

Canada
Oxford University Press
Toronto

U.S.A.
Oxford University Press Inc
New York

First edition, 1966
Reprinted, 1968

485 131188

First printed in Great Britain by
THE ALDEN PRESS
Oxford
Reprinted by photo-litho by
WILLIAM CLOWES AND SONS LTD
London and Beccles

ACKNOWLEDGMENTS

I SHOULD like first to acknowledge the gracious permission of Her Majesty the Queen to make use of material from the Royal Archives, Windsor Castle.

I am grateful to the following persons for allowing access to, and giving permission to quote from, the archives under their charge: the Marquis of Salisbury and the librarian, Christ Church, Oxford, for the papers of the third Marquis; the librarian, Birmingham University Library, for the Chamberlain papers; the Trustees, Mitchell Library, Sydney, for the Morrison papers; the Trustees, National Maritime Museum, Greenwich; and the Navy Department, Ministry of Defence. Unpublished crown-copyright material in the Public Record Office, London, is reproduced by permission of the Controller of H.M. Stationery Office. I have also to thank the Trustees of the British Museum for permission to consult the Balfour papers under their charge and the librarian, Cambridge University Library, for access to the Hardinge papers there.

I wish to convey my thanks to the staffs in these and other libraries where I have worked for their many courtesies.

My research was aided by the University of Sydney which generously granted me funds for the purchase of photographed material necessary for the preparation of this volume. For their assistance in financing its publication, I am grateful to the Principal and Councillors of St Andrews College within the University of Sydney and to the Trustees of the Isobel Thornley Bequest.

I should like to thank Professor W. G. Beasley, Professor of Far Eastern History, University of London, Professor Alun Davies, Professor of International History, University College, Swansea, and Professor W. N. Medlicott, Stevenson Professor of International History, University of London, who have encouraged my researches and judiciously commented on the present work in manuscript. A special debt is due to Professor Beasley, under whose supervision this study was prepared in one of its earlier manifestations as a thesis for the University of London.

Anyone who is foolhardy enough to enter the field of Japanese studies has to depend greatly on the labours of Japanese scholars and I am very conscious of my obligation to them. Among the many instances of co-operation which I have received, I should mention especially the help of Professor Oka Yoshitake of the University of Tokyo and Professor Imai Shōji of the Tokyo Foreign Languages University in making available to me material on the alliance. For assistance with translations, I am grateful to Professor Endoh Shinichi of Kagawa University and Professor Sugiyama Chūhei of Shizuoka University. For errors of fact and interpretation, I alone must be held responsible.

It remains only to express my thanks to the staff of the Athlone Press who have with great good nature guided me away from many pitfalls.

I. H. N.

London School of Economics
and Political Science
September 1965

CONTENTS

Abbreviations   xi
Introduction   1

PART I

The Background to the Alliance, 1894–1900

   I.   The Three Powers threaten Japan   23
  II.   The Powers take Compensation   46
 III.   Japan's Discreet Advances   63
 IV.   Britain, Japan and the Boxers   80

PART II

The First Alliance

   V.   The Anglo-German Agreement and Manchuria   99
  VI.   Germany, Russia and the China Problem   124
 VII.   A British Initiative   143
VIII.   The Alliance will be Pursued   163
  IX.   The Japanese Cabinet *versus* Itō   185
   X.   The First Alliance Concluded   204
  XI.   The New Alliance Considered   229

PART III

War with Russia and the Second Alliance

  XII.   Japan in Korea and Manchuria   247
 XIII.   Japan approaches Russia   262
 XIV.   The Russo-Japanese War   283
  XV.   The Alliance under Review   298
 XVI.   The Bargain Clinched   323
XVII.   Results of the Second Alliance   345
       Conclusion   365

Appendix: Translated Documents 378
Bibliographical Note 393
Select Bibliography 400
Index 414

MAPS

1. East Asia *facing page* 23
2. North-east Asia *facing page* 99

ABBREVIATIONS

BD	*British documents on the origins of the war, 1898–1914*, ed. G. P. Gooch and H. W. V. Temperley
DDF	*Documents diplomatiques français*
Fisher papers	Kemp, P. K. (ed.), *The papers of Admiral Sir John Fisher*
FO	Foreign Office, General correspondence, deposited in the Public Record Office, London
GP	*Die grosse Politik der europäischen Kabinette, 1871–1914*, ed. J. Lepsius, A. Mendelssohn-Bartholdy and F. Thimme
Hayashi Memoirs	Pooley, A. M. (ed.), *The secret memoirs of Count Tadasu Hayashi*
Inoue-den	*Segai Inoue-kō den*
Itō-den	Kaneko Kentarō, *Itō Hirobumi den*
Itō-hiroku	*Itō Hirobumi hiroku*, ed. Hiratsuka Atsushi
Katō	Itō Masanori, *Katō Takaaki*
Katsura-den	Tokutomi Iichirō, *Kōshaku Katsura Tarō den*
Letters of Spring Rice	Gwynn, S. (ed.), *The letters and friendships of Sir Cecil Spring Rice*
Meiji hennen shi	*Shimbun shūsei Meiji hennen shi*, ed. Nakayama Yasumasa
Mutsu-ikō	Mutsu Hirokichi, *Hakushaku Mutsu Munemitsu Ikō*
NGB	*Nihon gaikō bunsho* ('Japanese diplomatic documents')
Yamagata-den	Tokutomi Iichirō, *Kōshaku Yamagata Aritomo den*

Japanese names have been rendered with the surname or family name preceding the personal name in accordance with normal Japanese practice.

Introduction

THE signing of the Anglo-Japanese alliance in London on 30 January 1902 was a recognition of the importance which the far east had assumed in international affairs since 1895. It was also of unique significance for the two powers directly concerned. It was Japan's first alliance with a European power and therefore a token that she had reached the ranks of the world powers. For Britain, it was a departure from conventional policy, although it is a subject of dispute how far-reaching this was. It was a means by which the burden of maintaining the Pax Britannica, which had been the major external force in the far east since at least 1860, could be shared with another power. Important as it was to the signatories individually, it was important also as a contribution towards solving the most serious east Asian problem of the day, the weakness of Manchu rule in China and the desire of the powers to turn this to their own benefit. To this end, the treaty of alliance declared that Britain and Japan would co-operate to ensure that China was not deprived of her territory by the powers and especially by Russia. It was therefore part of an anti-Russian front in Asia.

Its importance was a continuing one. The first treaty of 1902 was revised during the Russo-Japanese war in 1905. It was revised again in 1911 and renewed for one year in 1920. It came to an official end only in 1923 as a result of the discussions at the Washington conference. Only a small portion of that history — the anti-Russian phase from 1902 to 1907 — is surveyed in this volume. In order to throw light on the state of relations between the two countries before the first alliance, the Sino-Japanese war of 1894 has been taken as the starting-point. In this introduction, it is necessary to examine the relationship between Britain and Japan at that time after almost forty years of contact.

Sir Claude MacDonald, who was Britain's representative in Tokyo for much of the alliance period, described it as 'that formal Alliance between the Island Empires of the East and the West'[1] — a phrase which has suggested the sub-title of this book. His phrase emphasizes the naval factor which was one aspect of the alliance throughout its history. Not only did the navies support the alliance, but the alliance also underwrote naval power in the Pacific. It was fitting, therefore, that it should be brought to an end at the Washington conference which was primarily convened to discuss naval disarmament.

DIPLOMACY IN JAPAN AND BRITAIN

In the years before the Sino-Japanese war, Japan had the reputation of being an up and coming nation speedily acquiring the attributes and machinery of western progress. She already had an efficient army and navy, a competent centralized administration and a growing industry. She seemed to be an apt pupil of the west. Since the Emperor Meiji had been enthroned in 1868, she had undertaken a systematic modernization under the skilled direction of a group of statesmen who had all come under some form of foreign influence. The most celebrated of these reforms was the constitution granted by the emperor to his people in 1889. From this time onwards, Japan had a Diet of two houses in which political parties were active. But this did not imply the advent of parliamentary democracy. Although parties had been set up early in the 1880s and were adept at public agitation, it was not the intention of those behind the constitution that parties should dominate the country's politics or that the prime minister should be the leader of the majority party in the Diet or should depend on it for support. Indeed, party cabinets were rare until 1900 and were not imperative even after that date. Thus, although Japan could claim to have many of the trappings of westernization and to have introduced many of its essential elements, she was certainly not operating within the liberal parliamentary tradition.

Japan was as ready to adopt western practices in the field of foreign relations as she was in the sphere of political organization. Since the Japanese had entered into diplomatic relations with foreign powers only since 1854, the Meiji administrators had had to build appropriate institutions from scratch. But they had set up a ministry of foreign

[1] C. M. MacDonald, 'The Japanese detachment during the defence of the Peking legations, June–August 1900', *Trans. Proc. Japan Society (London)*, no. 12 (1913–14), 19.

affairs and a diplomatic service without the reluctance which their counterparts in China showed. The new department or Gaimushō was set up in 1869; and the office of foreign minister (gaimu daijin) was established in 1885.[1] The minister was to be a senior minister, a member of the cabinet and was expected to have served abroad in a diplomatic capacity. With a few exceptions he was therefore a bureaucrat rather than a politician. By the 1890s he was assisted by a vice-minister, who was also an ex-diplomat, as head of the Foreign Ministry bureaucracy. Overseas Japan had diplomatic and consular representation from the early 1870s. Her practice was not strikingly different from that of other countries and was indeed devised with the help of foreign legal advisers, notably the Americans, Erasmus P. Smith for the period 1871–80 and Henry W. Denison for the period 1880–1914.[2]

In the making of foreign policy, the prime minister retained much practical control. Of course the independence, which a foreign minister enjoyed, varied with his personality and that of the premier. Since, however, the foreign minister was generally a prominent professional diplomat who had to be recalled from abroad to his new post and was not always conversant with home affairs or home politics, it was inevitable that he should be dependent upon the advice of the prime minister. On important aspects of policy the cabinet would be consulted, though consultation seems to have been less frequent than was the case in Britain. This might be expected within a system of government which was bureaucratic rather than democratic. In the period covered by this study, decisions would often be left to a sort of inner cabinet which generally included the prime minister, foreign minister and the war and navy ministers. In the main, the cabinet endorsed the recommendations of the prime minister and, when opposition arose, it came from outside the cabinet.

There were other institutions which affected the conduct of foreign affairs. Under the Meiji constitution of 1889, it was laid down that sovereignty vested in the emperor and that 'the respective Ministers of State shall give their advice to the Emperor and be responsible for it'. The Emperor Meiji, who was capable and experienced, was not often called upon to decide issues but he was consulted on important matters

[1] The best account in English is to be found in Takeuchi Tatsuji, *War and diplomacy in the Japanese Empire*, ch. 8.

[2] For a note on Denison, Shigemitsu Osamu, 'Nichi-Ei dōmei' ('Anglo-Japanese alliance') in *Kindai Nihon gaikōshi no kenkyū*, being studies presented to Professor Kamikawa, pp. 213–14.

of government policy. In emergencies such as the outbreak of war or the conclusion of peace or on major issues such as the making of a treaty, the emperor might, before giving his sanction, insist on consulting his advisers. By the later Meiji period these had come to be known as the genrō or Elder Statesmen, a loose body of leading statesmen who had taken part in the Meiji Restoration and had since guided the country's affairs. The genrō had no place in the constitution and owed their power to imperial prerogatives. Their main function had since 1892 been the vital one of advising the emperor on the person who might be appointed as the next prime minister, a person who until 1898 was invariably selected from among their number. They were gradually changing the form of their institution and broadening its functions. Since there were tensions among the Elder Statesmen, they were by no means a united group and were frequently critical of the ministry in power. While the genrō can be criticized as an extra-constitutional device, they did in practice introduce a review procedure on major aspects of policy by a group which contained much of the country's military, financial and diplomatic talent.

The prerogatives of the emperor could sometimes be turned to the advantage of the cabinet. By passing off their acts as those of the emperor, they could shelter behind the throne. Thus in 1895, when the ministers were forced to accept terms at the hands of the three powers which were generally regarded as humiliating, the decision was announced in the form of a rescript from the emperor which it would have been improper to dispute. The Meiji emperor was thus a factor in foreign policy-making but it cannot be said that he either invariably supported the ministry or habitually questioned its actions.

In view of the active role which the army and navy came to play in policy-making in more recent Japanese history, it is necessary to consider how influential they were at this time. It is first desirable to distinguish between three groups within the services: the army and navy ministers, the service chiefs and the 'military bureaucrats'. Within the cabinet, the war and navy ministers had a strong position and a growing voice in the formulation of foreign policy where it touched upon military interests. The strength of their position lay in the provision laid down in army and navy regulations in May 1900 that ministers and vice-ministers must be active service officers.[1] Thus they acted with the authority of the high commands. Through them the

[1] Yanaga Chitoshi, *Japan since Perry*, New York, 1949, p. 121.

service chiefs obtained a voice in affairs, although they had in any case the right of direct access to the emperor as commander-in-chief and the right of taking part in Imperial Conferences. In these ways the army and navy did have some say in the formulation of policy; but there is as yet no evidence that they exercised a sinister influence. Thus, during the negotiations for the Anglo-Japanese alliance, the navy was one of its strongest supporters but its views were voiced by the navy minister in the ordinary way. It would be wrong to read the character of Japanese politics in the 1930s into the situation of the 1900s.

Where the army and navy obtained rather special representation for their views was among the genrō. The clans which controlled the services also dominated the genrō council. It is possible to speak of the genrō being made up of 'civil bureaucrats' and 'military bureaucrats'. These terms are to some extent imprecise and unsatisfactory[1] but they rightly indicate that any policy which was accepted by the genrō, had been debated by the military leaders and in most cases met with their approval. But it would be misleading to suggest that there existed anything in the nature of a 'military party' at this time. In the existing state of national development, there was no politician who could afford to neglect the army or the navy; the only point of difference was over the amount of expenditure to be allocated to them. In these circumstances, there was no need for a military party. Many of the foreign policy issues during this period of expansion were strategic problems and it would have been unthinkable for the army and navy to have had no views. But in practice their views on China, Manchuria and Korea found expression quite effectively through existing channels.

It is illusory to look at Japanese policy at this period for constant elements or consistent themes. Japan was governed from 1894 till at least 1902 by a succession of short-lived cabinets, each with its own notions on foreign policy. While their policies doubtless had less variety than if they had been truly party cabinets, still they each had their idiosyncrasies. For all the elements of continuity which had grown up around the emperor and which the bureaucrats had written into the Meiji constitution, the degree of continuity in government was not marked during this period. There was, for example, no co-ordinated

---

[1] R. Scalapino, *Democracy and the party movement in prewar Japan*, Berkeley, 1953, p. 159, which contains the best account in English. See also J. A. S. Grenville, *Lord Salisbury and foreign policy: the close of the nineteenth century*, pp. 390–3; and Rōyama Masamichi, *Seijishi* ('Political history'), Tokyo, 1941, pp. 347–8.

B

view on the problem of a continental policy. Japan's foreign policy at
this time has to be regarded as a struggle between competing forces.

It is not necessary to analyse the structure of British policy-making
which has been ably described elsewhere.[1] But it must be observed that
there was not the same contact between London and Tokyo as there
was with the European capitals. While there was of course the telegraph
its undue use was discouraged by the parsimonious habits of the
Foreign Office and the Treasury.[2] Endeavours were always being
made to improve the cable systems in the Pacific. But the standard
channel of communication was still the dispatch, which took five weeks
to reach London from the far east via Suez or four weeks by the
Canadian Pacific Railway route though the time in transit was in due
course reduced to three weeks by the opening of the Trans-Siberian
Railway. What was most affected by the distance was the personal
contact between the Foreign Office and its representatives abroad:
representatives in the far east could not, as was the practice in Europe,
return at regular intervals for discussions at Whitehall. This was
unquestionably a disadvantage. But there were compensating advantages. There was not the complication of royal intervention which
occasionally altered the course of Britain's diplomacy with Europe,
where there were royal family ties and royal tours. Nor were there
many politicians or cabinet ministers with a knowledge of the far east.
This seems to have given the Asiatic Department of the Foreign Office[3]
a degree of independence which few other departments enjoyed and
seems to have allowed its permanent officials a greater measure of
specialization. Not that they were a law unto themselves over far-
eastern policy. Japan and the China problem were part of the larger
canvas of Britain's imperial interests where the Colonial Office and
Admiralty had to be consulted. And, since far-eastern policy was
closely linked to Russia's expansion in Asia, the departments responsible for the defence of India — the India Office and the War Office —
could not be ignored.

[1] Zara Steiner, 'The last years of the old Foreign Office, 1898–1905', *The Historica
Journal*, 6 (1963), 59–90.

[2] Even *The Times* rebuked its Peking correspondent for sending his reports too often
by telegraph as late as 1909. See the papers of George Ernest Morrison, *The Times*'s
correspondent in Peking, 1897–1912, deposited in the Mitchell Library, Sydney, 312/81,
3 April and 15 December 1909 (hereafter cited as 'Morrison papers').

[3] The Asiatic Department of the Foreign Office, more often described as the China
Department, was separated from the American Department in 1899 and dealt with the
business of China, Japan and Siam.

BRITAIN AND JAPAN BEFORE 1894

Like any other international device, the Anglo-Japanese alliance has to be considered in two aspects: first, the relations between the two countries directly concerned; second, the whole diplomatic situation existing within the relevant area at the time. On the one hand, it is hard to conceive of an effective and durable alliance coming into existence without a measure of friendship and a sense of common interest between the parties to it. Hence a study of the alliance cannot afford to ignore the relations between Britain and Japan on the broadest plane, whether military, industrial or commercial. At the same time, Anglo-Japanese relations were only a part of the complex network of international relationships in east Asia where the future of the Chinese Empire was being shaped. Let us consider first the state of feeling between Britain and Japan before the Sino-Japanese war in 1894.

Since 1868 there had been much mistrust of Britain in Japan. This was not unnatural. The Japanese considered that their country was insecure and vulnerable to attack from the sea; if Japan were to be attacked by any foreign power, it was likely to be by Britain, the strongest naval power in the far east. Moreover Britain pursued what seemed to the Japanese to be oppressive policies towards Japan.[1] On the other hand, Japan could not risk a disagreement with Britain. There were occasions when Britain's position could be turned to Japan's advantage. Such an occasion occurred in 1874 when Britain was able to mediate between China and Japan over a dispute in Formosa and to bring the two parties together to reach an agreement.[2]

The relationship of the two powers was more fruitful in the industrial than in the political sector. It was the main aim of the new Japanese government to modernize the country; and naturally it could not ignore Britain as the most economically developed country in the world. Japan's industrial missions, which went overseas, naturally sought advice in Britain where the industrial revolution had first taken root in Europe. In 1870 and 1873 the Japanese government concluded railway loans in Britain as the leading financial centre and a place with a zest for railway investment. Britain was ready to co-operate in these ventures in order to influence the Japanese in her favour.

[1] Kajima Morinosuke, *Nihon gaikō seisaku no shiteki kōsatsu* ('Historical reflections on Japan's foreign policy'), p. 49.

[2] *Nihon gaikō bunsho* ('Japanese diplomatic documents'), vol. 5, Ministry of Foreign Affairs, Tokyo, 1939, no. 194. Through the good offices of Wade, the British minister in Peking, a Sino-Japanese treaty was signed on 31 October 1874 (this series is hereafter cited as '*NGB*').

Britain was also eager to take a share in the modernization of Japan's military institutions for reasons of international rivalry, if for no other. Most European powers were trying to play some part in the reform of Japan's army and navy. The Japanese army was taken in hand first by French advisers and later, in the 1880s, by the Germans. The British government was invited to assist in the organization and training of the Japanese navy and agreed to do so. The new fleet was first placed under the guidance of Royal Navy officers who were seconded to act as instructors at the Tokyo naval college from 1873 to 1882. Thereafter it was possible, and indeed quite common, for individual officers to stay on as advisers. It was also common for Japanese naval officers to visit Britain for training: these included Tōgō Heihachirō, the victor of the battle of the Japan Sea, who studied at Greenwich Naval College from 1871 to 1878. The fact that these officers were trained on British ships and with British equipment had its effect on naval building: from 1870 to 1900 most Japanese battleships were built in British yards. France did some of the building and undertook the planning of the naval dockyards at Yokosuka; but this was short-lived. The collaboration with Britain was a continuing one, whose results are difficult to assess in political terms. But it is safe to conclude that Japanese naval officers as a group were favourable to Britain and that the creation of a modern navy in Japan by 1894 was due largely to the efforts and technical co-operation of Britain.[1]

It was essential for Japan's modernization and industrialization that she should engage in foreign trade. She required not only machinery, rolling stock and capital goods but also a wide range of raw materials. Naturally her imports were greater than her exports throughout the period of this study. Japan's trade figures for the not untypical year 1902 are given below:

Country	Exports		Imports	
	in yen	%	in yen	%
British India	13,336,895	5.16	50,977,168	18.76
Hong Kong	25,876,059	10.01	2,454,881	0.90
United Kingdom	17,346,149	6.72	50,364,029	18.53
France	27,283,458	10.56	4,745,776	1.75
United States	80,232,805	31.06	48,652,825	17.90
Germany	4,737,029	1.83	25,812,921	9.50

one yen = two shillings sterling approximately

[1] M. D. Kennedy, *Some aspects of Japan and her defence forces*, pp. 31–47.

As can be seen from these figures, the United Kingdom trade with Japan was one-sided: Britain's imports from Japan were much smaller than her exports to Japan and were very small by comparison with those of France and the United States. Britain's trade, however, cannot be realistically calculated without including the figures for British India and Hong Kong. When these are taken together, it is apparent that Britain had a considerable trade with Japan and the disparity between exports and imports is to some extent evened out. Moreover, Britain valued her stake in Japanese trade because of international competition in the far east.[1] Even so, her trade with China was probably five or six times the volume of her Japanese trade which was thus of much less significance to her. For their part, the Japanese found it convenient to trade with Britain and the British Empire though they were by no means dependent on it. All in all, the existence of a sizeable trade between the two countries led to a certain amount of cordiality but did not have great political significance.

British opinion was divided over Japan's modernization. There were many who recognized that Japan was a developing country with a strong central government, a growing industry and an increasing capacity for trade and who were prepared to assist in her development. But it was natural that there should come a time when this turned into a challenge to Britain herself as it did in the 1890s over shipping routes. A different view was expressed by the British merchants in the Japanese treaty ports or by the institutions at home, like the China Association, which defended their interests. They were sceptical of the modernization because they detected behind it so many remnants of the old Japan; they were aware of the anti-foreign feeling in Japan and expected at any moment a recurrence of the violence of pre-Restoration days which would be directed against themselves. They found it hard to recognize Japan's progress for, indisputable as it now seems, it was then less conspicuous than the instability of the rapidly changing governments. These groups argued for a policy of caution until the Japanese governments showed more signs of political stability.

Down to 1894, Britain's policy towards Japan was largely concerned with the maintenance of her treaty rights. It was precisely these that successive Japanese governments under pressure from xenophobic groups were trying to remove; and it was only natural that a running

[1] A. Stead (ed.), *Japan by the Japanese*, pp. 408–9.

battle should result. Britain had concluded the treaty of Edo in 1858, which defined the rights of British merchants on the same lines as those enjoyed in China: treaty ports, extra-territorial rights, and most-favoured-nation privileges for all trading countries. Thereafter, Britain's affairs were dominated by Sir Harry Parkes, her minister in Japan for sixteen years (1868–83). He was noted for the air of hauteur and condescension which he adopted towards the Japanese and left the impression that Britain had scant sympathy for the new Japan. Parkes was also considered to be the greatest obstacle to Japan's attempt to have her early treaties revised, though in the time of Parkes's successors, Britain's image in Japan improved: she seemed to become more accommodating and to be ready to make compromises with Japan's nationalist demands for treaty revision.

In 1893, the foreign minister, Mutsu Munemitsu, decided to grasp the nettle and attempted once again to revise Japan's so-called 'unequal treaties'. His strategy was to negotiate secretly with Britain a treaty which would remove her right of extra-territorial jurisdiction alto-gether. Despite a serious outburst of anti-foreign agitation in Japan, the British foreign secretary confirmed on 12 January 1894 that Britain would move in a leisurely manner towards revising her treaties.[1] This decision to support Japanese aspirations was not taken wholly from altruistic motives. Britain wanted to prevent the Japanese government from denouncing these treaties as the opposition was urging and thus depriving her nationals of these benefits. Britain was also trying to gain the co-operation of the Japanese government in keeping Russia out of Korea. Against this background, the Anglo-Japanese commercial treaty was finally signed on 16 July 1894. It postponed the ending of extra-territorial rights until 1899 but it did prepare the way for the immediate introduction of an *ad valorem* tariff. This set the pattern for Japan's later treaties with the United States, Russia and Germany, and with other countries with whom trade was smaller. It gave Japan an incentive to proceed with the introduction of a revised civil code and that portion of the commercial code, which remained incomplete, and thus to proceed further with her modernization.

Despite the fact that the commercial treaty was soon forgotten in

---

[1] Foreign Office, General Correspondence, *Japan*, vol. 445, minute by Rosebery, 12 January 1894 (hereafter cited as 'FO *Japan*'). I have dealt with this issue in more detail in my paper, 'Japan reverses the unequal treaties', *Papers of the Hong Kong International Conference on Asian History, 1964*, no. 20.

the outbreak of the war with China, it was an important turning-point in Japanese history. One official, Aoki Shūzō, who had taken a leading part in the negotiations, wrote that 'we may congratulate ourselves on having at one blow swept away the disgrace of the last 30 years and with one stride entered into the "Fellowship of Nations"'.[1] It was also a turning-point in Britain's attitude towards Japan. Sir Edward Grey, then parliamentary under-secretary at the Foreign Office, wrote that the government acted because 'the time had come when dealings with Japan might be put on the same equal terms as exist between nations of European origin'.[2] This was a great advance. While it was not a move towards an alliance, it is hard to see how a satisfactory alliance could have been achieved without the removal of Britain's extra-territorial privileges.

PRIVATE ADVOCATES OF AN ALLIANCE

If the history of the Anglo-Japanese alliance were merely a record of views which advocated an alliance, this study might start as early as the 1870s and become filled with talk of an alliance which appeared in the press in the 1890s. It was fashionable for nationals of either country who travelled to the other to express sentiments of goodwill long before the alliance was finally concluded. Often these were merely the sentimental reactions towards Japan which were common among Europeans at this time and had no political significance. But there were shrewd observers on both sides who saw the similarities between the two island empires; and it was by no means uncommon for them to describe Japan as Britain's 'natural ally'.[3] Moreover there was in Britain a patronizing admiration for Japan and her modernization which seemed to represent the culmination of the utilitarian and *laissez-faire* spirit which was still respected in commercial circles. Of course, the Japanese also had their critics but even they saw some merit in a political alignment between Britain and Japan.[4] It is hard to know

[1] *NGB* 27/I, no. 56, report by Aoki Shūzō, 19 July 1894.
[2] E. Grey (Viscount Grey of Fallodon), *Twenty-five years, 1892–1916*, i, 23.
[3] S. Gwynn (ed.), *The letters and friendships of Sir Cecil Spring Rice*, i, 145–6 (hereafter cited as '*Letters of Spring Rice*', Rice to Ferguson, 28 May 1893: 'In England we regard [Japan] as a practical joker. . . . The general feeling in Japan is that England is her natural ally.'
[4] J. Walton, *China and the present crisis*, pp. 257–90, especially p. 282. Walton, a Liberal M.P., argued that there was need for Japanese-Anglo-American co-operation but he was critical of Japanese mercantile ethics.

how important these advocates were because they were rarely politicians in office or diplomats in service and they hardly ever took the
trouble to formulate their ideas in detail.

On the British side, those who advocated an alliance without being
in a position to affect the course of events included a number of
journalists. One was Sir Edwin Arnold, publisher and one-time editor
of the *Daily Telegraph*. Then there was the Printing House Square
group: (Sir) Valentine Chirol, foreign editor of *The Times* from 1899,
Frank Brinkley, its correspondent at Tokyo from 1894, and Dr Ernest
Morrison, its correspondent at Peking from 1897. All three were
undoubtedly in favour of an alliance and frequently made this the
theme of their articles. The most influential of them was Chirol who
was in 1905 saluted by Theodore Roosevelt, the president of the
United States, as one of the originators of the alliance.[1] Chirol with his
vast experience as a diplomatic correspondent had the ear of the
Foreign Office and, when he paid visits to the far east in the eventful
years 1895, 1898 and 1901, authoritative reports from his pen were
published. He saw no prospect that Britain would obtain the co-
operation in the east of any other powers and became convinced of the
value of an alliance with Japan in 1901; but how he convinced the
Foreign Office of this — if he did — is not known.[2]

The idea can also be traced in the writings of that select circle of
politicians who travelled widely. It is interesting that Sir Charles Dilke,
when he originally wrote *Greater Britain* in 1875, foresaw that 'a time
will come when Japan might be a useful ally to us in the Pacific'.[3]
Another politician was Admiral Lord Charles Beresford, who visited
the far east in 1899 and advocated, like Dilke, an Anglo-Japanese
alliance which might be extended to China. He gave publicity to this
view in the book he wrote on his journeys.[4] In 1892, after a period in
office as under-secretary for India, George Curzon journeyed to the
east and recounted his findings in articles for *The Times* and later in
Problems of the far east. He did not mention the desirability of an
alliance with Japan, although he thought highly of the progress being
made there. 'Friendly relations between ourselves and Japan', he wrote,
'will assist her in that mercantile and industrial development, in which

[1] V. Chirol, *Fifty years in a changing world*, pp. 208–9.
[2] V. Chirol, *Far eastern question*, p. 193. 'If we are to hold our own in the Far East,
it is upon ourselves alone that we must rely.' Also, ibid., p. 195.
[3] C. Dilke, *Greater Britain*, London, 1875, p. 576.
[4] C. Beresford, *The break-up of China*.

she is following in our own footsteps, at the same time that it will confirm to us the continued command of the ocean routes'; Britain is, and can remain, 'the first Power in the East'; granted the continuance of peace, which Britain is not likely to break, she will be greater still.[1] Through these writings, Curzon acquired a reputation as an authority on the east; and, as under-secretary at the Foreign Office (1895–8), he was able to put his knowledge to some purpose. His standpoint like that of Dilke and Beresford appealed to those who were attracted by the call of imperialism.

Among Japanese statesmen, there was a group with experience of Britain. But the Japanese travellers were not the dilettante memoir-writers of late Victorian Britain who surveyed from a lofty eminence the upper crust of Chinese and Japanese society and rhapsodized about the scenery; they were men who had gone to Britain for training or for visits of inspection, who saw the grimy, sooty factory cities and reported on how far they should be reproduced in their homeland. Such men were Itō Hirobumi, Inoue Kaoru and Mutsu Munemitsu. These were men without illusions or sentimentality about Britain, although they retained an affection for her. Others were there for longer periods, mainly for education or in the diplomatic service, but few returned to Japan with pronounced pro-British feelings.[2]

Essential to the development of a favourable attitude towards Britain was the founding of the newspaper *Jiji Shimpō* in 1882. This was the act of Fukuzawa Yukichi, who had travelled widely in Europe from 1860 to 1867 and become imbued with much of the utilitarianism and liberalism then prevalent in Britain. He gathered around him at Keio a group devoted to economic and political thought in which English influence was marked. The newspaper *Jiji Shimpō* was the source of Fukuzawa's influence. Its editorials were more pro-British than those of any other newspaper; and, being an independent news-paper, it commanded great influence when all around was the 'yellow press'. This paper was used by those who favoured a British alliance,

---

[1] G. N. Curzon, *Problems of the far east*, pp. 413 and 426.

[2] For example, Mōri Arinori (1849–89) had been a student at London and later served as minister to London (1880–5). He was a protégé of Itō and was invited by him to return to Japan to reframe the education system but died long before the alliance became a practical issue.

More pro-British were Baron Suematsu Kenchō, minister of the interior (1900–1), who had been educated at Cambridge in the 1880s, and Baron Kikuchi Dairoku, minister of education (1901–5), who was also a Cambridge graduate.

like Katō Takaaki and Hayashi Tadasu, as a channel of publication for their articles.[1] There is also evidence that its offices were used as a rendezvous for sympathizers with these views.[2]

Thus the call for an alliance was heard from time to time in both countries. It was important after 1895, but it was not influential in the period before the Chinese war because its advocates rarely had the ear of government.

CHINA AND THE POWERS

The Anglo-Japanese alliance has implications, however, which are broader than the relationship between Britain and Japan. It grew eventually out of the situation in the far east as a whole: the need for an alliance was felt because it seemed necessary for them to have a common policy in China, Manchuria and Korea in order to resist the actions of the other powers there. It is necessary, therefore, to analyse the international situation in the far east in 1894.

In China the emperors of the Manchu dynasty had ruled since 1644. The zenith of their power had been reached in the eighteenth century but later the dynasty was content to stay on the throne and to rule in the traditional ways without seriously facing the challenge of modernization. For the better part of two decades China was in a state of turmoil from the Taiping rebellion which was not finally defeated until 1864. This uprising brought to the fore the economic dissatisfaction of the peasants, the hostility of the gentry and the animosity of the Chinese towards an alien dynasty; and these together almost succeeded in overturning the dynasty. But the Manchus managed to reassert their authority in the period of the 'T'ung-chih restoration' (1862–74) and took steps towards consolidation and modernization. They put down the great Muslim rebellions of the south-west in the 'seventies and re-established their suzerainty in the outlying tributary states of Indo-China, Tibet and Korea. They also set up armies and navies with modern weapons and western-style ordnance factories.

[1] Katō and Hayashi, who are both prominent in this study, were in Britain at formative stages of their lives. Katō (1860–1926) worked in Liverpool and London from 1883 to 1885. Hayashi (1850–1913) visited Britain as a student in 1866–7 and returned as minister in 1900. Both were relatives of Fukuzawa Yukichi.

[2] When Dr Morrison discussed a possible Anglo-Japanese alliance with Hayashi, who was then waiting to set off as minister to London, they met at the *Jiji Shimpō* offices in Tokyo. Morrison papers 312/60, 8 March 1900. See also A. M. Pooley (ed.), *The secret memoirs of Count Tadasu Hayashi*, p. 111 (hereafter cited as '*Hayashi memoirs*').

Their major test was to come with the Japanese war of 1894-5. Among the powers, there were those who prophesied China's doom before the war began but most were prepared to suspend judgment until the clash took place. It was soon plain that the Chinese northern fleet could not compare in quality, leadership or strategic understanding with the Japanese. When the army also collapsed, China was soon defeated and quickly came to be regarded as the 'sick man of Asia'. This was all the more ominous because the wave of expansion of the European powers which had started in the 1880s in Africa and the south Pacific, had absorbed most of the available territories there; and the danger arose that the powers might be tempted to take advantage of China's 'sickness' by diverting their energies to the orient. Britain, as the supreme power in the far east since 1860, had hitherto dissuaded others from making serious inroads into China proper and encouraged the growth of a stable administration. But Britain was no longer unchallenged there, as Russia took the lead in a new wave of expansionism. China had already suffered when the straggling branches of her empire — Indo-China in 1885 and Burma in 1886 — were lopped off the trunk. After 1895 China herself was in even greater peril.

The eastward expansion of Russia had taken place most significantly under the remarkable proconsulship of Nikolai Nikolaevich Muraviev, governor-general of east Siberia between 1857 and 1861. By the time of his retirement, he had established outposts on the Pacific, especially at Vladivostok, and had organized settlements along the Amur river. But his hopes were not fulfilled because the task of colonization without adequate land or sea transport from European Russia was formidable. For this reason the Russians seem to have concentrated until 1884 in central Asia, especially on the borders of Afghanistan, where their activities caused alarm to the authorities in British India. According to Dr Malozemoff, Russia's land forces in the far east at this time numbered only 15,000 men of whom 11,000 were stationed in the immediate neighbourhood of Vladivostok.[1] Considering the vast areas involved, this was a small force. But a new era had clearly arrived with the decision of the tsar in 1887 to proceed with the survey for a trans-Siberian railway. This reflected a shift of Russian interest to east Asia. In 1891 the building of the railway was inaugurated. Not only did the new means of communication offer the opportunity of stepping up the rate of colonization in Siberia but it also gave Russia a channel for

[1] A. Malozemoff, *Russian far eastern policy, 1881-1904*, p. 24.

increasing her armed forces in that area. There is evidence that this was accompanied by a more active diplomatic interest in the affairs of China, though many of Russia's ambitions could only be accomplished in the long term and had no obvious immediate effects.[1]

Russia could not embark on the trans-Siberian railway project without enlisting the support of French capital. This was assisted by political events when the Russian government entered with France into, first, an entente (1891) and, later, an alliance (1894). These arrangements offered political and defensive co-operation and smoothed the way for financial partnership. The question was how far the alliance would apply to the far east. The French had defeated the Chinese in the Indo-China war of 1884–5, had annexed Tongking as the price of peace and were penetrating into Siam and south China. But they were chary of extending their activities to northern or central China and of becoming involved in Russian adventures in Manchuria. They did not consider the alliance to be binding on them in the northern far east. Be that as it may, the other powers had to assume that France and Russia were working together in the far east and especially that their naval strength was being pooled.

Other powers were less active in China prior to 1894. Germany and the United States were already carrying on a considerable seaborne trade with the far east; but, apart from the American interest in Korea, they were not showing a particular political interest there. They had both taken territories in the south Pacific in the 1880s but had not yet built up their naval strength in Chinese waters or given any indication of their ultimate intentions there.

In the decade before the Sino-Japanese war, much international attention was focused on China's tributary territory, Korea. Korea had been opened to trade by the Japanese treaty of 1876. Since the appointment of Yuan Shih-k'ai as China's resident at Seoul in 1883, Japan had found herself increasingly opposed to China in the peninsula. When the situation seemed grave in 1885, they managed to avert war by signing the treaty of Tientsin which laid down that both powers should withdraw their troops and, in the event of disturbances recurring in the peninsula, should give written notice before sending forces there. The Korean king, naturally unwilling to be browbeaten by Japan or China, was persuaded by members of his court to turn towards Russia, which shared a frontier with Korea and had in 1884

---

[1] Cf. T. H. von Laue, *Sergei Witte and the industrialisation of Russia*, New York, 1963.

signed a commercial treaty with her. It suited Russia well to be invited to interest herself in Korean affairs. Rumours were at this time often circulated that Russia was seeking as a reward for her protection an ice-free port in south Korea for her far eastern squadron.

It was this that provoked an incident, which was of some importance in Anglo-Japanese relations. Under the impression that Russia was intending to take the lease of Port Lazareff (Gensan) on the east coast of Korea, the British government sent a naval squadron to occupy Port Hamilton on an islet off south Korea on 15 April 1885. Its avowed object was to check Russia's far eastern policy and to discourage her from taking possession of any naval base in Korea.[1] Russia made no countermove during the crisis; and it is claimed that she had no intention of making any forward move at this time.[2] Indeed she gave China an undertaking that, if Britain were induced to leave Port Hamilton, she would guarantee not to occupy any Korean territory, a guarantee which was to be of continuing importance down to 1904. When Britain received this undertaking from Korea and the suzerain power, China, she withdrew from Port Hamilton in February 1887.[3]

What light does the Port Hamilton incident throw on British policy in the far east? It suggests that there was an irrevocable rivalry with Russia there and that Britain was much concerned with Korea. If this was true of Britain's attitude in 1885, it did not hold good for the 1890s. Partly Britain learnt the lesson of the Port Hamilton incident; partly her leaders saw the need to give Russia some latitude in the far east. Britain had two major interests in Asia: the Indian Empire and the China trade. The first greatly outweighed the second. Both were affected by Russia's expansion in Asia; and it was thought that Britain's interests would best be served if Russia's attention were diverted from India. This could best be attained by not exaggerating Anglo-Russian rivalry in the far east. Similarly, Britain hereafter took only a secondary interest in Korea and Russia's actions there. The spirit of Port Hamilton never returned.

The Japanese had an ambivalent attitude towards this episode. On the one hand, they did not want to have the Royal Navy in a position

---

[1] E. V. G. Kiernan, *British diplomacy in China, 1880–5*, ch. 13. Also F. H. Conroy, *The Japanese seizure of Korea, 1868–1910*. Since the taking of Port Hamilton followed closely after Russia's seizure of Panjdeh on the border of Afghanistan on 30 March, it may have been inspired by the possibility of an Anglo-Russian war.

[2] Malozemoff, p. 30.

[3] Malozemoff, p. 32.

permanently to dominate the Straits of Tsushima. They told Britain during the crisis that they were most disturbed about Port Hamilton because the waters near Japan would become the centre of a dispute between the powers and it would only have the result of encouraging Russia to occupy Port Lazareff (Gensan) or Fusan.[1] On the other hand, they did not wholly regret Britain's willingness to involve herself against Russia. The Japanese were perfectly aware that Russia's ambitions were more likely to clash with those of Japan than were those of Britain. They had claimed to have a stake in Korea since the 1870s but had found their way barred by China and Russia. That Britain should take Russia's ambitions in the Korean peninsula so seriously as to occupy Port Hamilton secretly pleased Japan's leaders at a time when they considered their army and navy too weak to challenge Russia.[2] As the situation continued to be critical, the Japanese ministers discussed among themselves the possibility of practical co-operation with Britain. Ōkuma Shigenobu as foreign minister, wrote in January 1889 that Japan was now acquiring naval and military power which would commend her to Britain as an ally.[3] These ideas were carried one stage further under the succeeding ministry presided over by Yamagata Aritomo with Aoki Shūzō as foreign minister. They were much exercised over the attitude to be adopted towards Russia. In an exchange of memoranda round about May 1890, they explored the possibility of Japan allying herself with Britain and Germany in the far east. Yamagata was troubled with the prospect of Russia's position when the Trans-Siberian Railway was completed and favoured some combination in which the three powers could co-operate to secure their common interests against Russia.[4] He even approved overtures being made to this end. But, so far as can be traced, no formal approach was made; and the proposal probably perished with the collapse of the Yamagata ministry in May 1891.

From this it is clear that before 1894 there existed within Japanese government circles a group which favoured some arrangement with Britain. Individuals within the group changed their views from time to time. But there was a hard core of politicians who were consistently anti-Russian and reverted to these ideas when they returned to office.

[1] *NGB* 18, no. 335, Inoue to Kawase, 13 June 1885.
[2] Ōyama Azusa, 'Yamagata Aritomo ikensho' ('memorandum by Yamagata, home minister in Itō's cabinet, January 1888'), *Kokusai seiji*, no. 3 (1957), 186–92.
[3] *NGB* 22, no. 3.
[4] Ōyama, loc. cit., 192–5.

Yet, as on later occasions, the Japanese government fought shy of making overtures to Britain. British ministers, for their part, were not conscious of the need for any rapprochement with Japan until the defeat of China at the hands of the Japanese stimulated the powers to greater activity in east Asia. It was then that they became aware how far Britain's position of ascendancy in the far east had declined. It was already clear to some observers that the powers were 'too anxious to extend their European disputes to the East' and that 'the old concerted action is impossible'.[1] For all their rivalries, the powers had in the past managed to achieve some measure of co-operation on major issues in their dealings with China and Japan. So long as these dealings mainly concerned extra-territorial rights, the powers found it possible to stand together to promote their own interests. In this situation, Britain had the largest voice. Now, however, that extra-territorial rights in Japan were being given up, rivalries were increasing and the powers were seeking concessions in the east. Concerted action became impossible; and Britain's authority declined. On the other hand, disunity among the powers was not unwelcome to those in Japan who were looking forward to the day when their country could adopt a more independent foreign policy.

In the period before 1894, there had not been outright hostility between Britain and Japan, just as there had not been great warmth. Both in their direct relationship and in the context of international affairs, their governments were distant but not unfriendly. Their relations were distant in the sense that Britain could devote little attention to the affairs of Japan while Japan was only marginally interested in Europe. Whatever may have been the case among the merchants, relations at government level were not unfriendly as was shown by the commercial treaty of 1894. But, when war began between Japan and China, a new situation arose which gave a new dimension to their relations and introduced a new element of urgency.

[1] *Letters of Spring Rice*, i, 146, Rice to Ferguson, 1 August 1893.

PART ONE

The Background to the Alliance
1894–1900

I am very much impressed with Japan as a power, and it will be interesting to see what it turns out to be — bubble or nugget.

Cecil Spring Rice to Ronald Munro
Ferguson, 28 May 1893
*The Letters and Friendships of
Sir Cecil Spring Rice*, i, 145

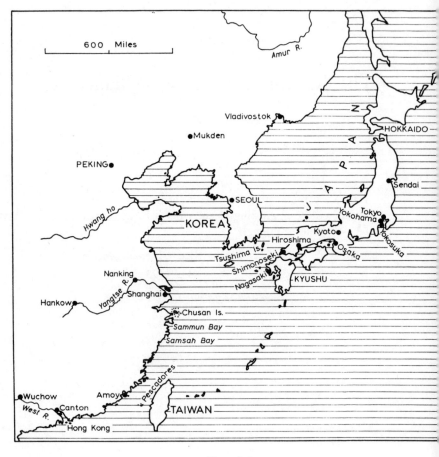

1. East Asia

CHAPTER I

The Three Powers threaten Japan

1894-1896

THE war with China was an intense experience for the developing Japanese state. The anxious excitement in August 1894 when Japan challenged the Middle Kingdom with all its resources of men and material, was soon followed by the exhilaration of victories. But even the decisive successes on land and sea were not without their tribulations, because the Japanese leaders knew that the more successful their country was, the more likely were the European powers to intervene. It will be the purpose of this chapter to consider the intervention of three of these powers and to indicate the state of Anglo-Japanese relations which had an important bearing on Japan's decisions during the crisis.

When war was declared on 1 August 1894, affairs were governed in Japan by the Itō ministry (1892–6) and in Britain by the Liberal ministry of Lord Rosebery (1894–5). Count Itō Hirobumi, one of Japan's Elder Statesmen, presided over a 'cabinet of all the talents' and was fortunate in having a skilful foreign minister, Mutsu Munemitsu. But his ministry was no more stable than that in Britain. After the defeat of his Home Rule bill for Ireland in March 1894, Gladstone had resigned the premiership and been succeeded by the foreign secretary, Rosebery. It was therefore left to a new foreign secretary, Lord Kimberley, to take the responsibility for Britain's decisions on far eastern policy in the testing period which followed.

BRITAIN AND THE SINO-JAPANESE WAR

It is first necessary to examine the view that the British government was anti-Japanese at the outbreak of the war. Since it had as recently as 16 July concluded the far-reaching commercial treaty, it does not seem to have had any basic prejudices against Japan. If it had been as pro-Chinese as is sometimes alleged,[1] it could have put pressure on Japan by withholding its signature from the treaty.

Kimberley prepared several schemes to prevent the outbreak of a war over Korea, where the Japanese were trying to advance their position against the suzerain power, China. But both China and Japan took up inflexible attitudes. On 28 June, Kimberley told Japan that the Chinese were asking for the good offices of Russia to solve the Korean problem and warned her that if she persisted in her present attitude, it could only lead 'to a serious quarrel in which Russia will be the only gainer'.[2] Russia took up China's invitation and informed Japan on 30 June that she would bear a great responsibility if she did not withdraw her troops. The Japanese decided to turn down the advice of both and to force China to yield. Kimberley accused Japan of unreasonably refusing discussions with China and, in a final effort, tried to secure the withdrawal of both armies in Korea to opposite sides of the 38th parallel. But it was too late for events were rushing towards war. There can be little doubt that Britain laid the failure of her mediation at the door of Japan, rather than China.

The Japanese were uncertain how pro-Chinese the British government was. Mutsu resented the protests which Kimberley had made but did not aggravate the situation. The Japanese minister in London was confident that he was having some success in keeping Britain detached from China. He was trying to convince British opinion that it was necessary for Japan's security that its army, either separately or together with China, should occupy Korea and claimed that he was 'using' *The Times*, *Daily Chronicle* and *Daily Telegraph* to that end. He was, he said, building up Britain's fear of Russia's southward expansion through Korea.[3] But there was still the deep-rooted suspicion in Japan that Britain might enter the war on China's side.

The Japanese tried hard not to alienate Britain in the problems which arose from the war. When before the outbreak of war, the Japanese navy sank the British merchantman *Kowshing* on its way from Taku to Korea with a complement of Chinese troops, Japan volunteered

---

[1] Chang Chung-fu, *The Anglo-Japanese alliance*, p. 14. 'At the beginning and the early stages of the war, British sympathy was clearly on the side of the Celestial Empire.' To a lesser extent, this view is found in A. L. Galperin, *Anglo-yaponskii soiuz, 1902–21 gg*, pp. 33–4, and W. L. Langer, *The diplomacy of imperialism, 1890–1902*, p. 173.

[2] FO *Japan* 439, Kimberley to Paget (Tokyo), 28 June 1894.

[3] *NGB* 27/I, no. 56.

to offer compensation if she was found to be in the wrong. The court held that Japan was not responsible and the sinking did not develop into a serious incident. Another issue arose over Shanghai, the centre of Britain's traditional trade in the Yangtse valley. It seemed likely that, as soon as war was declared, the Chinese would block the river approaches in order to ensure the security of their Shanghai arsenal. The only way to prevent the channels being closed was to obtain assurances from the Japanese. Mutsu guaranteed that 'no warlike operations shall be undertaken against Shanghai and its approaches'.[1] What was notable about Mutsu's promise was that it was unconditional and was kept throughout the war, despite the growing opposition from the military as the war developed.

Despite these gestures, it was a relief to many Japanese when Britain pledged her neutrality after war was declared. In fact, the Liberal ministry never considered intervening in a war which might be of long duration and would only harm the country's commercial interests. Britain's legal obligation under her treaty of 1883 with Korea was confined to using her good offices to bring about an amicable arrangement; and Britain had done this to no avail. But her overall commercial interest was to stop the war; and Britain took a prominent part in eight attempts by the powers to offer mediation. The Japanese prime minister, Itō, wrote in October that 'England is rousing the foreign powers against Japan' and seriously thought that armed intervention was contemplated to stop the war.[2] The fact was that every offer of mediation was seen by the Japanese as Chinese-inspired and as devised against Japan's true interest.

There is no evidence in the archives that Britain gave her favour either to China or to Japan. Britain, as a major power accustomed to having some say in the far east, made suggestions which were unacceptable to Japan. To that extent she might appear to Japan to be pro-Chinese. But this was an illusion. The actions which Britain took before and during the war were not so much pro-Chinese or anti-Japanese as pro-British. The Japanese historian, Kajima, has judiciously written that 'it was not as though Britain had hostile feelings towards our country or treated it as an enemy; she only thought that the war

---

[1] Foreign Office, General Correspondence, *China*, vol. 1213, note by Villiers, 29 September 1894 (this series is hereafter cited as 'FO *China*'); *NGB* 27/II, no. 735.

[2] *NGB* 27/II, no. 799; *Hayashi memoirs*, pp. 107-8, 'During the war with China, feelings in Japan were by no means friendly to England'.

would strategically and commercially have an adverse effect on herself and sincerely wished that peace in east Asia should not be broken'.[1]

In their desire for peace, Russia and Britain, though rivals in northeast Asia, made common cause. At a meeting on 21 August, the Russian ministers resolved to collaborate with Britain in efforts to restore peace by diplomatic means and to avoid active interference in the war. This need for collective action by the powers was also acknowledged by the British government. Thus, on 25 January 1895, Rosebery minuted that 'the importance of acting closely with Russia is in any case supreme'.[2] There was therefore a brief interval of co-operation between Britain and Russia during the war months.

JAPAN RECEIVES FRIENDLY ADVICE

The war with China was a real triumph for Japanese arms, all the more striking because few suspected that Japan's superiority would be so marked. The Japanese army advanced through Korea, crossed the Yalu river and occupied the south of Manchuria. Three divisions attacked the Liaotung peninsula and captured Port Arthur on 21 November 1894. Within six months of the start of the war, the Japanese had command of the sea and land approaches to the Chinese capital and were able to demand stringent terms.

While the Japanese people were agog with excitement, their leaders were worried. Firstly they were aware that their resources would be exhausted if the war lasted much longer. Secondly they realized that the sheer extent of Japan's victory had disturbed the European powers who were opposed to the disintegration of the Chinese Empire and also saw the defeat of China as a moment of opportunity for themselves. The Russians had hinted at their attitude by sending reinforcements from their modern Black Sea fleet to join their squadron in

---

[1] Kajima Morinosuke, *Nichi-Ei gaikōshi* ('History of Anglo-Japanese diplomacy'), p. 154. Kajima also argues that Britain in 1894 did not realize Japan's strength and probably expected ultimate victory to go to China. This was certainly not the official British view. Many of Britain's experts thought that the prospects of Chinese victory were exceedingly remote. E.g. FO *Japan* 478, note by J. H. Gubbins, 20 April 1894. On 24 September 1894, Sir Thomas Wade, the former British minister to China, informed the Foreign Office that despite China's many years of instruction, it had no one 'capable of commanding a battalion far less an army' (FO *China* 1213). On the other hand, Chirol, *Far eastern question*, p. 3, contends that Britain relied largely on China's latent resources as a fighting power but realized only very imperfectly Japan's 'national evolution'.

[2] FO *Japan* 455, minute on Kimberley to Trench, 25 January 1895; Malozemoff, pp. 57–60.

Chinese waters. The feeling among Japanese ministers was electric since their country was on the verge of a war more serious than that which had been fought with China.

It came as no surprise to Japan that the powers were anxious to have a say in the peace settlement. She had turned a deaf ear to their offers of mediation throughout the war. None the less the Japanese government decided to go some way towards forestalling opposition by giving to selected powers assurances about its intentions. The foreign minister, Mutsu, had discussions in February and March with the Russian minister, Khitrovo, and gained the impression that Russian intervention would not take place. Germany next offered advice on peace terms which would be suitable to the powers. While this action was taken independently, conversations were being held between the powers to decide on common action. But it was agreed that no scope for intervention existed unless the terms of the peace settlement, when announced, were found to be objectionable. Thus the notable feature of the joint intervention was that it took so long to mature and thereby caused a protracted period of suspense in Tokyo.[1]

China sought peace in the shadow of the great powers. The negotiators who were initially sent to Japan in February, were not properly accredited and the Japanese repatriated them when this was discovered. It was only when the leading Chinese statesman, Li Hung-chang, was appointed as negotiator that Japan would announce the terms of peace. At the height of the peace talks at Shimonoseki, however, Li was assaulted by a Japanese mob on 24 March,[2] and the Japanese negotiators, bowing before the sympathy which was widely shown towards China, urged the emperor to declare an unconditional cease-fire four days later.[3] They appear to have used the incident to make a planned withdrawal from Japan's strong position and to keep their people's high expectations within bounds. On 1 April they presented China with Japan's terms: Japan was to receive the territories of Formosa, the Pescadores and most of the peninsular part of

---

[1] NGB 28/I, nos. 561 and 571; Langer, p. 176.

[2] NGB 28/II, nos. 1052–3 and 1058.

[3] Kaneko Kentarō, Itō Hirobumi den, iii, 167–9 (hereafter cited as 'Itō-den'); Mutsu Hirokichi, Hakushaku Mutsu Munemitsu ikō ('Posthumous works of Count Mutsu'), pp. 476–7. This volume contains 'Kengenroku' ('memoirs') which Mutsu wrote at Ōiso after his final resignation from the Itō cabinet in 1896 as a documented account of the crisis of 1895 and a defence of his conduct of affairs (hereafter cited as 'Mutsu-ikō').

Another detailed account of the three-power intervention is found in a Foreign Ministry memorandum, NGB Meiji nenkan tsuiho, I, 679–723.

Liaotung together with an indemnity of 200 million taels (£30 million). The Japanese terms were leaked to the great powers by China who interceded for their intervention.

Suspecting a stratagem of this kind, the Japanese also confided their terms to the powers and the press. Their main object was to justify their claim to Liaotung which they considered to be a vital acquisition giving a strategic foothold on the Asian continent, and buttressing their interests in Korea. By these proposals they would obtain the peninsular part of Manchuria from the Yalu to the Liao river. This would give Japan not only Port Arthur but the most developed port in Manchuria, Newchwang, which was the terminus for Li Hung-chang's railway scheme of 1890. It was not unforeseen that such terms would meet with an ill reception from Russia and the powers.

On 6 April Japan presented to the powers the commercial demands which had been laid before China. They included the right of steamers to ply up the West river to Wuchow and the Yangtse to Chungking, a provision for fresh ports to be opened to foreign commerce and a provision that Japanese could freely engage in all manufacturing industries.[1] These terms naturally appealed to powers trading with China who would benefit under most-favoured-nation provisions. By divulging them, Japan hoped to prevent other governments from supporting China and also to mobilize world mercantile opinion in Japan's favour. The Japanese minister in London was instructed to pass them to the London press and to ensure that they filtered through to newspapers in Europe and America. With a quaint irony, he passed off his disclosure as being a secret emanating from Peking.[2]

Having been approached by China and the continental powers, Britain was called upon for an urgent decision. At a special cabinet on 8 April, there were divided counsels; but it was finally agreed that the Japanese terms did not justify interference on Britain's part, all the more so since much importance was attached to the commercial stipulations.[3] Later that day, Russia suggested to Britain that the powers should tell Japan in the most friendly manner that the acquisition of Port Arthur would form an obstacle to the maintenance of good relations between China and Japan and be a permanent menace to

---

[1] FO *Japan* 458, memorandum by Katō, 6 April 1895.

[2] *NGB* 28/I, nos. 610 and 618.

[3] FO *China* 1242, Kimberley to O'Conor, 8 April 1895; FO *Japan* 455, Kimberley to Lowther (Tokyo), 12 April 1895.

peace in the far east. Kimberley was able to announce that Britain would not take part in the protest. After Germany and France agreed to join in the 'friendly advice', Russia again asked Britain to join but again met with a refusal.

The continental powers decided to proceed with their 'advice'. The Japanese had stolen a march by inducing Li to sign the peace treaty on 17 April, subject to ratification. On 23 April the diplomatic representatives of Russia, France and Germany in Tokyo presented notes to Hayashi Tadasu, vice-minister for foreign affairs, advising Japan to return the Liaotung territory to China. In essence, it was a protest that Japan had dealt with the far eastern situation without consulting the powers; it was another link in the long chain of European interventions there but the first to be applied against Japan since the 1860s. To add persuasiveness to their message, the Russians mustered their squadron in ports close to Japan.

The 'friendly advice' was delivered at an inconvenient time for Japanese leaders. Hayashi was left in charge of foreign affairs in Tokyo, while the minister, Mutsu, was sick at Maiko near Kyoto and the prime minister was at Imperial Headquarters at Hiroshima, whither the court had moved to be nearer to the war front. An Imperial Council was held at Hiroshima on 24 April to consider the three powers' notes. There seemed to be three courses open to Japan: to refuse the friendly advice and risk hostilities against an even greater enemy; to settle the Liaotung problem at a special conference of the powers; or to return the peninsula to China.[1] The first course was ruled out when the military leaders said that most of Japan's forces were in action already and that they were weak in supplies, trained men and reserves.[2] The third alternative was rejected as being too humiliating. It was therefore decided to invite the powers to an international conference. Itō hastened to Kyoto to discuss the matter further at Mutsu's bedside. Mutsu was opposed to the conference on the ground that it would invite interference by the powers and reopen a range of subjects, which he wanted to keep separate from the Liaotung issue. His views were accepted and no immediate course was laid down except to delay Japan's reply for a while.[3]

Mutsu set about conducting an ingenious diplomatic offensive. He first tried to divide the continental powers but without success. He

---

[1] *Itō-den*, iii, 214–15.   [2] *Itō-den*, iii, 215; *Hayashi memoirs*, pp. 73–9.
[3] *NGB* 28/II, no. 678.

hoped to get Russia as the ringleader to reconsider her attitude but was told that the Russians were in earnest and that it was dangerous to reject their advice.[1] He also approached Britain, Italy and the United States to see if any practical opposition could be built up. All three were sympathetic; but Britain and the United States would not commit themselves to practical support and Italy, which was prepared to come out in favour of Japan diplomatically, would only act with the others.[2] Katō Takaaki, the new minister in London, was despondent.

It is clear that Britain's attitude was crucial in deciding Japan's course of action. Mutsu thought that Britain might be tempted to reverse her policy once the three powers had acted. The issue was considered by the British cabinet again on 23 April but it agreed to take an intermediate position. Kimberley told Katō that the government were 'animated by the most friendly feelings towards Japan and had no wish that she should be deprived of the reasonable fruits of her victories over China, although they would have preferred no disturbance of the *status quo*'. Asked what steps would be taken by the continental powers if Japan refused, Kimberley replied that the situation was undoubtedly a grave one.[3] On 26 April, Katō was asked to inquire how much help Japan could expect from Britain. Kimberley had discussions with Rosebery who confirmed that it was Britain's intention not to interfere at all. The foreign secretary therefore saw Katō on 29 April and told him that Britain could not give any tangible assistance. He informally advised Japan not to over-estimate the indignity of making concessions in answer to international protests as Russia had done in 1878 after San Stefano.[4] This response was a bitter, if not unexpected, blow to Mutsu. Yet he thanked Katō for his telegram which 'gave us a good guide in determining our action'.[5]

BRITAIN AND THE TREATY OF SHIMONOSEKI

There were two major factors which weighed with the British cabinet when it was considering its stand: the possibility of war; and the commercial benefits of the treaty.

---

[1] *NGB* 28/II, no. 707; *Itō-den*, iii, 215–20; *Mutsu-ikō*, pp. 510–12.

[2] *NGB* 28/II, nos. 666 and 725–8.

[3] Royal archives, A71/48, Rosebery to the queen, 23 April 1895; Itō Masanori, *Katō Takaaki*, pp. 248–9 (hereafter cited as '*Katō*'). FO *Japan* 449, Kimberley to Trench, 24 April 1895.

[4] *Mutsu-ikō*, pp. 515–16; FO *Japan* 449, Kimberley to Trench, 29 April 1895.

[5] *Katō*, i, 250; *NGB* 28/II, nos. 746 and 749.

The cabinet considered that, if Japan refused, war would result. Britain was under continued pressure from the continental powers to join the declaration since her absence would only encourage Japan to resist. But these powers would not commit themselves on whether they intended to use force against Japan or not. Kimberley therefore asked his Tokyo legation whether Japan was likely to give in if the three powers did not resort to force. The chargé d'affaires replied categorically — and probably incorrectly — that 'unless the warnings are to be followed by force, they will have no effect on Japan'.[1] Taking this along with his information that the Russian men of war at Kobe and Nagasaki were standing at the ready, Kimberley concluded that there might be a recourse to arms. The cabinet therefore took an intermediate position, neither joining the powers nor advising Japan to resist.

The Rosebery ministry was evidently influenced by considerations of international policy. This was a period when in Armenia, Siam, Africa and on the Indian frontier, Britain was trying to work with France and Russia. This made the cabinet reluctant to refuse Russia's request for co-operation in the far east; but the intervention seemed to Britain to be unjustified and contrary to her best interests in China. On the other hand, when Britain was asked by Japan for support against the Triplice, she naturally declined because she had no wish to risk an incident, which might provoke a war against them. Britain had no wish to become committed to Japan whose expansionist ambitions in China had already been reported by the Tokyo legation.[2] In these circumstances, it is not unexpected to find Sir Edward Grey, who was the ministry's spokesman for foreign affairs in the House of Commons, writing that his object was to keep his answers at question-time 'as colourless and neutral as possible' since he was trying not 'to give offence either to the Three Powers or to Japan'.[3] Clearly Britain was not willing to allow herself to be involved in any flare-up or any unpleasantness in the far east.

At the same time, Britain was attracted towards Japan by the commercial benefits which she hoped to derive from the treaty of

---

[1] FO *Japan* 456, Lowther to Kimberley, 22 April 1895.

[2] FO *Japan* 438, Trench to Kimberley, 16 November 1894. Printed for the use of the cabinet, 29 December 1894.

[3] Papers of Sir Edward Grey, consulted in the Foreign Office Library, London, note by Grey undated but evidently about 7 May 1895 (hereafter cited as 'Grey papers'); *British parliamentary debates*, 4th series, vol. 33, House of Commons, 7 May 1895, col. 638.

Shimonoseki. It was not that the treaty was deliberately worded so as to grant foreign powers special advantages; but these powers knew that, by the most-favoured-nation clauses of their existing treaties with China, they stood to gain by whatever fresh concessions Japan managed to extract. The commercial terms seemed to play into Britain's hands: they opened to steamers the Upper Yangtse from Ichang to Chungking and the Woosung from Shanghai to Suchow; and they gave the powers the right to engage in all kinds of manufacturing industries in all the open towns of China. Since British merchants were already established on the Yangtse and at Shanghai in great numbers, it seemed that they were well placed to profit most from these concessions in the short term.[1] Unquestionably they appealed to Britain and inclined the cabinet towards the treaty.

But Britain did not welcome these clauses without demur. When they were received, they were referred to the Board of Trade which in a memorandum reviewed them favourably though it doubted whether the advantages to British trade would come at all quickly. 'The opening of the Yangtse valley will be a good thing as a result of the peace but the indemnity is a commercial evil of a great magnitude', which must result in increased tariffs on goods in and out of China.[2] It was, it argued, to Britain's advantage that there should be an increase in the number of open ports on the Yangtse where its trading community was already strongly placed; it was also useful that the right to open factories in the Chinese concessions should be recognized. While the British government and merchants were in favour of these clauses for the benefits which they hoped to derive from them, the German government viewed them with apprehension because they seemed likely to result in the predominance of Japanese trade in China.[3] On the other hand, Britain was opposed to the large indemnity of 200 million taels which Japan demanded. It would be a crippling blow to China. Japan could not avoid making the demand since her treasury was exhausted by the war; but China's finances were even more shattered. A large indemnity could only be paid from a loan guaranteed by China's customs revenue which must inevitably lead to jostling among the lending powers. In the long term this would lead to demands

[1] *British parliamentary papers*, Japan no. 1 (1895), Cmd 7714, Treaty of Shimonoseki.
[2] FO *Japan* 495, note by Mr (later Sir) Robert Giffen, 17 April 1895. Giffen was chief of the Statistical Department, Board of Trade.
[3] Royal archives, Q 16/92, Gosselin to Kimberley, 9 April 1895.

for an increase in customs duty which would mostly affect Britain as the leading trading nation. Thus, Britain's reaction to the commercial aspects of the treaty was bitter-sweet and by no means as sanguine as some have thought.[1]

It is probably unrewarding to look too deep for the Rosebery ministry's reasons for not taking any part in the three-power intervention. In his memoirs, Grey denies that Kimberley had any ulterior motive in the decision he took: 'we did not consider that British interests required us to join in this interference with Japan's claims; the threat to her by the European Powers appeared harsh and uncalled for, and it was repugnant to us to join in it'.[2] While Britain probably thought the protest unnecessary, she had no primary interests at stake. This may be illustrated from an anecdote told by Katō. When he called on Kimberley at the height of the crisis, the foreign secretary admitted that he was not clear what districts Japan wanted to occupy in south Manchuria and had to have them pointed out on a map. Katō commented that if, as some British newspapers were suggesting, the country was greatly concerned over Japan's occupation of the Liaotung peninsula, Kimberley ought not to have been so badly briefed.[3] Although the Liberal ministry was worried about Russia obtaining a foothold in Korea or at Port Arthur, it did not consider that this was at issue in the three-power intervention which it treated as of secondary importance.

Britain's attitude destroyed any illusions, which the Japanese ministers had, that they would not have to yield. With this reaction from the most friendly power and similar reactions from the United States and Italy, the Japanese could not foresee any solution favourable to themselves. Thus Mutsu's policy of 'outpointing' the continental powers ended in failure.[4]

At an Imperial Council on 29 April 1895, the same day as Britain's reply, Japan agreed to modify the treaty of Shimonoseki. In a message to the powers next day, Japan offered to abandon the whole of the Liaotung peninsula, except Kinchow, one of the seven districts which she originally demanded but the one which included Dairen (Talienwan)

---

[1] Galperin, p. 39, claims that Britain intended with Japan's help to fortify her economic hegemony in China.

[2] Grey, *Twenty-five years*, i, 23–4.

[3] *NGB* 28/I, no. 640.

[4] Abe Kōzō, 'Nisshin kōwa to sangoku kanshō' ('The Sino-Japanese peace and the three-power intervention'), *Kokusai seiji*, no. 3 (1961), 52–70.

and Port Arthur.[1] This offer was rejected by the three powers. The Japanese army and navy were too exhausted by the war to test the bluff of the powers. On 4 May, therefore, the Japanese accepted the inevitable and decided on the permanent renunciation of the peninsula provided that China forthwith ratified the treaty of Shimonoseki and agreed to pay an additional indemnity. Ratifications were exchanged at Chifu four days later. Along with the treaty, Japan published on 13 May a proclamation by the emperor sanctioning the retrocession with the statement that the honour and dignity of the empire would not be 'compromised by resorting to magnanimous measures',[2] though even the emperor's intervention did not assuage the intense disappointment of the people and the general resentment against the Itō government.

The co-operation of the continental powers was an arrangement of convenience and its continuance was uncertain. They stuck together to keep Japan to its undertakings. In a further note on 31 May, they asked what amount of indemnity Japan wanted China to pay as compensation for Liaotung and how soon it proposed to evacuate the peninsula.[3] But in other respects the powers went their separate ways. The Chinese were negotiating a loan with France under the security of a Russian guarantee. This drew German financiers and politicians towards Britain which was similarly annoyed with these secret operations. Britain even urged Japan not to demand a monetary indemnity for the return of the peninsula but instead to obtain the opening to trade of the West river (Sikiang) which had been included in the original demands but had been dropped during the negotiations.[4] But Itō desperately needed the indemnity and could not agree. Later Britain tried to prejudice the Japanese against a French loan based on the Chinese customs and urged Japan not to evacuate the Liaotung peninsula without adequate security for the full indemnity. Although it was aimed against France, Germany made a similar recommendation. The Japanese prime minister rejected this reiterated advice because the indemnity payments were desperately needed for reconstruction, regardless of their source. On 6 July the contract for the Franco-Russian loan of about £16 million was signed to enable China to pay off part of the indemnity. But there was also an indemnity due for the retrocession of the Liaotung peninsula; and the three powers joined in urging Japan on 11 September

---

[1] *NGB* 28/II, nos. 750 and 757.   [2] *NGB* 28/II, no. 1130.
[3] *NGB* 28/II, no. 845; FO *Japan* 456, Lowther to Kimberley, 1 June 1895.
[4] FO *Japan* 452, Lowther to Kimberley, 18 June 1895.

that it should not exceed 30 million taels. This amount was accepted and eventually paid in November in London on China's behalf.[1] The Japanese troops left the peninsula early in 1896. The three powers had achieved their object but they could not rely on each other's unfailing co-operation. Thus in March 1896 Germany joined Britain in raising a further loan of £16 million for China.

ANGLO-JAPANESE RELATIONS
AFTER THE THREE-POWER INTERVENTION

The three-power intervention transformed the history of Japan. It retarded Japan's entry into international affairs and forced her to concentrate on building up her national strength. It also changed the configuration of powers in the far east in a way which was ultimately to affect Japan.

The Japanese had been taught the lesson that they must look to their defences. From being elated at their successes, they were utterly humiliated. They felt themselves to be deprived of the spoils of their victory and to be the victim of a conspiracy between the diplomats of China and Europe. The fact that the Japanese emperor assumed responsibility for the decision did not spare those responsible for the negotiations from vicious attacks in the Diet and the press. The position of Itō and Mutsu was unenviable: they had gone to war to satisfy the chauvinistic groups who were making government impossible by their disturbances; the army and navy were overwhelmingly victorious but the negotiators had to make a cowardly withdrawal. Mutsu confessed: 'in war we triumphed; in diplomacy we failed'.[2] But he blamed Japan's predicament on the jingoist groups which clamoured so much.

None the less the Itō ministry of 'all the talents' which had brought Japan through the war, managed to survive the unpopularity of the peace settlement and ran on until August 1896. Since the country had been financially crippled by the war, Itō's policy was necessarily devoted to reconstruction at home and disentanglement from foreign commitments. The ailing foreign minister, Mutsu, who had been consistently Anglophil, retired temporarily in June 1895 and was succeeded by Prince Saionji Kimmochi. Mutsu later returned to office but only for a short while (April–May 1896).

[1] FO *Japan* 454, Salisbury to Satow, 22 November 1895.
[2] *Mutsu-ikō*, pp. 556–8.

The Japanese leaders took the difficult decision to lie low for a while and retire into a self-enforced isolation. Japan would take no part in foreign adventures, while she built up her armed strength. Some would say that Japan became obsessed with the idea of revenging herself on Russia; certainly she became determined to avoid any further humiliation. In 1895 the government decided to double the size of the Japanese army and to increase the naval strength well beyond the targets set in the prewar shipbuilding plans. In the army its object was to improve the efficiency of its troops by giving them better weapons, firepower and artillery and to make certain administrative reforms, such as increasing the number of divisions.[1] Meanwhile the ministry of marine converted the existing shipbuilding programmes of 1893 into a ten-year planned expansion. With budgetary allocations on a vast scale in 1895 and 1896, Japan planned to convert her fleet into a balanced force of six modern battleships and six cruisers. As one commentator observes, the ease with which this programme was steered through the Diet, suggested that another age had come since the stormy scenes of 1893.[2] In the years that followed, most of the shipbuilding and machinery contracts for larger vessels were executed in British yards; and Japan spared no expense to ensure that they were modern in design. By 1900 Japan came to hold the naval balance between the Russo-French and British fleets in the far east and by the time this phase of her building programme was completed in 1902–3, her fleet was capable of dominating 'naval politics' there. Moreover, Japan enjoyed an advantage in that she could concentrate her vessels in the China seas at a tithe of the operating costs which a corresponding European squadron would have to bear. Thus, despite the considerable financial difficulties, which rearmament entailed, Japan's leaders achieved within a short period a remarkable national consolidation and emerged with the country's power re-established at a new level.

While Japan gained strength, the powers in the far east became roughly divided into two groups: France and Russia on the one hand, Japan and Britain on the other. These were years when the Franco-Russian entente blossomed in the far east,[3] the partners being especially active in offering loans to China. It could even be said that Russia made China her pawn, though not her voluntary ally. On political

---

[1] Itō Masanori, *Kokubōshi* ('History of national defence'), Tokyo, 1941, pp. 85–92.
[2] Ibid., 97–103; *Katō*, i, 357–9.
[3] Langer, pp. 411–12.

issues France and Russia were often reinforced by Germany but on financial issues she was more often on Britain's side. By contrast, the relationship between Britain and Japan was still a loose one. Since it had not joined the continental powers, Britain was in 1895 identified as the power most favourable to Japan's objects. Equally, Japan was drawn towards co-operation with Britain which was interested in maintaining the *status quo* in China and was less blatantly ambitious there. But there were many points of difference; and Britain had shown herself in 1895 to be shy of any entanglement in the far east. It is desirable to examine this new relationship in greater detail.

Mutsu, as part of his policy of improving relations with Britain, had raised the standing of Japan's legation in London. In the past the ministers there had been comparatively low-powered officials. So much so that Aoki, the minister to Germany, had had to be sent to London for the treaty revision negotiations in 1894. But part-time representation of this kind was false economy during a war; and Katō Takaaki was appointed as the new full-time minister. It was not that Katō was an experienced diplomat like Aoki: he had been a journalist, businessman and Foreign Ministry official and had served as secretary to Ōkuma when he was foreign minister in 1888-9. He was, however, influential, being the close friend of Mutsu and a protégé of Fukuzawa Yukichi, and was well known for his sympathy towards Britain, where he had earlier spent two years (1883-5). He received special instructions from Mutsu to convert Britain to Japan's cause: he tried to raise the confidence of Kimberley and the Foreign Office and was awarded a decoration for his contribution to Japan's war effort. He also set out to influence the general public through the press as his predecessor, Aoki, had done. He became an avowed inspirer of articles and, during his early months in London, the press there reported Japan more fully than ever before. From his arrival in January 1895, a new period of improved understanding opened between the two countries.

It is too early to conceive of an Anglo-Japanese alliance in the making. Sir Edward Grey rightly states that the Liberals in deciding not to join the other powers, had no thought of Japan as a possible ally.[1] It is unlikely that there was any inkling of this on the part of the Japanese government, which had asked Britain for help on an *ad hoc* issue and had been refused. The Japanese deduced that Britain was really determined not to fight Russia and France for the sake of her

[1] Grey, *Twenty-five years*, i, 24.

D

interests in the far east and that, if she were so inclined, she would not merely have looked on while Japan was being hard pressed over Liaotung.[1] In these circumstances it was premature to contemplate any arrangement for long-term friendship.

Yet there was some talk of an Anglo-Japanese alliance in the press. The *Jiji Shimpō* whose editor was the well-known Anglophil, Fukuzawa Yukichi, published articles in May and June 1895 in favour of an alliance. These had in all probability been written by Hayashi Tadasu who was vice-minister for foreign affairs at the time of the crisis.[2] Other papers of which the *Nichinichi Shimbun* and the *Kokumin* were prominent examples, were more wary of the suggestion, saying that Britain had shown 'supreme indifference at the recent juncture' and had given little evidence of pro-Japanese sentiments.[3]

The theme was also coming to be discussed unofficially, even at ministerial level. On the day that the Rosebery cabinet fell, 24 June 1895, Kimberley had a long talk with the Japanese minister in which he said that Japan would have to strengthen her armies and add to her naval power and expressed the hope that relations with Britain would always be those of warm friendship.[4] That Kimberley wanted to maintain close ties with Japan can be seen from his instructions to the new minister to Japan, Sir Ernest Satow. He spoke of the 'desirability of a close understanding between England and Japan in order to frustrate Russian plans for the acquisition of an icefree port' and confirmed that he had mentioned this to the Japanese minister.[5] The appointment of Satow was in itself a significant act. Sir Ernest Satow was an experienced diplomat and well qualified for his new post. He had joined the consular service in 1861 and gone to Japan as an interpreter. He had played some part in the hectic events of the Bakumatsu period which he later described in his book *A diplomat in Japan*. He

[1] FO *Japan* 453, Lowther to Salisbury, 9 July 1895.

[2] While the articles were published anonymously, Hayashi claimed to have written them, *Hayashi memoirs*, pp. 81–2, 103–9.

[3] FO *Japan* 453, Lowther to Salisbury, 9 July 1895, enclosing an assessment of Japanese press comment by J. H. Gubbins.

[4] *Katō*, i, 251–2; *NGB* 28/II, no. 870. There is no record of this discussion in the British archives, although it is known that Katō did call at the Foreign Office on that day, FO *Japan* 449, Kimberley to Lowther, 24 June 1895.

[5] Papers of Lord Salisbury, deposited in Christ Church library, Oxford, A/126, Satow to Salisbury, 15 August 1895 (hereafter cited as 'Salisbury papers'). Also in the papers of Sir Ernest Satow, deposited in the Public Record Office, London, PRO 30/33, vol. 14/8 (hereafter cited as 'Satow papers').

had seen at first hand the early years of the new Japan and had become an expert in 'things Japanese'. Later he had taken up diplomatic posts at Bangkok (1884–8), Montevideo (1888–93) and Tangier (1893–5). Now he returned to Japan where the men in power were those he had known as junior officials. Unquestionably Satow came closer to statesmen whose national character tended to make them secretive, than any other diplomat of the time. Beyond this, he was a careful and painstaking organizer of the everyday functions of the legation; and his dispatches and private letters are a model of conscientiousness and acute observation. His coldness of manner did not mar his services to Britain or to Japan.

The general election of July 1895 brought to power in Britain a new Unionist ministry with a substantial parliamentary majority. Lord Salisbury presided over the new ministry and himself acted as foreign secretary. But his health was indifferent and, during his frequent absences, his place was taken by Arthur James Balfour, then leader of the House of Commons, who took a considerable part in policy-making during the year of crisis, 1898. As parliamentary under-secretary, Salisbury chose George Curzon, traveller in China, Korea and Japan and author of the recent book, *Problems of the Far East.* He possessed a knowledge of the area which was exceptional in both Westminster and Whitehall. But Curzon was hardly consulted by Salisbury and was glad to resign in order to become viceroy of India early in 1899. Another figure, who was to count in policy-making, was Joseph Chamberlain, colonial secretary and a leader of the Liberal-Unionist faction. While it is arguable that Chamberlain was influential over policy towards Germany and the United States, it cannot be proved that he had as much effect on far eastern problems.

The change-over from the Rosebery ministry involved adjustments in Britain's eastern policy. The Liberal cabinet had in its last months suffered from considerable internal dissension over foreign policy and had been criticized for its weak handling of the far eastern crisis of 1895. Indeed Salisbury is quoted as saying in an unusually boastful mood that 'had he been in power he would for a start not have allowed the war at all' and that '*should that have proved impossible, he would under no circumstances have permitted the demand on Japan to give up the Liaotung Peninsula in Russia's favour*'.[1] Kimberley had worked for

---

[1] *The Holstein papers,* edited by M. H. Fisher and N. Rich, iv, no. 703, Hatzfeldt to Holstein, 6 August 1899. Italics in original.

co-operation between Britain and Japan on a modest scale. An opportunity for the new foreign secretary to explain his standpoint occurred when Satow wrote to Salisbury asking for instructions. Satow analysed the prevailing mood in Japan in August thus:

One or two Japanese have expressed to me their desire for joint action with Great Britain but I have not heard anything which would lead me to suppose that this is the wish of the Cabinet. From what I know of their character, I should expect them to prefer trying to get out of their present mess by their own skill in temporizing and that they would not readily enter into an alliance in which they would have to play second fiddle.[1]

In reply, Salisbury laid down the guiding lines of his policy in the far east and gave some interesting insights into eastern problems as he saw them. He wrote:

Our strategic or military interest in Japan can easily be over-estimated. She may no doubt be of use in hindering Russia from getting an ice-free port. But how long would her obstruction be effective? . . . Britain cannot rely on Japan's interest to oppose Russia. Maintaining amicable relations with Japan, the British Minister should with discretion explore the Japanese market. . . . My impression is that the shrewder Japanese ministers will not be sorry to see enough Russian power in those latitudes to counter-balance the powers of England. I would not therefore thrust upon them any advice or the hint of any naval or military cooperation either against Russia or China. But this will in no way hinder you from maintaining a most friendly attitude to the Japanese Government. . . . What you tell me about the apparent disinclination of the Japanese Government generally to cultivate our exclusive friendship, rather confirms the suspicion that in the end they will be convinced that it is rather their interest to join with Russia, and perhaps with France in cutting up China than to exchange platonic assurances of affection with us.[2]

This was not a statement of far-reaching political principles: it was astute, materialistic and down to earth. There is evidence that Salisbury was in practice to be guided in his policy by this general scepticism about Japan. Indeed he was to worry some of his colleagues during the crisis of 1898 by his sceptical inactivity. In 1898 as in 1895, Salisbury was discerning enough to realize that a localized agreement with Russia could be most valuable to the Japanese; he had no intention of

---

[1] Salisbury papers, A/126, Satow to Salisbury, 15 August 1895.
[2] Satow papers 5/2, Salisbury to Satow, 3 October 1895.

trying to tempt Japan away from reaching such an agreement. On the other hand, he seems to underestimate the extent of Japanese hostility to Russia after the triple intervention; the governments of Russia and Japan were generally on such unfriendly terms that their agreements were bound to be temporary. This might have been turned to Britain's advantage. But Salisbury was not prepared to do so. There is not a shred of evidence in this long memorandum that Britain's far eastern policy had been influenced by the result of the Sino-Japanese war and was now moving towards partnership with a victorious Japan. On the contrary. Salisbury's appraisal of the situation was lacking in positive ideas and was perhaps unnecessarily pessimistic.

Not all Salisbury's predictions have proved to be well-founded nor were all his judgments necessarily sound. He overestimated, for example, the scope for expanding British trade with Japan. More striking is his confidence that Britain still had an unquestioned supremacy in the far east. Many of his countrymen were beginning to feel that this assumption was losing its force and that Britain ought to be looking for an ally. But Salisbury was far from admitting any such need.

RUSSIA IN CHINA AND KOREA

Over against the Anglo-Japanese rapprochement — and more effective than it — must be set the Russo-Chinese rapprochement and the confrontation between Russia and Japan which was its inevitable consequence.

The Russians, who had saved China from the major consequences of her defeat at the hands of Japan, thought that it would be to their benefit to continue in a protective role. With the help of French finance, they had placed China under obligation by giving her a large loan in July 1895. Russia's various demands, which were foreshadowed in the Cassini draft convention in April, were finally accepted in the Li-Lobanov agreement of 3 June 1896. The Japanese historian, Kajima, has justly called this an 'anti-Japanese secret alliance'.[1] Under it, the allies would assist one another over a period of 15 years if Japan attacked either of them or took military action against Korea. China further approved the construction of a railway through northern

---

[1] Kajima, *Nihon gaikō seisaku no shiteki kōsatsu*, p. 62. The text is given in E. B. Price, *Russo-Japanese treaties of 1907–16*, Baltimore, 1933, pp. 101–2.

Manchuria to Vladivostok by the Russo-Chinese Bank. In September the contract for the construction of the so-called Chinese Eastern Railway was concluded at Peking between the bank and the Chinese government. Since the Russo-Chinese Bank was in effect an agency of the Russian Ministry of Finance, the Russians had virtually succeeded in extracting substantial railway rights in Manchuria, in return for the military assistance they promised against the Japanese.

Immediately after the Sino-Japanese war, the major confrontation between Russia and Japan took place in Korea. During the war there had been a formal alliance between Japan and Korea which had given the Japanese emergency privileges there. But the independence of Korea was recognized by the peace settlement. The Japanese exercised great influence there after the war since their troops continued to garrison many strategic points. By virtue of this, their minister, Inoue Kaoru, had great sway at the court. On 4 June 1895, however, the Japanese cabinet adopted a new policy: it resolved to eliminate intervention as far as possible and to encourage Korea to stand on her own feet.[1] If this was bona fide, it is odd that the next minister to be appointed should be General Miura, who arrived there in August. Certainly the Japanese position was weakened as a result of the unwise tactics of his officials. The Korean queen, who was the centre of anti-Japanese activity, was murdered by a group of Japanese patriots on 8 October and Miura was thought to be implicated along with a large number of Japanese. The Japanese government immediately recalled Miura and fifty others for trial by the Hiroshima district court. All the cases were dismissed on account of inadequate evidence but the accused were not reinstated.[2] The episode caused a revulsion in Korea against all things Japanese. Eventually in February 1896, the Korean king sought the protection of the Russians who had taken over the mantle of the Chinese in Korea. From the safety of their legation he passed sentences on a large number of Japanese for their misdeeds. So all-embracing did this protection become that it seemed as though Russia had ambitions to establish a protectorate there.

Japan had the alternative of making an approach to Russia or of reaching an understanding with other European powers, notably Britain. What was Britain's reaction likely to be? As early as May

---

[1] *NGB* 28/I, no. 298.
[2] Kiyozawa Kiyoshi, *Nihon gaikōshi* ('History of Japanese diplomacy'), 2 vols., Tokyo, 1942, i, 280.

1895, Mutsu had inquired whether Britain would support a proposal for a joint guarantee of Korean independence by the powers but had concluded that Britain was not likely to be interested.[1] The new Salisbury ministry was certainly not inclined to involve itself in Korean affairs. Balfour in what was obviously a policy speech on 3 February 1896, asserted that so far 'from regarding with fear and jealousy a commercial outlet for Russia in the Pacific Ocean which should not be ice-bound half the year, I should welcome such a result as a distinct advance in this far distant region'.[2] Japanese hearts must have frozen at what seemed to be a direct invitation to Russia, which could not be other than damaging to Japanese interests. Concluding that there was no help likely to come from Britain, the Japanese turned to the Russians and started negotiations in Korea in March.

On 1 May Salisbury inquired, like a bolt from the blue, whether Japan would agree to a declaration of Korean neutrality if such a proposal were advanced. The Japanese foreign minister replied bluntly that he had already approached Britain on this subject but, having received no encouragement, the Japanese were forced to negotiate with Russia and were on the point of signing something. Mutsu, however, gave Satow a note containing four questions to be referred to London for clarification; the questions were mainly intended to discover how far other powers were likely to accept the neutralization proposal. Mutsu rightly argued that if this proposal were accepted by Japan but met with insufficient support from the powers, it would recoil upon Japan, causing the failure of her talks with Russia and precipitating Russia's assumption of a protectorate.[3] Satow reported that a favourable reply from Britain might save Japan from having to accept any terms Russia chose to impose. But Salisbury replied that the object of his inquiry was simply to find out Japan's attitude and he had not communicated with other governments. Questioned further, Salisbury stated that the powers interested in Korea should combine to find a remedy for the anarchy in the country but the initiative 'should be with one of those specially interested: Japan, China or Russia'. Britain was interested, he added, but only in a second degree.[4] It was not a reply likely to encourage Japan to delay matters further with

[1] NGB 28/I, nos. 277–8.
[2] Langer, p. 400. Balfour confirms this view in G. P. Gooch and H. W. V. Temperley, British documents on the origins of the war, 1898–1914, i, no. 38 (hereafter cited as 'BD').
[3] NGB 29, nos. 300–3; FO Japan 468, Satow to Salisbury, 4 May 1896.
[4] FO Japan 471, Salisbury to Satow, 13 May 1896.

Russia. Indeed on the following day, 14 May, Mutsu instructed Komura, his minister at Seoul, to conclude the *modus vivendi* with Waeber, the Russian minister there: an on-the-spot administrative arrangement whereby the Japanese were forced to admit that Russia had equal rights in Korea.

Salisbury's unexpected intervention, though trivial in itself, is revealing. However much Salisbury might protest that Britain had no primary interests in Korea and was not worried about Russia having an ice-free port there, Britain was keen to prevent a possible Russo-Japanese agreement or a Russian protectorate over Korea. Despite this, Britain wanted to avoid too much involvement. Thus, Katō was told that Britain was perfectly aware that Japan was planning to send a special envoy to Russia for negotiations.[1] But Salisbury was not willing to prevent this: he was prepared to suggest an alternative solution, even if not to act as its sponsor before the powers. The incident also reveals Japan's motives and the keenness of Mutsu and Komura to enlist British support to improve Japan's position in Korea. Mutsu was apparently ready to throw over the Russian agreement, even at the last moment, if Britain had some practical offer to make.

The question arose whether talks with Russia at a higher level than the Waeber-Komura ones were necessary. The elder statesman, Yamagata Aritomo, who had been playing an increasing role in foreign affairs and had skilfully engineered his appointment as special emissary to the coronation of Nicholas II in June 1896, thought that, to avoid public notice, these could best be arranged during his visit to St Petersburg. Some days before the ceremony, he negotiated with Lobanov, the Russian foreign minister, the protocol which later came to be known as the 'Yamagata-Lobanov agreement'. The open part of the agreement laid down the financial and military aid which might be given to Korea and contained the undertaking that both would work for reforms there. The secret part, which only came to light much later, provided that they should both have the right to keep enough troops for protection of their interests and to send supplementary forces in an emergency.[2] Its effect was to place Japan and Russia on a footing of equality, not to say stalemate, and to set up two spheres of influence. The Russians, in what appeared to the Japanese to be a violation of the

---

[1] *NGB* 29, no. 311, Katō to Mutsu, 14 May 1896.

[2] *NGB* 29, nos. 475-8; *Itō-den*, iii, 282-5; Oka Yoshitake, *Yamagata Aritomo*, Tokyo, 1958, pp. 63-4.

treaty, appointed a large number of military instructors from among their own nationals and tried to bring Korean finances more under their control.[1] During the next two years, Russia was building up a superior position in the peninsula while Japan lay low.

Yamagata's visit to Russia was strenuously resisted by Itō and Mutsu. Itō as prime minister wanted to go himself. More significantly for present purposes, Mutsu, who had resumed as foreign minister in April 1896, objected to Yamagata's mission on the ground that he wanted to conciliate Russia by offering too many concessions. Mutsu therefore resigned over the Russo-Japanese treaty. But his resignation also betrayed an element of disappointment at his failure to get Britain to back Japan in taking a strong line towards Russia over Korea. Mutsu, whose attempt to follow a pro-British policy since 1892 has been a unifying factor in this chapter, felt some failure over this turn of events. In his retirement, he prepared his reflections on Japan's recent history under the title 'Kengenroku'. As the underlying theme of this political testament, Mutsu stressed that Japan should build up her strength and, as that strength increased, should woo Britain as her ally.[2]

[1] FO *Japan* 496, Satow to Salisbury, 26 March 1898.
[2] Kajima, *Nihon gaikō seisaku no shiteki kōsatsu*, pp. 84–5.

CHAPTER II

The Powers take Compensation

August 1896 – June 1898

'RUSSIA and Germany at the entrance of the Yellow Sea may be taken as represented by St George and St Michael shielding the Holy Cross in the Far East and guarding the gates to the Continent of Asia.'[1]

In such extravagant language, the German emperor congratulated the tsar on the arrival of the Russian squadron at Port Arthur. By March 1898 Germany had obtained the lease of Kiaochow; and Russia the leases of Port Arthur and Dairen (Dalny). Moreover they acquired rights in the adjoining peninsulas of Shantung and Liaotung. This was the outcome which had been expected since the Triple Intervention in 1895. The question which naturally arises is: what action did the other powers, and especially Britain and Japan, take in the face of this threat, which was by far the most serious issue in the far east at the time? This chapter will describe their actions during the period of suspense before it was known how compensation would be exacted and during the later months of crisis.

One of the factors which prevented concerted action between Britain and Japan, was the absence of political stability in Japan. There had been a rapprochement of sorts between the two powers, as the last chapter showed. Before this could be converted into an effective arrangement, the feeling of insecurity and impermanence from which most Japanese governments suffered, would have to be removed. In Britain, government between 1895 and 1905 was in the hands of conservative ministers, while foreign policy for most of that period was in the hands, or under the supervision, of Lord Salisbury. This imparted an element of continuity to British policy in the east. In

---

[1] *Die grosse Politik der europäischen Kabinette, 1871–1914*, edited by J. Lepsius, A. Mendelssohn-Bartholdy and F. Thimme, Berlin, 1922–7, xiv, no. 3739 (this series is hereafter cited as '*GP*').

Japan, however, there were five separate ministries as well as several cabinet reconstructions between 1895 and 1900.[1] Since the foreign ministers changed frequently, there was no scope for a long-term foreign policy. The sheer diversity of these cabinets certainly contributed to Japan's decision to lie low and complete her military and naval programmes.

What was the cause of this instability? Governments were generally dominated by bureaucrats; but they still had to face criticisms from political parties in the Diet. One means by which a bureaucratic ministry could avoid this opposition and keep itself in office, was to enter into an arrangement with the political parties or, more frequently, a private arrangement with their leaders. Commonly this took the form of offering the leader a place in the ministry. In the nature of things, it was a temporary expedient because it rarely satisfied the rank and file of the parties which were basically opposed to bureaucratic government.

The far eastern crises of 1897–8 had to be handled by two such coalition ministries and, in the emergency, the ministries were so involved with domestic problems that they could not take a long-term view of the international situation.

In September 1896 the Itō ministry, which had resigned because the Jiyutō (Liberal party) had withdrawn the support it had earlier promised, was replaced by a coalition cabinet presided over by the experienced elder statesman, Matsukata Masayoshi. Matsukata had managed to obtain the support of Ōkuma Shigenobu, the president of the Shimpōtō (Progressive party), by offering him a post in the cabinet as foreign minister. In this capacity, Ōkuma often rattled his sword in its scabbard but his pugnacity rarely came to anything, because Japan was not regarded as a first-class power. He was well disposed towards Britain and was ready to co-operate with her over east Asian problems. Matsukata was a specialist in finance and home affairs and was responsible for reforming the currency system and placing Japan on the gold standard. While he occasionally corresponded about the raising of a Japanese loan with the minister in London, he left Ōkuma a fairly free hand.

Rumours about the conclusion of an alliance between Britain and

---

[1] There were the second Itō (1892–6), second Matsukata (1896–7), third Itō (January–June 1898), Ōkuma (June–November 1898) and second Yamagata (1898–1900) ministries.

Japan were rife at the time of the diamond jubilee celebrations of Queen Victoria in July 1897.[1] The Japanese delegation, led by Prince Arisugawa, included Itō Hirobumi who was then out of office and had been specially invited by Ōkuma to go to Britain. The rumours were associated with the conversation which was known to have taken place between Itō and Salisbury. But there is nothing in the Whitehall archives or in Itō's writings to suggest that the conversations proceeded beyond the level of amiable platitudes. It was not beyond the bounds of possibility for Itō to take such an assignment upon himself; but in the absence of any evidence it must be assumed that the rumours were ill-founded. This was the time when the British ministers were engaged with the Colonial Conference and, had Japan wished to raise such an issue, a better time could have been chosen.[2]

Ōkuma resigned in November 1897 on the ground that Matsukata's pledges to his party had not been honoured. When the Diet met in the following month the ministry faced a motion of no confidence, dissolved the Diet and ultimately itself resigned on 25 December.

Itō was called to form the next ministry but could only do so by an arrangement with the other main party, the Jiyutō. The prime minister himself was fully engaged in preparing for the general election which was to take place in March. In these circumstances he left more than usual discretion to his foreign minister, Nishi Tokujirō, a career diplomat whose training and experience had given him sympathy towards Russia. A graduate from the university at St Petersburg, he was a fluent Russian linguist and had spent most of his diplomatic career there. Nishi was not exclusively Russophil; in a memorandum of 23 January 1896, he had argued for co-operation with Britain.[3] But, during his tenure as foreign minister, he kept clear of any course which was remotely anti-Russian and fought shy of any positive action which was beyond the resources of a virtually isolated Japan.[4]

It will be seen from this account how at critical moments in

---

[1] FO *Japan* 484, Lowther to Salisbury, 31 July 1897.

[2] Galperin, p. 61, footnote 2, using the archives of the Russian Foreign Ministry, also refers to reports that negotiations for an alliance were to be started by the Japanese mission to the jubilee celebrations. Japanese sources do not support this: *Itō-den*, iii, 303–4; *Katō*, i, 340–7. Indeed Itō's only important action during his visit to London was to warn Ōkuma strongly not to oppose the American annexation of Hawaii, which took place at this time.

[3] *NGB* 31/I, no. 195.

[4] Nishi had taken over as foreign minister on the resignation of Ōkuma in November 1897.

December and January, there were internal problems in Japan which diverted attention from foreign affairs.

KIAOCHOW AND PORT ARTHUR

While Japan was upset by this prolonged ministerial crisis, the long-awaited bid for compensation took place. The Germans took the lead by landing at Tsingtao, a town at the entrance to the bay of Kiaochow in Shantung, in November 1897. Already the French had been pushing forward their interests in south China during 1896 and 1897 but did not land at, and demand the lease of, Kuangchow until January 1898. Germany, therefore, set the pace among the Triplice. Using as his pretext the need for retribution after the reported murder of some Catholic priests in Shantung province who had asked for help,[1] the German emperor ordered that action must be taken against Kiaochow, which had a good harbour and was suitable as a fuelling point. By mid-January it became clear that the Germans proposed to establish a base in this area. Eventually China concluded an agreement on 6 March which gave Germany the lease of Kiaochow and privileges in Shantung province beyond. The German emperor had taken the precaution of trying to secure the prior assent of Russia for this act and received the grudging approval of the tsar personally. Meanwhile Chinese states-men were as usual looking around feverishly for defenders.

Despite a flurry of diplomatic activity, Japan did not make any protest against Germany's action. In deciding thus, the Matsukata cabinet was running in the face of press and public opinion but was probably justified because the ministry was shortly to give up office and was worried by Japan's isolation.[2] It might have followed a British lead. But Salisbury received assurances from Germany that any port it took would be open to foreign commerce and would not be used to acquire exclusive privileges for Germany; and, while he did lodge a protest when the negotiations for a lease began, he did not believe that it would so injure British interests as to justify interference.[3] With the

---

[1] *The Holstein papers*, iv, no. 630, supplies convincing evidence that the murder of the German missionaries only served to overcome the earlier opposition of the Foreign Ministry to taking a lease.

[2] Yamaguchi Kazuyuki, 'Kenseitō naikaku no seiritsu to kyokutō jōsei' ('The setting up of the Kensei party cabinet and the far eastern situation'), *Kokusai seiji*, no. 3 (1961), 89–90.

[3] The papers of George Nathaniel Curzon, parliamentary under-secretary for foreign affairs, 1895–8, deposited in the Public Record Office, FO 800/147, Bruce to Curzon,

coming of the Itō ministry in January, there was even less likelihood of Japanese intervention. Germany had rightly reckoned on the inertia of the two powers most likely to object.

The Russians took advantage of the situation created by Germany to send a squadron to Port Arthur early in December. It was normal for their far eastern squadron to use one of the China treaty ports for anchorage during the winter; and it was difficult for others to decide on their ultimate intentions. The Chinese negotiators, who were dragging on the parleys with Germany, were misguided enough to solicit Russian support. The Russians decided to capitalize on this by taking possession of Port Arthur. Towards the end of March, the lease of Port Arthur, Dalny (Dairen) and the tip of the Liaotung peninsula was formally granted.

To the Japanese, the occupation of Port Arthur was anathema for it was the hub of the territory of which Japan had been dispossessed three years before. It is remarkable that, in returning the peninsula to China, the Japanese had not taken precautions to prevent its being leased to a third power.[1] That being the case, it might have been expected that they would be the first to protest. But the Russians in a communication on 17 December, announced plausibly to Nishi that their squadron had anchored in Port Arthur in order to resist the occupation of Kiaochow bay by the German squadron. In these circumstances, it was not easy to take any action and Nishi accepted the statement.[2]

The foreign minister was subjected to contradictory advice from his representatives overseas. Katō discussed the matter with Salisbury on several occasions but found that Britain would not go beyond a policy of 'watchfulness'. Nevertheless he pressed upon Nishi the view that the Russian action would not be temporary and urged that Japan should make a strong protest.[3] Nishi, however, kept his counsel to himself and it was not until 18 February that he explained that Japan's internal condition was weak, both politically and economically: 'In the present situation, there are hardly any spare resources for use overseas.'[4] Japan, as he saw it, had no alternative but to accept the Russian *fait accompli*.

14 February 1898. Bruce pointed out that there were discrepancies between what Bülow was saying in the Reichstag and the assurances which Britain had been given. Curzon and Sanderson were forced to admit that there was some substance in this. *BD*, i, no. 3.

[1] Kajima, *Nichi-Ei gaikōshi*, p. 437.   [2] *NGB* 30, no. 241.
[3] *Katō*, i, 268–71.   [4] *Katō*, i, 332; *NGB* 31/I, no. 338.

Meanwhile from St Petersburg, the new Japanese minister, Hayashi Tadasu, who is later to play an important role in this study, urged that this was a good opportunity to consolidate Japan's position in Korea by obtaining Russian recognition for it. As early as 7 January Hayashi had been asked by the Russian foreign minister whether some arrangement could be reached to avoid complications there in the future.[1] A week later, the Russians proposed to enter into a new treaty over Korea; and Nishi agreed. On 16 February, Hayashi presented the Russians with an outline of the new agreement. In this way, the Japanese lost their chance to make a public protest over the occupation of Port Arthur and Dairen. They had been compromised in the hope of obtaining compensation in Korea for their connivance. In order to induce the Japanese to accept the position, the Russians felt that they could afford to dangle before Japan the possibility of improving their treaty position in Korea. This prospect commended itself both to Itō and his foreign minister and overcame any spirit of opposition to the seizure of these territories.[2]

Britain's attitude too was complicated by certain delicate negotiations which she was conducting with China for a loan of £16 million. Salisbury thought that the loan had little prospect of being concluded at Peking without Russian help or, at least, Russia's cognizance. In the cabinet an influential group, including Salisbury, Beach and Balfour, favoured an overture to Russia which might in the last resort offer to share the loan with her.[3] On 16 January the British minister to China recommended that Russia should be asked to collaborate in China. The next day Salisbury instructed O'Conor, his ambassador at St Petersburg, to inquire whether the Russian ministers favoured working together in Chinese affairs.[4] It was hoped that Britain might benefit from Russia's annoyance at Germany's action over Kiaochow where Russia claimed rights of first anchorage and whose seizure Witte had described as 'an act of brigandage'. The Russian leaders, for their part, saw in negotiations with Britain a way of gaining approval for their undisclosed ambitions at Port Arthur. By the middle of February little progress had been made: Salisbury admitted that some interchange of friendly language had taken place over an understanding with the

[1] *NGB* 31/I, no. 99.
[2] *NGB* 31/I, nos. 100–7; Langer, pp. 460, 471; *Hayashi memoirs*, pp. 95–9.
[3] The papers of Joseph Chamberlain, deposited in the University Library, Birmingham, 5/7, Salisbury to Chamberlain, 3 January 1898.
[4] *BD*, i, nos. 5 and 9.

Russians but said that their language was ambiguous and they were insincere.[1] The 'overture' broke down at the beginning of March. The Anglo-German loan was signed at Peking on 1 March and, shortly after, Russia showed her hand by demanding the leases in Liaotung. While there was still hope for success in these negotiations, Salisbury was compromised in his opposition to these leases.

Salisbury had exercised a remarkable restraint in order to quieten public opinion and create an atmosphere in the press suitable for conducting negotiations. He recalled two British men-of-war which had been sent to Port Arthur. He accepted an undertaking from Russia that any port which she might obtain leave to use as an outlet for Russian commerce would be made a free port.[2]

When all hope of a rapprochement had disappeared, Britain found that her efforts to organize opposition were too late. Through Chamberlain she asked the United States and Germany in March whether she could count on their co-operation in opposing action 'by which foreign powers may restrict the opening of China to the commerce of all nations'.[3] These countries showed little concern with the latest developments and little zeal to oppose them. Japan was displeased that Russia proposed to take a lease but was not prepared to take a strong line. On 12 March she asked Britain to join her in giving China an assurance that she had no aggressive intentions there, as this might strengthen China's hand in refusing Russia's demand for a lease. Britain replied that, without knowing Russia's exact intentions, she could give no guarantee. Japan therefore replied to Li Hung-chang who had initiated the move, that she could give no guarantee until Russia's intentions were accurately known.[4] Britain and Japan would not commit themselves not to take a lease in China and would not sacrifice their individual interests for the sake of joint action.

An agreement between China and Russia signed on 27 March, gave Russia the lease of Port Arthur and Talien for the same 25-year period as Germany had been granted for Kiaochow. China agreed to grant territorial concessions in the peninsula and permission for extending the Chinese Eastern Railway from Mukden through south Manchuria to these towns. The Russian announcement stated that Talien and Port Arthur would be open to foreign commerce; but in the former case

---

[1] FO *China* 1338, Salisbury to MacDonald, 11 February 1898.
[2] *NGB* 31/I, no. 216; *BD*, i, no. 1.   [3] Langer, pp. 472–3.
[4] *NGB* 31/I, nos. 233, 238 and 240.

this proved to mean only that foreign vessels of war could visit there to buy provisions, procure water and make repairs.[1] Port Arthur, which was purely a fortress and could not be described as a commercial port, was a different case; Russia's action there could not be justified as part of her search for a warm-water trading port. But protests were without avail. Russia had skilfully soothed Britain with promises and held out to Japan the hope of a *quid pro quo*. She had thereby neutralized all quarters from which practical opposition to her acquisitions might come.

Japan's reticence over developments in north China caused no little surprise in Britain. Could there be some truth in the view put forward by the British consul-general in Seoul that Japan was negotiating with Russia over Korea?[2] Satow was unable to confirm this. Instead he passed on the view of Itō's finance minister, the Elder Statesman Inoue Kaoru, that Japan would not take any part in the international affairs of the far east until its military and naval preparations were completed in 1902.[3] With most of Japan's leaders determined to shelter out of weakness, it was unlikely that they would challenge Russia over Port Arthur.

Kiaochow and Port Arthur provided the first opportunity for Britain and Japan to act together and show their solidarity as the powers most likely to oppose Russia and Germany. Instead, they acted separately and turned a blind eye towards these actions. Initially they both tried to negotiate with Russia for their own advantage and later asked China for compensation for the gains which the other powers had made.[4]

BRITAIN AND WEIHAIWEI

Having failed to reach any satisfactory agreement with Russia, the British government resorted to making demands on China. In February it secured an agreement for non-alienation of the Yangtse valley to any other power; in June it obtained the lease of the New Territories opposite Hong Kong. But symbolically the most important of its acquisitions was the lease of Weihaiwei. Under article VIII of the treaty

[1] *NGB* 31/I, nos. 260–4; *BD*, i, no. 1.
[2] FO *China* 1357, note by Bertie, 21 March 1898.
[3] Satow papers 14/10, Satow to Salisbury, 23 March and 6 April 1898.
[4] Kajima, *Nihon gaikō seisaku no shiteki kōsatsu*, p. 93, speaks of Britain's policy of 'compensation' over Weihaiwei.

E

of Shimonoseki, Japan's temporary occupation of Weihaiwei was due to end as soon as the indemnity provisions had been satisfactorily fulfilled. Weihaiwei was an island off Shantung province which lay midway between Port Arthur and Kiaochow and occupied a position of strategic importance at the gateway to Peking by sea. It was all the more significant after Germany and Russia had taken leases in that area.

The indemnity which was to determine the evacuation of Weihaiwei, had to be paid in three large instalments of which only the third was outstanding. China could only raise the sum by foreign loans and, after much manœuvring among the powers, a syndicate consisting of the Hong Kong Shanghai Banking Corporation and the Deutsch-Asiatische Bank, signed an agreement on March 1898 granting China a loan of £16 million. Out of this China was able to pay the outstanding portion of the indemnity. At the request of Japan, who was reluctant to accept a purely commercial settlement for such a large amount, the bond was inscribed in the books of the Bank of England — a reminder that foreign governments played a large part, financially as well as politically, in settling affairs between China and Japan. Eventually on 7 May, a bond for the formidable sum of £11,008,857 was passed over by the Chinese minister in London to his Japanese counterpart.[1] In accordance with their obligations, the Japanese withdrew their garrison from Weihaiwei by 23 May.

Three months earlier, Sir Robert Hart, the inspector-general of the Chinese Customs Service, had passed on to the British minister in China an unofficial offer from the Chinese Foreign Ministry that it was prepared to offer Britain the lease of Weihaiwei as soon as the indemnity was paid up.[2] Whether this was a means of enticing Britain's support against Russia, or of ensuring that the Japanese forces left when the indemnity was paid or merely of ingratiating themselves with Britain, cannot be known for certain. One authority thinks that it was a deliberate attempt of those Chinese officials who were impressed with the importance of Britain, to win her support even at the expense of further concessions. The offer of a lease of Weihaiwei was intended to serve as a check on Russia and was not given out of love.[3]

Although its initial reaction was that the time was not yet ripe, the

---

[1] A photograph of the original bond is found in *Katō*, i, opposite 264.

[2] FO *China* 1340, MacDonald to Salisbury, 25 February 1898; and 1338, Salisbury to MacDonald, 25 February 1898.

[3] E-Tu Zen Sun, 'Lease of Weihaiwei', *Pacific Historical Review*, xix, 281–3; and *Chinese railways and British interests, 1898–1911*, New York, 1954, p. 36.

British cabinet considered the proposal seriously. Balfour, who had taken over at the Foreign Office for the period of Salisbury's illness, wrote that if 'the Russians are to have a lease of Port Arthur and Talienwan on the same terms as the German lease of Kiaochow, the influence of those Powers over the Government of Peking will be so increased to the detriment [of Britain] that it seems desirable for us to make some countermove'.[1] The Admiralty took the view that, if Britain were to take a strategic base, it should be Chusan, the Thornton Islands or Weihaiwei (in declining order). But the ultimate choice rested with the cabinet and at its meeting on 14 March it decided tentatively to pursue the hint which Hart had passed on. For political rather than naval or commercial reasons, it opted for Weihaiwei, the small island and adjacent mainland territory at the lower lip of the Yellow Sea. It was reasonably close to the German leased territory of Kiaochow and commanded a strategic position opposite Port Arthur. As Balfour who had taken special responsibility for the decision wrote later, 'it was a strategic reply to Russia's strategic action in seizing Port Arthur'.[2]

Britain could not pursue this proposal without at least communicating it to Japan. At first, Britain encouraged the Japanese to stay on in Weihaiwei; but, although there was some support for this in the Japanese press, the Itō ministry was categorically opposed to it. Japan was in serious financial straits until the indemnity was paid and could not, in any case, have stayed on without meeting resistance from the three powers which had intervened in 1895.[3] The British minister then inquired whether Japan would object to Britain taking a lease of Weihaiwei after Japanese forces were evacuated, bearing in mind that Germany was otherwise likely to step in and consolidate her position in the Shantung peninsula. He received the evasive reply on 22 March that it had been Japan's desire that China should be able to take over Weihaiwei but 'from the moment that she is unable to do so, Japan has no objection to its possession by a Power disposed to assist in maintaining the independence of China'.[4] The delphic Itō had spoken.

[1] FO *China* 1338, Balfour to MacDonald, 7 March 1898.
[2] The papers of A. J. Balfour, deposited in the British Museum, London, Additional Manuscripts 49702, Balfour to G. S. Clarke, 11 October 1905 (hereafter cited as 'Balfour papers').
[3] *NGB* 31/I, no. 358.
[4] *NGB* 31/I, no. 361; FO *Japan* 501, Balfour to Satow, 15 March 1898 and 502, Satow to Salisbury, 17 March 1898.

Japan's minister in London was shocked by the unco-operativeness of this answer. He told his government that he found it 'inexplicable' and asked them to reconsider their attitude to Britain. In a lengthy memorandum of 26 March, he set out to show why the Tokyo policy of 'peace at any price' was short-sighted; he thought it was essential for Japan to cultivate the goodwill of Britain and urged Nishi to earn her gratitude by welcoming her occupation of Weihaiwei.[1] Britain was left without any real hope of advance encouragement from Japan and had to proceed on her own.

It took five meetings of the cabinet before it was finally decided to ask China formally for the lease of Weihaiwei. The delay may be explained by the frequent absences of Salisbury and the lack of unanimity among the cabinet. After 25 February, when he had a bout of influenza, Salisbury rested from his duties for a month and took a further month for recuperation in France. He was consulted at moments of decision; and this too accounted for some delay. There was also a basic disagreement. The cabinet met on 18 March and concluded that there were only two alternatives open to Britain: to urge Russia not to occupy any Chinese territory on the understanding that Britain would not do so either; or to let Russia proceed without any objection at Port Arthur and Dalny, while Britain took some place as compensation. The majority favoured the second course which had the backing of Balfour and Curzon who, as under-secretary at the Foreign Office, had some responsibility for the suggestion. Chamberlain, Hicks Beach and the service ministers, Goschen and Lansdowne, were not in favour of taking Weihaiwei. After a further meeting at which opinion was evenly divided, Salisbury wrote a minute recommending that it was not worth while becoming involved in war with Russia over Port Arthur and that Britain should secure from China some undertaking not to alienate Weihaiwei or at least to give Britain the first refusal.[2] When it became known that Russia had secured a lease at Port Arthur, the cabinet went beyond Salisbury's formula and, with Chamberlain alone dissenting, decided to ask China for the lease of Weihaiwei.[3] The British minister to China was instructed to obtain

---

[1] *Katō*, i, 298–306; *NGB* 31/I, no. 363.

[2] *BD*, i, no. 34. Cf. Gwendolen Cecil, *Biographical studies of Salisbury*, p. 5, claims that Salisbury wanted to avoid the risk of war with Russia because of the possibility of war with France.

[3] Royal archives Q 16/106, Balfour to the queen, 26 March 1898; Blanche E. C. Dugdale, *Arthur James Balfour*, 2 vols., i, 258–61.

the lease and the commander-in-chief was to move a naval force to the gulf of Pechili to check any Russian opposition. When MacDonald urged his home government to take Chusan rather than Weihaiwei, he received the reply that since Britain's objection to Russia's action was that it altered the balance of power in the gulf of Pechili, it would not meet the case to take Chusan. It was admitted that Weihaiwei might not be a makeweight for Port Arthur: 'it will depend on circumstances to what extent it may be necessary to use Weihaiwei.'[1] The British cabinet had knowingly asked for the lease of a second-rate base whose value would be confined to emergencies.

The government had come under attack for its inaction. After the Russian announcement, the protests were redoubled. Some, like Chamberlain, believed that Russia should be evicted from Port Arthur, even at the risk of war. The Weihaiwei party was the moderate group which felt that war was ill-advised. Indeed it was much concerned with the image of the government which was likely to face a storm of opposition after parliament reassembled. Curzon was able to announce on 4 April that the lease had been granted and, according to a report which was sent to Salisbury, 'everyone on our bench (including the anti-Weihaiwei party such as Chamberlain, Goschen, etc.) realised that but for Weihaiwei we should have fared badly'.[2] The demand for the lease had served its political purpose, although many doubted whether it would serve any strategic purpose.

JAPAN AND THE RUSSIAN AGREEMENT

On 1 April Japan was informed of Britain's intention to take a lease of Weihaiwei and was asked for her official approval. Since Japan had been putting out feelers to Russia, she was not in an easy position to reply. All the more so as Russia seemed to be in conciliatory mood: she promised in March to withdraw at Korea's request the military and financial advisers, who had been sent there in 1896, and seemed to be willing to reverse her forward policy in Korea while she established herself in Manchuria. This suggested to the Japanese that, instead of the unsatisfactory joint occupation which had existed since the 1896 treaty,

[1] FO *China* 1338, Balfour to MacDonald, 30 March 1898.
[2] (Lord) Ronaldshay, *Life of Curzon*, i, 285.

Russia might be prepared to accept a change in the *status quo*. On 19 March, after the new course had received cabinet approval, Nishi proposed to Russia that, if she would entrust Korea to Japan, Japan would in turn recognize Manchuria as being outside her sphere of interest. This was a formula which was to be repeated by Japan at regular intervals down to 1904 and came to be known as Man-Kan Kōkan (literally, the exchange of Manchuria for Korea). On this occasion Russia replied on 2 April that she could not consider excluding Russian power completely from Korea.[1]

A lengthy session of the Japanese cabinet was held on 2 April to consider its dilemma. It faced the alternative either of encouraging Britain in her overture or of pressing ahead with the Russian rapprochement despite setbacks. It was of course doubtful whether Russia could be trusted: she had announced her official lease of the Liaotung peninsula that day. But the stakes were certainly high. As against this, Katō was arguing from London that now was the time for co-operation between Britain and Japan in order to arrest the southward expansion of Russia.[2] It was, however, doubtful whether Britain might not capitalize on the crisis in China — as she later did by taking a lease on the New Territories beyond Kowloon — and could be fully trusted. In any case, co-operation with Britain might mean military action and Japan's financial difficulties precluded any such possibility.

The Japanese cabinet decided to compromise. It would give non-committal approval to Britain while it pursued its Russian negotiations, even if it was less hopeful of far-reaching benefits than it had originally been. Its reply to Britain on 2 April was the result of eight hours' deliberation in the cabinet.[3] One Japanese historian observes that, despite its cautious choice of language, the reply was intended to show that Japan really welcomed Britain's intentions over Weihaiwei: it agreed that Britain should take the lease, without indicating that it would support Britain's actions positively.[4] The Japanese, however, thought it was dangerous to become too much committed to closer relations with Britain, since it would prejudice their talks with Russia. For their part, the British regarded the message as less friendly than the Japanese intended. While Britain had asked for approval and support, Japan's reply offered merely 'concurrence' and pointedly avoided any

---

[1] *NGB* 31/I, no. 141.   [2] *Katō*, i, 302–6.
[3] *NGB* 31/I, no. 371; Satow papers 14/10, Satow to Salisbury, 6 April 1898.
[4] Yamaguchi, loc. cit., 92–3.

reference to 'support'. Moreover the Japanese asked for Britain's concurrence and support if they took similar measures.

This enigmatic request for support suggested that the Japanese were themselves looking for some territorial compensation in China during the crisis. This possibility, or at least the possibility that Japan might have made some bargain with Russia to obtain some compensation, had been foreseen by members of the British cabinet.[1] Indeed Japan did have such an intention, though it was no part of any bargain with Russia. On 22 April Japan asked China for a non-alienation agreement over the province of Fukien. The Japanese had discovered that their new territory of Taiwan and the province of Fukien opposite it were linked, both commercially and politically, and that many of the disturbances in Taiwan could be traced to organizers in Fukien. The Chinese agreed not to alienate the territory which thus became virtually a Japanese sphere of influence in China. The Japanese then asked for railway rights in the province but could only extract from China the verbal promise that, if she sought external aid in future for railway construction there, Japan would be the first to be approached.[2] Thus, unobtrusively and without objection from the powers, Japan turned the far eastern crisis to her advantage by securing exclusive rights in Fukien, though she was unable to exploit them because of slender resources.

The negotiations over Korea reached completion when the Nishi-Rosen agreement was signed on 25 April.[3] The final agreement came short of Japan's demand that she should be given a free hand in Korea; Russia admitted only Japan's special industrial and commercial rights in the peninsula. It made no concession on the main issue: it once again put the interests of Japan and Russia on an equal footing within an independent Korea. There was on the whole little advance for Japan over the 1896 treaty: joint occupation would continue as before. But, if in theory this was still so, in practice things were easier for Japanese in Korea after 1898. Japanese immigrants and traders entered Korea in large numbers and soon established themselves as the preponderant economic group in south Korea. From this point onwards, Japan's struggle with Russia over Korea was made very much easier

---

[1] FO *Japan* 501, Balfour to Satow, 22 March and 6 April 1898. Goschen reported that Japan's navy was making sinister movements which portended the seizure of Chinese territory. Balfour believed that there had been Russo-Japanese talks regarding Port Arthur and Weihaiwei.

[2] *NGB* 31/I, nos. 435-6 and 442.

[3] Roman Rosen was Russian minister to Japan (1897-1900, 1903-4).

because her nationals in Korea were so much more numerous than those of Russia.

There are widely differing assessments of this agreement. Those Russians who wished to build up their interests in Korea, thought that it was too favourable to Japan; but generally Russians were content to develop Manchuria and were satisfied with the treaty. Among Japanese, Komura, the vice-minister for foreign affairs, confessed that 'it amounted to nothing at all', although since it was the work of Nishi, who made a great mystery of his talks with Rosen, Satow thought that Komura was 'bound to treat it as insignificant'.[1] Certainly Nishi failed to win Man-Kan Kōkan but he won something equally valuable, *carte blanche* for Japanese enterprise and the Russian government's recognition of it.

In these two instances Japan took the opportunity to further her long-term objectives. To achieve this, she had to take up positions which were contradictory. On the one hand she wanted to avoid giving offence to Russia and therefore insisted that her limited undertakings over Weihaiwei should be kept secret. The Japanese were amusingly frustrated in this intention. Deputizing for Salisbury in the House of Lords, the Duke of Devonshire, in replying to a debate on Weihaiwei, was drawn into divulging that 'Japan had been consulted but, as she had requested Britain to treat her reply as confidential, its nature could not be disclosed except that it contained nothing to be taken as a remonstrance against the British Government'.[2] All the fastidious wording of the original Japanese note was shattered in a sentence. Japan lodged a weighty protest against this language but had to be content with the apology which was given.

On the other hand the Japanese did not act against British interests, even if they were cautious not to support them openly. On 30 April, after several earlier attempts, the Russian minister told Nishi that if Japan wanted to prevent China from ceding Weihaiwei to any other country after she withdrew, Russia would offer every assistance and would try to induce other powers to do likewise. The Japanese foreign minister, however, replied that, while Japan had from the start hoped that China herself would occupy Weihaiwei, she did not wish to impose special conditions on China.[3] Thus Russia's attempt to organize

---

[1] Satow papers 14/10, Satow to Salisbury, 5 May 1898.
[2] FO *Japan* 495, Satow to Salisbury, 9 April 1898; and Bertie to Satow, 19 April 1898.
[3] *Katō*, i, 308.

opposition to Britain over the occupation of Weihaiwei met with Japan's refusal.

Japanese co-operation was, moreover, useful to Britain in carrying out the eventual take-over of the island on 24 May, the day after the Japanese garrison was evacuated. The Japanese government volunteered to transfer the assets of the territory without demanding compensation. Its minister in London suggested that Japan should assist Britain as a means of restoring the goodwill which had been lost earlier in the crisis; he recommended that 'since Japan recognises the occupation of Weihaiwei by Britain as the best guarantee of Chinese independence, it should offer to pass over the barracks, etc., in Weihaiwei to Britain as they stand'.[1] His home government readily agreed that the facilities would be restored to the Chinese on condition that they should be placed at the disposal of the British forces which occupied the territory.[2] Japan handed over the barracks and other installations which might otherwise have been destroyed at the time of evacuation and also provided Britain with confidential information including up-to-date survey maps of the area. The smoothness with which British troops established themselves in Weihaiwei was largely due to the collaboration of the Japanese and British naval commanders on the spot.

The friendship of the Japanese military authorities towards Britain was much more warm-hearted than the official attitude adopted by the Itō cabinet. But this was probably the way in which the military cliques, who were notoriously anti-Russian, expressed their resentment at the politicians who had not taken their advice to continue in occupation of Weihaiwei. Certainly Britain's action was widely encouraged in military and press circles.[3] And the extreme caution, which the Itō cabinet showed, appeared as unreasonable in these quarters as it did to the British government. Yet the more that the attitude of the Japanese government is studied, the more it appears that, allowing for its domestic preoccupations and the difficulties connected with the treaty it was then negotiating with Russia, it did welcome Britain's acquisition of this strategic base.[4] Despite the coldness of his official communications, Itō told Satow privately that it

[1] *Katō*, i, 302.
[2] FO *Japan* 506, Katō to Salisbury, 11 May 1898.
[3] Satow papers 14/10, Satow to Salisbury, 14 April and 19 May 1898.
[4] Yamaguchi, loc. cit., 92.

gave him considerable satisfaction to know that Britain was 'represented' in the gulf of Pechili.[1] The underlying contradictions in Japan's attitude seem to suggest that her leaders did not yet consider their country strong enough to follow a single-minded policy which was liable to be resented in any quarter abroad.

Japan's conduct over Weihaiwei is an important pointer to the limitations on Anglo-Japanese friendship at this time. Her caution meant that in the major international issue of 1898 — the 'slicing of the melon' in China — the two countries were unable to work together effectively and had little impact on the course of events. Indeed they both contributed to the 'slicing'. For although the acquisition of Weihaiwei and the demand for a sphere of influence in Fukien were small matters compared with the leases of Kiaochow and Port Arthur, they were all part of a campaign of 'compensation' which was bound to cause further trouble in China. By the time the current crisis was ended, the Union Jack was planted between the standards of St George and St Michael at the entrance to the Yellow Sea.

[1] Satow papers 14/10, Satow to Salisbury, 14 April 1898. Satow reported that the Japanese cabinet was delighted at Britain's going to Weihaiwei because it kept the army and navy quiet.

CHAPTER III

Japan's Discreet Advances

June 1898 – June 1900

AFTER the lively tempo of events in the early months of 1898, there was a lull for almost two years. Between the cession of Weihaiwei and the outbreak of the Boxer disturbances, there was no international crisis in the far east and indeed no event of diplomatic importance to compare with the crises over Kiaochow and Port Arthur. The powers had sated their territorial appetites in China and were inclined to pursue their commercial enterprises and railway loans in peace. For Britain and Japan, this was a time, neither of great co-operation nor of serious disagreement. Both powers were called upon to define their policy towards the major happenings in the far east and, since their outlook on many points corresponded, there grew up a substantial community of interests. It will be the object of this chapter to examine these common interests.

1898 was an eventful year for the Unionist government under Lord Salisbury. Apart from events in the east, the overtures to Germany for some sort of agreement failed. In the autumn, Britain had a diplomatic clash with the French over Fashoda and, though it ended successfully for Britain, it showed the difficulty Britain would have in facing a continental coalition. With a war threatening in South Africa, which did eventually break out in October 1899, voices were raised about Britain's isolation in Europe. It is therefore understandable that British leaders should want to avoid trouble in the far east and should look for partners there.

KATŌ-CHAMBERLAIN CONVERSATION

It was in this context that the Japanese minister in London attached such importance to a conversation which he had with his host at a dinner party given by Joseph Chamberlain on 17 March 1898. Katō had been appointed in order to wean the British away from their supposedly pro-Chinese outlook and had come to set his sights on the achievement of an alliance with Britain. But this was the first occasion on which he had talked of the possibility of an Anglo-Japanese alliance to any British leader. He took away from his talk the impression that the time was ripe for an overture to Britain and that an important turning-point in his mission had been reached.

Chamberlain was well known for his public and private ruminations on foreign policy. In a letter to the prime minister during the far eastern crisis of December, he had written that the Japanese

are rapidly increasing their means of offence and defence, and in many contingencies they would be valuable Allies. They are at this moment much inclined to us and, being very sensitive, would appreciate any advance made to them. If we decided to take anything and were to inform them beforehand, I imagine that we should be sure of their support. I do not suppose that a Treaty of Alliance would be desirable, but I should hope that an understanding might be arrived at which would be very useful. In any case they are worth looking after as it is clear that they do not mean to be a *quantité négligeable* in the East.[1]

This is an important statement but it is too much to claim that Chamberlain became thereby the pioneer of the Anglo-Japanese pact among British statesmen, as does his biographer, J. L. Garvin. The idea was not new. A statesman of Chamberlain's broad sympathies would not unnaturally light upon such a proposal; but his major concern was to work with Germany or the United States.

As Katō and Chamberlain met, the far eastern crisis was at its height. Russian forces had just occupied Port Arthur; and the British cabinet had just asked Japan for her reaction to Britain's possible occupation of Weihaiwei. According to Katō's report, Chamberlain pointed out the dangers of the southward advance of Russia in the far east: if Japan decided to continue in occupation of Weihaiwei, Britain would approve since she realized that Japan had a special stake there; but if Japan were to hand it back, it might be worth while for Britain to occupy the territory and he hoped that this would not harm Japanese interests. Speaking more generally, Chamberlain said that he had been puzzled that Japan, whose interests were so similar to those of Britain, had never

[1] J. L. Garvin, *Life of Joseph Chamberlain*, iii, 249.

made proposals for co-operation in the defence of these interests. He assured Katō that Britain would welcome any such overtures.[1] It is impossible to judge whether the colonial secretary was making an officially-inspired inquiry or was merely offering an after-dinner blueprint for far eastern ills on which too great significance should not be placed. Since Chamberlain does not at this time seem to have commanded the full confidence of Salisbury or Balfour, the latter is more likely. At any rate, Chamberlain, for his own purposes, thought it worth while to goad Japan into making some approach.

On 26 March Katō followed up his glowing account of the conversation with a lengthy memorandum setting out his own views on the need for a British alliance and urging his superiors to adopt a stronger policy against Russia. He felt that Britain's decision to ask for the lease of Weihaiwei could serve as the ideal method of attaching Britain to Japan. He further set out his views on the nature of a suitable agreement based on combined naval power which would make the two countries guardians of China's shores.[2] Katō who was unaware of the secret negotiations then going on in Japan for some understanding with Russia over Korea, was bitterly disappointed that Nishi did not grasp this moment of opportunity. He therefore resigned his post, allegedly on grounds of ill-health, but really in protest against his government's disinterest. He was prevailed upon to stay in London until the following year.[3]

Katō was equally disappointed that Chamberlain could not be induced to take the initiative. In a letter to Salisbury on 29 April, the colonial secretary continued to press his ideas: as long as Britain retained her isolation, she was powerless to resist the ultimate control of China by Russia and should therefore aim at a defensive agreement with Germany.[4] In a speech at Birmingham a fortnight later, on the theme that 'who sups with the devil must have a very long spoon', he observed that if Britain was to preserve an equal opportunity for trade in China with all her rivals, 'we must not allow our Jingos to drive us into a quarrel with all the world at the same time, and we must not reject the idea of an alliance with those Powers whose interests are most nearly approximate to our own'. His reference to 'an alliance' was understood

---

[1] *Katō*, i, 293–7; *NGB* 31/I, no. 358; I have not found any record of the conversation in any British source or among the papers of Joseph Chamberlain at Birmingham University library.

[2] *Katō*, i, 302–6; *NGB* 31/I, no. 363.　　[3] *Katō*, i, 333–5.

[4] Joseph Chamberlain papers 11/6, Chamberlain to Salisbury, 29 April 1898.

by Salisbury and others as a public offer to Germany and the United States.[1] Katō, however, interpreted it rather as an invitation to Japan and the United States. Itō, who was supposed to have German sympathies, told Satow 'what he has never said before, that he was most anxious to be on the most friendly terms with England'. While Chamberlain did not stir his own government into preparing for an alliance with Japan — and probably never intended so — his Long Spoon speech did keep the subject before the Japanese leaders.[2] More probably it was merely another case of Chamberlain trying to play a larger part in foreign policy-making, as he had been doing since the beginning of 1898. With Salisbury ailing and frequently out of the country, this was a role which came naturally to Chamberlain and was not objected to by his colleagues. In this case, as elsewhere, his forte was informal conversation of which records were very rarely kept. Despite the lack of documents on his conversation with Katō, it cannot be doubted that Chamberlain did say something on these lines. The remarks are very much in character: he had the imagination to realize that one of the centres of international affairs had moved to the far east where Britain was isolated and vulnerable. Chamberlain had the flair, the politician's flair, which Salisbury for all his greater judgment lacked, for realizing that partners should be sought.

ŌKUMA'S POLICY

In Japan, policy towards Britain varied with the ministries, the short-lived Ōkuma cabinet (June–October 1898) and the more secure Yamagata cabinet (November 1898–October 1900). If the Itō ministry had, as the last chapter showed, been guarded and cautious in its attitude towards Britain early in 1898, the new ministers were considerably more ready to co-operate.

The experienced politician, Ōkuma Shigenobu, who combined the role of prime minister with that of foreign minister, was an admirer of Britain and wanted to keep in line with British policy. He presided over a Kenseitō (Constitutional party) cabinet, the first party cabinet in Japan. Office was thrust upon it within a fortnight of its formation which had been achieved by the amalgamation of the Liberal party (Jiyūtō) and the Progressive party (Shimpōtō). But the coalition broke

---

[1] Garvin, iii, 283; Salisbury papers A/106, Salisbury to MacDonald, 19 May 1898.
[2] Satow papers 14/10, Satow to Salisbury, 26 May 1898; *NGB* 31/I, nos. 402 and 403.

up before the cabinet was able to influence the country's foreign policy significantly.[1]

During this ministry, two events took place which were testing-points for Ōkuma's diplomacy. The first was the Spanish-American war. When Admiral Dewey destroyed the Spanish fleet at Manila on 1 May 1898, the Itō government had declared its complete neutrality. But the Japanese looked on with some vigilance; and when Manila surrendered on 13 August and Spain showed signs of abandoning sovereignty over the islands, Ōkuma had to rethink his government's position. In September he announced that he would welcome American sovereignty over the Philippines; but if this were not feasible, he would like to see a government formed under the joint control of Japan and the United States or, alternatively, with Britain as well.[2] When Filipino revolutionary leaders asked for Japanese help, Ōkuma turned a deaf ear. Within a month the Americans decided to demand the whole archipelago and this was eventually granted in the treaty of Paris.

The next Japanese government hinted to the British minister in Tokyo that the Americans seemed to be asking more from Spain than was justified by their military victories. But Britain, which had from the start supported America, showed no desire to question the settlement. The Japanese therefore cautiously accepted the inevitable American occupation. But Filipino nationalists had for some years obtained private support in Japan. When some of the insurgent leaders visited Japan in 1899 to ask for arms and ammunition, the government made it clear that it had no intention of antagonizing America and refused to allow export of these items. The American government twice protested against the shipment of coal and munitions by a private freighter, the *Nunobiki-maru*; but it is impossible to substantiate charges that the government was implicated in these attempts to support the Filipinos.[3]

The other event was the revolution of the Chinese intellectuals. In an initial wave of success, the reformers managed to convert the Emperor Kuang-hsu to undertake a programme of reform, later known as the

---

[1] An authoritative account of the Ōkuma ministry is Yamaguchi Kazuyuki, 'Kenseitō naikaku no seiritsu to kyokutō jōsei', *Kokusai seiji*, no. 3 (1961), 87–101.

[2] *NGB* 31/II, nos. 757 and 805. Good accounts are given in Josefa M. Saniel, *Japan and the Philippines, 1868–98*, pp. 216–21 and 'Okuma Shigenobu and the 1898 Philippine problem', *Papers of the Hong Kong International Conference on Asian History*, no. 28.

[3] *NGB* 32, nos. 561 and 566; FO *Japan* 499, Satow to Salisbury, 23 November 1898; FO *Japan* 512, Satow to Salisbury, 11 January 1899.

'Hundred Days', when blueprints for administrative, educational and military reforms were passed in profusion. The new leaders, who regarded Japan as the prototype of progressiveness and successful modernization, expected her encouragement and assistance. But the Japanese, while posing as the supporters of the reform movement, never alienated the conservative factions at court. Itō Hirobumi, who had not long given up the premiership, was touring China at the time and was careful to make friendly contacts with all parties, though he exerted his influence especially to ensure Japanese protection for the reformers when, after three months in office, they were crushed by the illiberal empress dowager and her party and the emperor was reduced to the status of a nominal ruler.[1] Ōkuma took special steps in October to grant K'ang Yu-wei, and other liberals who sought asylum in Japan, full protection.[2]

With China in such a weak state, Ōkuma wanted to bring China's military leaders under Japanese advice and guidance rather than Russian. On 4 September Japan suggested that Britain should share with her the task of reorganizing the defences of China, Britain advising the navy and Japan the army.[3] The proposal was seriously entertained in London. But, when the Japanese minister questioned Salisbury again in November, he was told that the recent *coup* at Peking had thrown the governing power in China into hands opposed to all foreign interference, although the British government was favourable to the idea.[4] Nothing came of the proposal; but it is typical of the constructive approach of Ōkuma and his more venturesome policy.

Despite his undoubted venturesomeness, Ōkuma has been criticized for neglecting openings for Japan's policy. He could, it is alleged, have taken up the case of the Filipinos and the reformers in China and followed an independent policy; instead, he chose to collaborate with the United States in the first case and with Britain in the second, thus aligning Japan with the acquisitive powers. These criticisms are very greatly exaggerated. Ōkuma could hardly have aided effectively

---

[1] *Itō-den*, iii, 397–402.　　[2] *NGB* 31/I, no. 583.

[3] The papers of Sir John Ardagh, Director of Military Intelligence, War Office, deposited at the Public Record Office, London, PRO 30/40, vol. ii, p. 40, contain a memorandum of 14 June 1898 on 'The future of China', which discusses a similar proposal. He considers that the Indian army could depute officers suitable for training the Chinese army. While the British at Weihaiwei did train a Chinese regiment under British officers, nothing came of the broader proposal and the Weihaiwei experiment was not a success.

[4] FO *Japan* 495, Salisbury to Satow, 16 November 1898.

either the Filipinos or the Chinese reformers with any chance of success and without risking a war which Japan could not afford. Be that as it may, the critics proceed to argue that Ōkuma's policy was a turning-point in Japan's diplomacy: in contrast to Itō's, it became anti-Russian and pro-Anglo-American. This conclusion seems to be justified. Indeed, this policy which favoured Britain and the United States rather than Russia, was officially accepted right down to 1905. Those who were pro-Russian tended to operate unofficially.[1]

JAPAN AND CONTINENTAL POLICY

The Kenseitō government was succeeded by a non-party ministry, presided over by General Yamagata. Yamagata shared with Itō the leadership of the genrō or Elder Statesmen.[2] Though they both belonged to the Chōshū clan, great rivalry developed between them. In so far as clan influence counted in Japanese politics, Chōshū supported Yamagata and oligarchic rule. Itō, by contrast, had favoured the growth of constitutionalism and more recently had been instrumental in giving the parties the opportunity of office. During Itō's absence in China, Yamagata, who had only consented to the party ministry with the greatest reluctance, contrived to upset the Kenseitō cabinet and take over as prime minister. He appointed as foreign minister Aoki Shūzō, who was an experienced diplomat and a previous foreign minister. Having spent much of his career at Berlin and having a German wife, Aoki was pro-German in his sympathies and was thought to be in accord with Yamagata who, like most military men, was believed to be favourably disposed to Germany. In practice, Aoki was also favourable to Britain and hostile to Russia. But he was held in check by Yamagata, who was a man of great caution. The prime minister appointed as vice-minister Tsuzuki Keiroku who was avowedly pro-French and pro-Russian; but this attempt at balance within the ministry was short-lived and Tsuzuki was replaced by Takahira Kogorō, a diplomat more suited to Aoki's temperament.[3]

Ōkuma's policy of looking for a foothold on the continent was continued tentatively by his successors over the next few years; but the

---

[1] Yamaguchi, loc. cit., 97–8.
[2] For a discussion of the genrō, see above, pp. 3–4, and below, pp. 158–60.
[3] Itō-den, iii, 404–8.

F

problem was whether this should be to the north or the south. Each course had its merits. The advantage of expansion into Korea was that it served the needs of Japan's own defence; but it could not be achieved without opposition from Russia. To the south, Japan could build on the non-alienation agreement which she had obtained from China over Fukien province. The advantage was that it would make control of Taiwan more effective as many of the dissident elements there came from Fukien; but it was remote and might cause difficulties with the other powers.

Japan's predicament was heightened when in February 1899, Italy, a newcomer in the search for spoils, asked China for an undertaking that she would not cede the province of Chekiang, adjacent to Fukien, to any other power. She further announced her intention of acquiring a naval station at Sammun bay.[1] Britain and Japan exchanged views in case their privileges were to be violated. Britain declared in March that she had no great objection to Italy's demand. Aoki also raised no objection to the Italian demand but warned enigmatically that 'Japan may, in future, find herself obliged to take similar action regarding the Province of Fukien in which she has already acquired certain rights'.[2] Japan did not try to dissuade Italy and was not inclined to oppose the Italian demand. In any case the demands were rejected by China. In August Italy requested Japan's support for renewed demands on China, this time for mining and railway rights. This was much more serious than the generalized demand in February. Thinking that this would conflict with Japan's own plans there, Aoki declined to offer any support.[3] Japan and Britain discussed their attitude. Because of the delicate situation in South Africa, Britain wanted to conciliate Italy and to prevent any counter-move by the Japanese; she gave Italy only luke-warm support and urged China to find the best solution she could. The Japanese minister at Peking was told to take the same course as Britain.[4] China eventually declined the Italian request and Italy did not pursue her demands.

Japan was tempted to consolidate her position in Fukien. Britain was worried that Japan might ask for a lease of some port there, for example Amoy. In December, Satow was instructed to tell the Japanese that any action against a treaty port would lead to serious international difficulties

---

[1] *NGB* 32, nos. 236 and 243.   [2] *NGB* 32, nos. 248 and 254.
[3] *NGB* 32, nos. 335 and 337.
[4] *NGB* 32, nos. 242 and 341; Satow papers 14/10, Satow to Salisbury, 23 March 1899.

and Britain hoped that any such idea would be abandoned.[1] There were formidable press campaigns in Japan for such a lease; but there is no evidence that the government was thinking of such an extreme move. Instead Aoki placed before the cabinet early in 1900 a lengthy memorandum proposing to ask China for rights of railway construction in Fukien and its neighbouring provinces, including Chekiang. The cabinet agreed to present to China a draft treaty on the lines of that which Germany had concluded for the laying down of railways in Shantung. Though the time was inopportune, these demands were presented to China on 5 June. Within a few days the Chinese, who were doubtless fortified by the anti-foreign activities of the Boxers, turned them down.[2] The significance of this incident is that Japan was acting in all respects like a European power in China, although her demands were more moderate and, in any case, failed in their object.

The Japanese were simultaneously pursuing the northern course without opposition from the powers. Since the agreement with Russia in 1898, they were infiltrating into Korea as fast as they could. The Russians were involved in Manchuria and left the way clear for Japan in south Korea. The other powers had little interest in Korea and were not much worried by Japanese ambitions there. Britain defined her position in the statement by the under-secretary for foreign affairs, Curzon, in 1897 that Britain wished to 'ensure that Korean territory and Korean harbours are not made the base for schemes for territorial aggrandisement so as to disturb the balance in the Far East and give to one Power a maritime supremacy in the Eastern seas'.[3] Britain thought the Korean government to be incurably corrupt and doubted the country's capacity to retain its independence: she was not prepared to interfere actively in Korean affairs to buttress a regime which was not likely to last. She was interested mainly in the international implications and only in so far as her naval and commercial interests were threatened or the peace of the far east was likely to be broken.

The Japanese proceeded to establish their commercial and industrial rights in south Korea, which had been recognized by Russia in the Nishi-Rosen treaty. Japan allowed her nationals to leave for Korea in violation of the treaty arrangements which limited them to the treaty ports; she encouraged the great expansion of Japanese trade with Korea

[1] FO *Japan* 515, Satow to Salisbury, 16 October 1899; 517, Salisbury to Satow, 9 December 1899.
[2] *NGB* 33, nos. 232 and 235.   [3] Langer, p. 457.

which took place between 1898 and 1900; she continued to give financial aid to the Korean court by way of loans. More important in the long term was her acquisition of railway rights. The Japanese had earlier purchased from an American promoter, James R. Morse, the rights for building the Seoul–Chemulpo Railway and had encouraged a group headed by Shibusawa Eiichi, the president of the Daiichi Bank, to take up the project. In September 1898, she also secured from the Korean government rights for the construction of the Seoul–Fusan Railway, a much more important arterial line. For various reasons, it was hard to arrange for the necessary surveying. Firstly, some of the genrō objected since they feared that it would only incite Russia; as against this, Yamagata and his war minister, Katsura, believed that the problem should be decided on military considerations and as part of an anti-Russian strategy.[1] Secondly, Japan was short of capital for investment overseas. The government had to attract a group of capitalists from the Mitsubishi interest, headed by Shibusawa, to form the company; but they were slow to take up the work.[2] There was, however, no shadow of doubt that the Japanese were the dominant commercial force in Korea in 1900.

Japan was also vigilant over territorial changes in the peninsula. In 1898 a pro-Japanese government was in power there but it was replaced in 1899 by (what seemed to the Japanese to be) pro-Russian ministers. In the summer of 1899 Japan approached Korea for a lease of Koje island for fishery and industrial purposes, the request being framed so as to give no pretext to the other powers to advance similar claims.[3] This was no mere commercial move since Koje was an important strategic position, commanding the entrance to Masampo and the Broughton strait. Meanwhile the Russians were seeking a site at Masampo for a coaling station and hospital for the steamship company which was to establish regular communication between Port Arthur and Vladivostok in connection with the Chinese Eastern Railway.[4] Here again the request was not as innocent as it appeared on the surface for Masampo was among the finest harbours in the far east and was clearly intended for use by Russian naval vessels. The Japanese were seriously worried; and private merchants, with the certain assistance of their government,

[1] Oka, *Yamagata Aritomo*, p. 79; Tokutomi Iichirō, *Kōshaku Yamagata Aritomo den*, iii, 386–90 (hereafter cited as '*Yamagata-den*').

[2] Maejima Shōzō, 'Nisshin Nichi-Ro sensō ni okeru tai-Kan seisaku' ('Policy towards Korea between the wars with China and Russia'), *Kokusai seiji*, no. 3 (1961), 79–81.

[3] *NGB* 32, nos. 101–9.   [4] Malozemoff, pp. 120–23.

bought up the land which the Russians sought, not without the judicious application of bribes.[1] These shady transactions recoiled on the Japanese because the Russians persisted in taking a lease, even although it was outside Masampo bay. The Japanese found that this would be more serious than in Masampo because it would be even nearer to Koje island to which they attached great importance.[2] Thus on 18 March the Russians after a naval demonstration, obtained the lease of a site between Masampo and its foreign settlement. A high-powered meeting of ministers took place in Tokyo on 27 March and decided to demand a lease of Koje island in order to resist the Russian demand for the lease at Masampo. The secret treaty between Russia and Korea was allowed to leak out: apart from the Masampo lease, the Russians had given an undertaking that they would not seek a lease of Koje island (Kargodo) and the Koreans in return promised that they would not alienate it to any other power. In the light of this disclosure, the Japanese decided not to press for a lease of Koje, which could in the new circumstances be acquired only at the risk of war.[3] As one Japanese commentator has observed, the Masampo incident was shelved because of the outbreak of the Boxer disturbances but it was in no sense basically solved; on the contrary, Russia's position at Masampo irritated Japan very much.[4]

The Japanese took a most serious view of Russia's long-term intentions. For them, Masampo was as serious as Port Arthur, because it might be the thin end of the wedge which would later enable Russia to command the Tsushima straits. Could Russia's promise not to take Koje island be trusted? The Japanese felt that they had no alternative because they still lacked the armed strength to resist Russia and had no hope of assistance from any other powers.[5] Malozemoff has contended, on the evidence of the deliberations which took place among the Russian leaders at the time, that 'neither an act of aggressive policy nor a secret move to infiltrate into a strategic position' was intended.[6] This is certainly not the impression left by the actions of the Russian minister in Korea or the naval commanders. It is also not the impression which the

---

[1] Tokutomi Iichirō, *Kōshaku Katsura Tarō den*, i, 872–3 (hereafter cited as '*Katsura-den*').

[2] *NGB* 33, no. 154. [3] *NGB* 33, nos. 166, 168, 169.

[4] Maejima, loc. cit., 82–3.

[5] Satow papers 14/11, Satow to Salisbury, 5 October and 2 November 1899 and 22 March 1900. These letters point out that Japan wanted to avoid a collision because of her weakness.

[6] Malozemoff, p. 122.

Japanese drew when they mobilized their fleet at the height of the crisis. It may be that Japan exaggerated her danger; but it is none the less a fact that this incident served to exacerbate Japan's feelings against Russia even before the Boxer disturbances broke out.

By 1900, Japan had acquired only a non-alienation agreement over Fukien and large commercial benefits in Korea. True, there were some groups in Japan, such as the Tōa Dōbunkai founded in November 1898, who were dissatisfied with this progress and wanted Japan to acquire territories on the coastline of Asia as the powers had done. But these sentiments were held in check by Japan's leaders who were anxious not to incur the open hostility of the powers. Partly this was tactical because they were keen to achieve a good reputation for Japan; partly it was financial because she could not afford expensive adventures; partly it was expedient because Japan could well wait since her geographical proximity conferred natural advantages upon her. In the first of these objectives, the Japanese scored early successes. During 1899 Japan secured international recognition as a world power. First, she achieved treaty revision; second, she became one of the Open Door powers in the far east; third, she was invited to send a delegation to the Hague conference on disarmament, being the only Asian power to do so. Thus, Japan's reticence and restraint were amply repaid by the international recognition and increased status among the powers, which she acquired.

BRITISH POLICY IN EAST ASIA

Britain's policy towards Japan was still subsidiary to her policy towards China which at this period was compounded of consolidation and caution. Britain sought to maintain her commerce with China undiminished and, despite the inroads of Germany and Russia, succeeded in retaining the major share in her expanding overseas trade. Despite opposition from the powers, Britain made a number of loans to China and acquired railway rights in several parts of the country. In these commercial transactions, there was a tendency for an alignment with Germany against Russia. Indeed Britain followed an equivocal policy towards Russia, at once working for some reconciliation with her and manœuvring against her at the Chinese court. Eventually after failing to reach agreement with Russia in 1898, Britain on 28 April 1899 exchanged notes with Russia whereby she undertook not to concern herself with railway concessions north of the Great Wall while Russia agreed not to place obstacles in the way of British railway enterprises in the Yangtse basin.[1] Salisbury had to face some opposition over this policy of caution; but he argued that, even though it bound British financiers to abstain from obtaining railway concessions in Manchuria, it was worth while.[2] The fact was that this sacrifice was no great loss since any British railway venture could succeed only with Russian co-operation in Manchuria and the agreement gave formal recognition to British predominance in the Yangtse basin.[3] The agreement applied to railways only; but there were those who felt that it represented a disclaimer of Britain's interest in the political future of Manchuria. This was a point which was to come up for discussion in 1901.

Another example of 'consolidation and caution' may be found in the evolution of the Open Door policy in China. On 6 September 1899, John Hay, the American secretary of state, distributed to Britain, France, Germany and Russia a note, calling upon them to give formal assurances that 'they will in no way interfere with any treaty port or any vested interest within any so-called "spheres of interest" or leased territory they may have in China'. Britain, France and Germany gave undertakings to adhere to the main contentions. Late in November, Japan which had not been approached in the first place presumably because she was not thought to have a 'sphere of interest', asked to be invited to subscribe to the note in view of her propinquity and her existing interests in China. Hay thereupon invited Japan which promptly adhered to the declaration.[4] Russia's ambiguous reply was for convenience interpreted by Hay as evidence of 'adherence' although Russia's real meaning was far from clear.

It was probably Britain that gained most from these notes. It might therefore be thought that the British government had in some way induced the United States to sponsor this 'standstill' policy in China, especially as Britain had encouraged the doctrine of the Open Door in China for some years. The only evidence that can be adduced to support this is that A. E. Hippisley, a British national who was on the staff of the Chinese Maritime Customs, had on his way to Britain visited W. W. Rockhill, who was in effect adviser on far eastern affairs to the State Department, and probably had an influence on the drafting. The most

---

[1] *BD*, i, nos. 57, 59 and 61.
[2] Salisbury papers A/89, memorandum for the cabinet, 15 February 1899.
[3] Joseph Chamberlain papers 5/7, Salisbury to Chamberlain, 19 February 1899.
[4] *NGB* 32, nos. 1–6 and no. 88.

that this evidence suggests is that the Hay Note owed much in its conception to the ideas of the Maritime Customs officials. It does not implicate the British government. On the contrary, the archives of the Foreign Office indicate that the distribution of the Note at this particular time owed nothing to officials there and that its form was such that Britain did not find it easy to reply. None the less, the Open Door Note helped in a theoretical way to safeguard British interests in China at a time when Britain was anxious to rivet her attention on Atlantic, rather than Pacific, affairs.[1]

Turning to Britain's relations with Japan, one obstacle to closer co-operation was removed in July 1899 when the revised treaties came into force and restored to Japan her rights of equality with other states. But the abolition of extra territorial rights affected British nationals in Japan who made representations on behalf of their 'perpetual leases' and complained volubly of Japan's municipal taxation. It is generally agreed that the visit to the far east early in 1899 of Admiral Lord Charles Beresford, the Unionist M.P., on behalf of the British Association of Chambers of Commerce had a pacifying effect: he spoke 'the language of reason and moderation to British residents' on treaty revision.[2] But the changes left a legacy of bitterness among the mercantile community in Japan. The British colonies, too, were not altogether pleased with the new position and suspicious of it. The British treaty of 1894, which was brought into force at this time, was not immediately applicable to the colonial territories, although they had the option of adhering to it. Most of these colonies preferred to forego prospects of increased trade for the sake of security as they conceived it. That is, most colonies in the Pacific area had devised immigration legislation to exclude first Chinese and later Japanese labour and feared that, by adhering to the treaty, they might have to withdraw their restrictions. Immigration legislation was an irritant in Anglo-Japanese relations at this time: the New South Wales restriction bill had brought Katō to protest to the London government in 1896 and 1898 that it would injure Japan's material interests and

---

[1] The best accounts of the formulation of the Open Door policy are given in C. S. Campbell, *Special business interests and the Open Door policy*, and *Anglo-American understanding, 1898–1903*, and in P. A. Varg, *Open Door diplomat: the life of W. W. Rockhill*.

[2] Satow papers 14/10, Satow to Salisbury, 25 January 1899. Beresford visited Hong Kong, Shanghai, Osaka and Kobe, stressing in his speeches the need for a three-sided alliance between Britain, China and Japan. See his book, *The break-up of China*. For the 1894 treaty, see above, pp. 10–11.

affect friendly relations.[1] This was certainly one of the few divisive issues then existing between Britain and Japan — and one which the London government could only partially rectify by suggesting the adoption in colonial legislation of restriction by dictation test rather than exclusion on grounds of race. This continued to rankle with the Japanese, although it was primarily a consular problem and probably weighed little at cabinet level.[2]

Another sphere in which the two countries were brought together was the financial one. In June 1899 the Japanese government secured a loan of £10 million at 4 per cent through a group of British banks. It was a government loan and was intended for a variety of public works, railways, steelworks and telephone installations. There had earlier been two small loans issued in London in 1870 and 1873. But the Japanese had generally found it hard to obtain foreign loans so long as silver was the basis of their currency and had deliberately adopted the gold standard in 1897 with the gold yen as the guarantee of a stable currency. The Japanese minister in London had then received confidential instructions to find out how much support there would be for a large loan to be raised there. By his efforts Japan gained access to the world's leading capital market.[3] In 1897 the government borrowed £4,300,000 in Britain and Osaka municipality obtained a harbour works loan through British bankers. But the 1899 loan was new of its kind and greater in scale. It was a turning-point for Japan which now felt that she could borrow abroad without being subjected to political pressures as China had been. It is hard to tell whether it had a precise significance for the political relationship of the two countries, though it was clearly a practical token of their mutual confidence. It was to be the first step in a period of increased foreign borrowing which was to last until 1913 and which therefore covered most of the duration of the Anglo-Japanese alliance. Indeed the co-operation between certain financial circles in the two countries is one of the most intriguing and least documented themes in the history of the alliance period.

While there was no real breach in Britain's friendship with Japan, there was not much enthusiasm for a closer relationship between them.

---

[1] *NGB* 30, nos. 414–15; *NGB* 31/II, no. 646–48.
[2] A. T. Yarwood, *Asian migration to Australia*, Melbourne 1964, pp. 10–15.
[3] *Katō*, i, 260–3. The success of the loan of 1899 should not be exaggerated, subscriptions in Britain covering barely one-third of the amount and the underwriters having to take up the remainder. Satow papers 14/10, Satow to Salisbury, 25 May and 15 June 1899.

Itō's foreign minister in 1898, Nishi, commented in a letter to Katō on the rumours about an alliance between Britain and Japan, which were then circulating:

It would not be possible for us, while the attitude of the powers is so uncertain, to enter into a special relationship with any one power or even to give a suspicion of doing so, since it would be frowned on by them. When a crisis comes along, Japan will probably co-operate with one or other of the powers but until such time it must remain uncommitted to any.[1]

This message was probably calculated to prick the exuberance of Katō whose frequent advocacy of a British alliance would appear to have been worrying his superiors. Nishi's view is borne out by Satow who wrote in April 1898 that the present statesmen desired that, until Japan was militarily prepared, she should abstain from opposing the plans of Russia by any overt diplomatic action: 'Unless it took the form of a defensive alliance, I do not think they would accept any proposition for joint action of any kind from our side.'[2] No Japanese government would take the initiative to approach a foreign country for aid or alliance until it could bargain independently from a position of strength. This was as true of the Yamagata ministry from 1898 to 1900 as it was of the Itō ministry to which both quotations have referred. Thus, Aoki Shūzō, when he assumed office as Yamagata's foreign minister, told Satow privately that he had made it a condition of his joining the ministry that good relations should be maintained with Britain: 'we must have *a* friend; . . . the only Power that can be a useful friend to us is England'.[3] Aoki sometimes overplayed his hand and his views often went beyond those of his colleagues. And even he did not advocate an alliance!

Much of the cordiality of Anglo-Japanese relations depended on the work of individuals. This was necessarily transitory. In the case of the individuals by whom this friendly feeling was most clearly shown, Katō and Satow, their terms of office were coming to an end. Katō left London on 15 April 1899 on furlough. Disappointed at the lack of progress towards the alliance with Britain which he sought, he left the diplomatic service early in 1900. Really a statesman with constructive views on policy rather than a conventional Japanese diplomat, he

---

[1] *Katō*, i, 311.
[2] Satow papers 14/10, Satow to Salisbury, 6 April 1898.
[3] Satow papers 14/10, Satow to Salisbury, 23 March 1899; and 14/11, Satow to Salisbury, 5 October 1899.

deemed it to be his function to pass to his government lengthy memoranda whose abiding theme was that more should be done to cultivate the friendship of Britain. Since his repeated requests for a more favourable attitude in such cases as the Weihaiwei incident and the Chamberlain talks, fell on deaf ears in Tokyo, he could scarcely be called a formative force in policy-making. His main contribution to the theme of this study was that over a period of five years his restless spirit did much to stir up forces favourable to Japan in London and kept the cause of a British alliance before the rapidly changing governments in Tokyo.

Sir Ernest Satow left Tokyo in the spring of 1900 on leave. Satow also played a significant role because his experience of Japan since the 1860s, his knowledge of the Japanese language and his friendship with most Japanese statesmen helped him to interpret the two governments to one another. Satow's parleys with Itō, Ōkuma and Aoki enabled him to report the frank views of these leaders in a way that was exceptional among British diplomats. While he cultivated good will on both sides, Satow never pressed on his government the idea of an alliance, which, as he knew, might not readily appeal to Salisbury.

Their tasks were passed to new hands. The new minister to London, Baron Hayashi Tadasu, arrived in May 1900; in Tokyo Satow's place was taken by Sir Claude Maxwell MacDonald in October. In each place there was a period of marking time before the new ministers took over. Both governments had other preoccupations; and Anglo-Japanese relations became merely one theme in the east Asian crisis of 1900 — the crisis of the Boxer disturbances.

CHAPTER IV

Britain, Japan and the Boxers

June–August 1900

1900 was another year of crisis in the far east. As in previous periods of emergency there, the alignments of the powers were thrown into clearer perspective by the crisis. It is not necessary for the purposes of the present study to examine in detail the nature of the Boxer disturbances — or the 'Boxer rebellion' as it is more often called under the assumption that it was a rebellion against the Chinese court — or the military action by the powers which they caused.[1] It will be sufficient to examine how far Britain and Japan were able to act together in face of Russia's actions during the crisis.

The Boxer disturbances were the work of a complicated heterogeneous movement which became prominent in north China in 1898. Whatever their origins, these movements were primarily peasant uprisings which attracted wide popular support by virtue of being anti-Christian and anti-foreign and were in certain manifestations anti-dynastic also. They were the cause of great civil unrest and were only half-heartedly suppressed by the provincial officials, since the court was undecided in its attitude towards them. The empress dowager and the reactionary officials, who came to power after the failure of the Hundred Days' Reform in 1898, eventually decided to divert the energies of the Boxers from themselves and turn them against the foreigners. Thus, by June 1900, the Boxers had enlisted the support of some high officials and courtiers and the movements spread like wildfire to the Peking area

---

[1] The Boxer disturbances are fully dealt with in studies by C. C. Tan, *The Boxer catastrophe*, New York, 1955, and V. Purcell, *The Boxer uprising*, London, 1963. British policy is treated in W. L. Langer, *The diplomacy of imperialism* and J. A. S. Grenville, *Lord Salisbury and foreign policy*. Among the studies on Japanese policy at this time are Kawamura Kazuo, 'Hokushin jihen to Nihon' ('The Boxer incident and Japan'), *Kokusai seiji*, autumn 1957, 93–118 and I. H. Nish, 'Japan's indecision during the Boxer disturbances', *Journal of Asian Studies*, xx (1961), 449–61.

itself with the altered battle-cry of 'uphold the dynasty and destroy the foreigner'.[1]

The Boxer activities against missionaries in the countryside and later against the legations in Peking affected Britain most among the powers. In the past, Britain had depended for her power in China on her naval strength in the far east; but, as soon as the South African war broke out in October 1899, a part of her naval squadron had to be withdrawn. As Britain became progressively committed in South Africa, a menacing European situation developed and threatened to disturb her security even more. Britain's mercantile interests in China continued without interruption; and Salisbury's aim appears to have been to turn a blind eye to China until he was forced to intervene. When, however, the lives of British nationals were at stake and the press was reporting tremendous atrocities, he was unable to remain inactive. At most he was able to send a force of marines and a section of the Indian army. Britain was therefore forced into the unusual position of urging the other powers to send large forces to China in order (as the German ambassador described it not inaccurately) 'to pull England's chestnuts out of the fire'.[2] The need was all the greater because Russia which had substantial troops readily available, was likely to take advantage of the crisis in China. Salisbury indeed wrote that 'Russia, not China, seems to me the greatest danger at the moment'.[3] The Russians appeared to have China at their mercy: either they could intervene by force or they could curry favour with the Chinese court by less vigorous military action while they took protective measures against the Boxer attacks which were menacing their railway interests in Manchuria. Britain's hopes naturally turned to Japan.

The Japanese leaders were in difficulties over sending a force to China. On the one hand, Japan was justified in sending troops because her diplomatic staff was affected by the siege of the Peking legations as much as those of the European powers. Further, she could send a large force to north China more speedily and more economically than the other powers; and Japan was not anxious to see Russian armies predominant in Manchuria and north China. As against this, in so far as the Boxer movement was anti-western and anti-Christian, it was not

[1] Tan, pp. 36–45.

[2] *The Holstein papers*, iv, no. 733, Hatzfeldt to Holstein, 19 June 1900.

[3] G. E. Buckle (ed.), *The letters of Queen Victoria*, third series, London, 1932, vol. iii, 561. Malozemoff, p. 134, estimates that there were 15,000 Russian troops in the province of Chihli late in August.

specifically anti-Japanese. Nor was there any reason why Japan should support European powers who, if past experience was any criterion, might well compensate themselves for the insult done them by demanding territorial concessions from China. Yamagata, the Japanese prime minister, commented as early as 8 June on the probability that the powers would compete against one another in a race for concessions.[1] Again, Yamagata's colleagues had no illusions about the hostility with which they would be met by the powers if they undertook a large-scale expedition to that very area of China from which they had been evicted five years before. The war minister, General Katsura, recommended to the prime minister that 'for diplomatic reasons it seems to be unwise for us to send a large force on our own' and urged him to await a request for support from the powers.[2] The policy of deliberate restraint which had been typical of Japan since the crisis of 1895 was therefore to continue during the emergency of 1900. This suited Yamagata's convenience because he had plenty of domestic problems and was in financial difficulties.

There are those who argue that Japan was trying to maintain a balance between her desire to help China and her responsibilities to the powers. Professor Kawamura has written that Japan's leaders did try to take an intermediate position and build a bridge between the powers and China.[3] This is difficult to assess. Probably the idea was not deeprooted in the minds of Yamagata or Aoki, who were both highly suspicious of Russia and anxious not to be left behind. But their wishes were generally modified by consultation with Itō. Late in June the emperor issued instructions that Itō should be consulted on the China question during the period of crisis. After his tour of China in 1898, Itō had been much in contact with Chinese leaders. In June he received a message from Chang Chih-tung, viceroy of Hankow, asking Japan to adopt a conciliatory attitude towards China: 'Japan has common interests with China and common sentiments, because both peoples are of the same race and of the same continent . . . Japan's policy toward China should be different from that of the other Powers.'[4] Certainly Itō did have some influence over Yamagata's policy; but it is hard to know how far the restraint to be found in Japan's policy was properly attributable to Chang Chih-tung and how far to the Japanese leaders' conception of their own interest. Itō agreed that limited forces should be

[1] *Yamagata-den*, iii, 407.   [2] *Katsura-den*, i, 893.
[3] Kawamura, loc. cit., 117.   [4] Tan, p. 87; *Itō-den*, iii, 429–30.

sent to north China but was not in favour of their being unduly increased. Under his influence, Yamagata seems to have adopted a middle-of-the-road course which tried to meet the wishes of the powers without antagonizing China.

THE POWERS SEND CONTINGENTS

The foreign diplomatic representatives in Peking were notoriously ill-informed about the stirrings in north China and only became belatedly aware of the dangers which they themselves faced from the Boxers. Admittedly they were deceived by the Chinese court which was vacillating in its attitude towards the Boxers and appeared to foreigners to be inscrutable. Thus, as late as the middle of May, the second secretary in Peking, writing ruefully to the Foreign Office about the Chinese, thought that 'there is something immensely attractive about these "rotters" — the only word — an Eton one — that I can find for them'.[1] On 28 May the diplomats called for reinforcements from their ships at the coast and a small force of 350 men reached Peking. On 4 June, after disjointed outbreaks in north China, members of the diplomatic body in Peking agreed to act together in reporting to their governments that they might be besieged in the Chinese capital. Salisbury therefore gave MacDonald discretion to provide for the safety of British nationals.[2] With this authority from London, he asked Admiral Sir Edward Seymour, commander-in-chief of the British far eastern squadron, who was then off Taku, for an expeditionary force. The other ministers endorsed the request. Seymour set off on 11 June at the head of an allied force of some 2000 men but was stopped midway to Peking by superior forces of Boxers and forced to retire to Tientsin.

Those in the legation quarter in Peking knew nothing of the fate of Seymour's expedition. The Boxers were at large in the countryside around Peking and had breached the railway and telegraph lines. Sugiyama Akira, the 'shokisei' (chancellor or senior clerk) of the Japanese legation, offered to make inquiries. On the evening of 11 June, he was killed by government troops on his way to the Yung Ting Men station on the outskirts of Peking in the hope of meeting the reinforce-

---

[1] Salisbury papers A/106, H. G. Dering to E. Barrington, private secretary to Salisbury 14 May 1900.
[2] FO *China* 1417, Salisbury to MacDonald, 7 June 1900.

ments.[1] His body was decapitated; and this made the attack much more than a mere violation of diplomatic privilege. It had the effect of persuading the Japanese to intervene more actively than they would otherwise have done. Although their forces had taken part in the Seymour expedition, they were not keen to be dragged in against the Boxers themselves. James Beethom Whitehead, who was deputizing for Satow in Tokyo, had earlier discussed developments with the Japanese foreign minister and been told that Japan would, if the necessity arose, 'mobilise and despatch a land force at short notice', provided she had the agreement of the powers.[2] But on 15 June Yamagata convened an emergency meeting of the cabinet and, after discussion with Itō, announced its decision to send two infantry battalions to China under Major-General Fukushima.[3]

In China the situation deteriorated rapidly. The Boxers entered Peking on 13 June when the court gave orders for any allied force to be resisted. The allied naval vessels in the Yellow Sea then seized the north and south forts at Taku at the mouth of the Peiho river, led by Japanese marines with great spirit. In retaliation for this 'invasion', the Chinese court decided to make war against the allies and authorized a siege of the legation area in Peking and the German minister, von Ketteler, the doyen of the diplomatic corps, was killed by the Boxers on 20 June.

Britain tried to muster support among the European powers for Japan to send a large force to China. After the cabinet on 22 June agreed to send reinforcements from India, Salisbury belatedly asked Russia whether she approved of 25,000 or 30,000 Japanese being sent. Russia took the line that she would not interfere with Japan's freedom to send troops provided they acted in accord with the other powers but that she was opposed to giving Japan a mandate for such an expedition. It was evidently not in Russia's interests to have her own predominance in forces undercut by an influx of Japanese troops. Nor could Germany be expected to approve because she had no troops in the expedition at this stage, although a special force was being sent out from Europe. Thus, the powers were not inclined to give the Japanese any encouragement by inviting them to play a special part.[4]

---

[1] NGB 33, no. 532, pp. 710–11. This document, 'Shinkoku jihen yōroku' ('An Account of the Boxer episode'), is a narrative account, compiled by the Japanese Foreign Ministry, of the powers' intervention in defence of the legations and at the peace-making.

[2] FO Japan 531, Whitehead to Salisbury, 9 June 1900.

[3] Itō-den, iii, 428–9; Yamagata-den, iii, 410–11.

[4] BD, ii, nos. 3 and 4; GP, xvi, nos. 4527–36.

The Japanese government, which was being urged by the Chinese not to intervene, wanted to ensure that any action which it took, would be acceptable to the majority of powers. It was pursuing conflicting objectives: it wanted to prevent any large-scale Russian infiltration into north China as a result of the crisis but it wanted also to avoid being in isolated antagonism to Russia there. On 23 June the foreign minister asked the powers what measures they favoured in the present crisis. The replies about Japan's role were as guarded as the earlier replies to Britain had been. It was at this stage that Britain threw over the idea of obtaining prior agreement from all powers and made to Japan her 'first appeal to send troops'.[1] Britain told Aoki' of the critical condition of the Legations and also of the force which has been sent to relieve them' and invited Japan to send a further relief force. Aoki replied frankly that Japan was not yet in a position to take an independent line of action in so grave a crisis: if Japan sent a large force, 'this will be resented by Russia and probably lead to a collision'; Japan could only take this risk if assured of the support of Britain and Germany hence the imperative necessity for an understanding between Britain, Germany and Japan to counteract Russian designs.[2] Aoki expected Britain, which most wanted Japan's intervention, to convert the other powers to this course.

Was Aoki's reference to an understanding between Britain, Germany and Japan of special significance? Aoki asked that it should be treated as 'most confidential' so that other governments should not hear of it. There is no Japanese version of this message, which suggests that it was the foreign minister's private initiative. He was given to pursuing personal schemes of 'high politics'; and this one is in keeping with the notion which underlay all Aoki's diplomacy, that what was needed was an anti-Russian front with Britain and Germany. But this could only be achieved if Germany were permanently detached from Russia. Since this was unlikely, Aoki's reference to an understanding between the three powers should be treated as a casual suggestion to Britain rather than a political proposal which was readily capable of fulfilment. In any case Salisbury took no special interest in the suggestion.

However much the Yamagata ministry might refuse to send a large force without the overwhelming support of the powers, there is the

[1] This phrase is taken from *Nihon gaikō nempyō narabi ni shūyō bunsho* ('Japanese diplomatic chronology and important documents'), 2 vols., Tokyo, 1955, where three separate British appeals are differentiated.

[2] Salisbury papers A/126, Whitehead to Salisbury, 25 June 1900. I think Grenville, pp. 311–12, may have read too much into the notion of an 'understanding' by suggesting

G

impression that it was not unwilling to intervene. Its problem was to choose the right degree of intervention and, in the solution, it had to take into account several domestic considerations. It had to win over political leaders like Itō and to influence opinion through the press; it had to examine the country's finances to find out how large an expedition Japan could afford.[1] For these reasons there were advantages in delaying a decision.

SIEGE OF THE PEKING LEGATIONS

The next phase of the Boxer disturbances is associated with the siege of the Peking legations by the Chinese army and the Boxers which lasted in violent form from 20 June to 16 July when it was temporarily relaxed. Tientsin too was in the hands of the Boxers so that there was little hope of any relief expedition being sent quickly. Moreover there was little reliable news of happenings in north China; and in the atmosphere of uncertainty which prevailed, governments in Europe were under strong pressure to send large forces.

On 3 July Britain pressed Japan to send all possible assistance — the so-called 'second appeal'. The following day the Foreign Office heard from Admiral Seymour at Tientsin that the legations were asking for help at once as conditions were desperate. Balfour and Brodrick who were left in charge during Salisbury's absence, passed this to Tokyo with a plea for help on the ground that Japan was the only power which could send reinforcements. Whitehead handed over this message — the 'third appeal' — on 5 July with the assurance that Russia was no longer opposed to Japan sending large forces.[2]

Yamagata could only respond to these appeals by handling the domestic situation carefully. He had no difficulty in his cabinet or with the majority of genrō who had to be consulted on an issue of such importance. But he was faced with opposition from Itō who was hostile to entanglements in China and was opposed to exhausting Japan's resources by rashly sending a large force because of his distrust of the foreign powers in China. Early in July, however, Yamagata managed to

that it was an 'overture'. See also Dr Grenville's article, 'Lansdowne's abortive project of 12 March 1901 for a secret agreement with Germany', *Bulletin of the Institute of Historical Research*, no. 27 (1954), 203.

[1] *Yamagata-den*, iii, 413–15.   [2] *NGB* 33/I, no. 574.

prevail on Itō that it was difficult to refuse foreign requests for support and that 20,000 men of the fifth division should be sent.[1] At the cabinet meeting on 6 July, it was resolved that 'it was desirable on military and political grounds to send troops urgently and so Japan should despatch without delay the division which has already been mobilised'.[2] Orders were issued for an expeditionary force of 22,000 men to be sent to China. This was a far-reaching decision because it associated Japan fully with the actions of the allied powers in China.

Britain felt that this number of troops might not be conclusive and offered to pay part of Japan's expenses if still more Japanese troops were sent to China. On 9 July the Japanese cabinet agreed to prepare one or two more divisions for China. Since Itō was again opposed to sending larger reinforcements, it was proposed that Lieutenant-General Terauchi Masatake, the deputy chief of the General Staff, should be sent to the spot to report on troop requirements. On 11 July the Japanese emperor received a communication from the Chinese emperor asking him to take the lead in restoring peace. If the tone of the communication was more friendly, it was in substance no different from that sent to the other powers. The Japanese reply was in line with that of the other powers in so far as it demanded that the siege of the legations must be ended before peace could be restored.[3] Meanwhile, pending Terauchi's report, the Japanese declined to send further troops, although they had the second division mobilized in case reinforcements were ultimately called for.

Britain could not understand what was deterring the Japanese from sending further troops. Could it be that her financial offer was too imprecise? At its meeting on 6 July the cabinet had agreed that, as Britain could not afford any more troops for China, it should offer Japan whatever financial support she required for an advance to Peking for 'the relief of the prisoners' (as Salisbury expressed it).[4] After a further cabinet meeting on 14 July, Britain undertook to afford the Japanese financial assistance 'up to a million sterling if they at once mobilise and send forward without delay for the relief of the Legations at Peking, Twenty Thousand troops' in addition to those already promised.[5] After discussion with the premier, Aoki replied that 'whether

---

[1] *Itō-den*, iii, 429–30; *Yamagata-den*, iii, 414–15.
[2] *NGB* 33/I, no. 592, pp. 572–3.   [3] *NGB* 33, no. 532, p. 723.
[4] Royal archives A 76/19a, Salisbury to the queen, 6 July 1900.
[5] Royal archives A 76/21, Salisbury to the queen, 14 July 1900; FO *Japan* 530, Salisbury to Whitehead, 13 July 1900.

Japan sends more troops or not will depend on the results of discussions between Terauchi' and other commanders. Since Terauchi eventually reported that the fifth division would be ample, the Japanese did not take up the offer and paid the expenses of their expeditionary force themselves from a supplementary budget. The Japanese rightly refused to be bribed to do something which they were reluctant to do and put military considerations first. Yet the offer of an outright grant was a significant gesture of Britain's confidence in Japan, of which it made no secret.[1] After it had been rejected, Britain did not renew her demand for Japanese troops.

The final phase of the Boxer crisis began with the occupation of Tientsin by the allied armies on 14 July — an important victory which demoralized the ill-disciplined Boxer levies. The Japanese fifth division reached there a week later. But there were disagreements among the commanders about the wisdom of an immediate advance on Peking where it was thought that the legations could not have survived.[2] Many commanders, including the Japanese, wanted to defer the assault until reinforcements from all quarters brought the numbers up to 50,000 men. Only an appeal from the legations, which were sorely tried by the more rigorous siege which confronted them from 28 July onwards, induced the commanders to venture forth. On 14 August the allied armies entered the capital and freed their nationals from the siege which had lasted nearly eight weeks. The superiority of western arms and discipline under fire made short work of the Boxers and confirmed the British contention that the commanders were being over-cautious in not advancing earlier on Peking.[3]

'LURKING EVIL INTENTIONS'

Jealousies which had earlier been submerged, burst forth as soon as the allied fortunes improved. The most prominent dispute arose over

[1] *NGB* 33/I, nos. 618 and 638. The British financial offer was made public in the British Blue Book, *China no. 3* (*1901*), after initial reluctance on Japan's part.

[2] After the British cabinet meeting on 20 July, Salisbury reported to the queen that 'it seemed too probable that the Legations have been slaughtered'. Royal archives A 76/20, Salisbury to the queen, 20 July 1900. The first message which got through from MacDonald was received on 30 July.

[3] In the end, the force which relieved the legations was estimated at 8000 Japanese, 4500 Russians, 3000 British, 2500 Americans and 800 French. With smaller contingents from other countries, this may have amounted to 22,000 men in all. But there were also large armies in Tientsin and elsewhere.

the appointment of a commander-in-chief for the allied contingents. Hitherto they had operated independently under a loose arrangement; but as peace was approaching and the number of troops growing, there was the danger that individual commanders might go their own way unless there was some central control. Germany argued that it should supply the commander-in-chief and put out feelers on behalf of General Waldersee. While Britain refused to sponsor him, the tsar was persuaded to do so, despite French misgivings.

An aspect of the Oberkommando question, which is specially relevant, is the reaction of Japan. On 7 August the Japanese emperor received a private telegram from the kaiser asking for his concurrence in the tsar's proposal. Japan replied that the emperor had no objection.[1] This decision was resented in Japan because the senior commander, both in rank and in the number of troops under his command, was the Japanese divisional commander in the field, Lieutenant-General Yamaguchi. It was a slight to Japan that the elderly Waldersee should at this late stage be proposed, although he was still in Europe. Japan's action was also criticized by Itō who rightly pointed out that, if Waldersee was indeed sponsored by the tsar, it was for the tsar, and not the kaiser, to recommend him to the Japanese emperor.[2] This episode has generally been recognized as a prestige-seeking manœuvre by Germany; but it was also regarded by the Japanese as an insult by Germany which seemed to have sinister ambitions in China. It was, however, unlikely that any European power would have placed its armies under the command of a Japanese general.[3]

After the legations had been relieved, there was in north China a group of foreign contingents, each with its own national objectives. Not content with freeing their nationals, many set about suppressing the Boxers; and the province of Chihli was overrun by foreign troops. Moreover, as the Japanese prime minister wrote on 20 August:

Although the powers try to disclaim their ambitions in China, Russia has quickly built up its forces and naval strength in Manchuria, Britain in the Yangtse and Germany and France likewise. All give abundant evidence of *lurking evil intentions*.[4]

---

[1] *NGB* 33/II, no. 996.　　[2] *Itō-den*, iii, 432–4 and 436–8.
[3] Cf. A. von Waldersee, *Denkwürdigkeiten*, 3 vols., Stuttgart, 1923, ii, 450: 'That we should give Japan the command, I consider to be out of the question, for Christian leadership must certainly be preferred.'
[4] *NGB* 33/III, no. 2370. Part of this document is translated in appendix A. My italics.

Early in August the British naval commander had sent troops from Hong Kong to protect British interests in Shanghai. On 25 August, Russia announced that she would withdraw her legation and contingent from Peking to Tientsin; many thought that the troops would be withdrawn further in order to concentrate in Manchuria, where Russia was already strongly established. It was not unreasonable to predict at the end of August that the powers with their armies at the ready would continue with the process of 'slicing the melon' which had not been completed in 1898. Such was the background of suspicion against which the diplomacy of the next four years must be set.

Japan which had the largest forces in north China, was eager to evacuate them as quickly as possible. Partly this was because of the great expense of keeping a large army in the field; partly because of the prestige which she would gain by a speedy withdrawal. Indeed, had it not been for the suspicious actions of the Russian force, the Japanese troops might have returned home sooner. The ninth brigade was eventually withdrawn in October. This reinforced the good reputation which the Japanese troops had earned by their discipline in China. It was the first occasion on which they had fought alongside European troops and they were quickly recognized as a well-organized military force.

While Japan's leaders were not so interested in north China, they were wondering whether they should be consolidating her interests in Korea or in Fukien in south China. They seem to have had the alternative of reaching an understanding with Russia over Korea and concentrating their activities in south China or of establishing their position in Korea while the emergency lasted, by armed force if need be, and ignoring the south. In July the Yamagata cabinet, which had for some months been much irritated by Russian actions at Masampo,[1] made an approach to Russia for some sort of bargain over Korea and Manchuria but did not receive an encouraging response. Even before this was completely rejected, the cabinet authorized a landing of forces from Taiwan on 26 August at Amoy. The exact purpose of the expedition is not known; but at least one object was to teach the local inhabitants, who were often responsible for creating trouble in Taiwan, a lesson.[2] Before the expedition had achieved anything, it was recalled

[1] Microfilm reproductions of selected archives of the Japanese army, navy and other government agencies, 1868–1945, reel T 178. See above, pp. 72–4.
[2] Ibid., reel T 154.

by Tokyo. This had been the course which Yamagata himself had favoured; and it is a problem to know quite why it was so soon given up. It is likely that the Japanese cabinet thought that Russia's withdrawal from Peking presaged a crisis in the north and that it would be unwise for its forces to be tied up in a southern adventure. It now seriously considered invading Korea, as many pressure groups were demanding, but decided as an act of caution to consult Germany first. The Germans lingered over their reply until a cabinet crisis in Japan made such an expedition impossible. Over a period of three months, the Yamagata cabinet had switched from one alternative to the other, watching cautiously the actions of the other powers and feeling uncertain where the true interests of Japan really lay.[1] Japan's conduct at the end of the Boxer disturbances was not entirely altruistic and might better be described as vigilant and indecisive.

ANGLO-JAPANESE PRACTICAL CO-OPERATION

The Boxer crisis gave a new dimension to the relations between Britain and Japan: scope for their friendship to be translated into practical co-operation. Among the various countries taking part in the operation, it was the British and Japanese forces which tended to act together. Sir Claude MacDonald, the British minister at Peking who virtually commanded the legations during the siege, later expressed the opinion that 'the memorable "Siege of the Legations" undoubtedly had the effect of bringing England and Japan into closer and warmer friendship and, to my knowledge, sowed the seeds of that formal Alliance between the Island Empires of the East and the West'.[2] This conclusion would exceed anything which a writer working from the archives could draw; but it is the verdict of one whose closeness to the Boxer disturbances and the later alliance entitles his view to be respected.

During the Boxer emergency, Japan's policy had been influenced more by Britain than by any other government. But that had been true for a few years past. The Japanese had responded favourably to Britain's urgent appeals as far as it suited them to do so. Similarly it must be assumed that Britain, in seeking Japan's intervention, had full confidence in Japan's integrity and military efficiency. At the same time,

---

[1] Nish, loc. cit., 451–5, gives further information about Japan's expedition to Amoy.
[2] MacDonald, 'The Japanese detachment during the defence of the Peking legations', *Trans. Proc. Japan Society (London)*, no. 12, 19.

Britain turned to Japan not as a power necessarily sharing her views, nor as a potential ally, but as the only country capable of giving timely support. In their co-operation the two powers had acted out of self-interest because they were linked by their opposition to Russia. As against this, Britain and Japan were not immune from suspicions of one another. The Japanese were among the powers who landed marines at Shanghai in August when Britain seemed to be threatening to become supreme there. Similarly Britain was suspicious about Japan's intentions during her expedition to Amoy and sent a ship to the scene. But these doubts were to be expected in the tense situation then existing in China and did not prevent the powers co-operating as far as possible, even though in the aftermath of the disturbances Japan tended to be more sympathetic to China than Britain was.

The factors which had affected east Asia since 1895 — the weakness of the Chinese Empire and the strength of Russia's position there — were now even more conspicuous and were likely to irritate the situation for some years to come. Nothing seemed so implausible in the immediate aftermath of the Boxer disturbances as the survival of China as an independent state. True, the Open Door doctrine had been reaffirmed in response to a circular letter issued by John Hay in July 1900; but few had confidence in its effectiveness. Joseph Chamberlain wrote in September:

I believe that [Russia] will ultimately secure North China and that the 'Open Door' will be a mere name as far as this part of the Chinese Empire is concerned. It is certain that we are not strong enough by ourselves to prevent her from accomplishing such an annexation.

In view of this gloomy forecast, what steps could Britain take? Chamberlain took the view that:

our policy clearly is to encourage good relations between ourselves and Germany, as well as between ourselves and Japan and the United States, and we should endeavour to make use of the present opportunity to emphasise the breach between Russia and Germany and Russia and Japan.[1]

For present purposes, it is sufficient to observe that Chamberlain had assigned a role in British policy to Japan. Indeed in order to attract the Japanese, Britain was to put no obstacle in the way of Japan's ambitions

[1] Joseph Chamberlain papers, memorandum by Chamberlain, 10 September 1900. The text is reproduced in G. W. Monger, *The end of isolation: British foreign policy, 1900-7*, p. 15.

in Korea. It is not possible to say that the colonial secretary's views were shared by any members of the cabinet when they were circulated to them. But at least they were the realistic and imaginative views of one of the most influential members of the Salisbury ministry and they contain one of the few indications that Britain felt powerless to cope with Russia in China on her own.

In the re-examination of policy in Japan, similar issues were discussed in a lengthy memorandum by the prime minister. Yamagata was trying to combat the argument that Japan should use the present crisis to consolidate her position in Korea before it was too late. This was a common enough view in Japan. The British military attaché, Colonel Churchill, asked himself the question: 'Can Japan afford to wait, her position in regard to Russia becoming relatively weaker the longer the delay?'[1] Yamagata, however, argued that the Japanese were not yet equipped to challenge Russia and would be well-advised not to raise the issue of Korea meantime. He argued:

Even if Britain privately agreed to it and the United States raised no objections, Russia, Germany and France would join together and oppose it. In event of war, would Britain still help us with her military forces? If we could not rely for sure on Britain allying with us, we would be forced to fight alone against a threefold enemy.[2]

Yamagata does not make his ideas altogether clear in these remarks. He apparently thought that Britain was the most favourable of the foreign powers towards Japan but could not be relied upon for armed support. He seems to have believed that the main danger to Japan was that the Dreibund of 1895 was still united against her. On these premises he argued that Japan should not advance in the north but should give first priority to the provinces of Fukien and Chekiang. As in the case of Chamberlain, there is no information to indicate how far his colleagues shared his views. But they are valuable even as the individual views of the prime minister.

Yamagata also referred to Russia's naval strength in north-east Asia. Britain's leaders were equally worried by this recent development. Russia was engaged in a large-scale naval building programme to cover the years 1898–1904. What was ominous for Japan and Britain was that, instead of keeping her battleships in the Baltic, she was sending them to the far east where Vladivostok and Port Arthur were being developed

[1] Morrison papers, 312/60, 5 March 1900.   [2] *NGB* 33/III, no. 2370. Appendix A.

as bases. To Japan they were a stimulus to her own shipbuilding programmes. To Britain, however, they were of great nuisance value because she had to send a corresponding number of battleships if she was to maintain the balance of naval power on that station. The Admiralty, which was faced elsewhere in the world by French naval building and by the new navies of Germany and the United States, was seriously disturbed. Every battleship sent to the China station reduced Britain's superiority in European waters which had been difficult enough to maintain since the outbreak of the South African war in October 1899. Thus, Russia's landward expansion was matched by her increased maritime strength in eastern waters, which was equally objectionable to Britain and Japan.

Yamagata's memorandum underlines a controversy which exists among Japanese historians of this period. Professor Furuya takes the view that from the cabinet decision in July 1900 to send troops for the Peking expedition, Japan must be treated as among the imperialist powers in the far east. By joining with the imperialist powers of Europe in what was a punitive expedition, Japan was identifying herself with them.[1] This was, in short, the point of take-off for Japanese imperialism. Other historians have argued that Japan was more moderate towards China than the vengeful European powers; that Japan was asked by China to mediate in July; and that during the peace talks the Japanese were able to lay before the allies the viewpoint of the Chinese side. In short, Japan was a bridge which spanned the gap between China and the powers and was well placed to use her good offices.[2] It is not the intention of this study to pronounce on this controversy. Truth seems to lie somewhere between the two views. On the one hand, the 'imperialist' criticism seems to ignore the fact that the relief of the legations was in part an international humanitarian operation. On the other, the 'bridge' argument seems to discount the great element of self-interest which prompted Japan's actions throughout the crisis and the peace conference which followed. Yamagata's memorandum seems to show that he was eager to take advantage of the crisis by acquiring either territory or a sphere of interest and does not indicate that Japan's attitude was really pro-Chinese. At the same time, while Japan was no

[1] Furuya Tetsuo, 'Nihon teikoku shugi no seiritsu wo megutte' ('About the development of Japanese imperialism'), *Rekishigaku kenkyū*, no. 202 (1956), 40–6.

[2] E.g. Kawamura, loc. cit., 117, claims that Japan's success in maintaining an intermediate position between the powers and China in 1900 was an historical fact of which Japan can still be proud.

better than the other powers in her ambitions, she was less determined than the powers in their pursuit. Considering that her armed forces were much more numerous, this indicates a degree of self-restraint on the part of the Japanese army and government.

The Boxer emergency was an important turning-point. It showed that Japan was already one of the powers and one of proven strength. Japan had for some years tried to be inconspicuous but she could no longer conceal her new strength after this crisis. Moreover she had reached marriageable age and might expect the attentions of several suitors. It was not unnatural that one of these should be Britain for whom this was a turning-point in middle age. Though Britain had previously been looking around for a partner, it had never been a matter of desperation until the Chinese crisis was added to the existing protracted South African crisis. The emergency was also a turning-point for the far east in general: China's resistance had broken down and her future integrity depended on the powers being able to ensure by their joint efforts that none of their number received preferential treatment there. It is within this context of power rivalries in north China that the Anglo-Japanese rapprochement had its origins.

PART TWO

The First Alliance

I do not pretend at all that it is one of the ordinary,
everyday diplomatic transactions between Power and
Power. But the reasons for it seem to me not to lie in
the secret archives of this or any other Foreign Office,
but upon the broad facts and the large necessities of
our interests and our policy in the Far East.

A. J. Balfour, House of Commons,
13 February 1902
British parliamentary debates,
4th series, vol. 102, col. 1294

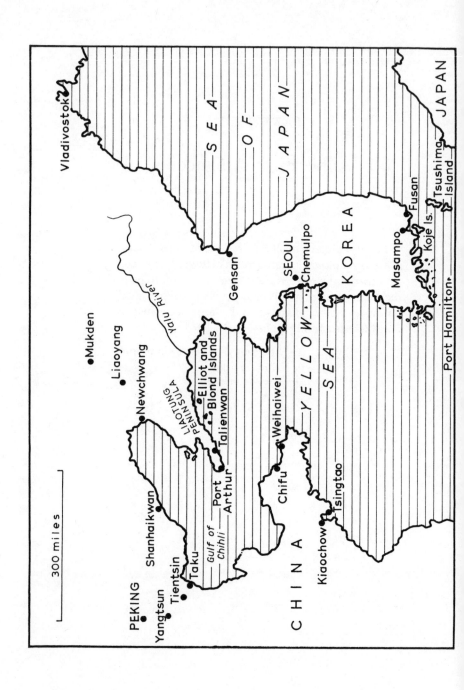

CHAPTER V

The Anglo-German Agreement and Manchuria

September 1900–April 1901

DURING the twelve months from August 1900 to August 1901, relations between Britain and Japan gradually improved. There was less evidence of misunderstanding than was observed, for example, when Britain occupied Weihaiwei. The two governments began to realize that their interests lay in challenging Russia, whose concentration in Manchuria and Korea seemed to have sinister implications for the future. None the less it takes more than an intangible identity of interest between two powers before they agree to merge in an alliance; and it is the slow process whereby this identity of interest was recognized which we must now examine.

There is a certain similarity between the period which we now approach and the years immediately preceding it. The events which we have so far described stemmed mainly from the Sino-Japanese war of 1894–5, which influenced international relations in the far east until 1900. The Triple Intervention, the Port Arthur crisis and indeed the state of Korea and south Manchuria throughout the period owed their origin to Japan's victory in that war. If the war had left China weak, the fury of the Boxer disturbances and the revenge which the powers took, left north China prostrate. Whereas Japan was forced to her knees by the powers in 1895, it may be said that Japan's stature among the nations grew immeasurably after the Boxer disturbances. While there were no victors in the crisis of 1900, Japan certainly gained a reputation as a military power. But there is this fundamental difference between 1895 and 1900: whereas the powers intervened in the Sino-Japanese war mainly by diplomatic protests, they intervened in 1900 by sending military and naval forces, albeit small ones, to China and

99

in the aftermath by keeping them there. Because of this, the powers despite all their mutual jealousies sought to prevent a recurrence of the 'free-for-all' in China which had been the characteristic of the previous five years and tried to bring about an international solution. The greatest obstacle to the accomplishment of this was Russia. While the press of the world found sensation in the steps which the allies were taking to save the Peking legations, the foreign offices of the world were more concerned with the steps which the Russians were simultaneously taking to consolidate their position in Manchuria in order to protect their South Manchurian Railway. Apart from the men seconded to the allied force in north China, the Russians sent vast forces into Manchuria in July and quickly disposed of the Tartar armies of that territory.[1] The key event was Russia's announcement that she proposed to remove her armies from Peking at the end of August. Did this mean that Russia proposed to occupy Manchuria with her armies and thus strengthen her grip on a territory where she had long claimed special rights?

CABINET RECONSTRUCTION

The situation in China had its effect on internal affairs in Japan. It threatened the existence of the Yamagata ministry which had been in office since 1898. In September its foreign minister, Aoki Shūzō, broke established practice by making a report direct to the emperor in which he expressed the opinion that Japan must not shrink from force in order to stop Russian aggression against Korea. Yamagata did not approve of this point of view and only learnt of it when the emperor questioned him about it. This episode which brought to a head disagreements between Yamagata and Aoki, served to divide the cabinet even further; and Yamagata placed its formal resignation before the emperor on 26 September. Apart from disagreements over resistance to Russia, there were differences over the abortive Amoy expedition in August in which the resignation of the influential governor-general of Formosa, Kodama, was only averted with difficulty.[2] There were also certain political developments in Japan which were disturbing for the non-party ministry of Yamagata. Marquis Itō, who had generally

---

[1] Tabohashi Kiyoshi, 'Giwa kempiran to Nichi-Ro' ('Japan and Russia during the Boxer disturbances'), *Tōzai kōshō shiron*, 2 vols., Tokyo, 1939, ii, 1051–105.
[2] On the cabinet crisis, *Itō-den*, iii, 465–6; *Katō*, i, 373–4; *Yamagata-den*, iii, 426.

opposed the ministry, was nominated as president of the Seiyūkai party which held its opening ceremony in Tokyo on 15 September. The new party absorbed the membership of the older Kensei party and thus became overnight a force in the land. Itō offered Yamagata an assurance of full support if he would continue in office.[1] But there is more than a suspicion that Yamagata, who was hostile to the growth of political parties in Japan and opposed their increasing influence, thought that it would be good tactics to give the Seiyūkai party a 'baptism of fire' by resigning forthwith and recommending that their president should be called upon to form a government. Since the invitation came within two weeks of the party's official inauguration, Itō refused more than once but was finally forced to accept under pressure on 6 October. No sooner had he accepted office than he fell sick and Saionji Kimmochi as vice-president of the Seiyūkai was called on to act as prime minister. Itō was not able to take up his duties until 10 December.[2] It is of some significance that Japan's decision on the Anglo-German agreement, was taken in Itō's absence and without his guidance.

The names of the first Seiyūkai cabinet were announced on 19 October. The portfolios of the army and navy remained in the hands of two non-party members, General Katsura and Admiral Yamamoto. The other non-party member was the foreign minister, Katō Takaaki, who had no Seiyūkai affiliation. The choice of a minister who was only 41 years of age, a supporter of Ōkuma and an avowed enemy of Russia — almost the antithesis of Itō — is not readily understandable. From Katō's biography it appears that he had as far back as June been offered the appointment if the Itō party came to power. The offer was renewed on 19 September and accepted on certain conditions. The most important were that the officials of the Foreign Ministry should not be changed on each occasion there was a change of foreign minister and that when diplomatic business was transacted with ministers of foreign countries, it should be done through him, however far-reaching it might be. These conditions were accepted and gave Katō an autonomy which had been denied to Aoki and his predecessors in office, who were liable to be overruled by the genrō.[3] Katō, who had been minister

---

[1] *Itō-den*, iii, 464, Itō to Yamagata, 9 September 1900.
[2] *Katō*, i, 389; *Rikken Seiyūkai shi* ('History of the Seiyūai party'), edited by Kobayashi Yūgō, 4 vols., Tokyo, 1924-6, i, ch. 1.
[3] *Katō*, i, 377-80.

to London from 1895 to 1899, was known to be an enthusiast for friendship with Britain and speedily adopted policies which were anti-Russian.

The foreign policy of the Itō ministry was conditioned by its domestic difficulties. The Itō cabinet had no difficulty in getting its finance bill which provided for increased excise duties, through the party-dominated lower house; but the House of Peers threw it out on several occasions. Itō requested assistance from several Elder Statesmen and from Prince Konoe, president of the House of Peers, but could not resolve the financial deadlock. He eventually resorted to using the discretionary powers of the emperor; and an imperial rescript was issued, instructing the upper house to accept the bill for tax increases. On this basis the budget was passed. But the revenue voted with such difficulty was insufficient to meet the nation's expenditure, especially that incurred in connection with the expedition to relieve the Peking legations. On 30 March 1901, the finance minister proposed to balance the budget by postponing certain public works. This gave rise to disagreement in the cabinet; and on 2 May Itō tendered his resignation. In the last months of his government's existence, foreign affairs had to take second place to domestic problems.[1]

There was also a major cabinet re-shuffle in Britain. After the relief of Ladysmith and Mafeking and several other victories in South Africa, the Conservatives decided to hold what came to be known as the 'khaki election' and dissolved parliament on 25 September 1900. The far east was not absent from the cabinet's calculations. The Leader of the House of Commons, Balfour, wrote in July that 'recent events in China have rather sharpened my desire for an early appeal to the country — we have evidently got before us a long stretch of troubled waters, which it would be much easier to navigate with a new H. of C. than with an old one'.[2] Successes in both South Africa and China stood the government in good stead and it was returned with much the same majority as it had hitherto enjoyed — no small achievement after five years in office.

The opportunity was taken to make certain adjustments in the cabinet which had their bearing on foreign affairs. It was the general feeling that Salisbury was no longer able to bear the double burden as premier and foreign secretary. Some thought that as prime minister

---

[1] *Itō-den*, iii, 505–9; *Katō*, i, 458–60.
[2] Salisbury papers, Balfour to Salisbury, 5 July 1900.

he was not sufficiently alive to party issues. He was criticized early in the election campaign for failing to convey his views to the country. Salisbury replied with characteristic wit that he did not do so for the simple but ample reason that he had nothing to say.[1] He did, however, eventually bow to his party's needs by issuing an address to electors. As foreign secretary also, he had fallen out of step with the views of most of his colleagues. Many of them wanted him to continue only as prime minister, if they could remove him from the foreign secretaryship without wounding him deeply. One alternative open, that of appointing Joseph Chamberlain to the Foreign Office, was not generally acceptable. After some deft manœuvring, Balfour hit on an arrangement which left Salisbury as prime minister but, as he explained in a letter, put 'the conduct of Foreign Office details into the hands of Lord Lansdowne'.[2] Towards the end of October, this solution was adopted. The new Salisbury ministry was announced with Lansdowne as foreign secretary assisted by Lord Cranborne, Lord Selborne at the Admiralty in place of Goschen and with St John Brodrick at the War Office.

The new foreign secretary had pulled through a trying, and not very successful, spell as secretary for war but he had definite qualifications for his new office. He was undoubtedly skilful in handling foreign diplomats and foreign powers. He was painstaking in administration and did not spare himself in learning about his new and unfamiliar office. With his experience as governor-general of Canada and later as viceroy of India, he brought to his task an appreciation of the wider world and an awareness of imperial issues. He was, moreover, a different kind of foreign secretary from Salisbury. Salisbury, genial as he was, kept his confidences to himself and often ignored advice. Lansdowne, on the other hand, was ready to receive recommendations and kept in touch with his advisers at home and overseas. But there is little evidence that any sharp change of policy accompanied the change of foreign secretary. Indeed, whenever a new approach was contemplated, the prime minister was always fully consulted.[3]

---

[1] Balfour papers, Add. MSS 49760, note by J. S. Sandars, 20 September 1900.

[2] J. M. Goudswaard, *Some aspects of the end of Britain's 'Splendid Isolation', 1898–1904*, Rotterdam, 1952, p. 50. For a different account, see Grenville, p. 323–5.

[3] On Lansdowne as foreign secretary, Zara Steiner, 'Last years of the old Foreign Office', *Historical Journal*, no. 6 (1963), 73–4. For further discussion of this topic, below, pp. 242–3 and 335.

ANGLO-GERMAN AGREEMENT ON CHINA

While this transformation was taking place, Salisbury was reluctantly engaged in negotiating an agreement with Germany over China. At the end of the relief expedition to Peking, Germany had been greatly irritated by the projected withdrawal of Russian troops from Peking and north China while Germany had a large expeditionary force on the high seas on its way to China. Britain was known to be suspicious of Russia; and Germany put out a few feelers. During a visit by the Prince of Wales to Germany on 22 August, the Kaiser mentioned that Britain would find Germany on her side if she gave a formal undertaking that she would maintain the Open Door policy in China. This was followed a week later by a request for a practical understanding over the Yangtse question.[1] Salisbury was rightly suspicious of these vague expressions which did not set out any course differing from that which had been pursued for some time. This attitude was criticized by other members of the cabinet who felt that this was an ideal moment to drive a wedge between Germany and Russia. When Salisbury left for a recuperative holiday on the continent, a small cabinet consisting of Chamberlain, Goschen and Lansdowne, met at the Admiralty on 3 September and drafted a joint telegram to the premier advocating the need for a gesture of goodwill towards Germany.[2] Beach and Balfour were not present but signified their approval. After stating that they did not favour the withdrawal of British troops from Peking, they stressed 'the importance of taking advantage of the opportunity offered by the recent action of Russia to detach the German emperor from Russia and bind him more closely to our interests'.[3] Salisbury agreed that there should be no withdrawal of troops from Peking but completely ignored the other suggestion. When he returned on 14 September, he found a strong note from Chamberlain emphasizing the need for good relations with the United States, Germany and Japan.[4] Salisbury also received a memorandum from Bertie expressing the contrary view: Germany was expansionist in China and not really hostile to Russia so that a *modus vivendi* with her would be dangerous.[5]

Unwillingly and with the cabinet united against him, Salisbury held

---

[1] *BD*, ii, nos. 8, 9 and 11.
[2] J. Amery, *Life of Joseph Chamberlain*, iv, 138–40.
[3] Salisbury papers A/89, Goschen to Salisbury, 4 September 1900.
[4] Joseph Chamberlain papers, memorandum by Chamberlain, 10 September 1900.
[5] FO *China* 1446, memorandum by Bertie, 13 September 1900.

talks with the German ambassador on numerous occasions. During the negotiations the German government stated that it could not press Russia for an extension of the principle of commercial freedom to portions of China in which that principle was not secured by any treaty, such as Manchuria.[1] This was one of the objectives at which Britain aimed. Eventually after considerable discussion it was agreed that the Open Door principle should apply to all Chinese territory so far as Britain and Germany could exercise influence. It was the vagueness of this phrase which prevented the treaty becoming effective. As signed on 16 October, the agreement was in the form of a joint undertaking to observe certain principles:

1. It is a matter of joint and permanent international interest that the ports on the rivers and littoral of China should remain free and open to trade and to every other legitimate form of economic activity for the nationals of all countries without distinction; and the two Governments agree on their part to uphold the same for all Chinese territory as far as they can exercise influence;

2. [Germany and Britain] will not, on their part, make use of the present complication to obtain for themselves any territorial advantages in the Chinese dominions, and will direct their policy towards maintaining un-diminished the territorial condition of the Chinese Empire;

3. In case of another Power making use of the complications in China in order to obtain under any form whatever such territorial advantages, the two Contracting Parties reserve to themselves to come to a preliminary understanding as to the eventual steps to be taken for the protection of their own interests in China.[2]

It is necessary to examine these terms in view of their bearing on the later Anglo-Japanese agreement. In the wording of the treaty, there was no limit to clauses 2 and 3 dealing with the territorial integrity of China: they applied to the whole of the Chinese Empire. But clause 1 relating to the Open Door was only operative as far as the signatories could exercise influence. Since Germany claimed that she did not exercise influence in Manchuria, she did not deem the clause to be applicable to the ports on its rivers or littoral, namely Newchwang and Talienwan. Since, however, Newchwang and Talienwan were already open ports, the effect of the German reservation was, to say the least, far from clear. It can only be assumed that the wording was intended

---

[1] *BD*, ii, no. 17.   [2] *BD*, ii, no. 17, enclosure.

to indicate that Germany was not prepared to take action to ensure that Russia kept these ports open; in what was to be a published agreement, Germany would not guarantee to oppose Russian activities in Manchuria. The more active group in the British cabinet whose ambition it was to embroil Germany with Russia in China, could not fail to be disheartened by the clause. But it was not surprising to Salisbury who could write on the day after the signature of the treaty:

Germany is in mortal terror on account of that long undefended frontier of hers on the Russian side. She will therefore never stand by us against Russia; but is always rather inclined to curry favour with Russia by throwing us over. I have no wish to quarrel with her; but my faith in her is infinitesimal.[1]

In such a spirit was this unhappy series of negotiations conducted on the British side.

The treaty had the appearance of being a one-sided arrangement. While Britain guaranteed that the Yangtse ports would remain open to trade, Germany's guarantees were limited to Tsingtao. Her privileges in the province of Shantung were not subject to any limitation under the treaty. While this apparent inequality gave rise to criticism from interested parties in Britain, it was no new thing for Britain to guarantee that the Yangtse ports would be open to trade. Indeed it would have been a flagrant violation of the Open Door principle if Britain had claimed to exclude others from them. It was not unnatural for the Germans to seek confirmation of this in the prevailing atmosphere of China when the powers were thought to be on the point of carving it up at any moment. Thus, the most important thing which Germany gained from its terms was an undertaking that Britain would not close the Yangtse to its commerce. In return, Britain hoped to obtain some assurance that Germany would co-operate against possible Russian expansion in north China and Manchuria. In the unsatisfactory compromise which resulted, the treaty became a joint undertaking, consisting partly of a restatement of Open Door principles and partly of a self-denying ordinance over territorial acquisitions in China.

It was hoped that it might also serve as a declaration in which all countries could join. The agreement was not published for ten days

---

[1] Monger, p. 17, quoting Salisbury to Curzon, 17 October 1900.

after its signature so that the text might be referred to powers with Chinese interests for the acceptance of its principles. Despite differences of language, none disagreed openly; and even Russia expressed her agreement in ambiguous terms.

JAPAN ADHERES

What gives the agreement special significance for this study is the form of Japan's response. Katō, who had only held office for a few days when the agreement was referred to Japan, wanted to turn it to his country's advantage. He hoped, by joining the agreement, to increase Japan's status as a world power; to establish a close relationship with Britain; and to detach Germany from her suspected friendship with Russia. He wanted Japan not merely to accept the principles of the agreement but also to undertake the responsibility for putting these principles into effect as a full contracting party to it.[1] Katō evidently wanted to convert it into a three-sided treaty. He inquired from Britain and Germany whether Japan could by adhering occupy the same position as one of the signatories instead of merely adhering to the principles. On receiving satisfactory replies on this point from both parties, Japan announced her complete adherence to the agreement on the above basis on 29 October.[2] Katō was confident that he could use this treaty to buttress the anti-Russian policy which he proposed to follow. He harboured the slight doubt that there might be some secret clause outside the treaty which had not been divulged to Japan but had to take on trust the assurances which he received that there was nothing secret about its contents. In the ten days available to him, he had neither the time nor the opportunity to inquire about the underlying assumptions of the two signatories or find out about the bargaining which had gone on. While there is inevitably an element of risk in all such transactions, it cannot be denied that Katō was rash in not probing more deeply into the complicated motives behind the agreement. This was a precaution which would have been expected of the prime minister, Itō, who was cautious to a fault, and it can only be assumed that he was too ill to be consulted about this decision. Indeed, he was later inclined to be critical of the transaction, hinting that, even though Japan had adhered to the Anglo-German agreement, it should

---

[1] *Katō*, i, 405–7.   [2] *NGB* 33, no. 57, Katō to Whitehead, 29 October 1900.

not be thought that she was going to pull the chestnuts out of the fire for Britain and Germany by opposing Russia's activities in Manchuria.[1] What emerged from Katō's initiative was virtually an Anglo-German-Japanese treaty. This fact has not always been appreciated. Partly this is because the Japanese had done something which was not expected of them. The signatories had not gone out of their way to invite Japan to take a part in the treaty which was different from any other power.[2] Japan's adhesion, therefore, was essentially the result of Japanese initiative. Partly too, this is a matter of terminology. Britain used the term 'adhere' to describe the actions of those powers who merely endorsed the principles contained in the agreement as well as the actions of Japan.[3] This has confused the issue. But there can be no doubt that Britain recognized Japan as a full party to the treaty. In a debate in the House of Commons on 26 July 1901, the parliamentary under-secretary at the Foreign Office, Lord Cranborne, said that the Japanese by their adherence 'entered into all the rights of the signatories; there is no question that they have all the rights which [we] ourselves and Germany have under the agreement'.[4] This is testimony to the uniqueness of Japan's action which is borne out by the records themselves.

Katō found the Anglo-German agreement very much to his liking: anti-Russian in intention, it would link Japan with Britain and detach Germany from friendship with Russia in east Asia, which had, he thought, prevailed since 1895. These were legitimate deductions for Katō to make from the text of the treaty and it was natural for him to associate Japan more closely with it. But Katō's hopes were not fulfilled. As we have seen, the treaty was less anti-Russian than the text implied. Britain had entered upon negotiations on the assumption that it would be aimed against Russia but, as negotiations continued, it became apparent that Germany did not share that assumption. The negotiators resorted to vague phrases; and it was only a matter of time before the parties drew differing interpretations from the treaty. Since

---

[1] Imai Shōji, 'Dai ikkai Nichi-Ei dōmei kyōyaku' ('First Anglo-Japanese alliance'), *Rekishi kyōiku*, no. 5 (1957), 59, quotes Itō's comment. *Itō-den* makes no mention of the Anglo-German agreement and does not claim credit for Japan's adhesion as part of Itō's policy.

[2] Ishii Kikujirō, *Gaikō yoroku*, pp. 34–5.

[3] Some confusion arises from the use of the term 'adhere'. Japan 'adhered' to the agreement as if one of its signatories, whereas the others 'adhered' to its principles.

[4] *British parliamentary debates*, 4th series, vol. 98, col. 267.

the agreement never became an effective instrument against Russia, Katō's hopes were frustrated.[1]

The Anglo-German agreement was important for the development of Anglo-Japanese understanding. To Japan and Britain, the agreement was first and foremost a challenge to Russia and acted as a natural counterpoise to Russian activities in Manchuria and north China which were already assuming a menacing form. It was, moreover, the first time that Japan had signed a treaty with Britain which concerned the far east as a whole and was not devoted to their commercial or domestic affairs.[2] One of the reasons why the Japanese government had not entered into alliance talks with Britain previously had been the fear that an agreement with Britain would only attract the joint opposition of France, Russia and Germany as in 1895. It was Katō's hope that the Anglo-German treaty made that alignment unlikely.[3]

In trying to associate Japan with an anti-Russian front, Katō was responding to much current thinking in Japan. One supporter of such views was the *Kokumin Dōmeikai* ('People's alliance') which was founded in September 1900 with Tōyama Mitsuru among its prominent leaders. At mass meetings, it worked up public opinion and urged the government to prevent Russian consolidation in Manchuria and to send troops to Korea. It was an influential body which had spokesmen in the Diet and carried on publicity campaigns in the press. Katō was more responsive to these anti-Russian views than was his prime minister because they fitted in well with his general thinking.

Perhaps it was under the influence of the *Kokumin Dōmeikai* that Katō consciously adopted a stronger policy towards Russia. This represented a fundamental change in the direction of his country's foreign policy. Since 1895 Japan had made compromise after compromise with Russia, particularly over Korea. As late as July 1900, the Yamagata ministry had tried to negotiate a settlement with Russia on the basis of the exchange of Korea for Manchuria; but Russia had not made a ready response. Itō, who succeeded Yamagata as premier, also favoured this line of approach; but Katō, by clever manœuvring, succeeded in getting his own way. In fact, he took a tougher line towards Russia than any foreign minister since Mutsu.

The Russians chose this moment to propose the neutralization of

---

[1] *BD*, ii, no. 38, enclosure 6. Salisbury told Hatzfeldt that Germany had 'altered it to make it agreeable to Russia'.

[2] *Katō*, i, 405–8.   [3] Galperin, p. 90.

Korea. This was not a new proposal: in September the Korean ministers at the instance of Russia had suggested making Korea a neutralized country but had not been taken seriously in Japan.[1] The idea was taken up by Witte shortly after.[2] On several occasions in November, Alexander Izvolskii, the Russian minister to Japan (1900–3), proposed that Japan and Russia should agree to the neutralization of Korea under guarantee of the powers. Katō agreed to examine any concrete proposal which the Russians put forward. It was in these circumstances that Izvolskii left a note with the Japanese foreign minister on 7 January 1901. Katō was most suspicious that Russia, which was thought to be consolidating her position in Manchuria, should take this moment to open discussions over Korea and claimed that Russia only displayed an interest in Korea when she wished to entrench herself more firmly in Manchuria. In his view, Japan had interests in both countries and Korean problems could not be divorced from Manchurian.[3] In this, he was supported by the *Kokumin Dōmeikai*, whose members got to know of the Korean proposals and tried, by organizing public agitation and even by threatening ministers, to put pressure on the government to transfer Japanese troops from China to the Korean frontier. This was one instance where a vocal group had some influence on the determination of foreign policy.[4]

On 17 January Katō replied directly to St Petersburg that, in view of Russia's temporary occupation of Manchuria, Japan felt it best to defer the neutralization plan until the situation returned to normal when talks might be resumed 'uninfluenced by any external considerations'. He added that the Russo-Japanese treaty of 1898 was still in force in Korea and seemed to work well.[5] When the Japanese chargé presented his government's reply, Lamsdorf told him that the neutralization plan was put forward tentatively as a friendly concession to Japan in the belief that it really represented Japan's ideas.[6] Izvolskii was gravely disappointed with Japan's reaction because he had been in touch with Inoue and Itō behind Katō's back and thought he had disposed them favourably to Korean neutralization. Indeed this story

[1] *NGB* 34, nos. 393 and 396.
[2] 'Boxer rebellion', *Krasnyi arkhiv*, no. 18 (1926), 42.
[3] *NGB* 33/II, nos. 1363, 1365; *Katō*, i, 411–13; Maejima, loc. cit., 84–5.
[4] M. B. Jansen, *The Japanese and Sun Yat-sen*, Cambridge, Mass., 1954, pp. 109–10.
[5] *NGB* 34, nos. 399–400; 'First steps in Russian imperialism in the far east, 1888–1903', *Krasnyi arkhiv*, no. 63 (1934), 9–11, Izvolskii to Lamsdorf, 14 January 1901.
[6] *NGB* 34, no. 404.

had circulated widely in Japan; and it may be that the *Kokumin Dōmeikai* put pressure on Itō. Certainly the draft reply was approved by Itō and the emperor on 16 January; and Katō got his way.[1]

By replying directly to Russia over the head of Izvolskii, Katō was inflicting what was perhaps a deliberate insult on the Russian minister. Katō had the idea that Korean neutralization was Izvolskii's own brainchild and that it was essential to know whether it was backed by the Russian authorities at home.[2] Whether the project was 'bluff' on Russia's part or not, it seems to have been ill-starred from the outset. The Russians seem to have overestimated the strength of their bargaining position in Korea which was now weaker than Japan's. The Japanese naturally rejected neutralization as a proposal which only weakened their standing in Korea and invited interference by the powers.

MANCHURIA

More serious were Russia's incursions into Manchuria. During the Boxer emergency, Russia had placed garrisons throughout Manchuria in defence of her railway interests. In her southward advance, she had occupied Newchwang, the main port of Manchuria, had taken over the customs and seemed likely to wrest the trade from the Japanese for her own nationals.[3] In all this Russia acted independently of the powers as though Manchuria were her own preserve. Indeed the Russian leaders declared that this was a matter to be settled between Russia and China in which other powers could have no say.

The trouble arose over the transfer of the civil administration of the southern province of Manchuria, Fengtien. On 26 November the local Chinese commander concluded an arrangement with the Russian commander, Admiral Alexeyev, whereby the Chinese might resume the administration under Russian protection. This temporary agreement, which did not entail the evacuation of Russian armies, was not

---

[1] It is known that a delegation of *Kokumin Dōmeikai* had an interview with Itō on 23 January 1901, led by Tōyama Mitsuru, but this was too late to affect the government's reply over Korean neutralization. None the less Itō could not fail to be influenced by their agitation. *Itō Hirobumi hiroku* ('Private writings of Itō Hirobumi'), edited by Hiratsuka Atsushi, i, 135–7 (hereafter cited as '*Itō hiroku*').

[2] *Katō*, i, 413–14; *Yamagata-den*, iii, 487.

[3] *NGB* 33/III, nos. 1840–5. What incensed Britain was Russia's take-over of the Yangtsun-Shanhaikwan railway, most of which was mortgaged to British bondholders.

ratified by Peking and was not pressed by Russia, provided formal negotiations were started. On 3 January, the London *Times* published the text of what purported to be an agreement between Russia and China but was in fact a garbled version of this arrangement. The report failed to indicate the temporary nature of the arrangement and suggested that the agreement was in reality the permanent seizure of Manchuria as a protectorate of Russia, which many had forecast. This article was the first intimation to reach foreign capitals and had the effect of generating the first 'Manchurian crisis' which lasted until April.

The information caused a furore in Japan. Katō asked Russia on 16 January whether there was any truth in the rumours about the treaty and, if so, what the details were. Lamsdorf gave assurances but firmly declined to give any positive information. A week later, Izvolskii handed over a note explaining the provisional nature of the *modus vivendi* and tried to remove Japan's suspicions.[1] But Japan was determined to make an issue of the treaty and gave the Chinese leaders and the Yangtze viceroys stern warnings about the consequences of signing such a treaty with Russia.

Japan's first approach was to Britain. On 12 January Hayashi suggested that Britain should protest to Russia like Japan; but Lansdowne declined. Instead he informed Russia in the most moderate language that questions would certainly be asked when parliament met and he would like to know what answer should be given.[2] Shortly afterwards Katō urged that a warning should be given by Britain to the Chinese court. Lansdowne confessed that he was disposed to humour Japan and gave China the necessary advice. This was followed by Germany which made a similar but separate declaration, though 'not without serious misgivings'.[3]

Lamsdorf gave Britain the assurance which he later agreed to have published, that Russia had no intention of seeking a guarantee against future attacks by any acquisition of Chinese territory.[4] To Britain and Japan, this statement did not square with Russia's actions. On 15 February Katō, who had just advised China against the Russian treaty, told Britain that he was 'anxious to inform the Chinese that

---

[1] *NGB* 34, nos. 84, 90 and 93.

[2] FO *Russia* 1625, Scott to Lansdowne, 11 January 1901; FO *Japan* 538, Lansdowne to MacDonald, 12 January 1901.

[3] *BD*, ii, no. 43; *NGB* 34, no. 102; *Katō*, i, 424.

[4] *British and foreign state papers*, xciv (1901), 1048, quoting Scott to Lansdowne 6 February 1901.

[the Japanese] will give them material assistance in case Russia insists on concluding an arrangement affecting territorial rights'. The following day Lansdowne prepared a memorandum for the cabinet commenting on the Japanese request that Britain should promise the Chinese material support. This was tantamount to offering China naval support if Russia demanded territory in Manchuria. Lansdowne thought that the elastic language of the proposal was dangerous and felt that Britain should not go beyond the Anglo-German agreement. Salisbury rightly pointed out the impossibility of Britain taking steps to defend the landward frontiers of China. He added that he was 'not opposed in principle to an engagement with Japan to join in defending the coasts in which we think we have serious interests in preserving from the Russian grasp'.[1] In short, a guarantee to China against Russia was not feasible; but an arrangement with Japan to protect Britain's interests on China's coastline would not be impracticable. Here in embryo is the Anglo-Japanese alliance. And by a strange irony it came from Salisbury's pen. But the idea was not followed up. The Japanese suggestion was, with the cabinet's sanction, turned down on the ground that it was difficult for Britain to deal with infringements of China's territory. Britain contented herself with renewed warnings to China.[2]

The important phase of the Manchurian negotiations started on 16 February when Lamsdorf passed over the Russian terms to China. While the twelve articles provided for the re-establishment of Chinese sovereignty in Manchuria and the demilitarization of the country, they laid down that Russia would receive certain exclusive privileges and that China would 'not grant in Manchuria and Mongolia any concessions for railway construction without Russian agreement'. On 1 March the Chinese asked for substantial revision of the draft and appealed to the powers for mediation in the dispute.[3] Three days later Britain responded by calling upon Russia to supply the text of the draft agreement and Japan consulted Germany and Britain about long-term action. On 6 March the Japanese minister to Germany obtained a statement from Mühlberg, the under-secretary for foreign affairs, that, if the Manchurian problem came to a crisis, Germany would observe

[1] FO *Japan* 542, MacDonald to Lansdowne, 15 February 1901; FO *China* 1500, minute by Lansdowne, 15 February; minute by Salisbury, 17 February.
[2] FO *Japan* 542, Lansdowne to MacDonald, 18 February 1901.
[3] Langer, pp. 714–16.

benevolent neutrality; and that Japan need have no worries since Germany's action would keep the French fleet in check and Britain would probably support Japan, if she was involved in hostilities with Russia. The same phrase — wohlwollende Neutralität — was also used on various occasions by the Kaiser and leading officials, though it was later withdrawn by the foreign minister, Richthofen.[1] Katō was suspicious about the extent of Germany's 'benevolence' and decided to question Britain. Hayashi, therefore, asked Lansdowne on 11 March whether Mühlberg's views revealed Germany's real attitude and how far Japan could rely on British help in the event of her considering overtures to Russia to be necessary. Lansdowne replied that he doubted whether Germany would go beyond strict neutrality in event of a crisis and that Britain could, on account of her South African commitments, give no practical assistance except to observe a strict neutrality.[2] None the less Lansdowne was eager to discover Germany's attitude since Britain might have been prepared to go beyond her strict neutrality if she could have relied on German assistance. The best answer to China's appeal for help was by way of international action and this depended largely upon Germany's reaction.

Moreover Lansdowne was worried that Japan's attitude was too extreme and incautious. Japan had in her message of 9 March mentioned the possibility that she might find it 'necessary to approach Russia'. On being questioned, Hayashi admitted that 'approach' probably meant 'resist'. As Salisbury was quick to point out, 'resist' implied not diplomatic, but military, action. Further questioned about the term, Hayashi replied that he had no instructions but from the context he imagined it to mean 'take strong steps towards' Russia. It is evident from the Japanese text of the telegram sent to Hayashi that Japan was thinking only of making 'overtures' by way of diplomatic negotiations. Clearly Hayashi was unwise not to inquire on this all-important point from Tokyo. By failing to do so, he unwittingly conveyed to Britain a false impression of his government's intention.[3]

---

[1] Hermann von Eckardstein, *Lebenserinnerungen und politische Denkwürdigkeiten*, 2 vols., Leipzig, 1919–20, translated as *Ten years at the court of St James, 1895–1905*, edited by G. S. Young (London, 1921), pp. 203-4, quoting Holstein to Eckardstein, 9 March 1901. Holstein uses the phrase 'wohlwollende Neutralität' to describe Germany's policy. Since Mühlberg's language to the Japanese minister was used also by his superiors, the notion that Inoue misunderstood what he was told does not hold water.

[2] *NGB* 34, nos. 159 and 171; the English versions in *BD*, ii, nos. 51b and 33.

[3] FO *Japan* 545, memorandum by Bertie, 9 March 1901. Japanese telegrams were at

In these circumstances, Lansdowne decided to devise a means for drawing out Germany. His staff was asked to prepare a draft declaration which Britain and Germany might sign jointly. Although it was never sent, it is interesting for the light it throws both on Britain's attitude to Japan and her suspicions of Germany. The draft read:

In present circumstances, the interests of England and Germany are not sufficiently involved to justify them in giving material assistance to the Chinese Government in resisting the conclusion of the Agreements. They admit, however, that the vital interests of Japan are thereby seriously jeopardised, and in reply to the enquiries of the Japanese Government as to what would be the attitude of England and Germany in the event of hostilities between Japan and Russia, they have to state that in such a contingency, which they would deeply deplore, it would be their object to limit as far as possible the extent of the war, and to that end they would remain neutral, reserving, however, to themselves absolute freedom of action should the course of events require them, in their own interests, to intervene on behalf of Japan.

In the event, however, of any Power joining Russia in hostilities against Japan, the British and German Governments will give naval assistance to Japan to defend herself against such attack.[1]

The draft was approved by Lansdowne and circulated to the cabinet. The intention behind the declaration was that Germany should be invited to join Britain in giving the undertaking secretly to Japan. Underlying it was the desire to elicit from Germany a distinct statement of her intentions. The step proposed was important enough to justify calling together the cabinet for a special meeting on 13 March. Salisbury's report on the cabinet states that several members were disposed to agree that Britain and Germany should join in undertaking to support Japan; but, in the absence of any indication that Germany would be willing to take part in such an alliance, it was thought better to defer any discussion until inquiries in Berlin had been made.[2] In the outcome, it was decided to ask Germany what she meant by

this time sent in English so that Hayashi had no access to the original Japanese words. *NGB* 34, no. 159, Katō to Hayashi, 8 March 1901, uses the word 'kōshō' which means only 'negotiation'.

[1] FO *Japan* 547, draft declaration by Bertie, printed for the cabinet, 12 March 1901. Text in J. A. S. Grenville, 'Lansdowne's abortive project of 12 March 1901 for a secret agreement with Germany', *Bulletin of the Institute of Historical Research*, no. 27 (1954), 210–12.

[2] Royal archives R 22/13, Salisbury to the king, 13 March 1901.

'benevolent neutrality'; and the draft declaration was scrapped. None the less it has an obvious significance for the story of Anglo-Japanese relations. Salisbury described the 'offer' to Japan as being one of alliance. Allowing for the flexibility with which he generally used this term, he was probably justified in this case where the powers were being asked to commit themselves to hold the ring for Russia and Japan. There is, however, no evidence that the cabinet was committed to the idea of an alliance at this stage. It seems to have been a cockshy declaration drafted to see if there was scope for an approach to Germany. For that reason, its terms were pitched high. Moreover, the cabinet was working from the false assumption that Japan planned to resist Russia by arms. Britain had no great interests in Manchuria and approached Japan's inquiry with natural caution. This attitude was confirmed when inquiries in Germany showed that she had no intention of upholding Mühlberg's undertaking of 'benevolent neutrality' nor would she risk conflict with Russia over Manchuria. Lansdowne accordingly told Hayashi that, much as Britain sympathized with Japan's cause, she would remain strictly neutral in the event of war between Japan and Russia.[1]

JAPAN'S LONE STAND

These intimations of strict neutrality on the part of Germany and Britain affected discussions proceeding in Tokyo. In answer to the appeal from China, Katō wanted to make a stand but he now found that, in any overt opposition to Russia, Japan's stand would be alone. On 12 March soon after Britain's preliminary reply, Katō, working on the assumption that Japan could not rely on external assistance, prepared a long memorandum for the prime minister, setting out three possible courses:

1. to make a public protest to Russia and, if that does not succeed, to settle it by direct resort to war;
2. to announce that Japan will take appropriate steps as a counterpoise to Russia and in self-defence and to act in disregard of the Russo-Japanese agreement on Korea;
3. to make an interim protest against Russia's activities which would merely reassert Japan's rights and, at a later date, to discuss suitable measures.

[1] FO *Germany* 1524, Lascelles to Lansdowne, 14 March 1901.

Such were the available alternatives set out by Katō in descending order of severity.[1] They were subjected to detailed scrutiny at several meetings of the Japanese cabinet without a definite policy emerging. While these deliberations were continuing, the note from Britain confirming her strict neutrality arrived and the Itō ministry became more inclined to adopt a less threatening attitude towards Russia.

On 17 March Katō received from Peking the draft of an amended agreement which Russia had presented to China, saying that it would be withdrawn, if not accepted within 15 days. Katō tried to impress the Japanese cabinet with the need for a moderate protest which would strengthen the hand of the anti-Russian party in China, especially the Yangtze viceroys with whom Japan was working closely. The cabinet agreed, firstly, to give another stern warning to China and, secondly, to draw up a declaration which could be made at St Petersburg. After several indecisive cabinet meetings Katō rallied his more cautious colleagues. On 25 March Japan which had advised China to reject Russia's time-limit, presented Russia with a note, stating that the agreement which was being negotiated with China contained clauses prejudicial to the sovereignty of that country and inconsistent with the treaty rights of the powers and should therefore be referred to the international conference at Peking. Lamsdorf refused to accept a memorandum on a subject of which Japan had no official cognisance but later replied, courteously enough, that it was inappropriate to discuss at the Peking conference a treaty which concerned only Russia and China.[2]

Meanwhile Britain urged China not to sign separate agreements with individual powers while the Peking conference was in session. Despite earlier disappointments, Lansdowne again asked Germany to support China in her resistance before the time-limit expired — but in vain.[3] In the labyrinth of diplomacy and intrigue which surrounded this crisis, Britain followed a moderate policy which was based on three main canons: to avoid antagonizing Russia; to encourage China to resist; and to restrain Japan from precipitate action. In the campaign against Russia, Japan was the leader, trying to enlist Britain's support, rather than the reverse.

On 23 March the Chinese court, relying on Japanese and British

---

[1] *Katō*, i, 434–7; *NGB* 34, no. 174.
[2] *NGB* 34, nos. 218, 228 and 231.
[3] FO *Japan* 538, Lansdowne to MacDonald, 19 March 1901.

I

support, issued a decree, directing that 'under the pressure of international opinion, the treaty cannot be signed'.[1] The Russo-Chinese agreement was dead for the present.

For the Japanese, the issue was far from dead. Japan was not only defending China, but also her own interests. Katō, in particular, was displeased with the terms of Lamsdorf's most recent statement which suggested that Japan was not a party involved in Manchuria and was not entitled to be consulted. Katō laid before Itō and the army and navy ministers the draft of a telegram to Russia, stating that Japan could not accept Lamsdorf's opinions and 'must indicate its general dissatisfaction with them'. The sting was taken out of this bold statement by the prime minister who redrafted it on 1 April and omitted the reference to dissatisfaction.[2] After approval by the full cabinet and the emperor, the message was passed over to Lamsdorf on 6 April. Again Katō's exuberance had been crushed; but his dynamism was still evident.

In the gazette of 5 April, Lamsdorf announced that the agreement which Russia was trying to reach with the Chinese in order to restore Manchuria to China, had fallen through. While asserting her right to negotiate separately with China, Russia cut off further discussions.[3] Russia had conceded nothing and continued to occupy Manchuria. She contrived to save face by pretending that her gesture was made in the interests of China and was not associated with the protests of the powers. Nevertheless Japan and, to a lesser extent, Britain had secured a limited victory. Russia knew that, when these issues were reopened, as reopened they must be, she would be faced by the same opposition which would only be the more bitter by the passage of time. Japan had not only challenged Russia but had given a taste of success to the anti-Russian party in China, especially the Yangtze viceroys.

The story of the Manchurian crisis is very relevant to the development of Anglo-Japanese relations. This is more due to a change in Japan's policy than to any change in Britain's. Katō liberated Japan from the spectre of Franco-Russian-German co-operation in the far east which had dominated Japanese thinking since 1895. On 8 April Katō described the whole Manchurian episode as a 'great victory for us' and his biographer points out that it was the first example of Russia giving way to Japan since the opening of the country.[4] In so far as

---

[1] Tan, *Boxer catastrophe*, pp. 198–202. [2] *NGB* 34, no. 256; *Katō*, i, 441–2.
[3] *NGB* 34, no. 265. [4] *Katō*, i, 446–7.

Russia gave in to pressure from the powers, she gave in to pressure from Japan and to resistance organized among other powers by Japan. There is little doubt that Russia was moved by Japan's complaints but it is less easy to decide to what extent. On the one hand, factors other than external pressure did affect Russia's action. Russia had imposed a time-limit on China and would lose her authority there if it was not enforced. On the other, Japan was unquestionably a thorn in Russia's ample flesh. Japan stood out as the only power with courage enough to voice her opposition directly to Russia rather than by merely issuing warnings to China. Allowing for the normal diplomatic courtesies, the language of Japan's messages was strong and threatening. But did these messages portend war? Izvolskii kept his government apprised of the dangers ahead and of the violence of Japanese military and naval opinion. Typical of Izvolskii's view was his conversation with the British minister on 5 April: he thought a collision between Russia and Japan was possible and indeed probable, the Japanese government was stubborn, the tone of the press provocative and he never left his legation without fear of being insulted. In St Petersburg Lamsdorf evidently took these warnings seriously and took account of the explosive situation. He later admitted that if Russia had not withdrawn the Chinese agreement at this time, 'Japan would not have hesitated to open hostilities against Russia'.[1] It may be concluded that Russia was seriously concerned with Japan's bellicose attitude.

There are reasons for believing that Japan could not have resorted immediately to war. Japan did not have the funds available for a continental campaign on a large scale. Indeed, that may not have been the intention: Katō, who was certainly the most resolute of the ministers, appears to have thought that, so long as Japan was bold and unflinching, Russia would climb down without opposition. There were admittedly several high-powered meetings of military leaders. On 31 March, the navy minister urged that nothing provocative should be done towards Russia, although the war minister was more confident. On 5 April at the board of marshals and admirals at which the army leaders, Yamagata, Ōyama and Saigō, were present, the strength of Russian forces in Manchuria was considered in the light of intelligence

---

[1] FO *Japan* 539, MacDonald to Lansdowne, 5 April 1901; Malozemoff, pp. 166–7, quotes military attachés' reports saying that Japan was not prepared to challenge Russia single-handed; but Lamsdorf's own statement must be more authoritative.

reports, although nothing is known of the decision taken.[1] Certainly Japan had not left unconsidered the military aspects of the crisis. Britain had made it clear that she could not offer any naval help; but it is doubtful whether this affected Japan's judgment unduly. On the whole, it seems that the Japanese leaders were preparing for an emergency but were incapable of engaging in an immediate war.

The Japanese government would not have been without popular backing had it taken any strong measures. Prominent groups in the Diet following the *Kokumin Dōmeikai* line and influential voices in the press were calling on Japan to undertake continental expeditions and place Japanese forces on the Yalu river in order to prevent encroachment by Russia on Korea.[2] It was with this backing that Katō warned China that, if it accepted the Russian agreement, Japan might make similar demands, possibly in Fukien.

THE ANGLO-GERMAN AGREEMENT WEAKENED

One consequence of the Manchurian crisis was that Germany clarified her view on the scope of the Anglo-German agreement. In a statement in the Reichstag on 15 March, Count Bülow said that the agreement 'was in no sense concerned with Manchuria', that 'there were no German interests of importance in Manchuria and the fate of that province was a matter of absolute indifference to Germany'.[3] It is outside the scope of this study to examine whether Bülow's standpoint was implicit also in Germany's attitude at the time of the negotiations or whether it was newly adopted because of the Manchurian tensions.

Bülow's view was not shared by Britain. Commenting in the House of Lords on the chancellor's remarks, Lansdowne said that Germany's interpretation was not acceptable to Britain; he maintained that Britain regarded the agreement as applying to Manchuria and would continue to do so. But he wrote privately to the ambassador in Berlin that

Lord Salisbury's illness made it impossible for me to obtain final instructions from him [about my House of Lords' statement] but of course the evidence to show that Germany had never regarded Cl. 1 of the Anglo-German Agreement as applicable to Manchuria was overwhelming.[4]

---

[1] *Katō*, i, 442–5.
[2] Jansen, *Japanese and Sun Yat-sen*, pp. 109–12.
[3] *BD*, ii, no. 32; *NGB* 33/III, no. 2363. Bülow was Chancellor, 1900–9.
[4] Lansdowne papers, Lansdowne to Lascelles, 1 April 1901.

In other words, Lansdowne felt that Germany was entitled to believe that Clause 1 did not apply to Manchuria if she insisted that she did not exercise influence there but that this did not apply to Clauses 2 and 3 which should still be supported by Germany. The application of the treaty to Manchuria became a subject of frequent parliamentary interpellations. Finally on 6 August, Lansdowne told the House of Lords that he had never felt that the point was one of substantial importance because

the only two places in Manchuria to which the Anglo-German Agreement really applied were the two ports of Ta-lien-wan and Niuchwang, both of which ports are open ports, quite irrespectively of anything contained in the Anglo-German Agreement.[1]

In effect, therefore, Lansdowne shrugged his shoulders. Britain had entered into the negotiations with Germany as a political gamble to detach Germany from Russia. But the gamble had failed: Germany would not rush into a quarrel with Russia over Manchuria. And there was nothing which Britain could do to cause Bülow to think differently.

The Japanese government was naturally disappointed at Bülow's declaration. It came as a shock to Katō who immediately asked Lansdowne whether Manchuria was excluded from the purview of the agreement because of some special understanding between the original signatories and whether it had been given 'a less general application than is fairly deducible from the terms of the compact'.[2] Lansdowne confirmed that nothing had been withheld from Japan and that he shared her regret at Germany's attitude. Katō never accused Britain of bad faith; he was even more convinced of Germany's unwillingness to antagonize Russia in the far east. For him, it was a complete volte-face: at the outset, Germany's entry into a treaty with Britain seemed to show that she had ended her collaboration with Russia which had lasted since 1895; by March Germany clearly (or so Katō thought) had entered into some sort of alliance with Russia over the far east. Katō refused to be consoled by the frequent denials which Germany gave him.[3] Germany's attitude helped to clarify the position of Japan:

---

[1] *British parliamentary debates*, 4th series, vol. 98, col. 1361. Also cols. 267–8, Cranborne's speech, House of Commons, 26 July 1901.

[2] FO *Japan* 545, Hayashi to Lansdowne, 22 March 1901; *NGB* 34, no. 224.

[3] *NGB* 34, no. 234, note on a meeting between Katō and the German chargé d'affaires in Tokyo, 28 March 1901. An anti-German interpretation of these events which may reflect that of Katō may be found in Ishii, *Gaikō yoroku*, 33–9: Germany's long-term plan

it drove Japan into the British camp. Katō believed that, now that Germany had defaulted, Japan because of her special commitment to the treaty was automatically drawn towards Britain in pursuing what he conceived as its objectives. Nothing could have accorded better with Katō's main objective in foreign policy: to forge closer relations with Britain.

None the less neither power could afford to displease Germany who still held a strong position in the balance of power in east Asia. British and Japanese ministers had to persevere in keeping Germany detached from Russia. They therefore kept their disappointment and disillusionment over the agreement to themselves. To Britain especially, Bülow's statement was a warning. Throughout the Manchurian crisis, Britain had made it clear that she would not act with Japan alone and had only intervened along with Germany or in anticipation of German action. Now, with little prospect of German support over Manchuria, Lansdowne would have to rethink his policy.

Britain's intervention was lukewarm and was more often directed towards China than against Russia. Britain could not adopt as extreme an attitude as Japan. Britain had already accepted Russia's railway rights in Manchuria. In a letter to his ambassador in Russia, Lansdowne wrote:

There is no desire here to be pedantic about Manchuria. We have already recognized its 'gravitation' for Railway purposes, and we should not fall foul of any reasonable arrangement of conditions under which Russian troops might be withdrawn. . . . With a little bonne volonté and mutual confidence the whole affair ought to be capable of settlement.[1]

This was a vastly different approach to that of Japan. While the Manchurian crisis embittered both the Japanese and the British against Russia, the courses which the two governments wished to adopt, diverged widely; and there was only a limited amount of co-operation. The reason was that Britain, unlike Japan, had always, before taking a strong line in the far east, to consider its European implications.

was to get Japan to join the Anglo-German agreement and then to ease herself out of the agreement so that Britain and Japan might be encouraged to set up an alliance; if this could be achieved, Germany's aim of keeping Russia and Japan at daggers drawn could be secured.

[1] Lansdowne papers, Lansdowne to Scott, 23 March 1901; and Lansdowne to Lascelles, 1 April 1901.

For Japan, the Manchurian crisis was like a coming-of-age ceremony. The power, which was later in 1901 to ask Britain for an alliance, was already a world power; Japan's voice could no longer be disregarded by countries with interests in China. What would have happened if the crisis had been magnified and the Russo-Japanese war been ante-dated by three years, one cannot tell. But Japan had fought a first-class diplomatic engagement, had tried unsuccessfully to marshal the raggle-taggle forces of opposition to Russia and, even if she did not in the end do battle, she did at least see the enemy retire.

CHAPTER VI

Germany, Russia and the China Problem

March–June 1901

A PROJECT for an Anglo-German-Japanese alliance was hinted at on several occasions by Hermann Freiherr von Eckardstein, who was first secretary at the German embassy in London (December 1899–1902). In this capacity, he was at crucial times early in 1901 required to undertake the duties of the ambassador, Count Hatzfeldt, who was prevented by sickness from attending to official business and was frequently absent from London. Married to the heiress of the Maple's fortune, Eckardstein was a prominent figure in English society in his own right and was invaluable to Germany. He was a frequenter of London clubs and had earned a reputation (among other things) for his formidable appetite. Having had no diplomatic training, however, he lacked the reserve and responsibility of the professional and applied the amateur touch to his activities which often led to complications in Berlin and London.

His project has to be seen in the broader context of the proposals for a rapprochement which were being scouted between Britain and Germany at this time.[1] These discussions were started about the time of the Kaiser's visit to the bedside of Queen Victoria in January and came virtually to an end late in May. It is not possible in a study of this kind to enter into the minutiae of German foreign policy. Suffice it to say that it is hard to know how far the Anglo-German alliance was really sought after by the German government and how far it was the personal inspiration of Eckardstein. In the end, the only basis on which the German Foreign Office would entertain the proposal was that of Britain's adherence to the Triple Alliance; and that condition was after sporadic talks not found to be acceptable to Britain.

Eckardstein's plan for Japan to be linked with Britain and Germany

[1] Grenville, ch. xv passim.

was associated with the negotiations for an Anglo-German alliance and moved in parallel to them. There was nothing specially original about the idea. Something of the kind was to be found in embryo in the Anglo-German agreement of October 1900. The subject was again raised during the Manchurian crisis. Something had to be offered to the Japanese if they were to be prevented from reaching an agreement with Russia. Holstein, the senior official of the Foreign Office, told Eckardstein on 2 March: 'Perhaps [Salisbury] will yet succeed in a grand finale to drive Japan into Russia's arms' by his policy.[1] This was a common theme of official thinking in Berlin and Eckardstein used it to urge Lansdowne to support Japan for fear of her entering into some arrangement with Russia.

It might be thought that, after Bülow's statement in March, there was little scope for the realization of such a proposal. Bülow had made plain that his country regarded the Anglo-German agreement as being inapplicable to Manchuria, thereby showing that Germany would not try jousts with Russia. Britain, who had throughout the Manchurian crisis refused to act without some assurance of German support, could no longer feel that there was much basis for such co-operation. Perhaps surprisingly, Germany followed up the Bülow statement by encouraging Britain even more strongly to get involved in the far east with Japan. What Eckardstein imported into the suggestion was that Germany might well join the others. Although Britain and Japan could not entertain these suggestions with much confidence, they could not afford to ignore any proposal coming from a German source. The position of Germany in the world balance of power and in the balance of power in east Asia was important enough to ensure that she would continue to be courted by Britain and Japan. Even though Germany had done much to alienate them, they did not turn down Eckardstein's initiative.

On 18 March 1901 Lansdowne told Eckardstein that Bülow's statement on Manchuria 'put an end to any idea which might have been entertained as to the possibility of England and Germany combining for the purpose of "keeping a ring" for Russia and Japan'. Eckardstein agreed that no proposal of that kind was likely to find favour at that time.[2] On the same day, however, he suggested to Hayashi, the Japanese minister, the conclusion of a triple alliance between Japan, Germany and Britain for the maintenance of China's integrity and the

---

[1] *The Holstein papers*, iv, no. 767.   [2] *BD*, ii, no. 77.

Open Door doctrine there.[1] On several later occasions he suggested that the three powers should establish a triple alliance in the east for five years and claimed that the idea would be supported by members of the British and German governments if Japan were to make overtures. On 11 April Hayashi finally asked for instructions to open discussions with Britain.[2] Katō reacted cautiously and took the unusual course of consulting his minister at Peking. Komura replied that it would be of immense advantage to Japan, strengthening her 'position vis-à-vis Russia as England in combination with Germany would be able to keep France neutral in event of conflict between Russia and Japan'. On 16 April, after consulting Itō and the emperor, Katō replied to London that there was no objection to Hayashi sounding the British government on his own responsibility and in a perfectly non-committal manner. It would be better, he added, 'not to inform the German chargé d'affaires of the receipt of this telegram', thereby suggesting that he did not genuinely believe in the Eckardstein overture.[3] Capriciously the Japanese dropped a hint to the German minister in Tokyo that Eckardstein had told Hayashi that Britain and Germany were working on an agreement over policy in the far east and intended shortly to invite Japan to accede. Naturally this caused consternation when it was passed to Berlin and to Eckardstein, who denounced the report as completely untrue.[4]

Eckardstein met Sir Thomas Sanderson, the permanent undersecretary at the Foreign Office, on 16 April and told him that Hayashi had mentioned 'an idea which he declared was a purely personal one — of an agreement between the Japanese government and Great Britain based on the Anglo-German agreement of October last but going further and pledging the three governments to support the integrity of China and the maintenance of the "Open Door" at existing Treaty Ports'.[5] It is not worth speculating whether the true originator of these ideas was Hayashi or Eckardstein; it is sufficient to observe that the proposals are not dissimilar in form from the ultimate alliance. Lans-

[1] Eckardstein, *Ten years at the court of St James*, p. 211.
[2] *NGB* 34, nos. 1 and 2.
[3] *NGB* 34, nos. 3 and 5. Cf. Lansdowne papers, MacDonald to Lansdowne, 16 February 1902: 'Kato told me confidentially that Ito is exceedingly cautious in all his dealings and it was with the greatest difficulty he could obtain permission to send instructions to Hayashi to open negotiations.'
[4] *NGB* 34, no. 6; *GP*, xvii, no. 5036, Wedel to the German Foreign Office, 15 April 1901.
[5] Lansdowne papers, T. H. Sanderson to Lansdowne, 16 April 1901.

downe received Sanderson's report at the same time as a detailed dispatch from Lascelles telling of the remarks which the German emperor had made to him 'freely and openly'. The Kaiser regretted that Britain did not afford more active encouragement to the Japanese, that Germany was treated with such suspicion and that Britain would not even answer his questions about her policy in the far east. He told Lascelles that:

it was painful to him to see the diminution of England's prestige which was merely due to the fact that His Majesty's Government would not take advantage of the opportunities offered to them. They had displeased the Japanese who now felt that they could not count upon the support of England against Russia. Was it likely His Majesty asked that so favourable an opportunity for resisting the encroachments of Russia would occur again? ... He thought he had made it clear that, in the event of complications arising in the Far East, he intended to observe a *benevolent but strict* neutrality and he had certainly understood that His Majesty's Government were prepared to do more than that.[1]

This resembled the view which Eckardstein had been putting over for some time; it suggests that his remarks were not merely personal aberrations but had been inspired from Berlin. The Kaiser's use of the phrase 'benevolent but strict neutrality' suggests that the German declarations to Japan in March may not have been so innocent and that Katō may have been right to believe that Germany's sole object was to implicate Japan in a war with Russia.[2] There is evidence that Lansdowne paid particular attention to this 'torrent of eloquence' (as Lascelles called it) and to the Kaiser's criticism of British policy. It seemed to show that Germany was favourable to an alliance between Britain and Japan and that Germany was never likely to join it.[3]

HAYASHI'S OVERTURES

Eckardstein was not the only person trying to insinuate his own ideas; Hayashi too was trying to impress his own views on the authorities in London and Tokyo. Baron Hayashi Tadasu (1850–1913) was born in Tokyo (Edo) and managed to visit Britain before the Meiji Restoration from 1866 to 1868, one of a select group who were then able to

---

[1] *BD*, ii, no. 72. My italics. Sir Frank Lascelles was ambassador to Germany, 1895-1908.
[2] *Katō*, i, 407.   [3] Lansdowne papers, Lansdowne to Lascelles, 3 February 1902.

leave Japan. As a result of this experience, he was asked to join the
Iwakura diplomatic mission on its journey round the world (1871–3).
After 20 years as a bureaucrat, he first came to prominence when he
deputized as foreign minister during the critical final stages of the war
with China in 1895. He then went as minister to China (1895–7) and
Russia (1897–9). From 1900 to 1906 he spent in London. On his return
to Tokyo, he took a number of government posts: foreign minister
(1906–8 and again in 1911) and minister of communications (1911–12).
He was less suited to high administrative office than to diplomacy. In
his last years he became increasingly disgruntled: during his period as
a minister of the government he considered himself to be the victim
of political intrigue and to have been denied his just rewards.

He was an avowed Anglophil. He spoke and wrote English better
than most Japanese and was described as an Englishman in mind and
almost in appearance.[1] Yet his conversion to the need for an alliance
with Britain came comparatively late. In 1897 he had been an advocate
of an agreement with Russia over Korea. But in March 1900, when he
was waiting in Tokyo prior to setting off for his new post in London,
he told G. E. Morrison, *The Times*'s correspondent in Peking, who was
in Tokyo on a short visit, of his ambition to achieve an alliance with
Britain during his period as minister there.[2] The ideas, which he was
to put forward, had their origins before he left Tokyo. This is confirmed by the evidence in his *Secret Memoirs* where he states that he
discussed the issue with Itō and Inoue and 'formed the impression
that they were in favour of an alliance with Great Britain'.[3] But there
is no sign that he received any warrant to put forward such views when
he left Japan.

Hayashi re-entered the lists at Lansdowne's diplomatic reception on
17 April. He asked whether it was possible to have some lasting
arrangement between Japan and Britain to safeguard their respective
interests. He avoided speaking of the Anglo-German-Japanese alliance
and confined his remarks to some permanent understanding between
Britain and Japan alone. Lansdowne, having perhaps been prepared for
these discussions by Eckardstein's remarks, suggested the extension
of such an agreement to Germany and later in the day mentioned

---

[1] *Hayashi memoirs*, p. 11. Also see biographical note, Grenville, pp. 394–5.

[2] Morrison papers 312/60, 8 March 1900.

[3] *Hayashi memoirs*, p. 110. For a comment on *Hayashi memoirs* as a source, see
Bibliographical note below, pp. 393–4.

Hayashi's overture to Eckardstein.[1] Lansdowne agreed to wait for some substantive proposal from Hayashi who still had to learn what the Itō government's policy was. The talks were personal, unofficial and exploratory and did not carry the alliance any distance. Britain's attempt to insinuate Germany into the arrangement received short shrift. Holstein told Eckardstein on 18 April that:

The Anglo-German-Japanese special Eastern Asia agreement that both [the Japanese] and the English desire would be quite against our interests because there would be no inducement for England to join Germany and the Triple Alliance in a general agreement. Until we are so joined, England and Japan must be satisfied with our neutrality.[2]

This private telegram, whose logic was irrefutable on German premises, could not fail to daunt even the buoyant Eckardstein. When the Anglo-German negotiations for a general agreement broke down in May, all question of Germany's adhesion to the Anglo-Japanese alliance lapsed.

Hayashi had to drink the bitter medicine of official neglect. On 17 April, after reporting his conversations, Hayashi offered his government detailed proposals for an alliance treaty with Britain, in order that Japan should be in a position to suggest 'some sort of a basis on which to negotiate'.[3] His recommendations were not acted upon. But they are interesting as an influence upon the Tokyo government and are set out below:

1. that the principles of the Open Door and the territorial integrity of China should be maintained;
2. that no grants of territory from China should be permitted apart from those obtained in the past by countries under treaties already published;
3. that Japan possessing superior interests in Korea to any other power, should be allowed freedom of action there;
4. that if one party to the alliance should be engaged in hostilities with another country, the other ally would maintain neutrality but if a third country should assist the enemy, the other ally would join in the struggle;
5. that the Anglo-German treaty would continue to be upheld;

---

[1] There are at least three versions of the Hayashi-Lansdowne conversation: Lansdowne's report to MacDonald (*BD*, ii, no. 99), Hayashi's account in *Hayashi memoirs*, pp. 116–18 and Hayashi's report to Katō (*NGB* 34, no. 7). These are in remarkable agreement on this exchange of views and even on its limitations.
[2] Eckardstein, *Ten years at the court of St James*, p. 219.
[3] *NGB* 34, nos. 8 and 12.

6. that the terms of the alliance relate exclusively to east Asia and the sphere of its operation shall not extend beyond the limits of east Asia.

These proposals had little immediate political effect. When Katō received the telegram, he took the opinion of the premier, Itō. Itō warned him that it was premature at this stage to enter into detailed negotiations and that he should try to find out Germany's intentions. He was afraid that some previous understanding existed between Germany and Britain which might have adverse consequences for Japan. Katō therefore replied that Hayashi should continue to make inquiries about the understanding between Britain and Germany.[1]

Itō, in avoiding a positive decision, was doubtless influenced by the financial and constitutional crisis which threatened the existence of his ministry. Since March, the Itō ministry had not been able to maintain solidarity on financial questions. On 10 May, Itō resigned from office and, while the successor cabinet was being formed, the head of the privy council, Saionji, was appointed prime minister. Katō continued in office for the time being but had little chance of carrying out policies according to his own wishes with only the authority of a caretaker ministry. As one study concludes, foreign minister Katō took 'Britain into his confidence on all matters and deepened the mutual trust between the two countries; and as an additional facet of this policy, he had the important side-effect of promoting an Anglo-Japanese alliance by resolutely putting a stop to Russia's advances and deepening the feeling of a "dependable Japan" '.[2] Understandably it was a great frustration for him not to be able to make a positive reply over the British alliance of which he had so long been the leading advocate in Japan.

While the ministry did not feel itself to be strong enough to take any steps, Yamagata, who had got wind of Eckardstein's parleys, did not let the matter slip. Not knowing the personalities of German diplomacy at first hand, he had to work on the assumption that Eckardstein's statements carried some authority. From his retirement, Yamagata sent the prime minister on 24 April a lengthy and most important letter in which he set down his views on 'Tōyō dōmeiron', the idea of an alliance for the east. He thought that the Eckardstein-Hayashi-Lansdowne talks had been carefully thought out by Britain

---

[1] NGB 34, no. 10.
[2] Katō, i, 450. Also Itō-den, iii, 517–18; Hayashi memoirs, pp. 118–19.

and Germany and that an anti-Russian alliance with them would be worth while for Japan.

We should seek Britain's views and devise with her a treaty of alliance in consultation with Germany . . . stipulating among its clauses our freedom of action in Korea.

It was, he thought, inevitable that there should ultimately be a war to uphold Japan's interests on the Asian mainland against Russia who was bent on a policy of expansion. Although the Manchurian agreement had been withdrawn as a result of Japanese protests,

Russia has for a long time been penetrating into Manchuria and the building of the Chinese Eastern Railway and the developments at Port Arthur and Dairen all indicate that she is intent on permanent occupation. From now on, she will use every opportunity to expand her sphere of influence and seize the rest of Manchuria.

This meant danger for Japan; and, after exploring the various courses open, Yamagata decided in future to lend his great influence to the cause of a British alliance.[1]

The consequences of this letter are clearer than its origins. Yamagata had at times favoured a stand with Britain, at times conciliation with Russia; but it appears that the tension of the Manchurian crisis, in which he had been involved through the genrō conferences, had made him again suspicious of Russia. This was a turning-point in his thinking because he came to lead the group which advocated some connection with Britain. This became a political force when Katsura who was Yamagata's protégé, took office as prime minister in June and showed that he was prepared to pursue this line of policy.

The talks with Britain might have died, had it not been for the determination of Hayashi. He could not extract any authority from Japan to present his 'six-point plan' but he had been told by Eckardstein that Devonshire, Lansdowne, Balfour and Chamberlain were in favour of a triple alliance and only Salisbury, who was not yet back from his holiday in France, was undecided.[2] He therefore determined to act on the vague authority which he had already been given to make further inquiries. Hayashi asked Lansdowne on 15 May if he had formulated any views on the proposed agreement between Britain and Japan since

---

[1] *Yamagata-den*, iii, 494–6. Translated in appendix B.   [2] *Hayashi memoirs*, p. 114.

Salisbury's return. Lansdowne had not, but he asked for Japan's views. Hayashi suggested that an agreement might follow the lines of the six-point programme which he had drawn up for Tokyo. Lansdowne commented that difficulties would arise when details came to be settled. Evidently the foreign secretary was still not taking a purely Anglo-Japanese agreement seriously and reported the conversation to Eckardstein as though he still thought in terms of a three-sided agreement.[1]

The results of this conversation were indecisive. Lansdowne showed little real enthusiasm. Only one of his actions bears any relation to these talks: on 20 May Lansdowne recalled the British minister in Tokyo to London 'to discuss various points connected with the Chinese question'. It may have been the alliance that was to be discussed. For his part, Hayashi recommended his conversation to the careful consideration of his government; but, as one observer commented, his telegram 'did not receive deep thought'.[2] When the new cabinet was set up on 2 June, Sone Arasuke became interim foreign minister until some permanent appointment could be made, and was naturally reluctant to embark on a major plan for future relations between Japan and Britain.

Most historians of the Anglo-Japanese alliance consider the doings described above as the direct precursor of the negotiations which ultimately took place. It would not be the contention of this study that Eckardstein or Hayashi played no part at this time, but the effectiveness of their personal diplomacy should not be exaggerated. Most studies rely heavily on European documentary sources and on the *Secret Memoirs of Count Hayashi*. Those based on the biography of Eckardstein, which was one of the earliest sources available, tend to err in inflating the role of Eckardstein; those relying on Hayashi's memoirs tend to exaggerate the part played by the early negotiations before Hayashi had the official backing of his government. In his memoirs, Eckardstein is generally thought to have distorted his conversations; Galperin describes him as 'the falsificator of documents'.[3] Hayashi's *Secret Memoirs* are a valuable source; but they convey a picture of Hayashi's own initiative beyond anything which would have been allowed to a minister in his country's foreign service. They lay stress

---

[1] *NGB* 34, nos. 13 and 14; GP, xvii, no. 5004. There is no document in the Foreign Office archives in which Lansdowne informed MacDonald of his discussions on 15 May.

[2] *NGB* 35, no. 25, pp. 64–5.

[3] Galperin, pp. 96 and 101.

on the progress made in these informal discussions and fail to show that Tokyo did not take a serious interest. Important as was Hayashi's persuasiveness with Lansdowne, he could make little headway in Japan on account of the government crises there during May and June.

Underlying these triangular conversations was the attempt of the two diplomats to make an impression upon the foreign secretary and induce him to take the initiative. Their importance depends therefore on the impact which they made on Lansdowne: in a letter to Mac-Donald, he described Eckardstein as being

very fond of discussing alliances, into which more than one combination entered, and at one moment he held out, I fancy without authority, to the Japanese the prospect of German support in the event of Japan finding herself aux prises with more than one antagonist, but it turned out that all he had to offer was neutrality, and the project went no further. Hayashi may have adopted what you describe as the 'motif of the agreement' from this source, but the idea is not a very original one.[1]

Lansdowne saw Eckardstein's tactics at close quarters and realized how he used the art of suggestion in the world of high society in which he moved.[2] But there were occasions when there was a resemblance between the chargé's views and those aired by the Kaiser. It was reasonable to conclude that he spoke with a certain authority, albeit from the German court rather than its foreign ministry. Even if there was only a remote possibility that he had such backing, Lansdowne could not afford to neglect it. The prospect of still involving Germany in an anti-Russian front in the far east, was so attractive to him that he could not reject any proposal, however implausible or seemingly unfruitful.

Similarly Lansdowne took up an ambivalent position towards Germany over the Japanese alliance. In the early stages of negotiation when the three-sided alliance proposals of Eckardstein came up for discussion, Hayashi tried to steer towards an alliance between Britain and Japan only but Lansdowne tended to bring Germany into the discussion. When the negotiations got under way later in the year, the Japanese government suggested that Germany might be consulted. Lansdowne never threw out the idea completely but never had

[1] Lansdowne papers, Lansdowne to MacDonald, 31 March 1902.
[2] The same scepticism over Eckardstein is found in countless letters, e.g. Royal archives W 42/43, Bertie to Knollys, 23 November 1901; and *BD*, ii, no. 81.

K

sufficient confidence in Germany to invite her to become a partner in the alliance.

Eckardstein was not the originator of the idea of the Anglo-Japanese alliance — a role which he himself would not have disclaimed. As Lansdowne rightly wrote, the idea of such an alliance was not a very novel one. Nor was Eckardstein the originator in the sense that the conversations in March and April in which he took such an active part, led inexorably to formal negotiations in October. That depended on whether the new Japanese government would follow up Hayashi's tentative discussions; and on the whole it let them lapse for a while. But within limits he did serve some purpose. Eckardstein was a useful mediator: he served as a clearing house in London for British and Japanese views. Neither side was too obviously anxious to take the initiative in the negotiations: both Britain and Japan used Eckardstein as a sounding-board for their views. In this capacity the German chargé had definite gifts. One Japanese observer could not fathom why he went around canvassing as he did.[1] But this was to Eckardstein one function of active diplomacy at the court of St James. He may have been open to criticism for misrepresenting his government; but he had a minor role in launching the Anglo-Japanese discussions.

It is wrong — but by no means uncommon — to exaggerate the steps that had been taken during the Eckardstein phase of the negotiations. On 29 May the British prime minister was sufficiently unconvinced of the need for any alliance that he wrote of Britain's isolation as 'a danger in whose existence we have no historical reason for believing'.[2] In Japan the new cabinet which came into office on 2 June, approached the subject cautiously and without preconceptions. Thus the discussions on the alliance, which took place in July, owed little to those held in April.[3]

AGAINST RUSSIA AT PEKING

Our preoccupation with Germany hitherto in this chapter should not mask the fact that the problem of the far east was mainly concerned

---

[1] Ishii, *Gaikō yoroku*, p. 45.   [2] *BD*, ii, no. 86.

[3] Chang, *Anglo-Japanese alliance*, p. 268, speaks of Eckardstein's suggestions as 'the starting-point of the negotiations' between Lansdowne and Hayashi. More recent accounts by Langer, Galperin, Monger and Grenville have drawn attention to the limited results of these early conversations.

with the dynamic actions of Russia. Germany was only important in so far as others were waiting to see whether she would take an active or a passive role; and the various Eckardstein overtures had tended to confirm the existing British and Japanese impression that Germany was not prepared to co-operate in putting restraints upon Russia. The focus of our attention therefore turns to Russia, who was evidently hoping to obtain secret benefits in return for her benevolence towards China at the Peking conference. Just as Russia had earlier provoked a crisis by her activities in Manchuria, so she was now making herself difficult by her diplomacy at the conference. Britain was not much affected by Russian moves in Manchuria but was gravely annoyed by her manœuvres at Peking. She therefore sought to build up an anti-Russian front at Peking and to this end tried to enlist the support of Japan.

In the settlement of the China problem, the representatives of the powers were faced with two major financial questions: how the powers were to determine their claims for compensation for their expenditure on the Boxer expedition; and where China would find the revenue from which to pay them. On the first question, it proved impossible for the powers to fix any criterion for compiling their indemnity claims and the conference agreed to leave the amounts submitted by the individual powers as they stood. When it was found that total claims amounted to 450 million taels, a sum which would cripple China, the United States proposed that the overall claim should be reduced and the individual claims proportionately scaled down. This proposal met with German opposition and was dropped on the strict understanding that Russia agreed to share in a joint indemnity instead of presenting her claims separately. Britain suspected that Russia and Germany had set their claims high in order to place China in a position of obligation to them. Lansdowne was worried lest an impoverished China might be forced to ask those powers which had filed the largest claims to forego payment in return for concessions. To avoid this, Britain sought to govern the method by which China paid off her indemnity by strict international arrangements.

Some long-term arrangement had to be devised to enable China to pay such a large indemnity. The Russians and Germans favoured an increase in Chinese customs duty from 5 to 10 per cent *ad valorem*. In March Germany sent Dr Stübel, the director of the colonial division of the Foreign Ministry, to London to show Britain how desirable this was. The Foreign Office was much irritated by this mission and Lansdowne told him pointedly that:

Considering our interests in Chinese trade, an interest which largely exceeds that of all other Powers together and our Treaty rights in regard to maritime customs, we were not at all likely to allow customs duties to be heavily increased merely for the purpose of enabling China to pay a large sum by way of indemnity to claimant Powers.[1]

Britain, whose merchants handled the great bulk of the import trade into China, objected to saddling them with additional duties in order to pay for the excessive claims of Russia and Germany. She eventually agreed to raise the duties to a real 5 per cent.

In April the Russians proposed that Germany and France should join them in guaranteeing a Chinese loan equal to the sum which they claimed as indemnity. Since this would have had the effect of resurrecting the so-called 'Triplice' of 1895, it created a great deal of suspicion. Russia then modified her proposal by suggesting that an international loan be offered to China under the collective guarantee of the powers and that each power should only pledge its credit for its own share of the indemnity. These suggestions struck Lansdowne as dangerous and he put forward on 15 May counterproposals for payment of the indemnity through the medium of bonds. To each creditor power China would give bonds bearing interest at 4 per cent which would correspond to its entitlement as recognized by the powers; revenue from Chinese sources would be paid regularly to a board of international character, which would distribute the proper amounts to the bond-holding powers and would itself meet any default in payment. Under this arrangement, it would be impossible for any one power to allow arrears to accumulate in order to force China to grant preferential concessions to it. The difficulty was that the bonds were intended to be put on the market by the powers, if necessary with their own guarantee, and this was not to the advantage of those with poor financial credit. Since interest was to be at the rate of 4 per cent, a power would lose if it could only offer its bonds on the market at a higher rate. Japan and Russia were the powers most adversely affected.

Britain took steps to persuade Japan of the advantages of her scheme. On 17 May Lansdowne explained that his proposals would avoid the risk of China becoming separately indebted to individual powers; and there is little doubt that the Japanese appreciated this.

[1] Salisbury papers, memorandum by Lansdowne, 30 March 1901.

But Katō, sensitive to Japan's financial difficulties, argued that, in order to obtain cash to repay the debt incurred by taking part in the China expedition, Japan had to put the bonds on the market and would receive less than their face value.[1] The British cabinet discussed whether it could guarantee the interest on Japan's share of the bonds but decided against it. Lansdowne admitted that the Japanese were 'a little sore, and perhaps not unnaturally' and added 'I wish I could help them financially, but it would be very difficult for us to guarantee their share of the bonds for them'.[2] While most powers were coming to accept the British bond proposal, Japan still stood out. The financial crisis which had contributed to the downfall of the Itō ministry in May, confronted the new Katsura ministry when it took over on 2 June. It authorized a statement to be made at Peking on 15 June that the Japanese were not opposed to bonds but wished to be compensated for the loss they would suffer by getting an extra share of the bonds. This was followed up by a memorandum on 21 June.[3] This setback for Britain's proposal was balanced by good news from an unexpected quarter: Russia announced that it was prepared to accept the bond proposals. So the British government which had hitherto been reluctant to assist Japan for fear of what Russia might demand, was free to reconsider Japan's case.

After consulting the Treasury, Lansdowne on 19 June prepared a note for circulation to the cabinet containing proposals to assist Japan. Lansdowne argued that Japan was inclined to think that he had not supported her sufficiently against Russia and that it was of 'the utmost importance that we should stand well with her in the Far East'. He thought that there were three courses available to Britain: to guarantee the Japanese bonds amounting to about £5 million; to give Japan a part of her own bonds; or to buy the Japanese bonds at face value. He favoured the last course.[4] Supporting this, Francis Bertie, an assistant under-secretary in the Foreign Office, set out his views the following day in a memorandum:

To satisfy Parliament that we get something for our purchase of the Japanese share of [the Chinese] bonds (£5,000,000) we might enter into an under-

---

[1] *Komura gaikōshi* (History of Komura's foreign policy,) 2 vols., Tokyo, 1953, i, 180–1. FO *Japan* 542, Lansdowne to MacDonald, 17 May 1901; MacDonald to Lansdowne, 20 May 1901.
[2] *BD*, ii, 58, quoting Lansdowne to Satow, 31 May 1901.
[3] *NGB* 33/III, nos. 2155–6 and 2174.
[4] FO *China* 1505, memorandum by Lansdowne, 19 June 1901.

standing with Japan that neither Power will without consultation with the other enter into a separate Agreement with any other Power with regard to China. . . . We might perhaps enter into a *secret* agreement with Japan that we will assist by sea in resisting any foreign occupation of Corea, Japan undertaking to give us armed assistance in resisting any encroachment by any Foreign Power on the Yangtse region and the South of China.[1]

This proposal, which contains the germ of the later alliance, probably did not reach anyone but the foreign secretary.

The report on the cabinet which was held on 21 June, states that 'it was desired by the Foreign Minister that the Chinese bonds should be taken by this country at a rate which would enable Japan to come out of the transaction with a financial result, which should not be inferior in value to that which had been accomplished by the other Powers'. There is no comment on what decision was reached, though it is implied that the foreign secretary's wishes were accepted.[2] But when, later in the day, Lansdowne saw Hayashi, he presented him with a memorandum offering to help the Japanese by transferring to them part of the bonds receivable by Britain. Questioned by Hayashi, he added that 'we should probably be able to place bonds worth, at their face value, say, £500,000 at the disposal of the Japanese government'.[3] It is not easy to account for this change; we can only speculate that the Treasury which had shown the greatest reluctance over these various unorthodox transactions, had ultimately refused to buy the bonds and thrown its weight on the side of the most innocuous alternative and one which would not require the sanction of parliament.[4]

The Japanese were already examining their financial position before this offer came forward. The finance minister in a detailed memorandum sent on 21 June to the prime minister, suggested that, if the bond proposal was finally adopted, Japan should ask for an increased indemnity out of the anticipated surplus. In the light of this, Hayashi replied to Lansdowne on 26 June, declining Britain's offer of help.[5]

---

[1] FO *Japan* 547, memorandum by Bertie, 20 June 1901.

[2] Royal archives R 22/31, Salisbury to the king, 21 June 1901. Britain's offer should have been printed as an enclosure to *BD*, ii, no. 100 but the editors by mistake stated that the enclosure was a memorandum by J. N. Jordan. The correct enclosure contains details of the financial offer from Britain to Japan.

[3] FO *Japan* 538, Lansdowne to Whitehead, 21 June 1901; *NGB* 33/III, no. 2184.

[4] FO *China* 1506, E. Hamilton (Treasury) to Bertie, 22 June 1901.

[5] *NGB* 33/III, nos. 2187 and 2197.

Presumably the new ministry was suspicious of accepting financial assistance when there might be political strings attached and did not believe that the addition of part of the British bonds would greatly relieve its problems. Moreover the Japanese were optimistic that there would be a surplus from the China indemnity on which they had a claim. They reckoned that there would be a balance of 34 million taels out of the total indemnity demanded of 450 millions. Britain was in no doubt that Japan's services during the Boxer crisis entitled her to special treatment and was ready to agree that Japan should have first claim upon any surplus which might be available.[1] But this was said without much confidence that there would be an indemnity surplus available for this purpose. Russia, however, let it be known that, if any power asked for special advantages for itself, she would also ask for them. The whole difficulty over the indemnity was on the point of being reopened. On 18 July, the Japanese government relieved the situation by agreeing to accept the bond scheme without demanding any extra indemnity.[2] Since there turned out to be no surplus, the Japanese had to bear any shortfall which there was on their bonds.

Even although they were not acted upon, the proposals of Bertie were significant. In his memorandum, Bertie showed that one section of the Foreign Office at least considered that this offer to Japan, coming as it did in a period of financial crisis, was more than a purely financial operation: Britain should get something in return by way of a secret agreement. This memorandum was chronologically the first statement from the British side in favour of some agreement exclusively with Japan and, brief as it is, it contains most of the salient features of the later alliance. It emphasizes Britain's distrust of Russian encroachments in Manchuria and Korea, about which Russia was rumoured to be negotiating with Japan at this time. Shortly after Japan turned down Britain's offer, Bertie was told by Eckardstein that Japan was using her share of the Chinese bonds as the security for a loan which she was trying to negotiate in Paris. For that reason Bertie did not let his views go by default. On 2 July, Bertie returned to the attack with a further memorandum in which he urged that 'the most tempting offer for Japan would be for us to purchase her bonds at face value and to promise her naval support in resisting a foreign occupation of Corea'. For Britain to buy Japan's bonds at face value was an alternative which

---

[1] FO *Japan* 538, Lansdowne to Whitehead, 21 June 1901; *NGB* 33/III, no. 2184.
[2] *NGB* 33/III, nos. 2209 and 2231.

the cabinet had earlier rejected; and it is doubtful whether it would have altered Japan's refusal. In view of the possibility that Japan might be obtaining financial help from Russia and France, it was, he argued, essential that Britain should show her willingness to come to an understanding with the Japanese and 'so keep them from gravitating towards our rivals'. In return for this help, Britain would ask for Japan's help in the Yangtse area.[1] Britain never offered to buy Japan's share of the Chinese bonds; but the other proposals which Bertie made were taken up during the re-examination of British far eastern policy which Lansdowne undertook in July.

PEKING SETTLEMENT

The bond scheme was only the symbol of anti-Russian feeling. It continued to have importance even after the principle of payment in bonds had been accepted by all the powers. On 10 July Lansdowne told Hayashi of his hope that, if the Manchurian question should come up again, the powers might find some means of avoiding the misunderstandings which arose earlier in the year. According to Hayashi's account of the conversation, Lansdowne asked whether some treaty could not be drawn up among the interested powers: while he recognized that Russia had to take certain measures for the preservation of her peculiar interests in Manchuria, it was desirable to devise a treaty which prevented Russia from annexing Manchuria or closing its doors to other countries. In his own account, Lansdowne made no mention of his proposing an anti-Russian treaty and recorded only his remark that the powers should seek a basis of agreement to counter any Russian breach of the Open Door in Manchuria. Even in its widest form, Lansdowne's proposal was for an international treaty and was limited to the commercial and financial implications of Russia's actions; there is no suggestion yet of a defensive alliance.[2]

The idea of guaranteeing the integrity of China appealed to the new Katsura ministry in Japan. The Japanese had been considering something of the kind for some time. Katō had presented just such a proposal to Britain early in May without receiving any definite encouragement. Katō was in communication with his minister in

[1] FO *China* 1506, memorandum by Bertie, 2 July 1901, enclosing minute by Hicks Beach.

[2] *NGB* 34, no. 292.

China on 31 May about putting a proposal of this nature before the Peking conference just before he left office. The gist of his proposal was that the powers should reach an agreement with China 'that, until China pays the total amount of the Boxer indemnity, no power shall acquire from China any exclusive rights, whether territorial or financial'.[1] Thus Lansdowne's fresh initiative accorded well with the sentiments of the Katsura ministry.

Shortly after, Hayashi received instructions that, while the project was still being studied in Japan, the good understanding which existed with Britain made it possible for Japan's initial conclusions to be passed over informally. The Japanese proposed to Lansdowne that the powers affected should get China to recognize the following two principles:

I. that it will not be permissible to convert, redeem or cancel the indemnity bonds except by the use of the sinking fund;
II. that, while the payment of any part of the bonds remains incomplete, China will not permit to any country any individual or financial advantages.

Even if some powers did not agree to the second principle, those powers which accepted it, might conclude an agreement with China that most-favoured-nation principles would be applied by China to any territorial or financial benefits which might be granted to any other power.[2] It was Japan's expectation that Russia might use the weakness of China to extort concessions and that China would only be prevented from offering these by a threat that other powers would seek similar benefits on a most-favoured-nation basis. Her main objective was to align the powers in an international agreement; but it would naturally depend on the attitude of Britain for its success.

The Peking peace conference closed with the signature of the peace protocol on 7 September 1901, almost one year after the conclusion of active hostilities. With all its bickering, this twelve-months' diplomacy was among the most unpleasant in history. But it cannot be denied that the peace conference was the focus of far eastern affairs at this time and Anglo-Japanese friendship was being forged there. This friendship was not automatic: Japan's interests sometimes dictated that it should follow a course which had been proposed by America or even Russia. The British representative claimed that Japan often took an

---

[1] *Katō*, i, 460; *NGB* 33/III, no. 2156.
[2] *NGB* 33/III, no. 2225; FO *Japan* 538, Lansdowne to Whitehead, 18 July 1901.

independent, and sometimes an obstinate, line on given issues.[1] But the powers which were most often prepared to adopt an anti-Russian stand at Peking were Britain and Japan.

There was collaboration, both on a policy and on a personal level. In these months Britain and Japan were trying to save the independence and integrity of China.[2] To this end, both powers worked through, and were influenced by, the Yangtse viceroys whom they regarded as the most stable elements in China. Japanese officials were in regular contact throughout 1901 with Chang Chih-t'ung, viceroy of Hankow, and Liu K'un-yi, viceroy of Nanking. At the same time, Lansdowne wrote that it was important 'that *we should keep well in with the Viceroys;* we have taken them a good deal into our confidence, and lent one of them a considerable sum of money'.[3] Britain and Japan were co-operating to keep the senior viceroys strong in order to counteract the influence of Russia in China. There was much consultation over the affairs of China and, even in the working out of policies which were contradictory, much mutual respect.

This consultation was in the long term of significance for the alliance. As soon as the conference ended, Komura returned to Tokyo to become Japan's foreign minister. Komura had gone to Peking from St Petersburg where he had favoured a rapprochement between Japan and Russia. But he appears to have become convinced during the Peking conference of the sinister implications of Russian policy in China and of the inevitable clash between Russian and Japanese interests. There was comparative harmony between the British minister, Satow, and Komura, who had been vice-minister for foreign affairs while Satow was minister to Japan. It seems that Komura's brief stay at Peking worked a transformation in his outlook which had no small effect on the later negotiations for the Anglo-Japanese alliance.[4]

---

[1] Satow papers 14/12, Satow to Bertie, 6 July 1901.

[2] Britain's policy for the conference was laid down in Satow papers 14/11, Satow to Lansdowne, 8 October 1900 (two letters) and confirmed by the foreign secretary.

[3] *The history of 'The Times'*, London, 1947, iii, p. 358, quoting Lansdowne to Bell, 18 February 1901. This refers to the loan of £75,000 which the British government arranged for Chang Chih-t'ung through the Hong Kong Shanghai Bank on 28 August 1900.

[4] *Komura gaikōshi*, i, 200–1.

CHAPTER VII

A British Initiative

July 1901

ONE factor which made the conduct of Britain's far-eastern policy different from relations with continental countries was that the Foreign Office had little personal contact with its diplomatic representatives who were posted in the far east. Given the limited resources of the Foreign Office budget at the time, it was not in the ordinary course of events feasible to discuss problems personally with the ministers to China and Japan, unless they happened to be in Britain on furlough and that did not normally occur more than once in five years. There were sometimes members of the Tokyo and Peking staffs who were to be found in London on their way to take up new posts and they generally, after an appropriate show of reluctance, jumped at the opportunity of prolonging their stay in the metropolis to advise the government in time of crisis. But their knowledge was not always up to date.

It was fairly rare for a minister to be recalled for consultations. Yet Sir Claude MacDonald, the minister in Tokyo, returned to Britain for a three-month visit at this time. There are many mysteries associated with his journey. Was it for leave or for consultation? Is there any truth in the claim made in *The secret memoirs of Count Hayashi* that MacDonald, during his visit to London, was playing a key role in the preparation of the Anglo-Japanese alliance? Since the opening of the archives on the British side, it has been possible to obtain a more complete picture of the circumstances surrounding his recall and to answer, even if only partially, some of the riddles which his mission presents.[1]

[1] Although MacDonald was a copious letter-writer, he has left no papers relevant to this study. But many of his private letters can be studied in the archives of their recipients, e.g. the Foreign Office, Lansdowne, Salisbury, Satow, Jordan, Dr G. E. Morrison.

SUMMONS TO MACDONALD

On 20 May, when Lansdowne was in the process of clearing up for the opening of the summer session of parliament, he agreed at the instance of Bertie to recall MacDonald from Tokyo for consultations — or, as it was officially expressed, 'on the public service to discuss various points *connected with* [*the*] *Chinese question*'.[1] This was only five days after the foreign secretary had had his exploratory talks on the alliance with Hayashi; and it may be assumed that this was one of the reasons behind the summons. At some inconvenience to himself, MacDonald sailed from Yokohama on 28 May, thus acknowledging that there was some urgency in the request. He travelled across Canada and reported at the Foreign Office on 3 July.[2]

Hayashi wrote of MacDonald being on leave. This was indeed the pretence which was made. MacDonald was certainly overdue for leave in 1901. After his experiences during the siege of the Peking legations when he was for a while thought to be dead, he had been instructed to 'come to England for a good rest, leaving Whitehead in charge at Tokyo'.[3] For some reason which is not clear, MacDonald went instead to his new post as minister to Japan, while Satow took over at Peking. The balance of evidence suggests that, though he was overdue for a rest, his visit from July to September was for political, rather than personal, reasons. Writing later to Sir Edward Grey, MacDonald recalled that he 'came home for a few weeks by order of the Secretary of State to consult on official matters in connection with the Anglo-Japanese alliance'.[4]

MacDonald was well qualified to make a special contribution to any fact-finding survey.[5] During his brief posting in Tokyo, MacDonald had made himself popular with both official and non-official Japanese, who regarded him as a friend of their country. But he also had experience of China and of the machinations of the powers there.

[1] FO *Japan* 542, Lansdowne to MacDonald, 20 May 1901 [my italics].
[2] FO *Japan* 542, MacDonald to Lansdowne, 23 May 1901.
[3] FO *Japan* 534, Salisbury to Satow, 22 September 1900.
[4] FO 371/272, MacDonald to Grey, 25 March 1907. Cf. Satow papers 9/14, MacDonald to Satow, 27 May 1901: 'This offer to come home on service was too good to refuse so we are off tomorrow. Needless to say my humble efforts at the F.O. will be entirely devoted to supporting you in every possible way.'
[5] A similar appreciation of Anglo-American relations, for which purpose Sir Julian Paunceforte had returned to London, was taking place in June and July. C. S. Campbell, *Anglo-American understanding, 1898-1903*, p. 231.

Moreover he had gained an international reputation during the Boxer troubles when he had in effect commanded the Peking legations. As an observer of the far east, he was less discriminating and penetrating than Satow, who had spent a large part of his overseas service there. But Satow was tied up with the intricacies of the Peking settlement and was not available for such an urgent summons.

Not that MacDonald's visit was shrouded in secrecy as befitted these conversations of which there is so little trace. On the contrary, he was accorded full honours and wide publicity as the most important survivor of the Boxer attacks. Shortly after his arrival in London, he was decorated by the king at Marlborough House and was given a civic luncheon by the Lord Mayor of London. These provided excellent camouflage for the true purpose of his visit.

These consultations on far eastern problems at the Foreign Office are unrecorded and can only be reconstructed in part. Bertie probably foreshadowed the discussions in his above-quoted memorandum of 2 July where he argued that, until Britain offered Japan something tangible like financial or naval support, Japan might make some arrangement with Russia involving the sacrifice of her position in Korea; but Britain should, before making specific offers of assistance, convince the Japanese that she would later on be willing to come to an understanding with them.[1]

What light do the new sources throw on the nature of the 'public service' which he undertook in Britain? In his letters, MacDonald has left a few shreds of information about his conversations with important people in the land. He claims to have spoken about Anglo-German relations in China 'to the King, several members of the Royal Family where strange to say it was listened to with eagerness and evidently created an impression, to Lord Lansdowne, Lord Salisbury, the Duke of Cambridge, &c. From my own particular platform, the Far East, I warned them and implored the powers that be not to allow themselves to be jockeyed by the Germans'.[2] It is noteworthy that MacDonald should lay stress on the wiles of Germany in the far east, although it may be assumed that he was also critical of Russia. His conversation with Salisbury is also of interest. He visited the prime minister at Hatfield 'for the purpose of talking the question [of the

[1] FO *China* 1506, memorandum by Bertie, 2 July 1901. Above, pp. 139–40.
[2] Morrison papers 312/63, MacDonald to Morrison, 20 February 1903. The Duke of Cambridge was a former commander-in-chief of the British army.

Anglo-Japanese alliance] over with him. (En parenthèse he was rather against the alliance)'.[1] And further 'bearing in mind what Lord Salisbury had said at Hatfield, I sounded Mr. Komura [on my return to Japan] regarding the possibilities of Germany joining in the arrangement'.[2] Can Salisbury have said that Germany would have to be invited to join any treaty with Japan over north China? There can be no definite answer to this; but it may have been the general line of discussion.

Salisbury's unaccustomed candour to MacDonald can only be explained by the fact that the prime minister held him in the highest regard. After a successful military career in Africa under Lord Cromer, MacDonald had been appointed Governor of the Oil Rivers in West Africa. After further success there, Salisbury sent him to Peking as minister in 1896. It was a time when the normal European attitude towards China was stern and hard-hearted; and by the standards of his time, MacDonald protected Britain's interests ably. In Japan he went to a post which was more relaxed; but there too he retained Salisbury's confidence, which his successor at Peking, Sir Ernest Satow, was unable to do. He may have lacked diplomatic finesse and been criticized by the career diplomats, but he was a sound and energetic British representative. His voluminous private letters to the Foreign Office from Tokyo have a racy quality and a salty humour which was rare in unofficial correspondence from other capitals.[3]

Before leaving Japan, MacDonald had informed the foreign ministry that he had been summoned for consultations.[4] The Japanese awaited developments in London with excitement. MacDonald talked with the Japanese minister on 15 and 16 July. In a later account of these conversations, he wrote that Hayashi told him that the Agreement was his own personal idea.[5] This is not the remark of a man who had been pressing his views on Hayashi. Evidently there had been an exchange of views in which both sides had taken the initiative and contributed their notions of the alliance which could be secured. It suggests that

---

[1] FO *Japan* 577, MacDonald to Campbell, 18 February 1904.

[2] Lansdowne papers, MacDonald to Lansdowne, 31 October 1901.

[3] Grey papers, MacDonald to Grey, 22 September 1912. MacDonald described the diplomatic service as a service 'in which I fear I am regarded as a "soldier outsider" '.

[4] FO *Tokyo legation* 844, MacDonald to Katō, 24 May 1901.

[5] Lansdowne papers, MacDonald to Lansdowne, 16 February 1902. 'I was under the impression that the "motif" of the Agreement as it now stands emanated from the brain of Hayashi or some one in the Japanese cabinet.'

Hayashi's claim, that he had been solely at the receiving end of the suggestions, is open to doubt.

The most detailed account of these interviews is to be found in Hayashi's telegraphic reports to his government. Hayashi reported that MacDonald came to see him on 15 July and told him that the highest authorities in the government, whom he later identified as the king and the prime minister, had expressed their opinion in conversation that a temporary understanding between Japan and Britain was not sufficient to meet the contingency which might arise in the far east and that the two powers should enter into some sort of alliance. On the following day MacDonald visited him again and said that his government was fully prepared to enter into an alliance with Japan but, since this would be a departure from its traditional policy, it required some time for the project to mature. Hayashi reached the conclusion that Britain was sincerely desirous of making an alliance with Japan but was afraid that Japan might enter into an arrangement with Russia before she could take the appropriate steps. He also thought that an alliance with Britain would be of great advantage to Japan and the present was the most opportune moment because, by fostering in Britain the fear of some Russo-Japanese agreement, Japan might be able to conclude it on favourable terms.[1]

On 17 July the Japanese foreign minister asked Hayashi to inquire, without committing his government, whether the present idea was to limit the understanding to Japan and Britain, or to include Germany and also whether it was intended to give such an understanding a limited territorial or geographical application, since the object of the proposed understanding was to meet contingencies in the far east.[2] Hayashi asked MacDonald about these points. On 19 July MacDonald referred them to Lansdowne. The next day MacDonald was authorized to reply that it was Lansdowne's intention that Germany would be included and that the zone to which the treaty applied, should be limited but that the foreign secretary had not yet formed any definite ideas. Clearly these preliminary inquiries were one avenue of approach to the informal negotiations between the two countries which started on 31 July.[3]

There are various explanations of MacDonald's role in these conversations with Hayashi. It has to be remembered that he was to some extent misrepresented by Hayashi and his language misunderstood.

---

[1] *NGB* 34, nos. 15 and 16; *Hayashi memoirs*, pp. 121–4.
[2] *NGB* 34, no. 17.   [3] *NGB* 34, no. 19.

He was misrepresented in the sense that Hayashi concealed many of his own ideas under the plaid of MacDonald to make them more acceptable to his government, as he had earlier done with Eckardstein. Some of the statements attributed to MacDonald may also have been misunderstood. Thus, MacDonald wrote that Salisbury was not keen on an alliance, while Hayashi informed Tokyo that Salisbury believed that an alliance should be made. Taken along with the premier's known reluctance to allow Britain to undertake overseas commitments, Hayashi's account seems far-fetched and implausible.

Making allowance for these misunderstandings and misrepresentations, there are two possible views of MacDonald's actions. The first is that his conversations with Hayashi were an indiscretion, the off-the-record effusion of an over-enthusiastic diplomat on leave. To pass on titbits from conversations with the king and Salisbury was certainly incautious. Indeed a Japanese foreign ministry official wondered whether it was a 'conversation in fancy dress' which was not properly authorized.[1] This cannot be proved from the documents. Such a view is upheld by one of Salisbury's biographers who argues that Mac-Donald's 'indiscretion' put a weapon into the hands of the Japanese government which they used cleverly to hasten negotiations.[2] Whatever the truth about the indiscretion, it can scarcely be argued that it enabled the Japanese to hasten negotiations, because the next moves on 31 July were made by Britain.

A second possibility is that MacDonald's remarks were a calculated leakage rather than a personal indiscretion. Judging from the fact that MacDonald was careful to report on his discussions to Lansdowne, it seems probable that MacDonald was charged with the task of keeping in touch with the Japanese minister. If this was his role, it probably sprang from Bertie's suggestion that some inquiries should be addressed to Japan 'as to their views in regard to China and the Far East so as to make them believe that later on, we shall be willing to come to an understanding with them.'[3] This is largely what Mac-Donald did. By using the arts of private suggestion, he let the Japanese know of the thinking within the British Foreign Office and prepared them for the official negotiations to follow. It is reasonable to suppose

[1] *NGB* 35, no. 25, p. 66. Shinobu Seizaburō and Nakayama Jiichi, *Nichi-Ro sensōshi no kenkyū* ('Studies in the history of the Russo-Japanese war'), Tokyo, 1959, pp. 120–1, supports the view that it was an indiscretion.

[2] A. L. Kennedy, *Salisbury, 1830–1903: portrait of a statesman*, p. 337.

[3] FO *China* 1506, memorandum by Bertie, 2 July 1901.

that, after the consultations in the Foreign Office, it was left to MacDonald to put forward the British case in a more non-committal way than could Lansdowne or Bertie. There were, of course, limits to the effectiveness of an approach to Hayashi who was already 'converted' to the cause. Britain wanted to convert Tokyo. Can it be that MacDonald was intended to convert Tokyo on his return there but that the pace of events was unexpectedly speeded up beyond the British government's intentions? This is probable. On the whole, therefore, it is the second alternative which fits the known facts better.

Naturally these doubts about MacDonald's role which afflict the historian, also afflicted the Japanese. When Lansdowne first undertook discussions with Hayashi on 31 July, it became an urgent matter for the Japanese to decide whether Lansdowne's proposals were really the same as MacDonald's. Lansdowne seemed to confine himself to talk of an understanding (*kyōchō*) over the Open Door and over Japan's interests in Korea, whereas MacDonald was talking of a *bōshū dōmei*, a defensive alliance. On 19 August Hayashi replied that he had no doubt that they were ultimately the same thing in different words.[1] After a comparison of the two views, Hayashi thought they were part of a co-ordinated plan; but his government was more sceptical and could only treat Lansdowne's pronouncements as authoritative. Japan, therefore, treated MacDonald's overtures with reserve; the Katsura ministry declined to take the initiative but was prepared to allow Hayashi to pursue discussions on a personal basis.[2]

MacDonald's approach to Hayashi was only a by-product of his recall, whose primary object was to advise his home government. One Japanese official, writing in 1902, admitted that Japan could not easily discern whether MacDonald's return was for his services at Peking to be recognized or for his views to be taken on the Japanese alliance which the British government evidently wanted to study. He was confident that, when MacDonald was consulted about an alliance, he recommended the proposal.[3] That was indeed likely. There lay unquestionably the major object behind MacDonald's recall.

JAPAN'S FINANCIAL PROBLEMS

There is one other aspect of MacDonald's role which merits attention. MacDonald brought with him first-hand knowledge of the Tokyo

[1] *NGB* 34, nos. 24 and 25.   [2] *NGB* 34, no. 17.
[3] *NGB* 35, no. 25, p. 65.

L

financial scene. Just a fortnight before he left, the Itō ministry had resigned, partly because of its financial problems. It was suggested that Japan's financial plight might be used by some of the powers for political purposes. Eckardstein, who was acting in charge of the German embassy, claims that Holstein bombarded him 'with private telegrams in which he expressed his fears lest Japan should make terms with Russia' in return for a possible Russo-French loan.[1] On 16 July Eckardstein told Lansdowne 'on absolutely trustworthy information that active negotiations were proceeding in Paris between the Japanese Government and French financiers for a Japanese loan' of about 10 million pounds on the security of the Chinese bonds. He formed the impression that Britain would come to Japan's financial aid and told Berlin that the articles which he had inserted in the London *Daily Mail* had had great influence in political and financial circles.[2] Certainly Lansdowne took the occasion to discuss with Hayashi on 18 July the loan alleged to have been offered by the Comptoir d'Escompte (Paris) but was told that nothing had been concluded nor was any arrangement likely to be reached. None the less Hayashi suggested to Tokyo that, by playing on Britain's fear of an arrangement between Japan and Russia, Japan might be able to conclude a treaty on favourable terms.[3]

It was extremely difficult for Britain to test the genuineness of these rumours about Japan's financial weakness. Every prominent Japanese who travelled abroad was assumed to be conducting negotiations for a loan. Viscount Watanabe, the finance minister in the former Itō cabinet, visited Europe in July and August for the purpose of removing 'obstacles which had deterred European financiers from investing their capital in Japan'. It was, in Hayashi's view, unlikely that any loan arrangement would be made until after his visit.[4] When Itō went abroad in September, he had to make in every European country he visited a public disclaimer that he was not intending to negotiate a loan. In September an industrial mission under Baron Iwasaki of the Mitsubishi group was negotiating in Paris. The financial implications of these visits naturally worried Britain; but there is no sign that any offer of a government loan emerged from them. Indeed the Japanese have consistently argued that the financial crisis in the summer of

---

[1] Eckardstein, *Lebenserinnerungen*, ii, 363–70.
[2] *GP*, xvii, nos. 5039–41.   [3] *Hayashi memoirs*, pp. 123–4.
[4] FO *Japan* 538, Lansdowne to Whitehead, 18 July 1901.

1901 was greatly exaggerated by interested foreign financiers and that the real problem was not financial but the political one of steering through the budget.[1]

Witte, the Russian finance minister who also played a dominant part in his country's foreign policy, certainly held that Japan's position was serious enough. He built his plans on the assumption that Japan was desperate for a loan. He himself was putting out feelers in Peking in July to settle the outstanding Manchurian problem by a new agreement with China.[2] He was keen to devise a means by which he could neutralize the opposition which might be expected from Japan; and that country's financial crisis was providential from his point of view. At the beginning of July when Russia's relations with Japan were particularly cordial, he gave Japan to understand that he was ready at any time to arrange for a large loan in Paris on behalf of the Japanese government. Witte was confident that he would have no difficulty in talking the French financiers into this. It was also suggested, equally unofficially, that Witte was prepared to do business over Korea and Manchuria: Russia would not object to Japan's administrative and financial advisers in Korea as well as police officials provided that Japan acknowledged Russia's position in Manchuria.[3] There is no sign that the Japanese paid particular attention to these unofficial suggestions, but it cannot be doubted that they partially explain why Marquis Itō decided in September to visit St Petersburg. Significant too was the campaign being waged at this time by *Novoye Vremya*, the paper sponsored by the tsarist government, for an improvement in Russo-Japanese understanding. It may be assumed that this sentiment was inspired; and it certainly fitted in with the known views of the French foreign minister. Taken together, this suggests that attempts were being made to re-establish relations between Russia and Japan which had been for a year at a low level.[4]

Much of this was based on the assumption that Japan was seeking financial assistance overseas. How far is this supported by the Japanese evidence? In official documents, in memoirs or in the press, the evidence is slight, presumably because talks on this subject are generally unrecorded or private in nature. It is likely that the Katsura ministry

[1] Cf. A. Stead (ed.), *Japan by the Japanese*, p. 67.
[2] *NGB* 34, nos. 288–91.
[3] B. A. Romanov, 'Proiskhozhdenie anglo-yaponskovo dogovora 1902 g.', *Istoricheskie zapiski*, no. 10 (1941), 54. Also *Rossia v Manchzhurii*, p. 316.
[4] Langer, pp. 749, 762. On *Novoye Vremya*, see *Katsura-den*, i, 1061.

on taking office wanted to improve the financial condition of the country by endeavouring to raise a foreign loan. Katsura asked his minister in Washington, Takahira Kogorō, to open talks with American capitalists with a view to raising a loan.[1] By mid-August this seemed to be hopeful. On 26 August some of the genrō met Katsura at Kanazawa, some ten miles from Yokohama, to discuss the question further. When it was learnt that Itō was likely to be travelling to the United States, it was determined to take the opportunity to enlist his assistance.[2] In America Itō made various speeches about Japan's need for aid of some sort. At the Metropolitan Club, New York, on 28 October, he openly admitted that his country needed a very large loan and could not raise it internally. Despite the joint efforts of Takahira and Itō, talks were broken off, largely because of the serious American steel strike.[3] It is interesting that these efforts were not particularly concealed from Britain. Thus MacDonald learnt at the end of November that Itō's visit to America was connected with the raising of a loan and had failed, while Itō evidently admitted in St Petersburg that he had not succeeded in America in raising a loan for his government.[4]

There is no evidence that the Japanese government sought a loan from France or Russia. Certainly Itō made no approaches in Europe. Since Witte's hints were offered as early as July, it appears that they must have been rejected by the Katsura government. It can only be assumed that Katsura who was involved in a bitter dispute with Russia at Peking, thought that the time was not opportune to conclude a loan arrangement with France and Russia. Britain too was excluded because the Treasury, despite its earlier offer of bonds, was known to be preoccupied with the costly war in South Africa and wanted to avoid any capital drain by way of foreign loan.[5] This explains why the United States was the only power approached and why, after refusals in that quarter, no official approach was made in any European capital. Eventually though not without difficulty, the budget was passed in

---

[1] *Katsura-den*, i, 1004–5.

[2] *Segai Inoue-kō den*, v, 22 (hereafter cited as '*Inoue-den*').

[3] *Shimbun shūsei Meiji hennenshi*, 15 vols., Tokyo, 1934–6, xi, 328 (hereafter cited as '*Meiji hennenshi*').

[4] FO *Japan* 542, MacDonald to Lansdowne, 29 November 1901; FO *Russia* 1625, Hardinge to Lansdowne, 30 November 1901.

[5] *Katsura-den*, i, 1005; Kuroha Shigeru, 'Nichi-Ei dōmei no seiritsu to kokka zaisei mondai' ('The alliance of Britain and Japan and their national finances'), *Rekishi kyōiku*, no. 5 (1957), 13–19 and 50–60.

December and no large foreign loan was arranged until the loan from Britain was completed at the end of 1902.[1]

It must be concluded that many of the rumours current in Europe were without substance. Many people in Germany, Russia and Britain believed in Japan's financial plight. In Germany especially, it was a convenient thing to believe and propagate, because it accorded well with Germany's political objective of involving Japan with Britain. Was it merely a political canard? No, it was a genuine belief, though Japan's need appears to have been exaggerated. The financial rumours were inflated to support the private scheming of Eckardstein and Hayashi. But the scare did not have a marked effect on Britain. MacDonald was briefed about loans by a few firms before he left Japan and made a point of approaching lending houses in London with results which he thought were encouraging.[2] The Hong Kong and Shanghai Banking Corporation took the opinion of its German associates about making a loan to Japan, although the proposal was not carried further.[3] But no suggestion of a government loan seems to have come to the notice of Lansdowne. While the foreign secretary discouraged Japan from taking up any Russo-French offer, he showed no signs of being rushed to a premature decision over the alliance on that account.

THE ROLE OF FRANCIS BERTIE

The far-eastern crisis of 1901 involved many and varied considerations, financial, territorial, strategic, whose only common feature was an expansionist Russia. If any countermove was to be made, who was to bring together these various considerations? On the British side, this role was taken by Francis Bertie, the shrewd, self-confident, petulant assistant under-secretary at the Foreign Office, who for all his faults had the great quality of building constructive plans out of a confused mass of material.[4] Bertie was in the fortunate position of being able to advise Lansdowne while he was still inexperienced as foreign secretary

---

[1] *Katsura-den*, i, 1014–15.
[2] FO *Japan* 563, MacDonald to Lansdowne, 24 October 1901; FO *Japan* 541, Whitehead to Lansdowne, 21 September 1901.
[3] *GP*, xvii, no. 5040.
[4] Francis Leveson Bertie (1844–1919), second son of the earl of Abingdon, entered the Foreign Office in 1863 and served primarily in Whitehall. He ended his career as ambassador to Rome (1903–5) and ambassador to Paris (1905–18).

and ready to accept ideas which were coherently expressed. Bertie's contribution to policy-making was considerable and not least in the formulation of the alliance with Japan. He was head of the Asiatic Department of the Foreign Office from 1898 till 1902 and had a large say in affairs during a period of crisis. He was, moreover, a man of deep-rooted prejudices:[1] hostile to Russia and to an entanglement with Germany, he was favourable to an arrangement with Japan. How and why he came by this idea is not clear but, having once determined upon it, he held to it most tenaciously. His knowledge of the far east was second-hand and was based on his assessment of the standing of the powers there rather than the rights and expectations of Japan or China. His judgments were not, therefore, particularly forward-looking.[2]

In a memorandum written after a private talk with Hayashi on 20 July, Bertie discussed how Britain should reply to Japan's suggestion in favour of an international agreement over China which Lansdowne had received two days before. Bertie doubted whether there was 'much probability of a far-reaching arrangement between Japan and Russia with the cooperation of France'. But two things modified his confidence. While Japan had refused Britain's financial offer, she may have hoped to obtain a large loan which was on offer at Paris with the ultimate object of forming a triple alliance in the far east between Russia, France and Japan. Secondly, it was possible, though not comprehensible, that Japan might be driven to accept Russian and French guarantees of the neutrality of Korea, if they were combined with a good loan on favourable terms. These doubts undermined Bertie's initial confidence that Japan would not fall in with France and Russia: 'an oriental state might act without caution if it found itself without funds or reliable friends.' He concluded that 'unless we attach Japan to us by something more substantial than general expressions of goodwill, we shall run a risk of her making some arrangement which might be injurious to our interests'.[3]

After analysing the difficulty, Bertie suggested a practical solution. Since the Treasury could not agree to the proposal that Japan's share of

---

[1] Steiner, loc. cit., 67–70.

[2] Morrison papers 312/65, 29 November 1905. Morrison who discussed the far east with Bertie that day, commented: 'what he said was so ignorant, so vulgarly expressed and so ill-considered that he wasn't worth listening to'.

[3] FO *China* 1507, memorandum by Bertie, 22 July 1901. Also FO *Japan* 540, Whitehead to Lansdowne, 22 July 1901, which passed on Tokyo newspaper rumours that a loan had been concluded in France.

the Chinese bonds should be purchased at face value, 'we should make an attempt to come to an agreement *without financial stipulations* and inform Japan that [we], knowing the vital necessity to her of Corea not passing under foreign control, are ready to undertake to give to Japan naval assistance in resisting any foreign occupation of Corea provided that Japan will promise to give to us, on our demand, *military and naval aid* in resisting foreign aggression in the Yangtse region and the South of China'.[1] Bertie has moved beyond the offer of financial support to Japan to a straightforward reciprocal undertaking. He is not thinking of a full-blown alliance such as MacDonald had discussed, so much as a restricted offer of help if Russia attacked Korea. It was to be a condition of this offer that neither party would, without consultation with the other, enter into a separate agreement with any other powers over the far east. Britain's offer would therefore be an alternative to any agreement which was offered Japan by Russia. It is hard to say what influence this memorandum had, for it was not initialled by the foreign secretary nor circulated to the cabinet. Yet the manner in which Lansdowne spoke to Hayashi on 23 July, suggests that he had read Bertie's proposals.

Lansdowne told Hayashi that, while he found Japan's ideas on an international agreement over Manchuria to be unrealistic, he was prepared to collaborate with Japan in her desire to prevent China from entering into exclusive arrangements with Russia. Lansdowne promised to place the proposals before the cabinet while they were being explored in Tokyo for he was sure they were agreed on the object at which they should aim.[2] And Hayashi was shrewd enough to reply to his government that, while Britain did not want to reject Japan's proposals, she had no intention of agreeing to them.[3]

The importance of these conversations for the Anglo-Japanese alliance might not be obvious, were it not that attention was focused on them by a further memorandum written by Bertie on 22 July. Bertie drew the wider implications of Japan's proposals by taking them out of the context of the Peking conference. The idea behind the earlier exchanges had always been: how can Britain and Japan act in such a way as to prevent Russia from bullying China into making concessions to her? The new memorandum lifted the issue to a new diplomatic level

---

[1] FO *China* 1507, memorandum by Bertie, 22 July 1901 [my italics].
[2] FO *Japan* 538, Lansdowne to Whitehead, 23 July 1901.
[3] *NGB* 34, no. 294; *NGB* 33/III, no. 2241.

and bore the significant title: 'Anglo-Japanese Agreement: reasons why one is desirable and why Germany should not be included.'[1] Japan, he argued, had just suggested an arrangement whereby the powers might guarantee that most-favoured-nation principles should apply to all grants of territory in China. In Manchuria, Japan seemed anxious, without going to war, to prevent Russia from acquiring permanent rights; in Korea, she took a more determined stand and might value an offer of British help to safeguard her security and interests there. Would Britain be wise to assist Japan in this? Bertie's conclusion was that the possession of Korea by Russia, taken in conjunction with her supremacy in Manchuria and her hold over any Chinese government, would be such a danger to British interests that Britain would in any case be forced to intervene. If Britain was bound to act thus in an emergency, she might as well support Japan in the ordinary course of events; such support would have to be tangible and practical and, bearing in mind Britain's limited power in the far east, would have to be restricted to naval, and possibly pecuniary, aid to Japan in resisting any foreign occupation of Korea.

This particular piece of Bertie's writing was influential in shaping the British proposals which were shortly placed before Japan. Many can be traced directly to this memorandum: the emphasis on naval co-operation, the shape of the alliance contemplated and the recognition of Japan's standing in Korea. Bertie with his known anti-German views also argued against the inclusion of Germany. Some of his proposals are not to be found in the treaty of 1902: the financial assistance which Bertie regarded as one of the inducements which Britain could offer to Japan. The memorandum did not represent the considered opinion of the cabinet or even of the Foreign Office: it must be described as an expression of individual views but the fact that so much was adopted is a measure of its importance. It was submitted to Lansdowne on 22 July and resubmitted after amendment on 22 September. Taken in conjunction with his other memoranda, it shows that British officials had for some time been seriously worried about the repeated far-eastern crises.

In a discussion with Hayashi on 31 July, Lansdowne took the initiative to break the ice. He told Hayashi that Britain and Japan should consider what line of conduct to follow 'supposing the balance of power in the waters of the Far East to be threatened with serious

---

[1] FO *Japan* 547, memorandum by Bertie, 22 July 1901.

disturbances'. He was worried by Russia's expansion in Manchuria, by her influence over Peking and by the possible naval predominance in the far east of France and Russia under the terms of their alliance. In the face of this, he thought that there might be an Anglo-Japanese understanding; but he seems to have had no clear idea of what the 'understanding' would entail. He did not propose an alliance, even a defensive alliance, nor did he specify naval assistance to Japan, as Bertie had in his memoranda. The most significant change in emphasis was Lansdowne's view that an international guarantee was less likely to be effective than an agreement limited to the two powers. This reflected his disillusionment with international conferences like that at Peking and his dissatisfaction with the Anglo-German agreement of 1900. Even though it was couched as Lansdowne's personal opinion, this was not a mere academic proposition but an offer of practical assistance.[1]

Two observations may be made about this conversation. First, Lansdowne's remarks were no mere flash in the pan. They had been preceded by a lot of preliminary discussion in the Foreign Office. He had seen Bertie's memorandum and, while he made no minute on it, he had at least been presented with the issues. Second, Lansdowne was not prepared to go ahead with an Anglo-Japanese rapprochement at which Bertie had been hinting without consultation with his colleagues. He had earlier promised the Japanese minister that he would lay his country's proposals for an international agreement before the cabinet but there is no evidence that he had hitherto done so. The talk on 31 July is sometimes described as the start of the official negotiations. But this was not so. Both Lansdowne and Hayashi were operating under a diplomatic smoke-screen of personal responsibility. Neither the British nor the Japanese cabinet had agreed in principle to enter into negotiations for an alliance. Although the stage of official negotiations had not been reached, it was important that the ice had been broken by British initiative.

DECISION-MAKING IN JAPAN

If July was for Britain the month for domestic activity on the alliance issue, August was the month for Japan. In reporting his conversations with Lansdowne on 1 August, Hayashi restated his conviction that a

[1] FO *Japan* 563, Lansdowne to Whitehead, 31 July 1901; *NGB* 34, nos. 20 and 371.

treaty of mutual assistance between Britain and Japan — or, if convenient, between Britain, Germany and Japan — would be of immense value to each in preserving Japan's strength in the far east.[1] But he was still without instructions and had no indication of the new government's attitude.

The conversation was considered at the highest level. Katsura, who had barely been in office two months and was uncertain of himself, decided to discuss the issue with Itō, the leading genrō who had retreated, as was the custom, from the mid-summer humidity of Tokyo into the country. On 3 August he visited Sōrōkaku, the marquis's residence at Ōiso, and had an exploratory discussion. On the following day, Itō paid Katsura a return visit at his country house, Chōunkaku, at Hayama.[2] Itō, who was among the leaders of the pro-Russian group in Japan, was doubtful whether Britain would sacrifice her isolation without expecting special guarantees in return. He thought it advisable to test Britain's intentions and on the spot jotted down Japan's minimum requirements, particularly in Korea. He felt that these would not be acceptable to Britain but that they might form the basis of Japan's reply.[3] On 5 August Katsura returned to Tokyo and invited the other genrō — Yamagata, Matsukata, Saigō, Ōyama and Inoue — to his residence to give their views on the draft reply which he had drawn up with Itō. This high-level consultation shows that Katsura realized that important steps were afoot and wanted to draw on the diplomatic experience of the genrō and to obtain as large a measure of support for his policy as possible. The genrō accepted Itō's proposals.

On 8 August, Sone, the Japanese foreign minister, replied to Hayashi approving his language to Lansdowne and authorizing him to tell MacDonald or, if he thought fit, Lansdowne that Japan was 'favourably inclined in principle to Britain's suggestion for a definitive understanding regarding the far east'. The telegram went on, presumably in the words of Itō, to lay down Japan's policy towards Korea and the minimum requirements which she would expect from an understanding with Britain. It stated:

The policy which Japan must always maintain, is to place Korea outside the scope of foreign countries' expansion policies, whatever dangers that

---

[1] *NGB* 34, no. 20.

[2] Ōiso and Hayama were resorts on the shores of Sagami Bay, some thirty to fifty miles from Tokyo, where senior statesmen had their villas and often transacted the more secret parts of their business.

[3] *Katsura-den*, i, 1055–6. [Appendix C].

may involve, however great the price. We must perforce pursue such a policy in the interests of our own security. In the view of the Japanese government, any extension of Russian power in Manchuria beyond her rights under existing treaties, would be a menace to Korean independence and would cause Japan itself grave concern. Such extensions of power and the advances made in establishing exclusive territorial, commercial and industrial interests in north China appear to be incompatible with . . . the policies of both Britain and Japan.[1]

Japan was staking her claim for recognition of her special position in Korea but was primarily concerned to get Britain to amplify her ideas on the scope and object of the proposed agreement. Needless to say, the tone of the reply, largely on account of Itō's intervention, was less favourable than Hayashi had hoped.

Armed with his new authority, Hayashi raised the subject with Lansdowne on 14 August. Still speaking unofficially, Hayashi explained Japan's attitude towards Korea and China and, according to Hayashi's account, Lansdowne stated that 'the vital objects of our agreement should be to preserve the Open Door into, and territorial integrity of, the Chinese Empire, as well as the interests of Japan in Korea'.[2] This version of Lansdowne's views is not to be found in his own account.

The reports of this meeting conveyed many wrong impressions. Hayashi, in rather coloured language, claimed that the word 'alliance' dropped from Lansdowne's lips several times — a phrase not calculated to give the cabinet an accurate idea of the British view. On the contrary, Lansdowne recorded that Hayashi thought — and he also agreed — that there could not be any question of an offensive and defensive alliance between the two powers. While some aspects of a possible alliance had been considered in the Foreign Office during July, it is unlikely that Lansdowne would hint at an alliance, even unofficially, at this stage. It was left to Hayashi to obtain definite instructions since Japan was thought to be more immediately interested than Britain. This was a natural precaution on the part of Lansdowne against any attempt by Hayashi to insinuate his own views without being properly authorized by his government. But it also showed that Britain was not prepared to set the pace and had little sense of urgency.[3]

Lansdowne promised to be ready with a proposal when Japan reverted to the subject and notified his cabinet colleagues. With the

[1] *NGB* 34, no. 21; *Itō-den*, iii, 520.   [2] *NGB* 34, no. 23; *BD*, ii, no. 103.
[3] *NGB* 34, no. 23.

approaching parliamentary recess, the cabinet was preoccupied with other matters and Lansdowne was only able to discuss the Japanese question cursorily on 16 August. Salisbury's report on the meeting read:

No matters of immediate importance were discussed. The Foreign Secretary explained some communications which he had had with the Japanese Minister but which had not reached any decisive stage. The negotiation has hardly yet proceeded further than the stage of asking for information as to our mutual assistance — but *it will be pursued*.[1]

Since the cabinet was not even asked for its views, it can be imagined how inconclusive Britain considered the overtures to date to be. Salisbury may have been less sanguine in his report than Lansdowne would have wished; but even the latter was guarded. He sums up the position at the end of August thus:

we sincerely desire to help the Japanese in the matter of their Bonds. The offer which we made to them was not favourably received but I am not without hope that we may yet have an opportunity of making good their loss. I have had some interesting conversations with Hayashi as to the possibility of a closer understanding between us, and I think it not at all improbable that we may succeed in arriving at this.[2]

Lansdowne was confident as he left for Ireland that something might come of the alliance and that financial assistance might be an inducement to Japan. The alliance would be pursued; but Japan must first show her hand.

Hayashi realized that, since the British ministers had scattered for the recess, there was little chance of much government business being undertaken for at least a month. He therefore asked his superiors to use that time to consider the question in detail. It was, he thought, a matter of indifference whether Japan or Britain took the next step: indeed it would be to the benefit of the party which first stated its terms and produced its draft.[3] Unexpectedly Hayashi managed on 30 August to have a farewell conversation with MacDonald on whose mediation the Japanese set such store. MacDonald had been in Scotland, had travelled on the continent and had indicated that he would not be in London for any extended period. Hayashi reported

---

[1] Royal archives R 22/51, Salisbury to the king, 16 August 1901. My italics.
[2] Satow papers 7/1, Lansdowne to Satow, 25 August 1901.
[3] *NGB* 34, no. 25.

only cursorily that MacDonald thought Lansdowne to be reluctant to make the first formal overtures.[1] MacDonald's report is more detailed and is worth setting out at length:

As to the Japanese 'understanding', Baron Hayashi begged an interview which I was of course only too pleased to grant. He seems just as keen and anxious to bring such an understanding about, as ever; my views on this point you know. Baron Hayashi seems to think that both England and Japan are loath to make the first *definite* move, and he is going to urge his Government strongly to do so and he has asked me to support him in private conversations with Marquis Ito and also with Komura, the new Foreign Minister [and] late Japanese Representative at Peking. I see no particular harm in my doing so for I think it would be useful that the first move should come from them. Of course I shall not go beyond saying that H.M.G. are very cordially disposed towards Japan. . . .[2]

This is MacDonald's only letter for the period of his stay in Britain which throws any light on the mysteries of his mission. It only survives because he was forced to write to Lansdowne who had already left for Derreen, his country house in Ireland. The foreign secretary replied that MacDonald should 'by all means encourage the Japanese ministers to tell us frankly what they want' and added that he was 'sincerely desirous to make something of the idea'.[3] Both Lansdowne and MacDonald felt that it was time for the Japanese to show their hand. Neither Hayashi nor MacDonald saw any early solution to this problem: it was not expected that any advance would be made until MacDonald returned to Japan on 23 October. There was in fact the predicted time-lag. But, by the time MacDonald reached Tokyo, the situation had changed: Itō had left Japan and Hayashi had been instructed to open negotiations in London.

What progress towards an Anglo-Japanese alliance had been made before August 1901? We have seen that there were many examples of good feeling between the two countries, of similar policies and of practical co-operation. These in themselves would not bring about an

---

[1] *NGB* 34, no. 27.

[2] Lansdowne papers, MacDonald to Lansdowne, 3 September 1901.

[3] Lansdowne papers, Lansdowne (Derreen) to MacDonald, 4 September 1901. Steiner, 'Great Britain and the creation of the Anglo-Japanese alliance', *Journal of Modern History*, no. 31 (1959), 29, wrongly describes this letter as 'Lansdowne to Bertie'. Cf. Monger, p. 43, quoting Lansdowne to Lascelles, 28 August 1901, in which he states that the alliance with Germany was still an open question.

alliance and gave no assurance that negotiations would inevitably end in success. Many in both countries felt that Russia's every act was a menace to British and Japanese interests and that only a united and positive approach would carry any weight with the Russian leaders. But there was a long way to go before an alliance could be achieved. The proponents of the alliance idea were prepared to let it take its course, while the antagonists in both countries — or those who were less than enthusiastic — had not yet been fully consulted. Britain was afraid that the Japanese might lead her a dance; the Japanese were doubtful whether Britain would pay their price. By August, Britain had taken a tentative initiative but Lansdowne was determined to leave the next move to Japan.

During the period since the Boxer crisis, Britain had followed a varied policy. In difficulties over the South African war, she had shown anxiety over events in the far east. She had entered into a localized agreement with Germany and Japan, had contemplated an alliance with these powers in March and finally had taken the initiative for an understanding — not necessarily an alliance — with Japan alone. In Japan there was a sharp break in foreign policy when the ministry changed in May. Under the foreign ministry of Katō, Japan had fallen out with Russia over Manchuria and things seemed to reach serious proportions. The change of cabinet led to a less active foreign policy and a greater preoccupation with financial problems. Perhaps for this reason, the Japanese leaders did not in August jump at Britain's proposals. It might be thought that the main driving-force behind an Anglo-Japanese alliance would be Japan's desire to secure Britain's friendship and that, as soon as Britain took the initiative, Japan would speedily seize the opportunity. This did not happen. The Japanese took their time to reply and then imposed awkward stipulations. Hence the progress which had been made by the end of August should not be exaggerated. Britain and Japan were still at the stage of exchanging views privately and had not yet reached the point where formal negotiations could begin.

CHAPTER VIII

The Alliance will be Pursued

August–November 1901

IN HIS report to the king on the cabinet meeting on 16 August, Salisbury affirmed that the alliance would be pursued.[1] It was not until 6 November that Britain passed over to Japan the first draft of the alliance. The question naturally arises: what accounted for the slow progress?

In both countries there was something of a diplomatic recess. Langer writes that 'despite this auspicious beginning [in mid-August], nothing further was done for almost two months' and 'we have no documents from either side which would explain the reasons for this delay'.[2] It is true that nothing was done to reopen discussions in London or Tokyo before 16 October and that no documents which passed through diplomatic channels significantly advanced the cause of the alliance. But documents have now appeared which show that the secretariats in both countries were studying the implications of a possible agreement and preparing to enter upon negotiations. It is understandable that the transition from private talks to official negotiations was the hardest step to take and could not be made without an exhaustive scrutiny. It was Japan's first major move in international relations while it was for Britain a rare diplomatic engagement. There was unquestionably delay; but it was mainly an administrative delay during which investigations within the two foreign ministries were pursued and experts consulted. This chapter will consider these internal developments, first in Japan, then in Britain.

FORMATION OF THE KATSURA MINISTRY

In Japan there had been a significant change of ministry which has not so far been adequately described. Early in May the Itō cabinet

[1] Royal archives R 22/51, Salisbury to the king, 16 August 1901.
[2] Langer, p. 751.

resigned on account of various financial and political difficulties. There followed an interregnum during which Prince Saionji acted as prime minister. Meanwhile endeavours were made by the genrō to form a cabinet by calling on one of their number, Inoue Kaoru. But Inoue was unable to form a ministry, largely because of the refusal of General Viscount Katsura Tarō to act as his war minister. Instead the imperial summons went to Katsura himself who succeeded in forming a cabinet on 2 June. Katsura was the protégé of Marshal Yamagata for whom his appointment was a personal triumph. Since Yamagata was assumed to be behind most of the decisions of the cabinet, it was given the nickname of the 'junior Yamagata cabinet'.[1] It also brought about a constitutional change. Katsura, who was not a genrō, was the first prime minister not to come from that group, apart from the short-lived premiership of Okuma in 1898. Since the Elder Statesmen were getting old and their ranks were not being augmented by younger statesmen,[2] there had to come a time when the prime minister would be drawn from elsewhere. Since, however, cabinets had traditionally been presided over by a genrō and contained at least one as a member, the Katsura cabinet set out with the stigma of being a second-rate one.

Katsura (1847–1913) belonged like Yamagata to the Chōshū clan. He was involved in the battles of the Meiji Restoration as a young soldier and devoted his career to the army. He spent two spells in Germany (1870–3 and 1875–8) to study military organization and there became an admirer of the Prussian reformers, Stein and Gneisenau. He accompanied a military mission to all European countries in 1883–4 and on his return became vice-minister for the army. In the war with China he was commander-in-chief of the third division. In 1896 he became governor-general of Taiwan (Formosa) and later minister of war under several premiers (1898–1901). From 1901 until his death he was prime minister on three occasions. Like Yamagata he had a hatred of party politics. He had undoubted ability and long experience in administration. As a member of the Japanese army his foreign connections were with Germany and he acquired, as did the army as a whole, a deep distrust of Russia. It may therefore

---

[1] Oka, *Yamagata*, p. 87. An illuminating study of the cabinet crisis of 1901 is G. Akita, 'Ito, Yamagata and Katsura: the changing of the guards, 1901', *Papers of the Hong Kong International Conference on Asian History*, no. 12.

[2] The only exception was that Prince Saionji Kimmochi became a genrō in 1916.

be said that his outlook on foreign policy was not so much pro-British as anti-Russian.

With the coming of the Katsura ministry, there were subtle changes in the activities of the genrō. Removed from the centre of the stage, they now began to guide affairs from behind the scenes. It was the genrō's duty to advise the emperor and their authority stemmed from the emperor's prerogatives. Hitherto their main function had been to advise on the choice of a prime minister who came almost invariably from among their number. Henceforward they would continue to select prime ministers but would also assert a right to be consulted at times of crisis. Under the Katsura cabinet, the prime minister maintained liaison between cabinet and genrō and took their approval for major cabinet decisions at a genrō conference. If the cabinet failed to consult the genrō, they could call on the emperor to direct the prime minister to do so. Now began what Professor Oka has called the 'period of genrō politics'.[1] One of its features was that during crises there seemed to outside observers to be voltes-faces in Japan's policy. But they were only the natural outcome of a dual diplomacy in which the genrō might step in, often at a late stage, and guide Japan's affairs along a course different from that which the ministry had been following.

Katsura's weakness was not only that he was subservient to the genrō but also that he had no automatic support from the political parties. He became the leader of a non-party government and naturally expected the hostility of the political parties and especially of the Seiyūkai of which Itō was president. There was indeed no reason why the Seiyūkai should look favourably on Katsura's 'cabinet of bureaucrats'.[2] The professional politicians considered that they were involved in a struggle with the bureaucrats in which no holds were barred. They exploited every political situation in order to improve the standing of their parties. Nor was there any reason why Itō should feel well-disposed towards Katsura. It was unquestionably a failure for Itō that he had been deprived of office and that Inoue had failed to form a cabinet only to make way for a Katsura cabinet. Moreover, in the events of May, Katsura had played a clever hand for, despite his good-humoured exterior and casual geniality, he had a reputation for intrigue which was second to none.

Similarly Itō was not on good terms with Katsura's protector,

[1] Oka, *Yamagata*, pp. 86–7.   [2] Rōyama, *Seijishi*, p. 352.

Yamagata. While they were both Chōshū men, they had been rivals for almost two decades and opposed each other on most political issues. Their influence over successive governments since 1890 had been evenly balanced but the emperor had more confidence in Itō. Their most bitter quarrel was over the constitution and the encouragement which Itō had given to political parties. Yamagata objected to parties, to the demagogic practices which party politicians had used in Japan since the 1880s and especially to party cabinets. In his view, Itō had transgressed by lending the support of a genrō to the political parties: not only had Itō accepted the presidency of the Seiyūkai in 1900 but he had also become premier of their first ministry.[1] For his part, Itō objected to the influence on government of the military bureaucrats, of which Yamagata was the leading exponent. Thus the two leading genrō were involved in a tussle to obtain control of the government and to have their own wishes on foreign affairs adopted as government policy.

Katsura only took up the premiership after he had received certain assurances from Itō. Even though Itō and the Seiyūkai seemed to be cast for the role of a natural opposition, their power was such that Katsura had to seek a settlement with them. Itō as a genrō was rather vulnerable to appeals of this kind: he felt it his duty to act in complete loyalty to the emperor and the state whatever government was in power. When he was approached by Katsura, he first convened conferences with the Seiyūkai leaders and devised a settlement whereby they consented to some increase in land tax and thus helped to overcome the budgetary difficulties which Katsura had inherited from Itō. Itō then agreed to give the prime minister advice on policy when it was required in the national interest. It was on this basis that Katsura had called upon Itō for guidance over the Anglo-Japanese negotiations in August. None the less, despite this general truce with the political parties and their leaders, Katsura required spectacular successes if he was to compensate for the fundamental weakness of his ministry in the Diet.[2]

These undertakings had their limitations. Itō had only doubtful control within his party. His leadership gave the Seiyūkai great prestige; but this did not help him to keep under control the more rebellious spirits within its ranks. When, as in September, Itō left the

[1] Oka, *Yamagata*, pp. 82–3.
[2] *Katsura-den*, i, 978–80; *Itō-den*, iii, 512–3.

country, his supporters sought every pretext to break the guarantees of long-term co-operation into which he had entered.[1]

Shortly after coming to power, Katsura set out a broad political programme for his cabinet. Its terms were: to strengthen the financial foundations of Japan and ensure industrial and commercial progress; to conclude an agreement of some sort with one European country since it was difficult for Japan to 'take charge' of the far-eastern situation single-handed; to make Korea a territory protected by Japan (hōgō-koku). In addition, he agreed to increase the navy to the level of 80,000 tons in order to meet one of the conditions laid down by Admiral Yamamoto for continuing in office as navy minister.[2] In view of the financial legacy of his predecessors, these objectives were bold and ambitious.

TWO VIEWS ON FOREIGN POLICY

Katsura's foreign policy was explicitly stated in his programme but here too he found himself opposed by other Japanese leaders. In a memorandum at that time, Katsura wrote that since early in 1901 Japanese statesmen had come to be divided into groups: those that favoured friendship with Britain and those that favoured friendship with Russia.[3] These were broadly defined groups but they were not exclusive, in so far as those who were pro-British were not necessarily hostile to Russia and vice versa. Until the Japanese knew what was available to them, they could not afford to view the British and Russian approaches as alternatives. Thus in August 1901, the distinction was really between those who felt that something would come out of an approach to Britain and those who disagreed. There was as yet no inkling that a full-scale alliance was on offer. It was only in November, when Britain presented the text of an agreement which contained the germ of an alliance, that the Japanese realized what was on offer. Even then they did not know what they could secure from an approach to Russia. In short, the Japanese leaders were not divided into committed groups; they were all seeking the most favourable opportunity for their country.

---

[1] Scalapino, *Democracy and the party movement in Japan*, p. 183.
[2] *Katsura-den*, i, 995–6.
[3] *Katsura-den*, i, 1055–6. Appendix C; Ōhata Tokujirō, 'Nichi-Ro kaisen gaikō' ('Diplomacy at the start of the Russo-Japanese war'), *Kokusai seiji*, no. 3 (1961), 107.

The most prominent members of the pro-Russian group were the two genrō, Itō and Inoue; Tsuzuki Keiroku, an intimate friend of Itō and son-in-law of Inoue; and Kurino Shinichirō, a senior diplomat who was on furlough from the legation in Paris. Their philosophy can be seen in a lengthy letter sent by Inoue to the prime minister on 26 August.[1] Impressed by a campaign in the Russian newspaper, *Novoye Vremya*, which often criticized Russia's far eastern adventures and now advocated a rapprochement with Japan, Inoue argued that something must be done to pursue this proposal if they were to avert the danger of war with Russia which had menaced them for the past year; that the Japanese could not afford a serious deterioration in their relations with Russia; and that Itō, who was going overseas in any case, should go to Russia, which would be much more rewarding than a visit to the United States, and appraise the situation there. Though this was not disclosed to Katsura, the group entertained the hope that Itō might ultimately conclude with Russia some form of entente which would safeguard Japanese interests in Korea in return for recognizing Russia's position in Manchuria.

The other group which favoured the pursuit of friendship with Britain, contained both Yamagata and Katsura. Yamagata had come out strongly for this course in April.[2] Equally convinced was Katsura who let some of this thinking creep into a long memorandum written at this time. He claimed that friendship with Russia who was determined to advance into Manchuria and improve her position in Korea must necessarily be temporary but that it was in Britain's long-term interest to remain friendly towards the Japanese.[3] Those who formed this group were not averse to some understanding with Russia but felt that with Russia in her present mood it was better to seek an entente with Britain in the first place. Their methods may have differed from the pro-Russian group but their ultimate aims were the same: to establish Japan's standing in Korea.

The cleavage between these groups was aggravated in August by the actions of Marquis Itō. He decided late in August to go abroad on a convalescent trip. It was his intention to go to the United States to obtain an honorary degree from Yale University and to proceed to Europe to examine the political situation there at first hand. He was also urged to go on to Russia by Count Inoue, who had been led by the

---

[1] *Katsura-den*, i, 1061-3; Galperin, pp. 63-4.
[2] *Yamagata-den*, iii, 494-6. Above, pp. 130-1.   [3] *Katsura-den*, i, 1055.

Russian minister to believe that Japan might find Russia ready to compromise over Korea and that this was an appropriate time for negotiation. At a meeting with Katsura and Inoue on 26 August to discuss ways of raising a foreign loan, Itō expressed the view that a link with Britain would be of minor benefit to Japan. The same day Inoue sent the prime minister a letter asking for the government to approve of Itō's visit to Russia.[1] On 11 September, Katsura agreed that there could be no harm in Itō's going and that he would be well placed to enquire unofficially since he had no government responsibility and was travelling in a private capacity. At a farewell party, Itō let it be known publicly for the first time that it was one of the objects of his journey to the Russian capital to have personal conversations about a possible Russo-Japanese understanding. Yamagata and Katsura asked that this should be done only after consultation with the government. This led to a heated exchange between Itō and Yamagata. The latter declared that if Russia was prepared to adopt Japan's demands over Korea, there could be no harm in discussions to that end but an agreement between Britain and Japan offered a settlement to which any approach to Russia must remain secondary. Katsura tried to win over Itō and asked for the co-operation of both elder statesmen in facing Japan's external problems.[2] It was in this situation of some uncertainty that Itō left Yokohama for Seattle on 18 September.

It is important for the purposes of the present study to know how far Katsura encouraged Itō in his intentions. This became a subject of great controversy in Japan and there are diametrically opposed views on the point. Kurino Shinichirō, who favoured Itō's going to Russia, has expressed the view that Yamagata urged Itō to go on to St Petersburg and that Katsura agreed to this because it seemed a good means of pushing through the British alliance in Itō's absence.[3] On the other hand, Tokutomi's biography of Katsura argues that the prime object of Itō's journey was to pursue his own idea of a Russo-Japanese agreement, while Katsura did not know how far Itō proposed to go and therefore encouraged the trip because of its good effects on Japan's reputation overseas and on the financial overtures which were then being made.[4] Perhaps the most judicious view is that Katsura

---

[1] *Katsura-den*, i, 1063.
[2] *Inoue-den*, v, 8–9; *Katsura-den*, i, 1061.
[3] *Itō-den*, iii, 529–30; *Rikken Seiyūkai shi*, i, 104–5.
[4] *Itō hiroku*, i, 349–54; Hiratsuka Atsushi, *Shishaku Kurino Shinichirō den*, Tokyo, 1942, pp. 284–7.

knew of Itō's proposal to go to Russia and approved of it but that Itō did not fully disclose his true intentions and that it is not clear, therefore, that Katsura was implicated in the schemes of Itō and Inoue.[1] Katsura did not entrust Itō with an official mission to negotiate with Russia. On the contrary, Itō wanted to find out the views of Russian leaders unofficially and there was no question of his going there to put forward official proposals. There is insufficient evidence to support the view that Katsura encouraged Itō to go away on a long journey because an agreement with Britain could not be achieved while he was in Tokyo. The British negotiations had not progressed far enough to make it necessary to get rid of Itō for a while. Moreover, if Itō had wanted to sabotage the alliance, he could have done so not unsuccessfully in Europe. On the whole, therefore, Itō's journey to Russia cannot be thought of as a deliberate official move to negotiate with the government there, after negotiations with Britain had been started.

KOMURA ASSUMES THE INITIATIVE

Just after Itō left Japan, Komura Jutarō, who had agreed to become foreign minister on the completion of the Peking conference, returned to Japan. Sone Arasuke, who had been combining the foreign ministry with the finance ministry, was conscious of the limitations of his interim appointment and had been content to keep things ticking over. At the age of 47, Komura who was educated at the Harvard Law School, was one of Japan's most experienced diplomats. He had worked with distinction as minister in Korea, the United States and Russia. More recently he had gained prestige and authority from his successful conduct of Japan's case at the Peking conference.

It is sometimes argued that Komura was predisposed to be hostile to Russia. This was certainly not true in 1900 when he advocated an agreement with Russia; but he certainly grew disillusioned with Russian actions during 1901. Thus, after their first meeting, the Russian minister in Tokyo, Izvolskii, reported that he was hopeful of some conciliatory settlement of outstanding problems: Komura was worried about rumours of a fresh Russo-Chinese agreement over Manchuria but still talked of a rapprochement. In the opinion of

---

[1] *Inoue-den*, v, 10–11.

Izvolskii and his French colleague in Tokyo, Komura approached the subject of relations with Russia with an open mind.[1] If Komura was not initially hostile to Russia, he was very suspicious of Russia's doings in China. In this he took a view similar to Katō Takaaki who had played a large part in getting him appointed. Katō and Komura had a good measure of mutual confidence: 'between Katō as foreign minister and Komura as minister to China there was complete unity and co-operation in dealing with the dual diplomatic crisis over Russia and China'.[2] Katō had recommended his appointment and urged that he should continue in China until his work on the Peking negotiations had been completed. When Komura finally took over, Katō was among the first to discuss policy with him. He shared with Katō a suspicion of Russia's recent activities in Manchuria and Korea. On his way from Peking to take up his duties, he visited Masampo and saw Russian activities there for himself.[3]

Komura was a comparatively 'new face' in the foreign ministry and his views on policy were not well known in Tokyo. Doubtless with this in mind, he made it one of his first tasks to prepare a lengthy memorandum of his views, entitled 'Opinions on a 10-year plan for internal affairs and foreign policy'. Among internal matters, he was concerned with the need to stabilize the country's finances, to increase the number of soldiers and sailors, to increase naval armaments and to improve communications of all kinds. In the foreign sector, he emphasized the need for the government to work for the development of overseas trade and for overseas investment in railways in Korea and China. To that end, there should be as much co-operation with China as possible.[4] The memorandum was not widely circulated and is therefore mainly important in so far as it illustrates the development of Komura's own thinking. Japanese marxist historians are inclined to depict it as one of the early examples of Japanese imperialistic thinking on foreign policy. True, some of his views were in line with the *Kokumin Dōmeikai*, whose avowed object was to encourage Japan towards a more active continental policy. At the same time, it could not be said that Komura's views about investment in Korea and China

---

[1] *Krasnyi arkhiv*, 'On the eve of the Russo-Japanese war', no. 63 (1934), 38, Izvolskii to Lamsdorf, 28 September and 6 October 1901.
[2] *Katō*, i, 459–60.
[3] *Komura gaikōshi*, i, 200. Above, pp. 72–4.
[4] *Komura gaikōshi*, i, 206–15, 'Naisei gaikō ni kansuru 10-nen keikaku iken'.

were basically dissimilar to those of other powers which had interests in east Asia.[1]

The memorandum throws no specific light on Komura's attitude towards Britain. Yet indirectly it shows that Komura was suspicious of all powers in China and Korea. The fact that he was later to be the leading advocate of the alliance with Britain must be attributed to his political calculations rather than any special attachment to Britain. Indeed he was not well liked by the British or by foreigners in general. While they found him to be highly intelligent and a tough negotiator, they thought him proud, stubborn and secretive. If he was lacking in warmth, this may be attributed to the illness from which he was already suffering and which was to take him to a premature death in November 1911.

As soon as he took up office in September, Komura made an exhaustive study of Anglo-Japanese negotiations. It will be recalled that, when Katō approached Britain in May, Komura had been consulted in Peking and been found to favour an alliance with Britain.[2] As part of his investigation in September, he asked Ishii Kikujirō, then a departmental head in the Foreign Ministry, to find out whether Britain had ever violated her obligations under an alliance. Ishii reported that there were probably occasions when Britain had violated international obligations as in the case of Denmark; but she was not known to have fallen short of any obligations as an ally.[3] This illustrates the painstaking and cautious way in which the Japanese approached the alliance.

On 2 October Hayashi reported that Lansdowne had returned from his holiday in Ireland and that the time was ripe for further negotiation. As a first step Komura discussed with Denison, the American adviser to the Foreign Ministry,[4] the terms which Japan might demand on

[1] Shinobu Seizaburō, *Nihon no gaikō*, Tokyo, 1961, pp. 63–4.

[2] *Komura gaikōshi*, i, 253.

[3] Kiyozawa, i, 293, quoting Asahi Shimbunsha, *Gaikō yōroku*, p. 105. Ishii refers presumably to the British attitude to the Danish crown in the accession dispute over Schleswig and Holstein in 1863–4. Though Britain was bound by the treaty of London, 1852, to acknowledge the two duchies as part of the dominions of the king of Denmark, she did not support Denmark against Prussia by force of arms.

[4] Henry Willard Denison (1846–1914), an American lawyer who after some years' practice in Japan, was given a three years' contract as legal adviser to the Foreign Ministry in 1880 which was continued until his death. He was responsible for drafting diplomatic documents in English and took part in all the major treaty negotiations of the Meiji period. It is impossible to estimate his real influence. There were many cases where he was overruled, as in the Weihaiwei debate of 1898. None the less there is much evidence,

entering the contemplated agreement and drew up a statement of government policy for presentation to the country's leaders. Komura presented this document to a meeting at the prime minister's residence on 7 October at which Katsura, Yamamoto, the navy minister, and Kodama, the war minister, attended, and obtained their approval. What emerged was the first official expression of Japanese opinion on a possible future alliance. The statement was embodied in a telegram sent to Hayashi on 8 October, informing him that Japan had given most careful consideration to Britain's proposals for a 'defensive alliance' and wished to establish close co-operation for the preservation of their common rights and interests. To that end Japan welcomed a defensive treaty with Britain. Hayashi was given authority to open negotiations by such means as he thought fit but was warned that any communication to the British government should be verbal until there was a real prospect of bringing about the alliance. The use of the phrase 'defensive alliance' is significant since both sides had assumed in August that an alliance was not contemplated. For a week, Hayashi was unable to comply with his instructions because of the ministerial absenteeism which was notorious at the court of St James. Then on 16 October Hayashi met Lansdowne and put forward Japan's proposals on an unofficial and personal basis without disclosing the terms suggested in the telegram from Tokyo.[1]

Japan had taken up the initiative which Britain had left with her in August. There had been delay in replying. But when we analyse the two factors contributing to this delay — the departure of Itō for Europe and the advent of a new foreign minister — it is clear that the latter was more important. The absence of a full-time foreign minister had left things at a standstill. As soon as Komura took over, he began clearing up like the proverbial new broom. Whereas his predecessor had been prepared to drift, Komura thought it wise for Japan to take the initiative and to proceed with the British approach. An element of chance creeps into the story in the fact that Komura did not meet Itō before the latter's departure. This was pure coincidence. Had the Peking protocol been signed earlier, Komura could have returned to

e.g. in the biography of Shidehara, that he was much trusted both by ministers and officials. It is, however, wise to bear in mind the quip made about the foreign advisers whom the Japanese employed at that time: 'they were on tap but never on top'. This was certainly true of Denison. Cf. Grenville, pp. 408-9.

[1] *NGB* 35, no. 25, pp. 67-8. *Hayashi memoirs*, p. 128.

Tokyo before Itō set off and might have had discussions with him. In fact, however, Komura went ahead with his assessment of Japan's future policy without the advantage of learning Itō's intentions at first hand.

BRITAIN'S NAVAL PROBLEMS

That Britain thought nothing amiss in the two months' delay over Japan's reply which was received on 16 October, can only be explained by the migratory habits of British statesmen during the sacred summer recess. At the close of the summer session of parliament, Salisbury repaired promptly to Hatfield. Lansdowne left on 16 August for a month on his estates in Ireland. Shortly before Lansdowne was due to return to London, the prime minister left for over a month's holiday on the Riviera. No cabinet meeting was planned before the end of October. Even exploratory talks could not take place on a major aspect of foreign policy in Salisbury's absence; and Lansdowne could not have taken an important step without the authority of his colleagues who were in September or October absent from London.

None the less Anglo-Japanese relations were being studied. Before leaving London in August, Lansdowne promised Hayashi that he would study the question during his holiday. Lord Selborne, the First Lord, prepared a memorandum of the Admiralty's views on 4 September. He argued that the two-power standard was beyond Britain's strength if the United States were to use all their resources or if applied to a possible war against France in alliance with Russia. In considering the value of some sort of naval alliance with Japan, he thought that there were strategic reasons for keeping British naval strength in Chinese waters as low as was compatible with the safety of the empire. But there was a point below which it would be dangerous to go: Britain could not afford to see her Chinese trade disappear or see Hong Kong and Singapore fall. He estimated that, in a few months' time, Britain would have four first-class battleships and sixteen cruisers in Chinese waters as against a combined French and Russian strength of seven first-class and two second-class battleships and twenty cruisers. These odds would be too great unless Britain were assured of an alliance with Japan. Britain and Japan together would in 1902 possess eleven battleships there against the French and Russian total of nine, as well as a preponderance of cruisers. Selborne concluded that an alliance with Japan would add materially to Britain's naval strength and would effectively diminish the probability of a naval war with France or Russia singly or in combination.[1]

The Selborne memorandum was a document of first importance but little is known of its origin. The Director of Naval Intelligence stated that the Japanese alliance grew 'out of arguments and facts which emanated from the Naval Intelligence Department'.[2] He presumably means that the alliance owed much to the Selborne memorandum, which in turn drew on the arguments and facts worked out by his department. These cannot be traced. But after the Navy League storm of July 1901 it is not unexpected to find that the Admiralty was endeavouring to find ways and means of combating Franco-Russian naval power.[3] It is on the basis of this examination, of which so little is known, that the First Lord issued his review of naval strength in the far east in the light of demands made on the Royal Navy elsewhere. His aim was to achieve the greatest measure of security for Britain's interests consistent with economy. Clearly a naval agreement with Japan, which now possessed the strongest fleet in the far east, would meet the Admiralty's objectives by ensuring Britain's security while conserving her naval resources.

The need for economy had been impressed on the service ministries by the Treasury throughout 1901. The chancellor of the exchequer, Sir Michael Hicks Beach, held orthodox Gladstonian views on finance and had met the demands of the South African war by means of increased income tax and war loans which were not to his liking. He now sought to end emergency expenditure and to restore army and navy finance to a peacetime footing. He had no alternative but to accept

[1] FO *Japan* 547, memorandum by Lord Selborne, 'British naval policy in the Far East', 4 September 1901. Text is reproduced in Steiner, 'Great Britain and the creation of the Anglo-Japanese alliance', *Journal of Modern History*, no. 31 (1959), 29-31. Grenville, p. 404, has rightly criticized the fallacy of relying solely on statistics of ships by zones for a comparison of naval strength.

[2] Papers of Admiral Sir Cyprian A. G. Bridge, deposited in the National Maritime Museum, Greenwich, Custance to Bridge, 25 February 1902 (hereafter cited as 'Bridge papers'). Since Custance became D.N.I. in the summer of 1899, he had produced plans for naval redistribution which described *inter alia* how Britain was losing her superiority in far-eastern waters to Japan.

[3] After a press agitation by the Navy League, there was strong opposition to the weakness of the Royal Navy in debates in both Houses early in July. Replying to the criticisms, both Arnold-Forster and Selborne admitted that the navy was not as strong as they would like. *British parliamentary debates*, 4th series, vol. 96, cols. 708-66 and 955-71.

Boer war expenditure without demur and so it was the China expedition which came under his axe. In the summer of 1901 he objected to the expense of maintaining large British forces in China for fear of international complications there. He campaigned in the cabinet from May to September for the return of a large portion of the British force to India where it would be paid from Indian revenues; but his colleagues only went part of the way because of opposition from the Foreign Office.[1]

Beach was also opposed to expenditure on army and navy reforms to remedy the faulty organization revealed by the South African war. In April he had yielded to the ill-starred army reorganization scheme put forward by St John Brodrick. But he resisted the plans of the Admiralty to embark on a building programme. 'What I want to stop', he wrote, 'is the increase in the estimates not due to war.'[2] His attitude had its effect on the course of the Japanese alliance: the only way in which a policy of economy in the far east could be reconciled with a policy of resistance to Russia there, was by cultivating the friendship of one or other of the interested powers. Under pressure from the Treasury, therefore, the Admiralty drew attention to the benefits which could be gained from Japanese co-operation. In September, Beach circulated two cabinet memoranda, recommending that 'the financial situation should be met by imposing a real check on the increase of expenditure', and proposed that the cabinet should refuse any increase in the navy estimates.[3] Beach reinforced his view by threatening to resign if his proposed economies were not upheld. Salisbury replied, consoling him, in the following vivid passage:

When I saw how blindly the heads of our defensive departments surrendered themselves to the fatal guidance of their professional advisers, I realised that we were in the face of a Jingo hurricane, and were driving before it under bare poles.[4]

Other members of the cabinet were less sympathetic and only Beach's loyalty to the prime minister induced him to stay on until Salisbury's own resignation in July 1902.

Against this background, Selborne's memorandum took on added

---

[1] Balfour papers Add. MSS 49727, Beach to Lansdowne, 9 May 1901; and Lansdowne to Balfour, 10 May 1901.

[2] Salisbury papers, Beach to Salisbury, 9 September 1901.

[3] Salisbury papers, Beach to Salisbury, 13 September 1901.

[4] Victoria A. Hicks Beach, *Life of Michael Hicks Beach, Earl St Aldwyn*, ii, 152–3.

significance for the cabinet. The document was intended for Lansdowne and it was not circulated to the cabinet before 28 October. None the less Selborne's observation that a treaty with Japan might secure economy without reducing naval security, would naturally attract support among those who were trying to preserve cabinet solidarity.

LANSDOWNE RESPONDS WITH CAUTION

On his return to the Foreign Office, Lansdowne called for a fresh draft of the memorandum written earlier by Francis Bertie. The manuscript with only slight re-editing by Bertie was submitted on 22 September, two months after its original composition. It was Bertie who had first drawn Lansdowne's attention to the naval benefits of an agreement with Japan; and his views had now been confirmed by the First Lord himself. The foreign secretary made no minutes on this memorandum but added several marginal notes which indicate the form in which the alliance was taking shape in his mind: the treaty would contain a promise of ships and money to Japan in resisting the occupation of Korea, would define the policy of both powers in China and Korea, and would prevent either signatory from signing separate agreements with other powers. The parties, he thought, would communicate about measures to be taken, such as docking, repairs and reliefs, which would be outside the agreement and arranged afterwards. These notes by Lansdowne about what he described as a 'Japanese entente' were the skeleton for the later alliance. This means that Bertie's memorandum has a special place in the growth of the alliance in so far as it convinced Lansdowne. At the same time, it was never circulated to the cabinet as was Selborne's memorandum and did not play a part in its conversion. Some of Bertie's ideas, such as the offer of money, were subsequently dropped but the main structure held good.[1]

Lansdowne had sketched the general lines of a possible agreement before he held the crucial discussion with Hayashi on 16 October. So indeed had the Japanese but Hayashi was told not to be precise about terms. He merely told Lansdowne that Japan wanted to maintain her interests in Korea and to prevent other powers like Russia from disturbing them. Lansdowne recognized that Japan by her agreement of 1898 with Russia enjoyed 'rights of industrial and commercial

[1] FO Japan 547, memorandum by Bertie, 22 September 1901.

expansion' there, the exercise of which might lead to the establishment of political influence, but Lansdowne did not commit himself to any view. On China, the two powers were already in agreement. Japan, Hayashi said, thought that the alliance would only come into effect if one ally were attacked by two or more other powers. Lansdowne accepted this and added that neither signatory should, without consulting the other, come to separate understandings with another power as to Chinese or Korean affairs. Hayashi seems to have urged that Germany should be made a party to the treaty but Lansdowne replied that, in the first instance, it would be an advantage for Britain and Japan to arrive at a clear idea of their requirements without reference to any other power. In addition, Lansdowne's version of the conversation contains his remark that the two navies might with advantage work together even in time of peace, not just when the alliance was called into being in time of emergency, and that each power might afford the other facilities for the use of docks, harbours and coaling stations. This suggestion is clearly related to the Selborne and Bertie memoranda.[1]

The discussions on 16 October were necessarily general but they show how far ideas on both sides had developed since August. A great deal of rethinking had been done in London and Tokyo; and it had revealed how closely related many of their interests were. Thus, the alleged 'delays' were more apparent than real.

It was left with Lansdowne to consult Salisbury and prepare a draft of the proposed treaty. The draft was passed to the foreign secretary as a 'preliminary sketch' on 23 October. When Salisbury returned to Hatfield from his holiday two days later, Lansdowne placed before him the rough draft together with an account of his recent conversation with Hayashi and Selborne's memorandum. The prime minister was asked for permission to raise the question with the cabinet. Lansdowne wrote that the draft 'will require a good deal more revision but, before we go further, I should like to know whether you concur in the general idea'. Salisbury agreed 'generally with the despatch and draft treaty'.[2] This remark invalidates the conclusions of those who have held that Salisbury was opposed to the alliance from its early stages.[3]

---

[1] FO *Japan* 563, Lansdowne to Whitehead, 16 October 1901; *NGB* 34, no. 28; *Hayashi memoirs*, pp. 128–31.

[2] FO *Japan* 563, Bertie to Lansdowne, 23 October 1901; FO *Japan* 547, Lansdowne to Salisbury, 25 October 1901.

[3] J. T. Pratt, *War and politics in China*, London, 1943, p. 138.

This draft agreement with the supporting documents was laid before the cabinet on 28 October but was not discussed at its meeting on that day. When Hayashi inquired about the progress being made, he was assured that the position of the alliance was hopeful. Similarly, when Komura attempted to press MacDonald who was by this time back in Tokyo, Lansdowne replied that the question would come up for discussion by the cabinet shortly.[1]

Lansdowne treated this unprecedented excursion of British diplomacy with due caution. One illustration of that caution was the re-examination at this time of the possibility of an Anglo-German alliance.[2] Another is the important approach which Britain made to test Russian opinion on matters in dispute.

In October there was a new development in the far east when Russia again tried to reach an agreement with China over Manchuria. On 5 October Russia proposed that the restoration of Manchuria to China should be conditional on her conferring mining concessions in Manchuria on the Russo-Chinese Bank, an agency of the Russian Finance Ministry.[3] Japan, which had been the most active opponent of the earlier arrangement, delivered a strong note of warning to China and tried to unite the powers against Russia's latest move. On 30 October, Lansdowne replied that he opposed Russia's demands on railways and mining rights and would communicate his views to the Yangtse viceroys, whom Britain regarded as her allies in China. But before the Manchurian incident could reach the same serious proportions that it had in March, the negotiations were brought to an end by the death of Li Hung-chang.[4]

Although Lansdowne was not prepared to give Japan offers of whole-hearted support, he was seriously worried. The British press was suggesting that Russia was proposing to obtain unilateral concessions now that the Peking conference had ended. Lansdowne admitted that Russia's proposals were clearly opposed to British interests and Britain's declared policy in the far east.[5] On 22 and 24 October he had held exploratory talks with the Russian ambassador

[1] *BD*, ii, nos. 107–9; FO *Japan* 547, memorandum by Bertie, 31 October 1901.

[2] Royal archives W 42/42, memorandum by Bertie, 27 October 1901, reproduced in *BD*, ii, no. 91 under the date 9 November. Bertie criticizes the tortuous policy of Germany and advises against an alliance with her, whereas 'a formal understanding between England and Japan is of the utmost importance to both countries'.

[3] *NGB* 34, no. 306.   [4] *NGB* 34, nos. 309, 318, 319, 337.

[5] FO *China* 1510, notes by Lansdowne, 19 and 25 October 1901.

in London in an endeavour to gain assurances that Britain's treaty rights throughout China would be respected under the new agreement but had found that the ambassador was unaware of any Russo-Chinese agreement and was not authorized to give any assurances. Lansdowne, however, deferred action 'pending a reference to the cabinet as to the line to be taken with regard to the Manchurian question'.[1] The foreign secretary then obtained the special sanction of the cabinet at its meeting on 28 October for his proposal to follow up these conversations in St Petersburg, asking Russia for a broad reciprocal settlement covering China and Persia and wherever else their interests conflicted. In Persia, he proposed that Russia and Britain should jointly make an offer to provide a foreign loan 'by a mutual arrangement which would specify strict guarantees'.[2] This came to nothing because Witte, the finance minister, who had a large say in Russian policy at this time, seems to have arranged the Russian loan beforehand. Over China, Lansdowne asked for suitable assurance for British interests in Manchuria and suggested that 'the same principles as those by which we might be guided in our dealings with Persia, might well guide us in our dealings with China'. Lansdowne evidently wanted direct talks over Manchuria bearing in mind the terms of the Anglo-Russian convention in 1899: Britain had no objection to the exercise of Russian influence in north China so long as Russia did not infringe Britain's rights in central and south China. The Russian ministers did not accept the suggested compromise and the British cabinet decided on 5 November to take the matter no further.[3]

This approach was not wholly concealed from Japan. On 31 October, Bertie informed the Japanese minister of Britain's endeavour to elicit assurances about the Russo-Chinese draft agreement and of Lamsdorf's stout refusal.[4] While Britain did not take Japan into her confidence over the minutiae of the approach to Russia, the fact that its existence was disclosed to the Japanese suggests that Britain's object was to obtain assurances from Russia which would complement, rather than replace, a possible agreement with Japan.

At the same time there is evidence that Britain made this approach partly on its own merits. Selborne may have been expressing the view

---

[1] Salisbury papers, Royal, Salisbury to the king, 29 October 1901.
[2] FO *Russia* 1624, Lansdowne to Hardinge, 28 October 1901.
[3] Salisbury papers, Royal, Salisbury to the king, 5 November 1901.
[4] FO *Japan* 547, memorandum by Bertie, 31 October 1901.

of the cabinet when he wrote that, with the signature of the Peking protocol, Russia would be occupied in developing 'her hold over Manchuria, an operation which we can no more prevent than Russia could prevent our conquest of the Transvaal'.[1] Since Russia's action in Manchuria was something which Britain could not control, the best course for Britain was to recognize this fact by making concessions gracefully in Manchuria, while demanding concessions in return in Persia. If this was truly Britain's motive, the approach should not be seen exclusively in the context of the Japanese alliance.

None the less it is hard to discount the notion that one of Britain's motives was to come to an understanding with Russia which would avoid the risks inevitably associated with a Japanese alliance. Each was a subject reserved for cabinet decision and it is known that the cabinet decided to put out feelers to Russia before clinching the Japanese alliance. The alliance was not discussed at the first of the autumn cabinets on 28 October but the approach to Russia was. At its meeting on 5 November, the cabinet heard a report on the failure of the Russian discussions and examined the draft proposals for the Japanese agreement. It may be concluded that, while Britain did not conceal this half-hearted Russian approach from Japan, it was in part at least a device to see how the wind was blowing in Russia before commitments were made to Japan which must by their nature be offensive to Russia. By obtaining Russia's reaction, Britain was assessing her bargaining position before deciding on the nature of the alliance to be offered.[2]

BRITAIN'S FIRST DRAFT

On 5 November Lansdowne presented the cabinet with his draft of the projected agreement with Japan 'which he had been negotiating since last June'. Its object, he said, was 'that in any war between Japan and one other Power *we* should be neutral: and similarly if we were at war. If war involved *two* Powers against Japan we should then be bound to join her: and similarly Japan would be bound to help us

---

[1] Bridge papers 15, Selborne to Bridge, 4 November 1901. The government was, in any case, under pressure from some sections of the press to work for a settlement with Russia.

[2] Britain's overtures to Russia are dealt with in Monger, pp. 50–6 and Grenville, pp. 401–2.

N

against any two Powers'.[1] The large majority of the cabinet was in favour of this proposal but there were certain dissenting voices. Some members held that the draft was unequal in so far as it conferred larger benefits on Japan than it did on Britain. They hoped that the scope of the agreement would be extended beyond the far east to cover Britain's territories in India, because of recent Russian pressure in Persia and Afghanistan. It was agreed to meet this point by a verbal communication to Japan. The suggestion came from the War Office and the India Office which were particularly concerned with supplying India with army reinforcements and which had been harassed by the difficulty of doing this during the war in South Africa. Thus, Hamilton and Brodrick are likely to have viewed Japanese help as a means of solving these difficulties, but there were also those who thought the alliance should be extended to India to avoid giving it the appearance of being a one-sided bargain. But the atmosphere within the cabinet is uncertain. The only eyewitness account is given by Balfour who wrote:

I was a few minutes late, and found the brief debate already in full swing, and the Cabinet not very anxious to hear any views on the general aspects of a problem, which they were treating in the main as one confined to the Far East.

Balfour, who was anxious to extend the discussion to the world-wide responsibilities which Britain would assume through the alliance, was taken by surprise and did not take part in the cursory debate.[2]

The draft treaty was approved by the cabinet and passed to Hayashi on 6 November. After the conventional alliance clauses, the draft provided that neither party would, without consulting the other, enter into separate arrangements with another power; and that, when their interests were in jeopardy, they would communicate with one another. After the large support which the Admiralty had given to the idea of a Japanese alliance, it was natural that there should be naval provisions and these were contained in the following 'separate article':

The naval forces of the two Powers shall, so far as is possible, act in concert in time of peace; and mutual facilities will be given for the docking of vessels of war of the one Power in the ports of the other and also for the use of coaling stations and other advantages conducing to the welfare and efficiency of their respective navies.

[1] Salisbury papers, Royal, Salisbury to the king, 29 October and 5 November 1901.
[2] Balfour papers, Add. MSS 49727, Balfour to Lansdowne, 12 December 1901. Other parts of the letter are reproduced in Monger, p. 64.

Each of these phrases crystallized a British naval interest: Britain wanted to ensure Japan's naval co-operation in peacetime (such was the theme of the Selborne memorandum); if Britain could obtain docking facilities from Japan, she might avoid the construction of new docks at Hong Kong; and coaling facilities at Hong Kong were most unsatisfactory and had been condemned in several Admiralty reports.[1] The naval clause was, therefore, practical and entirely devoted to serving British interests.

Hayashi accompanied the text by his own recommendations to his government. He reported Lansdowne's remark that, while the draft had been prepared on the assumption of its limitation to China and Korea, some sections of the cabinet preferred to extend its scope to India and the Malay peninsula. Indeed Hayashi advised his government to accept this extension. But it was evidently not regarded as *sine qua non* by Britain and was not taken seriously by the Tokyo authorities, which naturally wanted to avoid far-flung obligations. Another point which struck Hayashi was that Japan's relationship to Korea had been left unspecific in the draft. He had earlier asked that words should be included to convey the idea that Britain acquiesced in the adoption by Japan of suitable measures for the maintenance of her interests in Korea in view of her preponderant stake in the country. But Britain deliberately omitted any such phrase from the first draft and confined herself to the pious hope that Korea should not be absorbed by any other power — an acknowledgment of Korean independence.[2]

The first draft was that of a broad-minded and sensible agreement designed to meet the objects of both parties as far as possible. It was filled with obvious signs of a conciliatory spirit on Britain's part; and Lansdowne probably expected an early favourable reply from the Japanese in view of their statements that they wanted to settle the matter urgently.

The Foreign Office and the Admiralty were the strongest proponents of the alliance in Britain. As Balfour's remarks suggest, at the crucial cabinet meeting those in favour of the alliance were organized and left those with doubts divided and incoherent. The Admiralty was hoping that foreign policy might help to cure its naval

---

[1] E.g. Salisbury papers, Foreign and Imperial, memorandum by Pretyman, 4 December 1900.

[2] *NGB* 34, nos. 30–1; FO *Japan* 563, Lansdowne to MacDonald, 6 November 1901; *Hayashi memoirs*, pp. 132–4.

predicament: the First Sea Lord wrote: 'foreign navies grow by leaps and bounds; we must look to diplomacy or alliances to help us out'.[1] Since the far east was one of the zones where it was most difficult for the Admiralty to cope with foreign strength, it advocated strongly the need for a Japanese alliance and was a consistent backer of the Foreign Office.

The dispute between Selborne and Beach had by no means ended with the so-called Selborne memorandum of 4 September. In a memorandum on the Estimates for 1902–3 which was circulated to the cabinet in October, Beach again inveighed against the Admiralty: 'the rate at which we have been increasing our expenditure on new construction and in the number of men, might now be lessened with perfect safety'. Such a policy, he added wrily, would doubtless excite 'the wrath of the Navy League, the "Service Members" [in Parliament] and the *Daily Mail*'.[2] He therefore urged the cabinet to refuse any further increase in naval expenditure. Selborne reacted quickly. On 1 November he prepared a counterblast to the chancellor of the exchequer; he could hold out no hopes of a slackening of new naval building; 'to do so would surely entail our falling into an inferiority of strength in respect of France and Russia'. With specific reference to the far east, he argued that the most powerful portion of what was formerly the Baltic fleet had been moved to far-eastern waters and concluded that 'our own interests in Chinese waters and our possessions there are too valuable to enable us to ignore the presence of such an important Russian squadron'. The Japanese navy was 'good of its kind' but unfortunately Russia had the longer purse; 'while Russia is continuing her building policy, Japan has for want of funds come to the end of her building programme'. The memorandum was circulated to the cabinet on 16 November and discussed at two meetings.[3] Thus, Admiralty opposition to Beach's retrenchment policies was constantly before the cabinet as long as the Navy Estimates were undecided. By chance, this corresponded with the period that the Japanese alliance was under the scrutiny of the cabinet.

[1] Bridge papers 15, Kerr to Bridge, 29 November 1901.

[2] Salisbury papers, Foreign and Imperial, memorandum on the growth of expenditure by Hicks Beach, October 1901.

[3] Selborne papers, deposited in the Naval library, Ministry of Defence, London, memorandum on the Navy Estimates, 1 and (revised) 16 November 1901. It was discussed at cabinet meetings on 19 and 25 November.

CHAPTER IX

The Japanese Cabinet *versus* Itō

November 1901

IT WAS not until 12 December that Japan replied to Britain's draft of 6 November. But Japan's delay during this period, which has been commented on by all writers, should not be mistaken for inactivity. Her ministers and experts were busily engaged in studying the British draft and re-examining the bases of Japanese foreign policy. There were indeed three distinct phases of activity on Japan's part: first, the preparation of a Japanese counterdraft within the foreign ministry; second, the approval of the counterdraft by the cabinet; and third, its approval by the genrō and emperor. The last of these involved a detailed consideration of Japan's overall foreign policy and was associated with the discussions which Marquis Itō held in Russia.

THE JAPANESE CABINET DECIDES

When the two telegrams containing the British draft and Hayashi's account of his talks with Lansdowne reached Japan on 8 November, they were studied by the foreign minister. Komura replied that he was working on an amended draft which would have to be submitted to the cabinet and that, in view of Katsura's absence from Tokyo, it might take some time before a reply could be sent.[1] This was the time of the north-eastern (Tōhoku) autumn manœuvres at Sendai; and General Katsura had gone north in attendance on the emperor. He returned to Tokyo on 11 November and was shown the telegrams. He quickly cabled to Itō in Paris that negotiations with Britain had progressed and that the Japanese government was now required to take a decision urgently. He requested Itō to remain in Paris until he received further news.[2] The prime minister also convened a cabinet

[1] *NGB* 34, no. 33.   [2] *NGB* 34, no. 34.

meeting on 13 November which heard an interim report from Komura about the exchanges leading up to the present draft. The cabinet was not called upon for an immediate decision but was asked to consider the question in time for a later meeting. Unfortunately Komura fell ill that day and was confined to bed for more than a fortnight.[1]

Katsura and Komura recognized that a decision by the cabinet would be worthless unless contact could urgently be established with Itō. Komura therefore instructed the Japanese minister in London to 'go immediately to Paris or wherever Marquis Itō is staying and show him the whole range of recent telegrams . . . to get his consent in principle for the British proposals'.[2] When Katsura reported developments to the emperor on 14 November, he was told that it was essential for Itō to be consulted and that his action in doing so was approved. Hayashi accordingly proceeded to Paris where Itō had been for ten days while he was having interviews with President Loubet and the foreign minister, Delcassé. In various discussions with the Elder Statesman, Hayashi only succeeded in obtaining Itō's consent to go ahead with the British approach in the most general terms and could not talk Itō out of going to Russia. After studying the telegrams which had been exchanged with Britain, Itō cabled to Katsura on 15 November that he had no objection to the agreement in principle but was not satisfied with Britain's attempt to exclude Germany nor with the British draft of the clauses regarding Korea. He further suggested that it would be 'sound policy to delay coming to any definite decision until I carry out an exchange of views with the Russian government'.[3] Whatever doubt there was about Itō's intentions before this, it was now plain that he proposed to conduct talks at St Petersburg.

After his discussions with Itō and his travelling companion Tsuzuki,[4] Hayashi gave vent to his resentment in telegrams to Tokyo. Hayashi could understand Itō wanting to go to Russia in the state of

---

[1] *Komura gaikōshi*, i, 275; *NGB* 35, no. 25, p. 70.　　[2] *NGB* 34, no. 35.

[3] *Itō Hirobumi hiroku* ('Private writings of Itō Hirobumi'), edited by Hiratsuka Atsushi, 2 vols., Tokyo, 1928–30, vol. i, appendix, no. 16, Itō to Katsura, 15 November 1901. The appendix to vol. i contains a collection of memoranda written by Itō during his visit to Europe and of telegrams exchanged with Tokyo, under the title 'Nichi-Ei dōmei to Nichi-Ro kyōshō' ('The Anglo-Japanese alliance and Russo-Japanese agreement'). This collection is hereafter cited as '*Itō hiroku*, appendix', followed by the number of the document.

[4] Baron Tsuzuki Keiroku, who accompanied Itō as his secretary, was widely known for his pro-Russian views. He had been Japan's vice-minister for foreign affairs (1898–9) and was then regarded as being hostile to Britain.

mind in which he had left Japan; but that he should persist in going when he saw the draft treaty which Britain had offered could only imply some double-dealing which would stain the good name of Japan. Hayashi viewed Itō's activities partly as a slight against his own doings in London and partly as a plot by one set of genrō in Japan. He was also indignant at the indecisive attitude of his home government in letting Itō proceed as far as he had.[1] On his return to London, Hayashi visited the Foreign Office and met with a broadside from Bertie: he was told that Britain would be very indignant, were Japan to conclude a separate treaty with Russia at a time when negotiations had progressed so far. Hayashi's assurances that Itō's visit was purely private and gave no indication of official Japanese policy, did not ring true. The Foreign Office never doubted Hayashi's intentions and probably realized that he was powerless. Hayashi reported on 21 November that Britain was keeping 'vigilant eyes on the movement of Marquis Itō' and even sent a copy to Itō in Berlin in the hope that it might induce him to cancel his journey to Russia.[2]

Komura, though far from well, tried to clear the air with Hayashi by refuting any charge of duplicity on Japan's part. Itō, he said, was not entrusted with any official or diplomatic duties and anything he did in the Russian capital was on his own personal responsibility. Hayashi gave Lansdowne an assurance on these lines on 26 November. Foreign ministry officials in Tokyo were also trying to impress the British minister with the good reasons behind the delay. Lansdowne, however, minuted that he doubted the truth of these.[3]

This was virtually the first occasion on which Katsura had had to come to a decision on Itō's visit to Russia. In September he had given general approval to Itō's going there; but the itinerary was then tentative, Russia was far away and the prospect of a British alliance was still uncertain. Now, with circumstances changed, the moment for decision had arrived. Would Katsura try to persuade Itō to abandon his trip? Katsura's problem was that Itō was in no sense his subordinate and, now that he was in Europe, he was even less likely to listen to any persuasion. Deducing that nothing would deflect Itō from his purposes, Katsura urged him on 22 November to proceed

[1] *NGB* 34, nos. 36 and 38; *Hayashi memoirs*, pp. 138–44.
[2] *NGB* 34, no. 42.
[3] *NGB* 34, no. 45. Lansdowne's minute on FO *Japan* 563, MacDonald to Lansdowne, 25 November 1901.

to the Russian capital with all speed instead of waiting a while in Berlin as he intended.[1] Itō followed this advice and went straight to Russia, only changing trains in Berlin. Meanwhile Komura made it clear to the Japanese legation in Russia that Itō had no official mission but could discuss with the Russian leaders 'freely and without reservation'.[2] Itō asked Tokyo's views on the nature of the conversations which he would hold; and Katsura replied that he should confine himself to 'private and personal conversations' with the Russian ministers which would not be inconsistent with Japan's acceptance of the British proposals.[3] When the moment for decision arrived, Katsura found that he had not the power to prescribe Itō's movements or to restrict his actions and thought it best to urge him to go on to Russia for unofficial talks.

Because of the foreign minister's continued sickness, the cabinet met at his residence on 28 November to discuss the next step over the British treaty. A revised draft of the English version was approved with slight amendments. Special endeavours were made to ensure that the cabinet decision was unanimous. But, when the prime minister reported to the emperor next day, he was told that the redraft should be referred to the genrō, including Itō in Europe, and confirmed by them before he would give his assent. Katsura, therefore, resolved to consult Itō by messenger and to convene a meeting of the genrō later when Itō's views were received.[4]

By the end of November, the Japanese cabinet was definitely committed to accepting a treaty with Britain. News of the cabinet's commitment was allowed to leak out judiciously. Komura took the opportunity to inform MacDonald on 28 November — an action which Itō described as 'very hasty'. The foreign minister also passed the counterdraft to Hayashi so that he too was made aware of the position.[5] In order to consult Itō, Hayashi was told to send the draft agreement by the hand of some responsible person to wherever Itō was. On 1 December, Matsui Keishirō, the first secretary at the London legation, was delegated to take the draft to St Petersburg where Itō

[1] *Itō hiroku*, appendix, no. 19, Katsura to Itō, 22 November 1901.

[2] *NGB* 34, no. 44.

[3] *Itō hiroku*, appendix, no. 20, Itō to Katsura, 26 November 1901; no. 21, Katsura to Itō, 27 November 1901.

[4] *NGB* 35, no. 25, pp. 73–4. Grenville, pp. 406–7, mentions a genrō meeting on 30 November of which I have found no trace.

[5] *NGB* 34, nos. 50 and 51.

then was.[1] It was, of course, an exceptional procedure for Komura to follow but in no way extraordinary or unreasonable. The emperor had directed that Itō be consulted as he would automatically have been consulted had he been in Japan. The only peculiarity of this method is that Itō was being consulted at such a distance on a matter so detailed as the text of a treaty. The reason why someone from London was sent was largely to prevent a leakage. It was insecure to send a telegram of this nature to St Petersburg, since the Russian postal authorities had a reputation for prying into foreign cables and the Japanese staff there, who were not aware of the secret negotiations with Britain, might let the matter leak out. Motives of security and secrecy thus combined to induce Komura to use this devious method. It was Hayashi's decision to entrust the mission to the most senior member of his staff. It may seem strange that Hayashi, who was only told to send a member of his staff, should have entrusted the mission to one who was his deputy. The probability is that Hayashi wanted not merely to deliver the telegram but also to find out the nature of Itō's talks and current thinking. In a rank-conscious society like that of Japan, this could best be uncovered by the most high-ranking official available.

WAITING FOR ITŌ

It is important to analyse Britain's attitude to Itō's journeying. As Hayashi reported, Britain was keeping 'vigilant eyes' on the marquis's movements. On 20 November Lansdowne asked MacDonald whether 'Japanese delay in coming to a conclusion on our alliance can be in any way connected with Itō's journey' and received the reply that it was unlikely that it had any connection with the delay which he attributed to the fact that Komura had been laid up with pneumonia and was not allowed to receive anybody.[2] Evidently Lansdowne did not accept this and questioned the British embassies in France and Russia. Hardinge reported from Russia that Itō 'received encouragement from the French Government to come to St Petersburg in order to obtain assurances from the Russian Government which may satisfy French financiers and thereby facilitate the raising of a Japanese loan

---

[1] *NGB* 34, no. 53. Langer, p. 764, seems to be unduly harsh in describing the action of sending Matsui across Europe as 'just another way of gaining time'.

[2] FO *Japan* 563, Lansdowne to MacDonald, 20 November 1901; MacDonald to Lansdowne, 22 November 1901.

in Paris'. The Russians hoped that Itō's visit might facilitate an arrangement 'by which Japanese obstruction to Russian projects in Manchuria may be withdrawn in consideration for concessions to Japan in Corea'.[1] But Hardinge's report seems to be discredited when it is compared with what is known from Japanese sources which suggest that Itō had no special financial commission to raise a loan in France.[2] Indeed Hardinge's remarks were not more informative than a great deal of speculation which was circulating in Europe about Itō's purposes.

Hardinge further claims that it was at his instance that 'a message was promptly sent to Marquis Itō in Berlin inviting him to come to London'.[3] This suggests that Itō's decision to visit London was only reached early in December, whereas it was known much earlier. Before Itō left Tokyo in September, he called on all the diplomatic missions of the countries which he was proposing to visit. He told the British chargé d'affaires that he would visit London early in 1902, as in fact he did.[4] Moreover when Hayashi met Itō in Paris, he established that the Elder Statesman would come to London at the end of his European tour in January. There was always the possibility that Itō would be diverted from this plan by invitations to return by the Trans-Siberian Railway, although this would have exposed the falsity of his claim that he was going abroad for his health. In fact he turned down several such invitations and showed no keenness to return by this route. It also seems unlikely that the British government at this stage sent Itō a specific invitation, since his arrival in Britain at the Christmas season unquestionably caught the Foreign Office unprepared. It seems to have left the initiative to Itō himself. This does not imply that Britain was reluctant to have a visit. On the contrary, it was greatly relieved.

Lansdowne took Itō's journey to Russia fairly philosophically. In his attitude, he seems to have combined scepticism with reserve. He was sceptical in so far as he questioned the accuracy of Japanese assurances that Itō had no official mission.[5] He was reserved in circumstances where it would have been natural for him to have reacted more

---

[1] *BD*, ii, no. 76. Charles Hardinge was chargé d'affaires in Russia in 1901.

[2] FO *Russia* 1625, Hardinge to Lansdowne, 30 November 1901; and Scott to Lansdowne, 17 December 1901.

[3] Charles (Lord) Hardinge, *Old diplomacy*, p. 77.

[4] FO *Japan* 541, Whitehead to Lansdowne, 20 September 1901.

[5] FO *Japan* 563, minute by Lansdowne, 25 November 1901.

violently. There were certain factors which gave him confidence. First, the fact that Itō intended to visit London meant that he did not hope to do anything conclusive in Russia. Second, Britain having recently made overtures to Russia, he might assume that Itō would find the Russian leaders equally intransigent. Third, Lansdowne recognized Hayashi's sincerity of purpose and could only trust that he was representative of opinion within the Tokyo cabinet and that Itō was unrepresentative.

Some historians claim that Itō's talks in St Petersburg had an immediate bearing on the alliance. Professor Yanaga writes that Itō's 'visit to Russia stimulated the British into action and actually hastened the conclusion of the treaty of alliance'.[1] But there is little evidence to support this. When Lansdowne handed over the first British draft on 6 November, it was not known that Itō was planning to go to St Petersburg. Its timing was determined by internal considerations within the government and was not hastened by any outside stimulus. From this time until 12 December, the effect of Itō's doings was not to spur on Britain but to slow down Japan. The Foreign Office was already committed and had no alternative but to await Japan's reply. Lansdowne never protested formally to Tokyo and never threatened to break off negotiations. After 12 December, when Itō was sojourning in Berlin waiting for the Russian reaction to his proposals, British ministers did not panic by concluding the agreement prematurely nor did they accept any of the Japanese terms, which they thought to be undesirable, for fear of repercussions in Russia. There was no sign of undue haste in the negotiation. Indeed the consideration of drafts continued slowly during December or January; and there was no guarantee that the talks would not break down. It would be wrong to pretend that Lansdowne was not apprehensive; but he was not hurried into the alliance by the prospect of Itō's success.

It is interesting that the Japanese government was quick to give Britain assurances that the delay was not caused by Itō's activities. In effect, it admitted that there would be something improper and injurious to Japan's honour if talks were pursued with Russia at an official level while the country was negotiating with Britain. The Japanese rightly claimed that Itō's conversations were not official. But

---

[1] Yanaga, *Japan since Perry*, p. 301. Others who seem to overstate the case are Langer, p. 771, 'there was much uneasiness in London on account of Itō's peregrinations' and Monger, p. 56, '[Lansdowne's] anxiety became acute'.

the various disclaimers, which they offered, were not equally valid. The most valid of their arguments was that the Foreign Ministry was in some disarray for most of November. Komura's attack of pneumonia led to his absence for three weeks. Normally his duties would have been undertaken by the vice-minister or the prime minister. But the vice-minister, Uchida, left for his new post at Peking early in November; and Chinda, his successor, did not arrive until the end of the month. This, coupled with the absence of Katsura from Tokyo for a short while at the autumn manœuvres, accounted for much of the delay in November. After the cabinet's decision had been taken, the delay could no longer be attributed to the ministers.

Those who sympathize with Itō in this crisis argue that the ministry, after initially encouraging him to go to Russia, tried to disown him and ignore his views. In other words the whole manœuvre was undertaken merely to get Itō out of the way while the alliance was being negotiated.[1] It can only be said that, if it was in Katsura's mind to by-pass the genrō and Itō in particular, he was naïve and did not succeed in achieving his purpose. In the end the Japanese decision was deferred until Itō had had discussions in Russia and had reported on his findings. By doing so, Japan got the best of both worlds. But this was not really Katsura's doing. His views were sacrificed to a higher national interest which was interpreted by the emperor and genrō.

CONSULTING THE GENRŌ

The emperor had ruled that, even though Itō was in Europe, he should still be asked for his views on the alliance. It should be observed that the matter was referred to Itō for his views on the counterdraft to Britain, not for his views in the light of his discussions in Russia. That it did in practice amount to the same thing was due to the fact that he lost no time in arranging his interviews with Russian leaders. He had in fact almost finished these by the time the counterdraft reached him. But there was no reason why the Tokyo authorities should have foreseen this; Itō might have been as dilatory in holding these talks as he had been in Paris. Thus those in Tokyo cannot altogether be accused of holding up the British negotiations while they saw what Russia had to offer Itō.

[1] E.g. *Itō hiroku*, i, 350–4, memorandum by Kurino. The literature on this controversy is large: among Itō's supporters, there are biographies of Itō, Inoue, Kurino and Tsuzuki; on Katsura's side, there are biographies of Yamagata, Yamamoto Gombei and Katsura.

Itō, who had reached St Petersburg on 27 November, had been lobbied about the alliance by Count Inoue, one of the sponsors of his visit. Inoue cabled that he was puzzled why Britain should offer an alliance, although it was a complete break with her established policy: was Britain intending to enveigle Japan into her own particular difficulties? For Japan to conclude an alliance with Britain might induce Russia, France and Germany to join together in the Dreibund; and the Japanese must take account of this danger in advance and examine the attitude of Germany. He felt, therefore, that Japan should only proceed with the British negotiations after she had found out how far Russia would give way on the Korean question and acknowledge Japan's commercial and industrial position there.[1] This was advice very much after Itō's own heart; but it was not the view of the government.

The first secretary at the London legation reached the Russian capital on 3 December, deciphered the telegram there and delivered it to Itō. The marquis left for Berlin on the following evening, while Matsui took the train the next day in order to avoid attracting attention. Itō studied the draft in Berlin and sent two telegrams to Tokyo containing criticisms.[2] He also had detailed conversations with Matsui before the latter returned to London on 11 December and reported that Itō wanted to make amendments to Japan's counterdraft and still thought that it was premature to make an agreement with Britain, without opposing it outright.[3]

While Katsura was waiting for Itō's opinion, he made elaborate arrangements to lobby the other genrō, Yamagata, Inoue, Matsukata and Saigō. On 30 November, Matsukata called on Komura to inquire about his health and the foreign minister could not lose the opportunity of explaining the need for pursuing the negotiations with Britain. After a further talk with Katsura on 5 December, Matsukata was completely convinced. Yamagata and Saigō were privately lobbied by the prime minister and expressed their approval.[4] This left only Inoue who, as a former foreign minister, was the most knowledgeable

---

[1] *NGB* 34, nos. 47–8, Inoue to Itō (Russia) and reply, 28 November 1901. Shinobu, *Nichi-Ro sensōshi no kenkyū*, p. 129–30, says that Katsura tried to stop Inoue's telegram being sent but that Inoue insisted.

[2] *NGB* 34, nos. 55 and 56, Itō to Katsura, 6 December 1901. [Appendix E].

[3] *Hayashi memoirs*, pp. 150–8. A Japanese version of Matsui's report is in *NGB* 35, no. 25, pp. 41–3.

[4] *NGB* 35, no. 25, p. 74.

of the genrō about world affairs. Inoue admitted that by 4 December the majority of the genrō supported the idea of an alliance, while he still felt that Japan's counterdraft was lacking in clarity.[1] The task of converting Inoue was allotted to Denison, the American adviser to the Japanese foreign ministry. On 5 December, the two discussed the diplomatic, military, commercial and financial aspects of the alliance for more than four hours. Inoue appears to have been worried that, if Japan allied herself with Britain, Germany would join the Franco-Russian alliance and that this would impose additional obligations and worsen Japan's naval position in Chinese waters. On the following day, they compared the draft of the British alliance with the text of the triple alliance and concluded that it was a straightforward peaceful alliance.[2] The extent of Inoue's conversion is doubtful since he still held out hopes of Itō's success in Russia. But it was a great strength of the genrō arrangement that the draft was given such an exacting examination by one who had no ministerial or constitutional responsibility.

Even though Itō's comments had not been received, the genrō council met at Katsura's country house at Hayama near Tokyo on 7 December. The previous day Katsura had informed the British minister that he had sounded the genrō and found them favourably disposed to the agreement.[3] MacDonald was impressed with Katsura's determination that, whatever Itō's attitude, the cabinet would proceed and believed that Katsura and Komura would resign if the cabinet decision did not prevail.[4] In this atmosphere of determination, Yamagata, Inoue, Matsukata and Saigō assembled and were presented with a memorandum drawn up by Komura which compared the value of a British treaty with a Russian one. It pointed out some of the disadvantages which might result if the Russian negotiations were pursued. An agreement with Russia would only bring about a temporary peace in the far east, would hold out only minor commercial advantages for Japan, would gravely impair Japan's long-term interests by destroying China's goodwill and would force Japan to keep her naval strength on a parity with Britain's. On the other hand, an agreement with Britain would ensure a relatively long-term peace in the far east, identify Japan with the Open Door powers and bring financial and commercial

---

[1] *NGB* 34, no. 54.   [2] *NGB* 35, no. 25, p. 76.
[3] FO *Japan* 563, MacDonald to Lansdowne, 3 and 6 December 1901.
[4] *NGB* 34, no. 57, memorandum by Komura, 7 December 1901. [Appendix D].

benefits, improve the standing of Japan in China and help in solving the Korean problem. Finally the task of maintaining naval parity with Russia would be less formidable than with Britain. Komura argued that the treaty with Britain which was on offer, would enable Japan to put pressure on Russia and serve her interests best. This memorandum is full of rare insights into the making of Japanese policy.

It was only when Inoue was shown the history of the project from the start that he agreed with the others to proceed with the London talks. He justified his change of front by cabling to Itō immediately after the meeting that, when he saw the telegrams which Itō had sent to Hayashi in May and which Katsura had sent after discussions with Itō in August, he discovered that negotiations had more or less been started from the Japanese side. He therefore saw no alternative but to concur in the majority view of the genrō. Inoue felt that Japan which had initiated the talks could not draw back now that Britain had responded.[1]

While Katsura obtained the genrō's approval to proceed with the talks, he agreed to wait a few days for a communication from Itō. The telegram containing Itō's comments on Japan's counterdraft was badly delayed: it reached Tokyo on the evening of 8 December and was decoded overnight. While Itō offered a number of drafting improvements, he also made some criticisms on grounds of principle. He thought it unwise either to leave Germany out of the British treaty or to entrust negotiations for the inclusion of Germany to Britain. Since a British treaty would make any arrangement with Russia difficult, he recommended that it should not be concluded until after it was known whether an understanding with Russia was possible or not.[2] While Itō had a different notion of priorities from the cabinet, it would be wrong to say that he denounced the treaty.

When the matter was referred to the emperor, he ruled that the genrō should be consulted over Itō's views. Katsura accordingly held further discussions with Matsukata and Inoue as the senior genrō at Matsukata's house at Mita on 10 December. They concluded that it was not possible to foresee a Russo-Japanese agreement materializing and further delay would only bring Britain to withdraw her proposals so that Japan might, if she delayed further, lose the sympathy both of Russia and Britain and find herself in complete isolation. They recommended that it would be best to conclude an agreement with

---

[1] *NGB* 34, no. 58, Inoue to Itō, 7 December 1901.　　[2] *NGB* 34, nos. 55–6.

Britain on the lines of the earlier decision.[1] Katsura and Komura immediately sought another audience with the emperor who decided that Japan must pursue her talks with Britain without further delay. That same evening, Komura instructed Hayashi to pass on to Britain the Japanese counterdraft which had already been sent to him and explained the reasons for Japan's amendments so that they too might be conveyed to Lansdowne.[2]

Itō knew that he had been out-manœuvred and suspected that his views were being unceremoniously shelved. He therefore sent a telegram from Berlin telling Hayashi to take no action on any instructions received from Tokyo without referring to him. On 11 December when Hayashi received instructions from home to go ahead, he referred to Komura for confirmation. Komura replied that he was to comply with his earlier orders without delay. Katsura took the occasion to inform Itō that his views had been placed before the emperor and duly considered before Japan's decision was taken. So Hayashi, while preserving the courtesies by informing Itō of his action, passed over to Lansdowne on 12 December Japan's revised draft and four days later the note of explanations.[3] Thus ended a most illuminating phase of Japanese statecraft, which illustrates the effect which the genrō could have on the formulation of policy and the extent to which the final decision rested with the emperor.

ITŌ AND RUSSIA

We have hitherto considered Itō's journey from the viewpoint of the British alliance. We must now turn to examine the talks he had in the Russian capital. Since they were abortive, they did not have much practical effect on the first alliance; but they are of interest for the present study because they foreshadow the lines of Japan's approach to Russia before the outbreak of war in 1904. An exhaustive study of these important talks which will clear away the many misunderstandings associated with them, is long overdue but cannot be given here.

Shortly after his arrival at St Petersburg, Itō received a message from Tokyo containing a request from the prime minister that he would

---

[1] *NGB* 34, no. 66.   [2] *NGB* 34, nos. 67 and 60.
[3] *NGB* 34, nos. 62, 63 and 65.

confine his conversations in Russia to an informal exchange of views, since Japan could no longer delay negotiations with Britain.[1] He told his friend, Inoue, that he saw no alternative but to bow to Katsura's wishes although he considered them to be in flat contradiction to the original objects of his going to Russia. He thought that Russian opinion was ready for an understanding with Japan and asked Inoue to consult the premier again.[2]

On 28 November, accompanied by Tsuzuki Keiroku who had travelled with him as interpreter, Itō went by rail to Tsarskoe Selo palace for an interview with the Emperor of the Russias. He was received cordially but nothing of great political import was discussed. More significant were two conversations he had with the foreign minister, Count Lamsdorf (2 and 4 December), although Lamsdorf admitted rather unkindly to the French ambassador that he had had the impression he was speaking to a deaf-mute[3] — surely not a description of talks which were world-shattering in their implications. The fact was that the talks had been marred by language difficulties, Itō speaking indifferent English and Lamsdorf replying in indifferent German. Since attention was concentrated in the talks on Manchuria and Korea, it was natural that he should arrange to have a conversation with the influential finance minister, Count Witte (3 December). He was careful in these discussions to say that he was offering personal and unofficial opinions. Itō's purpose was to find out how much Russia would be prepared to concede to Japan in Korea. Lamsdorf reminded him that the existing treaty gave the Japanese equal rights in Korea and continued: 'If we delegated Korean affairs exclusively to Japan and accepted even her right to send troops there, we should naturally require some guarantee that Japan did not turn Korea to her strategic advantage on any pretext. If Japan were to construct bases on the Korean littoral, this would threaten communications between Vladivostok and Port Arthur and, for reasons of self-defence, Russia could not look on disinterested.' None the less, Lamsdorf asked Itō to prepare a memorandum containing his proposals for a Russo-Japanese agreement on Korea. This document was handed over to Lamsdorf

---

[1] *NGB* 34, no. 46. 'An informal exchange of views' conveys the colourlessness of the Japanese original better than Professor Langer's phrase 'harmless gossiping' (p. 763), which implies a studied insult to Itō which Katsura could scarcely offer.

[2] *NGB* 34, no. 48.

[3] *Documents diplomatiques français*, 2me serie, i, no. 548 (this series is hereafter cited as 'DDF').

O

at the final interview on 4 December. The draft, which was in English, set out Japan's optimum demands in Korea as follows:

Russia vouchsafes to Japan freedom of action in Korea in all matters, political, industrial and commercial, and recognises her special right to assist by advice and support in making Korea accept the obligations of better government and, in the case of civil disturbance, to settle incidents which threaten to disturb the peaceful relations prevailing between Japan and Korea, using such military strength as the exigencies of the situation may dictate.

Since Lamsdorf could not discuss the proposals with his colleagues or the tsar before Itō's departure, he promised to send on his considered views to Itō in Berlin.[1] Thus Itō did not secure the immediate encouragement in Russia which might have turned the scales in his favour.

The prime purpose of Itō's sojourn in Berlin was not to negotiate with Germany but to study the political climate and await Russia's reply. He was received royally and granted an audience with Kaiser Wilhelm II at Potsdam on 14 December. He also sampled the night life which he remembered from earlier visits there. In due course Russia's reply was handed over on 17 December and Itō left for Brussels forthwith.

The most important of Russia's counterproposals, which had mainly been drawn up by Witte and Kuropatkin, were those dealing with Japan's rights in Korea. Russia would admit that Japan possessed freedom of action in Korea in respect of industrial and commercial arrangements and that Japan had superior rights, after prior consultation with Russia, to help Korea by active support and thus make her conscious of her responsibility to maintain good government and, if necessary, to send military help to quell disturbances which hindered peaceful relations. But these concessions were limited in certain respects: Japan must not use Korean territory for military objectives; military installations which endangered the passage through the Korean straits would not be built; Japan should not send forces greater than the situation warranted.[2] These limitations went far towards curbing

---

[1] *Itō hiroku*, appendix, nos. 28 and 30, meetings with Lamsdorf.
[2] *Itō hiroku*, appendix, no. 51, Lamsdorf to Itō, reaching Berlin 17 December 1901. For the text, Langer, p. 768–9.

the 'free hand' which she had earlier offered. The Russians, feeling that Itō had pitched his demands high, had decided also to set out their maximum demands with the result that their counter-proposals appear to be uncompromising. In short the Russians' reply implied that they were entitled to a completely free hand in Manchuria whereas Japan could only operate in Korea under distinct limitations. Witte had overplayed his hand. Itō was undoubtedly disappointed to receive such unconciliatory terms.

Itō informed the prime minister of this development without delay.[1] Four days later Katsura replied making it clear with the smoothness of which he was a master, that the government was not prepared to support Itō's overture. The Elder Statesman had offered to barter Manchuria for Korea but, argued Katsura, Japan had since March given guarantees to China against Russia's occupation of Manchuria and could not now encourage Russia's actions there without loss of national honour.[2] Itō replied to Lamsdorf on 23 December that he could not countenance any agreement which did not acknowledge Japan's freedom of action in Korea which, he claimed, was incompatible with consulting Russia beforehand. Itō added that, on the basis discussed, 'there was little hope of our countries easily reaching an agreement of any permanence. . . . These first impressions have raised doubts in my mind about the advantages of referring your draft to the Japanese government as the basis for further negotiation'.[3] Probably Itō would have taken this view regardless of the reply from Tokyo; but he did in fact delay until Katsura's reactions were known. Itō was as disgruntled with Katsura as he was with Russia. He hotly defended his search for an understanding with Russia.[4] But he was in a weak debating position and had to acknowledge that he had been outpointed.

Itō had a different notion of priorities from the Japanese cabinet. He favoured an approach to Russia before being involved in entanglements with Britain. He was not in a position to carry on his talks with Russia in the face of a veto from Tokyo, although he continued to cherish the hope of doing so. But, at the same time, it would be wrong to imagine that Itō was opposed to the alliance with Britain. He has

[1] *Itō hiroku*, appendix, no. 53, Itō to Katsura, 17 December 1901.
[2] *Itō hiroku*, appendix, no. 58, Katsura to Itō, 21 December 1901. [Appendix E].
[3] *Itō hiroku*, appendix, no. 60, Itō to Lamsdorf, 23 December 1901.
[4] *Itō hiroku*, appendix, no. 59, Itō to Katsura, 22 December 1901.

the reputation among Meiji statesmen of being vacillating,[1] of following elastic policies and of being ready to compromise when he found himself in a vulnerable position. It was so in this case.

In this sense, there was not really a sharp division between the Japanese leaders. Katsura, who had succeeded in having his policy adopted, could now afford to be charitable. On 28 December, he assured Itō that there was scope for resolving the problem of Korea and Manchuria on a reciprocal basis with Russia; the restrictions which were to be imposed on Japan in Korea must also apply to Russia in Manchuria. If the Manchurian problem could be solved on such a basis, he thought that other countries, including Great Britain, would be grateful to Japan. But he was hoping to bring to completion as quickly as possible the negotiations then proceeding with Britain before opening discussions with Russia.[2] In short, Katsura admitted that he was ready to follow up these talks with Russia and felt that Britain could not object since the end was peaceful. It was to be the policy of the Katsura cabinet to achieve an alliance with Britain but to continue to negotiate with Russia over Korea. When Kurino Shinichirō was newly appointed minister to Russia in November 1901, he was told that his duty would be to work for an understanding with Russia in the far east. In January 1902, Kurino challenged Komura on this point after a discussion with Itō in Paris and was told that the cabinet 'desired to come to an arrangement with Russia over Korea' but it did not at present intend to give final orders for the conclusion of a treaty.[3]

Of course, Itō had no intention of acting as Katsura's lackey and replied that he could do nothing further with Russia until he returned to Japan to explain some of the intricacies of the Russian situation which were apparently incomprehensible to those in Tokyo.[4] He did not return to Russia as Witte had hoped but went through Brussels to London where he was received as cordially as in any European capital. He then repaired to Paris and to Italy before leaving by steamer

---

[1] Oka Yoshitake, *Kindai Nihon no seijika* ('Statesmen of new Japan'), pp. 33–4. I differ from Dr Grenville's view (p. 411) that Itō's failure in Russia did not deter him from opposing the British alliance.

[2] *Itō hiroku*, appendix, no. 61, Katsura to Itō, 28 December 1901.

[3] *Itō hiroku*, appendix, no. 71, Kurino to Itō, 20 January 1902. Kurino left for his appointment in Russia on 17 November. He paused in Paris for a while to straighten out his affairs and there met Itō.

[4] *Itō hiroku*, appendix, no. 63, Itō to Katsura, 30 December 1901.

from Naples on 23 January. He reached Nagasaki on 25 February just a fortnight after the British treaty was published. From 4 December when Itō had the crucial discussion with Lamsdorf, his journey had only slight political significance and that was in Britain.

'INSURING IN BOTH OFFICES'

While Itō was in England, he had two meetings with the foreign secretary, one at Lansdowne's country seat at Bowood on 2 January 1902, the other at the Foreign Office four days later. They had conversations which were unofficial but are none the less significant.[1] Itō turned the discussion to the question of Korea; and the resulting dialogue was fully reported by him:

Itō:—There is in being an agreement between Russia and Japan regarding Korea; and Japan is at present much restricted by it but cannot revoke it. This agreement is something which Japan has borne long enough and cannot continue. If we changed this agreement to our benefit by mutual consultation between Russia and Japan, Your Lordship would surely be in sympathy with us.

Lansdowne:—I can't fully understand your view. Do I gather that you mean to arrange a Russo-Japanese agreement similar to, but separate from, the Anglo-Japanese agreement?

Itō:—I am very anxious not to leave any misunderstanding on this point. I have no thought of any two-faced policy towards Britain and Russia nor do I support a Russo-Japanese alliance. I only desire to try by the most peaceful method to reach a complete agreement with Russia by moving the milepost of the existing Russo-Japanese agreement just a step forward in order to safeguard our interests in Korea. To my mind, this is something which would increasingly secure true peace in the far east in the future.

Lansdowne:—I do not disagree. But if Japan were to come to terms with Russia which were inconsistent with what Britain was prepared to give Japan in Korea, Britain could not agree to it. So long as it does not infringe

---

[1] There is no support for the view that Itō's reception in London was not so cordial as in continental capitals and that Itō was cold-shouldered because of his suspected doings in Russia. He was granted an audience with the king and given interviews by Salisbury and Lansdowne (twice). He was entertained at the usual banquets, country-house weekends and diplomatic luncheons and was awarded decorations and academic degrees equivalent to those which he received in Russia and Germany. Never the less his arrival late in December made it difficult for these functions to be arranged; and his decoration had to be awarded at the British embassy in Paris. *Itō-den*, iii, 570, for the photograph.

our commitments, there ought not to be the slightest difference of opinion and, on the contrary, it would coincide with Britain's peaceful intentions.[1]

This reveals that Lansdowne did not think there would be anything amiss if Japan were to pursue a treaty with Russia over Korea simultaneously with the British alliance. While this was not reported to the Japanese government until after Itō's return to Japan, it amounts to an important gloss on the later alliance. Disappointed as he was, Itō was still eager to pursue an agreement with Russia and wanted to remove any objection from Japan's future ally. Itō was surprisingly outspoken in telling Lansdowne of these ideas, which were not likely to be palatable to Britain in the first instance. Writing later to MacDonald, the foreign secretary recalled that 'in my conversations with Itō and Hayashi, I detected a desire to come to an understanding with Russia as well as with us, and, so to speak, to *insure in both offices*'.[2] And with reservations Lansdowne was prepared to go along with this proposal.

This leads us in conclusion to the question: what influence did Itō have on the British alliance? A senior Japanese official, Ishii Kikujirō, who was responsible for writing a report on the negotiations shortly after the event, remarked that whether the British agreement came about or not 'really hung by a thread'. He describes the events of early December as 'a grave national crisis' and attributes this to the actions of Itō.[3]

It is not quite clear what Ishii means by a national crisis but presumably he is referring to the crisis of decision which faced the leaders in Tokyo. It was not the crisis which prompted them to consult Itō in St Petersburg. Had he been in Japan, he would certainly have been consulted on such a matter of high policy. He was the leading genrō and the confidant of the emperor with whom the final decision rested. As the father of Japanese foreign policy, he was the statesman with the greatest grasp of foreign countries' aims and ambitions. It was natural for him to be consulted. His presence in Europe was certainly a complication but it gave him the opportunity to judge European diplomacy at first hand and hence increased the value of his opinions on the current issue. It is not so easy to explain why Itō was consulted on the detailed terms of the treaty; but it may be that Itō, who

---

[1] *Itō hiroku*, appendix, no. 64 and 65, conversations with Lansdowne. Also *BD*, ii, no. 120, which was circulated as a cabinet paper on 8 January 1902.

[2] Lansdowne papers, Lansdowne to MacDonald, 31 March 1902. My italics.

[3] *NGB* 35, no. 25, p. 70.

possessed special skill in drafting agreements, was expected to be a useful critic and commentator on Japan's counterdraft. Judging from his comments, he was not so much a critic of the alliance as an advocate of delay in concluding it. This was the point of disagreement between him and Tokyo. It can hardly be described as a 'crisis of decision'. Nor is there much ground for saying that the alliance 'hung by a thread'. Itō ultimately found himself without support among the genrō. Had the other genrō or a majority of them sided with him, the alliance would indeed have hung by a thread; it would certainly have developed into an interesting dispute between genrō and cabinet whose result would have been uncertain. But it was not so. So long as Itō was alone, the obstacles which he could place in the way of the British alliance were not insuperable provided the cabinet was determined. Indeed Itō's activities were obstructive rather than destructive; and it is doubtful whether they were ever so important that the alliance was really in question.

So much for Itō's role during the negotiations. But what of his attitude towards the alliance? During his interviews with Lansdowne, he denied that he was one of 'those who distrust the negotiations'.[1] He was probably quite sincere in this statement. He had just seen the Russo-Japanese agreement, which had taken first priority in his thinking, fail to materialize; but he still pursued it as a long-term objective. This did not mean that he was hostile to the concept of a British alliance. His objection was more to the haste with which Katsura was trying to rush it through. He was neither Anglophobe nor Russophil; he pursued Japan's interest as he conceived it. He wrote:

If you examined the status and renown which present-day Japan has won in the diplomatic arena of Europe, you would find that isolation need not be detrimental to Japan.[2]

Like Salisbury, he could not appreciate the danger of his country's isolation. He was therefore averse to concluding a treaty with Britain on easy terms.[3]

[1] *Itō hiroku*, appendix, nos. 64 and 65. *BD*, ii, no. 120: '[Itō] was in entire sympathy with the proposal, and trusted that the Agreement would be concluded'.

[2] *Itō hiroku*, appendix, no. 48, Itō to Katsura, 13 December 1901.

[3] When the conclusion of the first alliance was announced, Itō was in Singapore as the guest of Sir Frank Swettenham, governor of Straits Settlements, who remarked to him that 'the hand which had guided it was Ito's'. Itō declined to take the credit for it. Morrison papers 312/65, 18 October 1905.

CHAPTER X

The First Alliance Concluded

December 1901–February 1902

On 12 December, when draft and counterdraft had been exchanged, the parties became locked in negotiation and the bargaining phase had begun. Although the need for an agreement had already been accepted in principle on both sides, the bargaining proved to be unexpectedly hard. The Japanese cabinet, whose counterdraft had ultimately been accepted, made demands which appeared to Britain to be very stiff and on which she was reluctant to make concessions. The Japanese, far from being willing to conclude a treaty on any terms in order to attract Britain as a partner, were most tenacious of their claims and ambitions.

Even before Hayashi passed over the counterdraft officially, Britain heard of Japan's amendments direct from Tokyo. On 9 December, Lansdowne received a telegram from MacDonald setting out the amendments of which Katsura had rather improperly given him advance notice. The Japanese wanted the treaty to lay down that the naval forces kept by the two powers in far eastern waters should exceed those of all other powers and that Britain should recognize Japan's special sphere of influence in Korea.[1] This telegram was circulated to the inner cabinet and caused some misgiving.

Balfour, who as the Leader of the House of Commons was the most important member of the government apart from Salisbury, called on Lansdowne on 11 December and criticized the alliance on various grounds. The foreign secretary asked him to put his views in writing and Balfour prepared a weighty memorandum.[2] His view was that Britain should not have offered to enter into an offensive-defensive

---

[1] FO *Japan* 563, MacDonald to Lansdowne, 6 December 1901.

[2] Balfour papers Add. MSS 49727, Balfour to Lansdowne, 12 December 1901. Text in Monger, p. 64.

alliance with Japan without considering how she was placed with Germany, owing to her 'rejection' of German advances at the very moment she was secretly making similar advances to Japan. During November the cabinet had been considering the pros and cons of an understanding with Germany on a regional basis which was advocated by Lansdowne but was opposed by Salisbury and finally rejected.[1] But Balfour argued that the dangers from joining the Triple Alliance were less and the gains greater than from a Japanese alliance. The enemy in each case would be Russia and France and the conflagration in the event of an emergency would not be any the less in the case of a Japanese alliance. Lansdowne was inclined to deny this, claiming that the chances of a *casus foederis* arising under a Japanese alliance were much fewer than under an Anglo-German agreement and the 'area of entanglement' was much more restricted under the former. The question, he added, was whether Britain should allow Japan to be wiped out by France and Russia in certain given circumstances: 'If the answer is "no", may we not as well tell her so beforehand and get what we can out of the bargain?'[2]

Balfour also touched on an issue which had been raised before by members of the cabinet and would be raised again before the alliance was approved: that Britain was vulnerable in India in event of war with Russia and that Britain should ask for Japan's help there. Balfour's letter stated:

The weakest spot in the Empire is probably the Indian frontier. . . . A quarrel with Russia anywhere, about anything, means the invasion of India.

This was a gloomy forecast in which Balfour was probably exaggerating his fears. None the less Indian security was the cause of considerable anxiety at the time. During the war in South Africa, the army in India was short of 11 thousand men and the defence of the country might become perilous in the event of an attack over the north-west frontier. Russian troops were thought to be concentrated beyond the frontier and to be ready to attack at short notice, while France was thought to be sufficiently unfriendly to join Russia if a crisis arose. In August 1901 a report on the 'military needs of Empire in a war with France and Russia' had been submitted by the War Office and had underlined the fact that reinforcements for the Indian

[1] *BD*, ii, nos. 91–4.
[2] Balfour papers Add. MSS 49727, Balfour to Lansdowne, 12 December 1901.

and Colonial garrisons were seriously deficient.[1] The secretary of state for India had therefore set up a further committee to consider the military defence of India. Since there was a difference of opinion between Calcutta and London, the issue was one of some delicacy; and several members of the cabinet were sensitive to the needs of Indian defence. The committee report was not issued till 24 December and cannot therefore have prompted Balfour to mention the matter.[2] But Indian defence was a perennial problem during the South African war; and it was natural that Balfour should draw attention to the danger which Britain ran in concluding an anti-Russian treaty with Japan. This exchange of views between Lansdowne and Balfour was followed up at a discussion before the cabinet meeting on 13 December; but its results are not known.[3]

The Japanese counterdraft was finally delivered by Hayashi on 12 December. The only two clauses which represented a substantial change were those in the 'Separate Articles' which it was intended to keep secret. These read:

Article II (new clause)
Each of the High Contracting Parties shall endeavour to maintain in the Far East at all times naval forces superior in efficacy to the naval strength of any other Power which has the largest naval forces in the Far East.

Article III (new clause)
Great Britain recognises that Japan may take such suitable measures as she deems necessary to safeguard and promote the preponderating interests which she actually possesses in Corea.

Lansdowne, who had had the benefit of advance information from Tokyo, told Hayashi that some of the clauses were unacceptable.[4] When the British cabinet met on 13 December, it decided to defer discussion on the new Japanese terms until 19 December. The cabinet was informed that Lansdowne hoped to see the German ambassador and 'to give him a general indication of our views on this question of Japan, in order that Germany should have no ground for complaining that we had observed undue reticence towards her'.[5]

[1] Cabinet Office, Miscellaneous records, deposited in the Public Record Office, London, Cabinet 3/1/1A, War Office report, 12 August 1901.
[2] Cabinet 6/1/1D, India Office report, 24 December 1901.
[3] For the notion that Balfour was favourable to the alliance, *Hayashi memoirs*, p. 114. It is known that Balfour's letter was not printed for the cabinet.
[4] *BD*, ii, no. 115; *NGB* 34, no. 65.
[5] Salisbury papers, Royal, Salisbury to the king, 13 December 1901.

Lansdowne did meet Count Metternich, the new German ambassador, during the cabinet meeting on 19 December and, in the course of a discussion on the Anglo-German alliance project, asked whether:

it might not be possible for the two countries to arrive at an understanding with regard to the policy which they might pursue in reference to particular questions or in particular parts of the world in which they were alike interested?[1]

Metternich replied that no such minor proposal was likely to find favour with the German government. This discussion clarified Lansdowne's position. Balfour's hope that Britain might be able to join with Germany in some way was frustrated. Hereafter Balfour does not emerge as a critic of the Japanese alliance. Japan had not been explicitly mentioned during the discussion with Metternich; and it is hard to say whether Lansdowne was carrying out his promise to the cabinet. At any rate, Lansdowne established from the ambassador that Germany was not prepared to arrive at understandings for particular parts of the world and it was safe to assume that she would not wish to join with Britain and Japan in an understanding over the far east. Moreover, this was the end of the road: Lansdowne did not propose to pursue an arrangement with Germany. If, therefore, Britain wished to avoid isolation, the only partner immediately available was Japan.[2]

Along with the counterdraft, Hayashi had received an elaborate memorandum containing an explanation of the amendments which Japan had made. Hayashi handed this over on 16 December and argued strongly in favour of the amendments. When the criticisms made by Lansdowne were reported to Tokyo, Komura prepared a further detailed note which he sent to Hayashi for delivery before the final cabinet meeting for the year on 19 December.[3] The Japanese were rather over-anxious that the alliance should be concluded quickly and urged upon Britain the need for speed. The reason was that the Japanese government was involved in a serious political crisis. Since the opening of the Diet early in December, the Seiyūkai opposition had campaigned against the budget arrangements. There was a series of meetings at which the ministry tried to win over the Seiyūkai recalcitrants who had in Itō's absence abroad gone back on the guarantees which he had given the government. By 22 December no progress

---

[1] *BD*, ii, no. 94. [2] *GP*, xvii, 112–14.
[3] *NGB* 34, nos. 70–2; *Hayashi memoirs*, pp. 166–70.

had been made and there was talk of Katsura having to call for a dissolution of the Diet. On 26 December, however, a compromise solution was reached; and the storm abated slightly. For internal reasons, therefore, Japan was anxious for an early settlement of the alliance.[1]

At its meeting on 19 December, the British cabinet made no definite progress towards approving the Japanese treaty. But, as Salisbury's report significantly stated, the differences of opinion were more in respect to details than to substance. 'Especially', it continued, 'was the Cabinet disposed to reject a proposal that each Power should bind itself always to keep in Japanese seas a fixed naval force. We could not sacrifice the free disposal of our ships: and the Japanese Treaty would not repay us for the surrender. On the other hand many members of the Cabinet thought that the terms offered to us were hardly equivalent to the practical guarantee which we were offering to Japan: and desired that the Japanese engagements should extend to India and Siam'. Further discussion with Japan was held to be necessary.[2] When Hayashi called to hear the cabinet's findings, Lansdowne told him that it was decidedly opposed to a binding distribution of British naval forces in any part of the world and to the Korean article which was liable to be misconstrued as abetting the aggressive policy of Japan in Korea.

There was a short respite in negotiations because of Lansdowne's absence for Christmas. But Hayashi met Lansdowne on 31 December and handed over yet another explanatory memorandum from his government.[3] As Japan was asking for all possible haste, Lansdowne thought it desirable to consult his cabinet colleagues urgently. In a letter to Salisbury on New Year's day, Lansdowne wrote that he feared 'that the Cabinet of 13th [January] may have so much business before it that the Japanese Agreement will stand a poor chance'. With the prime minister's consent, he circulated the Japanese note to the cabinet with his own comments and a request for the views of his colleagues. Selborne, Lord James of Hereford and Lord Balfour of Burleigh agreed with Lansdowne. But the more important members of the cabinet were dissatisfied with the treaty as drafted. Hicks Beach, Joseph Chamberlain and C. T. Ritchie offered amendments which were

---

[1] *Meiji hennenshi*, xi, 349–54.
[2] Salisbury papers, Royal, Salisbury to the king, 19 December 1901.
[3] *NGB* 34, no. 73.

fundamental, although it is doubtful whether they opposed the alliance outright. As befitted his nature, Beach was the most extreme in his criticisms:

The treaty is really a new departure in our foreign policy. I do not myself think that we gain enough from the treaty to outweigh the obvious objections to it.

He insisted that it should be considered again at a cabinet meeting.[1] Chamberlain's anxiety was over public reaction:

The natural objection which will be taken to the Japanese Treaty is that it is too one-sided. We give the Japanese everything in regard to Corea — they say we are equally advantaged in regard to the Yang-tsze but this does not appear on the face of the treaty.[2]

He asked for a bilateral appearance to be given to the treaty though he was not basically opposed to it. None the less this casts doubt on the view that Joseph Chamberlain was one of the main forces in the cabinet favouring the Japanese treaty.

Far outweighing these in importance was the long note which Salisbury prepared, the last major statement of his thinking on foreign policy. Unlike the other letters, Salisbury's was issued as a circular to the whole cabinet on 7 January. He referred to Japan's naval demand and commented that 'it may hamper us greatly if we have need for the use of our forces in some other service with which it may be Japan is not connected. The reason for making it is not easy to guess, for every conceivable motive might be relied upon to secure that if we were fighting on the side of Japan we should not stint the number of our ships'. Japan's refusal to extend the treaty beyond the far east, he claimed, 'deprives us at all events of a plausible defence for the great dangers and costs which we are running for the sake of Japan'. There remained one more consideration of 'a much graver character': Japan's claim that she had the right 'to take without our permission measures [in Korea] which we might regard as provocative'. Salisbury defined the danger thus:

It involves a pledge on our part to defend Japanese action in Corea and in all China against France and Russia, no matter what the *casus belli* may be. There is no limit: and no escape. We are pledged to war, though the conduct of our ally may have been followed in spite of our strongest remonstrances,

---

[1] Lansdowne papers, Beach to Lansdowne, 2 January 1902.
[2] Lansdowne papers, Joseph Chamberlain to Lansdowne, 5 January 1902.

and may be avowedly regarded by us with clear disapprobation. I feel sure that such a pledge will not be sanctioned by Parliament, and I think that in the interests of the Empire it ought not to be taken.

. . . If the Treaty imposes on us the liability of being committed against our will to a dangerous policy in Corea, it will be no consolation that Japan is committed against her will to a dangerous policy in the Yang-tsze. Japan offers us 'a formal declaration of non-aggressive policy'; but that will give us no security. It is a sentiment; not a stipulation.

Nor can I attach great importance to the plea of Japan that troubles are apt to break out on short notice, and that in case they should occur Japan may be compelled to adopt a line of policy without having time to consult us on the matter. The necessity for a decision so sudden that the telegraph will not be able to cope with the emergency is not a very probable contingency, and certainly does not furnish a justification for surrendering without reserve into the hands of another Power the right of deciding whether we shall or shall not stake the resources of the Empire on the issue of a mighty conflict.[1]

Salisbury thought that it would not be wise to give Japan the right of committing Britain to a war, unless the policy which Japan was pursuing had been approved by Britain. He could not believe that 'Japan will definitively refuse us some discretion on the question whether the *casus belli* on which she is joining issue with France and Russia is one on which we can properly draw the sword'. So he concluded that there was still a need for further negotiation.

This was a great memorandum, thoughtful, constructive and logical. It cautioned Lansdowne against accepting the Japanese demands too easily. It was a commentary on the draft treaty by a skilful draftsman, not an outright attack on the concept of an alliance, as in his earlier memorandum on the German alliance. It is a good example of Salisbury as a flexible statesman and gives no indication that he felt an underlying opposition to the alliance.

These various cabinet memoranda confirm that the conclusion of the alliance was not a matter of precipitate decision in Britain. But what significance had they? Was the alliance in the balance as late as the first week of the New Year? These memoranda have to be read in the light of Salisbury's report on the cabinet meeting of 19 December that 'differences were more in respect to details than to substance'.[2] By

---

[1] Salisbury papers, Foreign and Imperial, memorandum by Salisbury, 7 January 1902.
[2] Salisbury papers, Royal, Salisbury to the king, 19 December 1901.

inviting written comments on the draft treaty, Lansdowne had re-opened the matter; but the comments were still made within the context of substantial agreement, even though they were highly critical on detail. The alliance was not in doubt; but Britain was still dissatisfied and cautious over several clauses; and much patient and skilful redrafting was still required.

It was possible to meet most of the objections raised by altering the British draft circulated on 8 January. Beach agreed to the revised draft. Lansdowne then reported to the prime minister who offered amendments to the first article. In this form the draft was passed to Hayashi on 14 January without being discussed on the previous day by the cabinet. Now that the British counter-draft had been handed over, the end of negotiation was in sight.

BONES OF CONTENTION

There were certain points on which both sides had strong convictions that were holding up the achievement of the alliance. It will be convenient to consider these topics of greatest controversy separately under three headings: the scope of the proposed agreement; Japanese demands in Korea; and naval strength in the far east.

First, the scope of the agreement. When Britain's first draft was handed over, a proposal was mooted that, since British interests in the Yangtse valley were not as great as those of Japan in Korea, Japan should be asked to extend the agreement to cover south-east Asia and beyond. This point was not embodied in the draft itself but was strongly held by the British cabinet and may be ascribed among others to Balfour. If war should arise out of the Japanese alliance, Balfour argued, the forces Britain would have to fight would be Russia and France; the quarrel might be confined to the east but, so far as Britain was concerned, the theatre of war would be the English channel, the Mediterranean and the frontier of India.[1] This meant that Britain's involvement would be much greater than that of Japan and that Japan might not unreasonably be asked to give assistance outside the far east. Lansdowne told Hayashi that it was important that 'neither of them should be overwhelmed by a combination of foreign Powers. The disappearance of Great Britain as a sea Power in the Far East would be a calamity to Japan, and it would make no matter to her whether such

---

[1] Balfour papers Add. MSS 49727, Balfour to Lansdowne, 12 December 1901.

a calamity were to be brought about by a quarrel originating in the Far East or by complications in some other part of the World'.[1] Japan, however, tried to confine the alliance to the far east. Komura claimed that the Yangtse region was an adequate *quid pro quo* for Korea and argued that, while the situation there was quiet at present, it could give rise to grave difficulties at any moment. Hence the so-called 'equality of interests' contemplated by the agreement could not be said to act in favour of Japan.[2] On 19 December Lansdowne again urged that it was desirable to give a wider scope to the agreement but Hayashi replied that it would be fruitless to pursue this proposal. Britain reluctantly accepted this and the alliance was confined to the 'extreme east'.[3]

The second bone of contention was Japan's request that Britain should acquiesce in the adoption by Japan of suitable measures for the maintenance of her interests in Korea. Lansdowne chose to ignore Japan's aspirations in his first draft. The Japanese replied by inserting clauses giving them the right to prevent 'the occupation of any part of the territory of Korea by another power'. Lansdowne was chary of giving the Japanese 'a free hand to make a *casus foederis* out of any Russian encroachment in Corea [otherwise] Japan will be free to embark upon hostilities in which we may become involved over some comparatively insignificant local question'.[4] Britain was determined not to be the catspaw of Japan and was dissatisfied with Hayashi's assurance that Japan would not lightheartedly involve herself in war there for any but the most amply sufficient reasons. Britain insisted that in any Korean outbreak she should take part in joint consultations. But this was not acceptable to the Japanese who argued that 'disorders in Korea always break out suddenly; and speedy measures are needed to quell them. On most occasions it would be most difficult to consult Britain. . . . Britain need not be afraid that, in recognising Japan's freedom of action in Korea, it will encourage aggressive tendencies in that peninsula'.[5] Lansdowne wanted to avoid involving Britain in what might be mere expansionism on the part of Japan but he appreciated that a guarantee over Korea was from Japan's standpoint the most tempting part of the treaty. Eventually he devised a formula which

---

[1] *BD*, ii, no. 110.   [2] *NGB* 34, no. 71.
[3] *Hayashi memoirs*, pp. 167–8.
[4] FO *Japan* 547, note by Lansdowne for the cabinet, 16 December 1901.
[5] *NGB* 34, no. 71.

satisfied both sides and consisted of three propositions: Japan declared herself to be entirely uninfluenced by any aggressive tendencies there; Britain acknowledged Japan's interests politically as well as commercially and industrially; Britain recognized that it would be admissible for Japan to take measures to safeguard these interests if threatened by the aggressive action of any other power. Thus Britain ensured that she would not be dragged into an unnecessary war on account of some minor Korean dispute — and such a circumstance never in fact arose.

Thirdly, naval strength in the far east. In his memorandum, Selborne had indicated that, if a naval agreement were to be concluded, Britain and Japan together would in 1902 'show eleven battle-ships against the French and Russian nine, as well as a preponderance of cruisers'. The Admiralty believed that Britain could in this way avoid increasing her squadron in the far east and possibly reduce it in the long term. None the less, Britain made no mention in her first draft of numerical strengths and dealt solely with aspects of naval co-operation in time of peace like repair and coaling facilities. In Japan, the concern was more with naval tonnages than with these facilities; the navy minister, Baron Yamamoto, suspected that Britain might be intending to use the treaty to switch her naval strength to another sector. Inoue studied naval strengths early in December since he was afraid that an alliance with Britain might land Japan with increased obligations against Russia, France and Germany.[1] The Japanese counterdraft, therefore, contained a more rigorous clause, committing each ally to 'preserve in the far east at all times a fleet more powerful than the greatest oriental squadron of any other power'.[2] The Japanese intention was that Japan and Britain should each keep there a fleet of greater strength than the Russian far-eastern squadron. Lansdowne promptly informed Hayashi that Britain could never entertain any provision which might interfere with her discretion in determining the strength of her naval force in any given area. Britain had many commitments in South Africa and Europe and could not guarantee to maintain a fixed naval force in China. Turning down Japan's request, he remarked rather bluntly that, if Japan found the naval support which she eventually derived from the alliance to be unsatisfactory, she could always bring the agreement to

---

[1] *NGB* 35, no. 25, pp. 75–6. Whether on the basis of tonnage or the number of vessels, Anglo-Japanese naval strength exceeded that of Russia, France and Germany.
[2] *NGB* 34, no. 49.

P

an end after its allotted term of five years. Furthermore, if the Japanese persisted, the negotiations would be prejudiced.[1]

Not to be brow-beaten, Japan insisted upon a naval undertaking of some sort and, faced as she was with a domestic crisis over naval building, proposed that each power should in future maintain in the far east a force as far as possible superior to the oriental fleet of any third power.[2] This was more acceptable to Lansdowne who with the help of Selborne transposed the phrase negatively into the form that was adopted in the final agreed version:

Great Britain/Japan is resolved so far as possible never to neglect the maintenance of supremacy of its naval forces, which may be apportioned for service in Eastern waters, over the forces of any third power.[3]

Such obligation as remained was a vague one and was open to a variety of interpretations. The Admiralty set great store on the phrase 'so far as possible' and judged 'supremacy' by 'the aggregate tonnage of all classes of ships on the China station'.[4] Japan certainly did not interpret the phrase in this way and was not explicitly told how Britain regarded it. Although the clause has the marks of being salvaged from basic disagreements, the Japanese expressed their high appreciation of Lansdowne's efforts to meet their wishes 'especially in the matter of maintaining naval strength to which the Japanese Government attach importance'.[5] Britain may have appeared to yield to Japan on this point but the British archives show that this was illusory. Since the naval provisions were contained in a diplomatic note which was kept secret, rather than in the agreement itself, the extent of the obligation never became the subject of public censure.

These three points of difference which were discussed extensively during December and January, contained the essence of the treaty. Many of its clauses were routine and prosaic and ultimately had little effect. But the clauses about Korea and about naval power had an important bearing on the future history of the far east. They were most keenly argued and sometimes seemed to threaten the agreement itself. Thus Lansdowne complained that 'the Japanese are pressing hard to insert inconvenient stipulations about Britain's naval strength' and

[1] *BD*, ii, 115–17.
[2] FO *Japan* 563, Hayashi to Lansdowne, 30 December 1901.
[3] FO *Japan* 563, Lansdowne to MacDonald, 14 January 1902.
[4] Lansdowne papers, Selborne to Lansdowne, 2 and 7 January 1902.
[5] *NGB* 35, no. 2.

wanted 'to keep for themselves an absolutely free hand . . . as to
Corean affairs. I hope we shall come to terms but they are very stiff'.[1]
Never the less by perseverance, by draft and redraft, he worked out
a formula on these points. There remained a measure of disagreement
with the result that the clauses were emasculated and it rested with the
parties to construe them as they thought fit. Japan went her own way
with *carte blanche* in Korea; Britain pursued her naval destiny according
to her own lights.

The last lap in the negotiations had been reached. Japan was bargaining hard but was determined to push through the treaty quickly. In
Britain there was a similar urgency. Parliament opened on 16 January
and the pressure of its business on the cabinet was bound to be an
obstacle to complex negotiations like the alliance, as the session
developed. Again, secrecy could not be maintained indefinitely.
Further the Manchurian situation was again looking grave and the
announcement of the alliance might serve as a sobering warning to
Russia. For these reasons, Lansdowne evidently wanted to complete
the talks with haste, despite Japan's intransigence, and was giving the
text almost daily study.

On 14 January, Lansdowne made it clear to Hayashi that Britain had
gone to the limit of concession and would be unlikely to accept further
modifications.[2] Japan, however, pressed her rights in Korea and also —
and this was a new demand — in China. These points were the subject
of six papers circulated to the British cabinet and were discussed at
the cabinet meeting on 24 January which took exception to 'some
phrases which would have imposed upon Great Britain the obligation
of assisting Japan in case of a quarrel with Russia and France even
though Japan should have been the aggressor'. Japan was willing to
correct this defect up to a certain point.[3] Over China, Lansdowne was
reluctant. Japan's proposal, he claimed, would destroy the idea of the
agreement as one of mutual advantage; if it were amended, Japan
would be bound to Britain only in respect of interests which were
common to both powers but Britain would be bound to Japan in
respect of interests peculiar to Japan.[4] None the less, Article I was
amended to accord some recognition in a rather clumsy way to Japan's

---

[1] Lansdowne papers, Lansdowne to MacDonald, 9 January 1902.
[2] *BD*, ii, no. 121.
[3] Salisbury papers, Salisbury to the king, 24 January 1902.
[4] *BD*, ii, no. 122; *Hayashi memoirs*, pp. 174–5; *NGB* 35, no. 2.

interests in China. The British ministers were evidently worried not only about the amendments needed but also about the reaction of public opinion and were anxious above all to create the impression that the alliance conferred equivalent benefits on both signatories.

In Japan, it appears that the foreign minister was given a large measure of discretion to handle the last stages of the negotiations with Britain. After the Japanese leaders had made their decision on principles early in December, there does not seem to have been any consultation with the genrō or much with the cabinet. It was on 25 January that Japan accepted the revised formula whereby Britain recognized her political, commercial and industrial interests in Korea. When this was granted, Komura placed the final text of the alliance before the cabinet on 29 January, secured its approval and obtained the imperial assent. He then sent Hayashi powers to sign the treaty and diplomatic note on behalf of his government.[1] The English text, which was to be the authoritative text of the treaty, was signed by Lansdowne and Hayashi on 30 January. It read as follows:

The Governments of Great Britain and Japan, actuated solely by a desire to maintain the *status quo* and general peace in the extreme East, being moreover specially interested in maintaining the independence and territorial integrity of the Empire of China and the Empire of Corea, and in securing equal opportunities in those countries for the commerce and industry of all nations, hereby agree as follows:—

Article I
The High Contracting Parties, having mutually recognised the independence of China and Corea, declare themselves to be entirely uninfluenced by any aggressive tendencies in either country. Having in view, however, their special interests, of which those of Great Britain relate principally to China, while Japan, in addition to the interests which she possesses in China, is interested in a peculiar degree politically as well as commercially and industrially in Corea, the High Contracting Parties recognise that it will be admissible for either of them to take such measures as may be indispensable in order to safeguard those interests if threatened either by the aggressive action of any other Power, or by disturbances arising in China or Corea, and necessitating the intervention of either of the High Contracting Parties for the protection of the lives or property of its subjects.

Article II
If either Great Britain or Japan, in the defence of their respective interests

---

[1] *NGB* 35, nos. 7, 9 and 11.

as above described, should become involved in war with another Power, the other High Contracting Party will maintain a strict neutrality, and use its efforts to prevent other Powers from joining in hostilities against its Ally.

Article III
If in the above event any other Power or Powers should join in hostilities against the Ally, the other High Contracting Party will come to its assistance and will conduct the war in common, and make peace in mutual agreement with it.

Article IV
The High Contracting Parties agree that neither of them will, without consulting the other, enter into separate arrangements with another Power to the prejudice of the interests above described.

Article V
Whenever, in the opinion of either Great Britain or Japan, the above-mentioned interests are in jeopardy, the two Governments will communicate with one another fully and frankly.

Article VI
The present Agreement shall come into effect immediately after the date of its signature, and remain in force for five years from that date.

In case neither of the High Contracting Parties should have notified twelve months before the expiration of the said five years the intention of terminating it, it shall remain binding until the expiration of one year from the day on which either of the High Contracting Parties shall have denounced it. But if, when the date fixed for its expiration arrives, either Ally is actually engaged in war, the alliance shall, *ipso facto*, continue until peace is concluded.

The treaty which did not require ratification, came into force immediately after its signature. The diplomatic notes, containing the naval agreement, were signed and exchanged by Hayashi and Lansdowne on the same occasion. By the notes each government recognizes that its naval forces:

should, as far as is possible, act in concert with those of [its ally] in time of peace, and agrees that mutual facilities shall be given for the docking and coaling of vessels of war of one country in the ports of the other, as well as other advantages conducive to the welfare and efficiency of the respective navies of the two Powers.

At the present moment Japan and Great Britain are each of them maintaining in the Extreme East a naval force superior in strength to that of any other Power. [Each ally] has no intention of relaxing her efforts to maintain, so far as may be possible, available for concentration in the waters of the Extreme East a naval force superior to that of any third Power.

This note was kept secret by the two powers.

How did Britain and Japan fare during the negotiation of the treaty? On the whole, both powers secured their essential objectives and fostered their interests by the treaty. Britain benefited by being responsible for the preparation of the initial text and for most of the later drafting. Britain was left to express Japan's interests in the wording and, in so doing, avoided phraseology which did not suit herself. None the less, the Japanese government did its share of hard bargaining and rightly insisted on stating what it wanted. As a result, Britain sometimes sought refuge in vagueness of wording and the final treaty, which was notoriously complex in its phrasing, did not represent a complete accord. Yet, for a treaty negotiated at immense distances and in two unrelated tongues, it was a creditable piece of work which largely succeeded in meeting the genuine wishes of both parties.

PUBLICATION

Since most of the European powers had entered into secret alliances, some interest attaches to the publication of the new treaty as an open alliance. It was, of course, negotiated privately and strict precautions were taken against leakage, as might be expected in an atmosphere of secret diplomacy. Yet it was always intended for publication, since secrecy could not be effectively preserved after the treaty had been signed and since it was normal in British parliamentary procedure for the treaty to be placed before the Houses after signature. As a result, the wording of such passages as Britain's recognition of Japan's rights in Korea had to be minutely considered from the point of view of a wider audience and the negotiations were probably prolonged on that account. It had originally been proposed that there should be certain unpublished articles but this idea was dropped. Instead, matters concerning the navies were contained in diplomatic notes which were exchanged at the time of signing and were not disclosed to the public. It was finally agreed to publish the agreement on 11–12 February, as far as possible simultaneously in the two capitals.

Britain and Japan had divergent views about publicity. British statesmen did not favour undue prominence being given to the Japanese agreement. Partly this was because it was not usual for this to be done; partly it was because the cabinet feared that public opinion would regard the agreement as a sacrifice of Britain's independence in the far east and a blank cheque for Japan there. Since there might well be opposition in press and parliament, the terms of the treaty could best be bruited abroad delicately and unobtrusively. The circumstances of the Katsura ministry were obviously different. It was a non-party ministry with strong party opposition in the Diet. If it was to consolidate its position, it had to advertise its successes. The Katsura ministry was conscious that it had scored a triumph. It had secured a victory in obtaining recognition of Japan's interests in Korea and had successfully tied her future fortunes to an old-established empire. Nor was there any reason for the ministry to fear the repercussions of publicity; the small, effervescent groups which occasionally stirred up trouble were mainly nationalistic and were not likely to be opposed to a British alliance. While Britain would have been content to let the treaty leak out, the Japanese government was determined to announce it with a fanfare of trumpets.

The date of publication was chosen so as to allow a fortnight in which the treaty could be communicated as an act of courtesy to other interested powers. It was generally agreed that it should be made known to Germany and the United States.

Throughout the negotiations Japan had been consistently in favour of consulting Germany. From Europe Itō had recommended — and Katsura agreed — that Germany should be introduced into the negotiations. Inoue had opposed the British alliance because he felt that it would push Germany into alignment with Russia and France and resurrect the Triplice in east Asia which had been a danger to Japan since 1895.[1] The attitude of Germany towards the alliance was therefore critical. The Japanese cabinet felt, however, that it could not have the major say in an issue whose implications for Britain were world-wide but for Japan were merely confined to the far east. Any approach to Germany was left to Britain's discretion; and the negotiations were concluded without any approach being made to Germany. Komura then proposed that 'the invitation to Germany should be given

---

[1] *NGB* 35, no. 25, pp. 75–6.

without unnecessary delay'.[1] There is a hint that he believed that Germany might be prepared to adhere to the agreement as Japan had adhered to the Anglo-German agreement of 1900.

Britain seems to have been in a dither over the approach to Germany. After a period of uncertainty, Lansdowne had finally satisfied himself from his conversation with Count Metternich on 19 December[2] that Germany would not enter an alliance with Japan. He therefore kept the alliance from Germany as a closely guarded secret. When Eckardstein entertained Itō in London, the Foreign Office asked that Itō should be specially briefed not to divulge anything about the state of the negotiations to the German officials. With the coming of the new year, Britain's relations with Germany, which had been strained since Chamberlain's Edinburgh speech on 25 October, further deteriorated. In a speech to the Reichstag on 8 January, Bülow made unhappy references to the actions of the British armies in South Africa which were greeted in the British press with a tumult of fury. Two days later Bülow spoke again in a slightly more conciliatory tone. The British ambassador urged that this should not be used as a pretext for the cancellation of the visit to Germany by the Prince of Wales.[3] The arrangements went forward as before and the prince's short stay was most cordial. There were thus contrary influences at work: the heated hostility of the press on both sides and the more moderate attitudes of the two governments who were unable to control the press. Influenced by the newspaper campaign, Lansdowne told Hayashi on 30 January that 'the feeling of the British people having been so hurt, ... overtures of the kind to the German Government are injudicious at the present moment'.[4]

On 31 January, the day after the signing, the British cabinet decided that the agreement 'should be announced to Germany within the next few days: and after that an interval of at least a week should be allowed to elapse before it was generally announced'.[5] This cabinet resolution preceded the King's minute which read:

---

[1] *NGB* 35, no. 11, Komura to Hayashi, 29 January 1902. On the basis of this telegram, I have discounted MacDonald's report that Komura told him that 'he did not think it would be advisable to take the German Government into our confidence', *BD*, ii, no. 127.

[2] *BD*, ii, no. 94.

[3] Lansdowne papers, Lascelles to Lansdowne, 11 January 1902. Langer, p. 775, takes a more severe view of Bülow's statement.

[4] *NGB* 35, no. 14, Hayashi to Komura, 30/31 January 1902.

[5] Salisbury papers, Royal, Salisbury to the king, 31 January 1902.

There should be no loss of time in informing German Government of the Anglo-Japanese Agreement — or else they will hear from some other source — secrecy being *almost* an impossibility. The Emperor will be much interested in hearing the news as he has strongly advocated a close alliance between Great Britain and Japan.[1]

But there was a last-minute hitch. On 2 February, the day before the communication was to be made, Lansdowne wrote to Hayashi that 'for reasons which I shall be glad to explain to you when we meet, it has been decided *not* to announce the Agreement to the German Government just yet'.[2] By the time that Hayashi's message reached Tokyo, Komura had already passed it over in outline to the German minister. This left Lansdowne with no alternative but to follow suit. He told Lascelles on 3 February to communicate the substance of the agreement at once to the emperor. Lascelles was to use his discretion about reminding the Kaiser of their conversation of 11 April 1901 when the emperor had criticized Britain for not affording more active encouragement to the Japanese. Lascelles passed over the message on 5 February, the same day that Lansdowne informed Eckardstein in London. Germany showed no interest in joining, but expressed her appreciation of the advance information. In one of his well-known epigrams, the Kaiser commented: 'At last the noodles have had a lucid interval'.[3]

Not every move in this puzzle nor every motive can be fully explained in the present state of our knowledge. There is no adequate theory to account for the last-minute hitch of 2 February. Certain broad conclusions can be reached. The Japanese government was more anxious to enlist the support of Germany than the British. Metternich reported that Britain wanted to encourage Germany to become a party to the alliance up to the last moment.[4] This is doubtful: Britain was prepared to dangle the carrot before the emperor to see what reaction it would have in that most unpredictable quarter; but she had no

---

[1] *BD*, ii, no. 126.
[2] Lansdowne papers, Lansdowne to Hayashi, 2 February 1902; *NGB* 35, no. 19.
[3] Lansdowne papers, Lansdowne to Lascelles, 3 February 1902; FO *Japan* 560, memorandum by Bertie, 6 February 1902. For the Kaiser's observations in April 1901, see above, p. 127.
[4] *The Holstein papers*, iv, no. 799, Metternich to Holstein, 21 February 1902. 'On the day that Lord Lansdowne had asked me to call in order to inform me of the Agreement, Lord Salisbury and Mr Chamberlain had been to see him immediately before my visit, and I believe that it was only at this meeting that it was decided not to suggest to us that we should join.'

intention of making an overture. Even this course was forced upon Britain by the swift action of the Japanese. This issue was not just the simple act of 'communicating' a treaty. It was complicated by the fact that Britain and Japan were both uncertain about Germany's true sentiments: had Germany encouraged the idea in order to become a partner in it? Because of its doubts on the subject, the British government treated this approach as tentative and non-committal. But it had the good effect of discouraging Germany from joining Russia and France in any counteraction.

The approach to the United States is by comparison straightforward. The agreement was akin to the Open Door policies of the United States and Komura felt that she should receive advance notice of the treaty. There was no likelihood of the United States joining the alliance and the advance notice was therefore only a token of goodwill. Moreover the American government had just made it clear to Russia that it took a serious view of her actions in Manchuria and of the Russo-Chinese banking agreement. Sir Claude MacDonald urged London to inform the United States in order to encourage her in her attitude. But the Foreign Office was worried that the American ministers would divulge the alliance to the press before its final publication.[1] None the less Lansdowne ultimately relented and agreed to overlook the State Department's inclination to disclose other people's secrets to American pressmen.

In communicating the treaty to Germany and the United States, the allies were dealing with powers which were likely to welcome it. There were also powers whose reactions towards it would be either hostile or cold. The Japanese government thought that it was desirable to reassure these powers, while Britain wanted especially to avoid upsetting France and Russia by thrusting the treaty too blatantly before them. In the haste in which they were forced to act, the two governments acted at cross purposes.

On 10 February, Japan instructed her ministers to Russia, France, Austria, Italy, China and Korea to communicate the treaty to their governments on the day of its publication.[2] They were to give suitable assurances that the treaty was peace-loving and would not harm their interests. The Japanese hoped that misunderstandings would be avoided if governments were informed in this way rather than through

[1] FO *Japan* 563, MacDonald to Lansdowne, 7 February 1902.
[2] *NGB* 35, no. 25, p. 87.

the press. Britain protested that it was not customary to communicate treaties to foreign governments unless it was a question of securing their adhesion, which was not the case in this instance.[1] It is likely, however, that Japan acted from lack of knowledge and experience of international procedure rather than from any intention of stealing a march on Britain. The Foreign Office was annoyed that it had not been consulted by Japan so as to enable steps to be taken for the British ministers overseas to present identic notes about the alliance simultaneously with their Japanese colleagues. This was doubly embarrassing because, by a peccadillo of the Foreign Office clerks which brought down upon them the thunder of the permanent under-secretary, the text of the treaty had not even been sent to ministers abroad for their private information so that they were in no position to take remedial action. The Japanese representatives at the major European capitals acted unilaterally, a situation which was naturally most unfortunate in the case of Russia. This incident suggested that there was a lack of understanding between Japan and Britain but it really only reflected the difference between the publicity-minded Japanese and the more reticent British.

Both signatories were basically agreed that the treaty should be published. Since it was impossible to keep the treaty secret for long after signature and was in any case highly desirable to prevent any 'exaggerated and mischievous reports concerning its object and scope',[2] both parties favoured early publication. Parliament was in session in both countries; and it was natural that the announcement should first be made there. Publication was roughly synchronized. In Britain, the text was laid before parliament on the evening of 11 February along with an explanatory dispatch by Lansdowne. In Japan, it was published on 12 February, because the previous day was the Japanese *kigensetsu* or national anniversary.

The British procedure was to let the news leak out in an indirect manner. Lord Cranborne, who as parliamentary under-secretary was responsible for Foreign Office business in the House of Commons, considered that the whole idea was 'to treat the whole thing as quietly as possible. No splash, not even a statement in both Houses until we are asked'.[3] The ministers, who evidently expected some criticism,

---

[1] FO *Japan* 563, Lansdowne to MacDonald, 12 February 1902.
[2] *BD*, ii, no. 126.
[3] FO *Japan* 560, Cranborne to Barrington, 10 February 1902.

wanted to avoid any discussion until members of parliament had had time to study the text and to avoid any formal statement until it was seen how the press reacted. The question of the Japanese treaty was in fact raised in the Commons on the motion for the adjournment on 12 February by Sir Henry Campbell-Bannerman as leader of the opposition. But he elicited little information from Balfour as Leader of the House. The government seemed to be determined to make no premature statements and certainly took no steps to herald it as a triumph for British diplomacy. Nor did it give a hint of the naval provisions from which it hoped to benefit.

When parliament debated the treaty, reaction followed expected lines. The government case was persuasively defended by Lansdowne in the Lords and by Cranborne and Balfour in the Commons. For the opposition, Campbell-Bannerman and Sir William Harcourt attacked the alliance as an unnecessary departure from existing policy and as limiting Britain's freedom of action. To some extent, this was echoed by other Liberals. At the same time, many were rather attracted by the idea of a treaty with Japan. Thus, the Liberals as a mercantile party tended to respect Japan's development and value her adherence to the Open Door policy; and the spokesmen of its China 'lobby', like Henry Norman[1] and Joseph Walton, expressed surprise but were not hostile to the treaty. In the Lords, Lord Spencer and Lord Rosebery, who had been associated with the Liberal ministry which had first called Japan into the comity of nations by the treaty of 1894, were inclined to support the new measure. Further, the 'Liberal imperialists' like Sir Edward Grey spoke in favour of Japan becoming Britain's partner. Since the Liberal opposition was divided on foreign policy, there was not the full-blooded opposition to this measure which its importance would have justified.[2]

By contrast, Japan's policy was one of 'splash'. After the emperor had held an emergency meeting of the Privy Council on 12 February to hear reports on the alliance, Katsura announced it in the House of Peers and Komura in the House of Representatives. In tones of great satisfaction, Katsura described the alliance as an 'internationally important matter' which would also secure Japan's objects in east

[1] Norman, who was knighted in 1906, was the author of several travel-books dealing with Japan, in which he praised the progress she had made but made no reference to an alliance. They were *The real Japan*, London, 1892, and *The peoples and politics of the far east*, London, 1895.

[2] *British parliamentary debates*, 4th series, vol. 102, cols. 1260–1300.

Asia.[1] There was very little opposition to the treaty. There was in Japan little well-informed opinion on foreign affairs among the political parties and the comments made were in general unanalytical and uncritical. It might have been expected that Itō's followers in the Seiyūkai would show hostility. But the Seiyūkai was in an unenviable position: it could not be certain that Itō had not during his visit to London taken some part in formulating the final treaty. Its doubts were played on by the government newspaper, *Kokumin Shimbun*, which, in tracing the history of the alliance in its issue of 15 February, mentioned that long telegrams had passed between the government and Itō in Europe and hinted that he had been kept fully informed of developments. In any case, argued the *Kokumin*, the alliance was a national issue of which all parties must approve.[2] The Seiyūkai withheld its criticisms until Itō's return. Arriving back at Nagasaki on 25 February, Itō was met by Katō Takaaki who showed him how enthusiastically the British treaty had been welcomed by the people and tried to argue him out of any opposition to it. Katō's motive cannot be stated for sure since he was not a Seiyūkai member and it is not known whether he was the emissary of the Katsura ministry or not.[3] At any rate, at a dinner held in his honour, Itō delivered a speech which must be regarded as public-spirited, if rather ironic. Speaking of the alliance, he said:

I hope that we shall remain on friendly terms with Britain, the ally of our people, and cultivate increasingly good relations with other peoples and avoid any breach with them so that we may achieve progress for our commerce and industry.

Diplomatic affairs are not the preserve of parties or political groups but the concern of the whole country. If political differences are to give rise to divergences in foreign policy and if factions, pro-British or pro-Russian, pro-German or pro-French, are to grow up among our people, it will in effect destroy the unity of our country and be most unfortunate. A contract concluded between one country and another is binding on the peoples themselves and can as a rule never be altered during the period of its validity, regardless of party or of the cabinet of the time.[4]

This seems to be a sincere statement of Itō's viewpoint: he was not enthusiastic about the alliance without necessarily being hostile to it;

---

[1] *Meiji hennenshi*, xi, 380, quoting *Jiji Shimpō* for 13 February 1902.
[2] *Meiji hennenshi*, xi, 381, quoting *Kokumin Shimbun* for 15 February 1902.
[3] *Katō*, i, 477-8.
[4] *Itō-den*, iii, 555-7.

he claimed that the Seiyūkai was committed to the treaty on constitutional grounds. But there were in any case strong practical reasons against their opposing the alliance because of its sheer popularity: the treaty has been greeted by the Japanese people with acclamation.[1]

PRESS REACTION

Press reactions were also important. In Britain, the response to the treaty depended upon the political complexion of the journal. Among the daily papers, the Liberal newspapers like the *Manchester Guardian* and *Daily News* gave prominent coverage to the criticism made by the Liberal leaders that the treaty was unnecessary. *The Times*, the *Scotsman* and the *Glasgow Herald* accepted it thoughtfully; but their tone fell short of enthusiasm. Among the periodicals, whose writers had more time to study the treaty than was available to the dailies, it would be surprising not to find some note of criticism. Yet only a few periodicals such as the *Spectator* and the *Monthly Review* were hostile. The *Spectator*, one of the leading weeklies at the time, had for long supported the cause of a rapprochement with Russia and was naturally worried that closer relations with Japan would prevent the cherished improvement in Anglo-Russian relations and add to Britain's overseas liabilities. On the whole, however, there were few columnists who made an all-out assault on the new alliance. Lansdowne, who had confessed on 9 January that he was 'a little nervous as to the manner in which the new departure may be regarded in Parliament and by the public',[2] was later able to write, in reply to a congratulatory note from Joseph Chamberlain, that he 'had no idea the Treaty would be taken so well'.[3] When it is recalled that some criticisms of substance had been made, it may well be imagined what a storm of protest Lansdowne had expected to face.

The Japanese press was almost unanimously in favour of the alliance. The *Jiji Shimpō*, which had always been one of its strongest advocates, and the *Asahi Shimbun* were inclined to write of the great honour conferred on Japan by her alliance with a leading world power. But some papers had their reservations. Tokutomi Sohō (Iichirō), a famous columnist, writing in the *Kokumin Shimbun*, the newspaper of

[1] FO *Japan* 563, MacDonald to Lansdowne, 13 February 1902.
[2] Lord Newton, *Lord Lansdowne*, London, 1929, p. 224.
[3] Amery, *Life of Joseph Chamberlain*, iv, 165.

the Katsura ministry, praised the alliance but argued that the Japanese should not be lulled into a false sense of security by relying too much upon Britain; they must continue to build up Japan's national strength. Further the *Nippon*, an independent nationalist newspaper, devoted an editorial to warning the Japanese people that they should think of the alliance in terms not of honour but of national interest; unless Japan exerted herself and became self-reliant, the treaty of alliance would become purely nominal. In these statements, the press was echoing the government's own exhortation that the people should not rest on their laurels but devote themselves to further efforts for the sake of national development.

The Japanese press also declared that the effects of the alliance on the far east generally would be beneficial. Korea's territorial integrity would be guaranteed, while the dissolution of the Chinese Empire would be prevented. Thus, the prospects for peace in east Asia were greatly improved. These countries, wrote the *Nippon* in a series of articles on 'the Alliance and Business', presented a challenge to Japanese businessmen who could now penetrate commercially into them; they could invest with security in these countries and, with the help of local capital, build up industries.[1] The *Jiji Shimpō* also reported that the alliance had nowhere been more cordially welcomed than in industrial circles.[2]

The reaction of the Japanese people was also favourable. Although Japanese public opinion was not a force to be unduly reckoned with, the public — and especially the Tokyo populace — was subject to great bursts of enthusiasm; and the announcement of the first alliance gave rise to just such an outburst. There were hosts of dinners and public meetings held throughout Japan at which politicians extolled the virtues of the twin island empires and the guarantee of peace which their new partnership gave.[3] Katsura, who relied on this favourable reception for the popularity, and indeed the continued existence, of his ministry, bathed in a fleeting glory.

From this it can be seen that the governments which had concluded the alliance, were broadly supported by parliamentary and press reactions. Yet there is a marked contrast between the reticence of the

---

[1] *Nippon*, 15–21 February 1902.
[2] *Meiji hennenshi*, xi, 380, quoting *Jiji Shimpō*, 13 February 1902.
[3] Lansdowne papers, MacDonald to Lansdowne, 16 February 1902. MacDonald reported that the alliance had been 'received with immense enthusiasm'.

British reaction and the largely favourable Japanese reaction. Did this not imply that it was the Japanese who really wanted the alliance? For contemporaries, this was one of the mysteries associated with the alliance. Defending the Foreign Office estimates during a debate in the House of Commons on 3 July 1902, the government spokesman, Lord Cranborne, said:

It is not for us to ask for treaties: we grant them. We are only too delighted to have the opportunity of granting this Treaty to a Power whose interests are so much in conformity with our own as are those of Japan.[1]

This remark, made in the heat of debate, was incautious, not to say positively mendacious. It prompted Cecil Spring Rice to make the irreverent aside:

Cranborne seems to have been putting his foot in it a good deal lately and to be a worthy son of his father.[2]

Be that as it may, Cranborne was reflecting a common misconception in Britain at the time: that Japan had taken the initiative in asking for the alliance and that Britain had merely responded. As this study has shown, the position was rather different. In April, Lansdowne had been presented with Japan's ideas in the distillation favoured by Hayashi and gathered the impression that this was an overture from the Japanese government of some sort. But this was not so. In July Lansdowne seemed to take the initiative but it was again on a purely personal basis. In October Japan took up the initiative and this proved to be the crucial approach because it induced Britain to pass over her first draft. The position was therefore obscure; and contemporaries were naturally ill-informed. But Cranborne was wrong to imply that Britain merely granted the alliance in response to a Japanese petition. Both sides had taken the initiative at different times; but Britain had generally assumed the leadership in the discussions.

---

[1] *British parliamentary debates*, 4th series, vol. 110, col. 734.
[2] *Letters of Spring Rice*, i, 353, Rice to his sister-in-law, 17 July 1902. Lansdowne inquired from MacDonald (FO *Japan* 563, 14 July 1902) whether Cranborne's statement had been received by the Japanese 'with dismay or resentment'; but this was denied.

CHAPTER XI

The New Alliance Considered

THE Anglo-Japanese agreement of 1902 was a limited and temporary alliance. It was limited to the far east; but this geographical limitation did not give complete satisfaction even at the time of signing and revision was called for. It was temporary in the sense that it was due to run for five years. But, once the first alliance had been signed, it was easier to continue the treaty than it was to terminate it: it was continued in revised form in 1905 and 1911. So the decision of 1902 was a more important step than the later ones. None the less the first alliance remained distinct from the later treaties in its form and in its motives. It is therefore convenient to pause at this stage in the narrative to consider the various historical problems which arise from the 1902 alliance.

For this purpose it is worth while to examine some of the considerations advanced in an illuminating dispatch which Lord Lansdowne himself drew up to explain his actions to the British minister in Tokyo. After it had been circulated to the cabinet on 8 February, it was published along with the Agreement as a parliamentary paper.[1] It was written to present the British government's intentions at their most persuasive and to disarm foreign countries of any suspicions which they had. As the last chapter showed, Lansdowne was expecting criticism when the alliance was first published. His intention, therefore, was to issue his defence in advance. For all that, the dispatch is a thoughtful and discriminating document; and, taken together with the corresponding Japanese documents, it offers a useful framework for considering the motives of Japan also.

Lansdowne's dispatch throws some incidental light on the origins of the alliance. Observers have traced its origin variously to the Sino-Japanese war period, to the far-eastern crisis of 1898 or to the Boxer

[1] *British Foreign and State papers*, xcv (1901–2), 83–6, Lansdowne to MacDonald, 30 January 1902.

emergency. Unquestionably there was developing over this period a common interest between the two powers. But common interests are not necessarily accompanied by common policies nor do they invariably lead to an alliance. What is of interest to the historian is the point at which the British and Japanese governments decided that it was necessary to codify their common interests in the diplomatic language of a treaty and to define the obligations of one party to the other which had hitherto been imprecise. Certain points in the development of the alliance are not really in dispute: the official negotiations started in November 1901; and the preliminary parleys can be traced to the conversation between Hayashi and Lansdowne on 16 April. But this is to look at the alliance from a narrowly diplomatic standpoint and it is less important to find out its diplomatic origins than to establish what brought both sides to realize the need for such a treaty. In this study, we have taken the view that the major factors were suspicion of Russia and the awareness of the military and naval challenge which that power presented in the far east. Since Japan would probably have been prepared to receive overtures for an alliance at any time, the problem is really to establish how Britain came to acknowledge the need for co-operation with Japan. This took place about July 1901 when a wave of assertiveness on Russia's part in Manchuria and at the Peking conference reached a high point and drew Britain towards Japan. The British government was moreover worried that Japan might be induced by the promise of financial aid to go over to the Russian side; and, while it did not believe that there could be a Russo-Japanese alignment for long, it was naturally anxious to keep the Japanese and the Russians apart. Britain's conversion cannot therefore be traced to any given incident; it is attributable to many motives: diplomatic, strategic and financial. In short, it was as complex and varied as the alliance itself proved to be.

This view is in general supported by Lansdowne in his dispatch and independently endorsed by Katsura. For Lansdowne, the agreement was 'the outcome of the events which have taken place during the last two years in the Far East and of the part taken by Great Britain and Japan in dealing with them'.[1] Throughout the complications in China since 1900, the two powers had, he considered, been in close and uninterrupted communication and had been actuated by similar views. Lansdowne thus rejects the notion of an earlier origin for the alliance

[1] *BD*, ii, no. 124.

and seems to consider that it started with their practical co-operation in the months following the Boxer disturbances and especially with their joint action over Manchuria. This assessment seems to be confirmed by the Japanese prime minister's statement that the joint warnings which the British and Japanese governments gave to China over Manchuria, 'have had great influence on the course of the present negotiations with Britain'.[1] Katsura too saw the origins of the alliance in the Manchurian crises of March and October 1901; and this is supported by such evidence as has been adduced in this study. In these crises the two powers came to recognize that their far-eastern policies had a remarkable similarity and could conveniently be defined in an international treaty. None the less a general concurrence of ideas does not automatically lead to the creation of an alliance; and certain differences of a fundamental nature arose during the course of the negotiations.

Lansdowne's statement that the alliance was the outcome of events in the far east gives the lie to the frequently heard view that it was merely the offshoot of European diplomacy.[2] It would be a distortion to imagine that the affairs of the far east were being decided in Europe or were being resolved in accordance with European relationships. To be sure, the actions of diplomats of the outside powers were determined by the courts which they represented. But European alignments were not necessarily carried over to the far east; nor were far-eastern alignments necessarily carried over to Europe. France had frequently refused to carry the obligations of the Franco-Russian alliance beyond Europe to the northern parts of the far east. In 1895 Germany had refused to carry the friendship of the far-eastern Dreibund of that year into European affairs. Britain entered into the alliance largely by reason of her eastern, rather than her European, interests. Similarly the Japanese were not entering into it in order to secure some standing in Europe or indeed the world — that was still remote in their thinking. For the present their leaders were content with limited objectives in the far east.

Lansdowne's statement also involves a judgment on the theory that Germany was the ultimate originator of the alliance. The early

---

[1] *Itō hiroku*, appendix, no. 58, Katsura to Itō, 21 December 1901.
[2] Cf. Romanov, *Rossiya v Manchzhurii*, p. 354 'After the conclusion of the Anglo-Japanese alliance, the [Manchurian] question entered the realm of European power politics.'

publication of *Die Grosse Politik* and of Eckardstein's *Lebenserin-nerungen* gave many observers the impression that Germany was the vital link in the diplomacy of the Anglo-Japanese alliance. It has been argued that she was instrumental in bringing about the alliance.[1] This was not so. Germany was not cognizant of it until she was privately informed of its signature on 7 February. Nor had she any part in its negotiation since Eckardstein had no authority for his actions from the German government. Having said this, it must be admitted that there was considerable shilly-shallying over Britain's attitude towards Germany. Lansdowne could not be sure, in the strange state of German foreign policy-making, that Eckardstein was not the recipient of private instructions from the Kaiser. Lansdowne had to assume that Germany was not ill-disposed to the alliance: he was convinced that the emperor, Bülow, Holstein and others contemplated such an alliance.[2] What he could not decide was whether Germany had any wish to join such an alliance and whether the opportunity should be given to her at the risk of receiving a snub. Lansdowne and the cabinet seem to have been in two minds about consulting the Germans. Eventually it was probably the anti-British outcry among the German people at the time which convinced the British government that the atmosphere was not suited to an initiative of this kind. There was not the slightest suggestion that Germany had really been the initiator of the alliance, only that Germany might possibly wish to become a party.

It would be equally wrong to imagine that the alliance with Japan was only taken up by Britain after an understanding with Germany had failed to materialize. These were not alternatives. Britain's approach to Japan has to be regarded as complementary to anything which emerged from Anglo-German negotiations in 1901.

In his dispatch Lansdowne proceeds to set out the aspirations of Britain in three statements which may serve as the framework for this analysis. He hopes that the agreement may be found of mutual advantage to the two countries, that it will make for the preservation of peace and that, should peace unfortunately be broken, it will have the effect of restricting the area of hostilities.

---

[1] This view seems to be held by Soviet historians like Romanov and Galperin and by a wide range of Japanese historians, including Eguchi Bokurō in *Shigaku Zasshi*, no. 44 (1933), Tokinoya Tsunesaburō in *Tōzai kōshō shiron*, and Kuroha Shigeru in *Bunka*, no. 16 (1952).

[2] Lansdowne papers, Lansdowne to Lascelles, 22 April 1902.

MUTUAL ADVANTAGE

Firstly, Lansdowne points out that the provisions should be of mutual advantage but does not imply that they were necessarily of equal advantage. The main benefits accruing to the two powers through the alliance were that Japan gained recognition by Britain of certain rights in Korea while Britain obtained corresponding recognition by Japan for her rights in the Yangtse valley. Recognition implied that, if these rights were menaced by the aggression of two or more powers, the alliance would come into play and these rights would be defended jointly. The general feeling is that Japan gained more from this bargain than Britain.

The safety of Britain's interests in the Yangtse valley may easily be exaggerated. British merchants often complained that Britain had not obtained the privileges there which the other powers had gained in their spheres of influence, though the government had no intention of altering the position. What was more worrying was the economic encroachment of other trading powers there. Perhaps it was unlikely that any *casus belli* would arise between the powers on that account; but it would be wrong to suppose that Britain was without fear for her vulnerability there or that these fears were without foundation. Indeed Japan was involved in the defence of Britain's interests in the Yangtse region in October 1902, when Germany opposed Britain's efforts to evacuate foreign troops from Shanghai and insisted upon receiving special guarantees.[1]

Britain's obligation to recognize Japan's position in Korea probably involved a greater commitment. At the same time, Britain was only recognizing and supporting those rights which Russia had in the main already recognized in 1898. The effect of the alliance was not to advance Japan's economic rights in her sphere of influence but rather to assert her political rights in Korea.[2] Japan received from a third power the recognition of her rights, especially her right to intervene there in the event of Russia causing trouble or of the Koreans themselves opposing Japanese interests. Britain, albeit reluctantly, accorded a certain formal recognition to Japan's commercial and political inroads in the Korean peninsula, while paying homage to the shibboleth of Korean independence. This must be viewed in the light of Britain's gradual

[1] *BD*, ii, pp. 138–53, deals with the evacuation of Shanghai.
[2] Papers of J. N. Jordan, minister to Korea 1901–6, deposited in the Public Record Office, London (FO 350), vol. 3, Jordan to Bertie, 22 February 1902.

désintéressement in Korea. In 1885 she had thought it merited the naval occupation of Port Hamilton. In 1896 Salisbury had tried to prevent Russia and Japan from getting together over Korea but had very quickly retreated when he was asked what practical help he would give to Japan instead. Progressively Britain had disinterested herself. This was only natural because her commercial interests there were so small.[1] She had less interest there than Japan had in the Yangtse valley and had nothing to sacrifice by giving the guarantee. Moreover, it was Korea's strategic importance that mattered most to Britain; and this was best secured by encouraging Japan to keep a foothold in the peninsula, even though this was inconsistent with a full measure of independence for Korea.

Did the alliance also improve Japan's status in Manchuria? Certainly British ministers twice confirmed in the House of Commons that the alliance applied to Manchuria.[2] Professor Langer, however, has argued that the statements were made chiefly to stifle opposition: 'Manchuria really had nothing to do with the Alliance. Neither Japan nor England would fight to keep the Russians out of those provinces.'[3] It is true that Britain had made it abundantly clear on many occasions that, as Russia had a special interest in Manchuria, she was not keen to become involved there, while Japan was not as interested there as in Korea and was not prepared in 1902 to resort to force to uphold her policy. But it is surely untrue to claim that Manchuria had nothing to do with the alliance. It has been argued in this study that the alliance stemmed from the Manchurian crisis of 1901; and it would be surprising if Manchuria was not affected by its terms. The phrases in the preamble were at least partially devised to apply to Manchuria at whose ports Russia was depriving the powers of equal opportunities of trading and whose territorial integrity was at stake. These terms were a challenge to Russia in Manchuria; and, as future developments were to show, they were also a convenient bargaining-counter in Japan's negotiations with Russia.

[1] Lansdowne papers, Sanderson to Lansdowne, 4 May 1901:' There is only one British firm [in Korea] — no British ships visit the ports — and all British trade is in the hands of Chinese pedlars'.

[2] *BD*, ii, nos. 132–3.

[3] Langer, p. 782. That Manchuria was more prominent in Japanese thinking than Professor Langer would lead us to believe, may be seen in Appendix E, Katsura to Itō, 21 December 1901. Katsura writes that 'since the crisis in Manchuria developed, we have by our policy given guarantees to various foreign powers that we will assume responsibilities which cannot be neglected'.

Criticisms about the one-sidedness of the alliance have mainly been directed at the British government rather than the Japanese. Even during the negotiations, some members of the British cabinet complained about the substantial and unequal gains which Japan was making and wanted to secure greater equality by extending the scope of the treaty to cover south-east Asia or even India. Lansdowne did not try to equalize the benefits; this was done in the Anglo-Japanese treaty of 1905 and was later regretted. Lansdowne seems to have been aware that alliances do not resemble balance sheets in which the benefits can be foreseen, precisely calculated and set off one against the other. As it turned out, the alliance was never put into practice in a military sense so that the question of advantage was hypothetical and merely raised for reasons of national prestige. Lansdowne claimed that the alliance was of mutual advantage; and for him that was enough.

There was also the other side to the alliance — the side concerned with the Open Door doctrine, which was partially a declaration of a self-denying kind. The powers declared that they were specially interested in maintaining the independence and territorial integrity of China and Korea and in securing equal opportunities in those countries for the commerce and industry of all nations. It cannot be suggested that these were not the genuine aspirations of the signatories. At the same time, these phrases were carefully worded since the powers were committed to observing them for five years.[1] Moreover, these declarations which appear in the preamble were much less important than the remainder of the treaty. The alliance was so geared to the self-interest of the two signatories that the Open Door objectives took second place.

It is in this connection that serious criticisms have been made of the alliance. It has been said that it is an imperialistic treaty. Thus Professor Furuya takes the view that from the Japanese cabinet decision in July 1900 to send troops for the Boxer disturbances 'Japan laid claim to a position among the imperialist powers in the far east'. He also contends that 'from the Boxer episode to the conclusion of the Anglo-Japanese alliance can be regarded as Japan's period of conversion to an imperialist country, that is the point of departure for Japanese

[1] Shigemitsu Osamu, 'Nichi-Ei dōmei' ('Anglo-Japanese alliance') in *Kindai Nihon gaikōshi no kenkyū*, Tokyo, 1956, p. 182. Shigemitsu states that Komura instructed Denison, the American adviser to the Foreign Ministry, to avoid in his drafting of the treaty the use of the phrase 'Open Door' but to employ instead the words 'equal opportunities for the commerce and industry of all nations'.

imperialism'.[1] In so far as imperialism is concerned with the security and defence of an empire, the alliance was connected with imperialism. In so far as imperialism involves the acquisition of territory, the alliance was not imperialist. There is nothing in the terms of the treaty to give the allies warrant for territorial expansion of any kind. The view held in this study is that the alliance was primarily intended to preserve the *status quo* and generally succeeded in achieving that object.

PRESERVATION OF PEACE

In his dispatch, Lansdowne's second hope was that the alliance 'would make for the preservation of peace'; and it must ultimately be judged by the extent to which it achieved this objective. How far were Britain and Japan honest when they claimed that they wanted to maintain 'general peace in the extreme East'? Many have criticized them on the ground that this object was bogus. In the early years of the League of Nations, there was a prevalent idea that alliances could not contribute to peace since they were associated with secret entente diplomacy and had at their roots the seeds of war. This has influenced some of the historical studies on the alliance. Thus Professor Dennis wrote:

The world is sick of the old diplomacy of which the alliance was such a marked example. If I have written an indictment of that diplomacy, I hope that it is also an obituary.[2]

Dr Chang wrote that the treaty hastened the war in the far east and that 'an instrument which ordered a third Power, Russia, to get out of Manchuria and out of Korea . . . while at the same time asserting the allies' special interests in China . . . could not be said to be purely defensive'.[3] A more general criticism from a different standpoint is given by the Soviet historian, Galperin, who criticized the aggressive character of the first alliance and claimed that it was the decisive step on the way to war between Russia and Japan.[4] Each of these writers brings special prejudices to his task and it is necessary to see what truth lies in these charges.

[1] Furuya Tetsuo, 'Nihon teikoku shugi no seiritsu wo megutte' ('About the development of Japanese imperialism'), *Rekishigaku kenkyū*, no. 20 (1956), 43–4.
[2] A. L. P. Dennis, *The Anglo-Japanese alliance*, Berkeley, 1923, preface.
[3] Chang, *The Anglo-Japanese alliance*, pp. 96–7.
[4] Galperin, *Anglo-yaponskii soiuz*, pp. 160, 177.

Was the alliance a failure because Japan two years after the signing took up arms in a war which might have spread outside the limits of the far east and become a world conflict? Did it make war with Russia inevitable? The first alliance could not claim to be peaceful if it closed the door on negotiations between Japan and Russia for a peaceful solution of their disagreement and in other ways discouraged a peaceful settlement. On the other hand, the alliance could not be shown to be warlike unless the motives of the leaders on either side *at the time of signature* were in favour of a settlement by battle; it is not enough to show that the Japanese leaders late in 1903 decided to make war in order to prove that the alliance was not peaceful in intent.

Did the alliance rule out negotiations between Russia and Japan? There has been a great deal of misunderstanding on this point. Article IV of the treaty laid down that separate agreements should only be reached after joint consultation; but negotiations with Russia were not thereby ruled out. On the contrary, Britain agreed with Japan that agreements could be concluded without prior consultation if the objects were not incompatible with the terms of the alliance. How far-reaching this concession was, may be realized from Lansdowne's reply to proposals which Itō made during his stay in Britain:

If the Marquis merely suggested that in the interests of peace Japan should do her best to obtain from Russia a recognition of the interests which we were ready to join her in protecting, a source of danger would be removed;

and he saw no reason why Britain should disapprove.[1] In saying this, he virtually gave Japan *carte blanche* to negotiate with Russia. It was probably in the knowledge of this that Katsura told Kurino, Japan's new minister to Russia, that there was no reason to diminish efforts to find a *modus vivendi* with Russia on far eastern problems.[2] Clearly the Japanese did not feel themselves impeded by the alliance in making overtures to Russia and were even encouraged by their improved bargaining position to do so. While entering into the alliance with Britain, they were trying to avoid falling out with Russia. Theirs was a policy of reinsurance which was inspired by a desire for Japan's advantage and for a peaceful settlement.[3]

Kurino Shinichirō had for a long time cherished the personal

---

[1] FO *Japan* 563, Lansdowne to MacDonald, 7 January 1902.
[2] *Itō hiroku*, appendix, no. 70, Kurino to Itō, 20 January 1902.
[3] *NGB* 35, nos. 90 and 92.

ambition to maintain good relations with that government and urged Komura on 5 February to pass over the alliance to Russia as soon as possible with suitable assurances. The foreign minister decided that Kurino might pass it over on the day of publication with the statement that the treaty was entirely peaceful in its objects and would not prevent the complete fulfilment of the hope that the two governments would reach an amicable settlement of their divergent interests.[1] Before doing so, the Japanese minister informed the British ambassador there, who was instructed by London to try to dissuade his colleague from making the intimation.[2] But without success. While the Japanese justified their action to Britain on the ground that it would remove the fear that the full text had not been published, they also claimed that to communicate the treaty directly to Russia might help in relieving the tension which Russia was causing over Manchuria — surely a diametrically opposed view. Japan's action was thus intended both as a demonstration of goodwill and as a judicious warning.

The Russians, against whom the alliance was clearly aimed, immediately set about devising some counter-measures. Within a week of the signature, the Russian foreign minister, Count Lamsdorf, asked France to join Russia in a counter-declaration, in which they would endorse the general spirit of the Anglo-Japanese treaty but reserve the right to discuss means for the safeguarding of their interests if they were disregarded by third powers or thwarted by China herself. After some hesitation on the part of the French foreign minister, Delcassé, the Franco-Russian accord was signed on 16 March. It received the assent of Austria, but not of Germany. The declaration was a sign both of strength and weakness. It was strong in so far as it showed the world that Russia had no thought of being browbeaten by threats from Britain and Japan. But it also exposed the weakness of the Franco-Russian alliance: the French would not agree to extend their obligations to the far east by guaranteeing in advance to take action to defend Russian interests; and even subsequent discussions in May did not convert them to this need. In effect, the French declined publicly to be implicated in any adventures which the Russians undertook in the far east.[3]

Despite this, Japan was already engaged in parleys with Russia. When Lamsdorf was approached in February, he was sceptical and

---

[1] *NGB* 35, no. 25, pp. 89–90.   [2] *BD*, ii, no. 130.
[3] *DDF*, 2me serie, ii, no. 84.

asked whether a separate treaty with Russia would be possible in view of Article IV of the alliance. On 12 March Komura told Kurino that the Japanese government earnestly wished for an understanding with Russia over Korea and that the Anglo-Japanese alliance would not hinder its realization; the only problem would be to find a satisfactory basis.[1] Shortly after, Izvolskii told Komura that he had heard of Itō's conversations with Lamsdorf and wanted to know how the foreign minister felt about them. Komura repeated that Japan was hoping for an agreement with Russia over Korea. There was naturally some delay in these parleys when the Russo-French declaration was published. But from July onwards the subject was again prominent. On 1 November Komura passed over unofficially a skeleton of a possible agreement whereby Japan would gain rights in Korea while Russia would gain rights in Manchuria.[2] Thus the alliance was not in practice a drawback to talks with Russia. While Langer doubts whether an agreement over Korea could possibly have been made to conform with the alliance,[3] this study has argued that Article IV of the alliance has to be read in the light of Lansdowne's assurances that he had no objection to other negotiations provided they were not adverse to the alliance. In all these ways, the Japanese seemed to be exploring the path of negotiations after the signing of the alliance.

As against this, it can be argued that the conclusion of the alliance played into the hands of the military party in Japan. This is true inasmuch as it gave strength to the ministry of General Katsura. What it ignores is that military bureaucrats like Yamagata and Katsura were cautious men who were by no means set on a programme of war and continental expansion. In any case, the treaty was carefully worded so as to give Katsura only limited scope in Korea.[4]

Certainly Britain's intentions seem to have been genuinely pacific. Britain was not unaware of Japan's military and naval strength, although she may have regarded it as less formidable than Russia's. Japan had already demonstrated in March 1901 that, if the circumstances justified it, she was prepared to go to war. In Britain's eyes, one of the objects of the alliance was to act as a restraint upon a wilful Japan whose strength was acknowledged but whose self-control was

---

[1] *Komura gaikōshi*, i, 297.
[2] *Komura gaikōshi*, i, 297–300; *Katsura-den*, i, 1128; Imai Shōji, 'Dai-ikkai Nichi-Ei dōmei kyōyaku', *Rekishi kyōiku*, vi (1957), 66–7.
[3] Langer, p. 771.   [4] Cf. Grenville, pp. 390–1, with which I disagree.

thought to be doubtful. That this was so may be seen in a private letter from the permanent under-secretary:

The Agreement will have a steadying effect on Japan. There was a certain risk that she might at some emergency have a *coup de tête* and go for the Russians, which is certainly not desirable if pacific pressure would afford a solution, or lose heart and give way more than would be desirable either for herself or for us.[1]

The alliance was a military alliance and war could not be ruled out. But both signatories seem to have determined to seek out peaceful solutions wherever possible.

Linked with this issue of war and peace was Lansdowne's third hope that, if hostilities did break out, the alliance would have the effect of restricting the area of hostilities. It appears that Lansdowne was not convinced that the alliance would inevitably result in an enduring peace — only that it was peaceful in intention. British military authorities had for long been worried that a minor episode perpetrated by Russia in Asia would, by virtue of the Franco-Russian entente, be turned into a world-wide conflagration. If Britain made it clear that she would support Japan in the far east in certain eventualities, the likelihood was that France would think twice about supporting Russia in that area. By announcing her commitment under the alliance, Britain would make it plain to France which was thought to be lukewarm in support-ing Russia's adventures in the far east, that she wanted to see any conflict confined and to that end would be glad if the French would join her in holding the ring for Russia and Japan. Lansdowne probably hoped that France and Britain might be drawn together to reach an understanding of their own. Certainly the entente of 1904 together with the arbitration treaty which preceded it, had the effect of narrow-ing the range of Anglo-French disputes and thus restricting the area of hostilities in the Russo-Japanese war.

The notion that the alliance was one of restricted scope in peacetime, is of prime importance. Balfour wrote that the British cabinet at the time was not 'anxious to hear any views on the general aspects of a problem which they were treating in the main as one confined to the Far East'.[2] This was in conformity with Lansdowne's view that

---

[1] Satow papers 7/2, T. H. Sanderson to Satow, 9 May 1902.
[2] Balfour papers Add. MSS 49727, Balfour to Lansdowne, 12 December 1901.

Britain's aim should be to enter into regionalized pacts, whose objects and obligations were limited to one particular area.[1] The alliance was the first of these regional pacts and, since the Anglo-German agreement on China (1900) was still-born, the earliest to be effective.

BRITAIN AND ISOLATION

In his dispatch Lansdowne did not mention that the alliance marked the ending of British isolation. This was obviously the criticism which he most expected to hear from his political opponents. It was a factor that also affected Japan but was more open to criticism in Britain than it was in Japan. For Japan, to be sure, it was a change from isolation but it was also an alignment with the world's leading power which was unquestionably regarded as an honour. For Britain, it was a 'departure from isolation' that implied a weakening of that self-sufficiency which had characterized Britain during the nineteenth century and also an alignment with Japan which was scarcely recognized as a world power. For Japan, it was promotion into the ranks of great powers and therefore a natural progression. For Britain, it could have been portrayed as the reverse, a sign of decadence.

Lansdowne repudiated this view. In defending the first alliance in the House of Lords, he urged his hearers not to be prejudiced in considering the Japanese alliance by 'any musty formulas or old-fashioned superstitions as to the desirability of pursuing a policy of isolation'.[2] In later years he amplified this statement in what was almost his last speech as foreign secretary, that to the Junior Constitutional Club on 6 November 1905. He was speaking in retrospect of the alliance which had by then been renewed for a further ten years; but his arguments applied also to 1902. Lansdowne claimed that 'the time for objecting to alliances as entanglements had passed by and the price of a policy of isolation was more than we could afford to pay'.[3] He argued that Britain had abandoned the policy of isolation not only in Asia by the Japanese alliance but also in Europe by the French entente and that Britain had to do as other powers did who were distributed in groups. Britain was a power, distributed in Europe

[1] *BD*, ii, nos. 92 and 93.
[2] *British parliamentary debates*, 4th series, vol. 102, 13 February 1902, col. 1176.
[3] *The Times*, 7 November 1905.

and Asia; she should co-ordinate her foreign policy objectives with her security needs by concluding regional agreements as required. These remarks seem to be consistent with the stand which Lansdowne had taken several times in 1901.

Lansdowne's statement that he had initiated a change of policy, did not go unchallenged. Lord Cranborne in a letter to the prime minister took some exception to Lansdowne's speech. His conception of Britain's previous foreign policy, predominantly that of his father, was different:

For the last twenty years we have been engaged with different Powers, notably with Germany and with France, in adjusting conflicting claims, and in bargaining so as to get rid of causes of friction.[1]

He was thinking back to the policy of the Mediterranean agreements which lasted for most of the decade after 1887 and, while he asserted that the policy towards Japan had special features, he considered that Lansdowne's policy should properly be regarded 'rather as a development of past policy than as a new departure'.[2]

These remarks raise two questions: what was the elder Salisbury's attitude towards the Japanese alliance? was the alliance such a radical departure from Britain's previous policies? On the first point, Salisbury with his pragmatic approach to policy-making, was not averse to making agreements if circumstances warranted but was suspicious of long-term entanglements. Certainly he was less 'alliance-minded' than other members of the cabinet like Chamberlain, Balfour and Lansdowne; but he did in fact commit himself to the Japanese alliance, although he was suspicious of an agreement with Germany in 1901. Salisbury was by nature disinclined to follow other than an empirical, hand-to-mouth, policy. Thus, he was able to adapt himself to a far eastern alliance in the same way as he conceded the need for the Anglo-German agreement of 1900. His note of 7 January 1902 did not reject the alliance, although he was fully aware of the risks involved.

Was it such a radical departure from Britain's previous policies?

---

[1] Balfour papers Add. MSS 49758, Cranborne to Balfour, 9 November 1905. Cranborne had by this time succeeded his father as Lord Salisbury but is here referred to by his former title for the sake of clarity.

[2] Cf. *BD*, viii, no. 1, note by T. H. Sanderson, 1 July 1902, written just before the elder Salisbury's final retirement.

In a speech in the House of Commons after the publication of the alliance, Balfour said that it was:

We have made what I quite admit is, at all events in recent years, a new departure. I am not prepared to minimise in the slightest degree the importance of the steps we have taken. I do not pretend at all that it is one of the ordinary, everyday diplomatic transactions between Power and Power.[1]

Recent studies have tended to show that there was a group within the Salisbury cabinet of 1900 which wanted a break with the old policy and turned their backs on the policy of isolation.[2] It would require a study broader in its scope than this one to make an adequate comment on this complex issue. It is, however, fair to say that there is an ambivalence about the term 'isolation'; and that Cranborne and Balfour are using it in different senses.[3] Balfour implied that Britain's isolation entailed the absence of foreign entanglements. Cranborne suggested that Britain's traditional policy, while it may have avoided entanglements, none the less showed willingness to sort out differences and that this could not reasonably be described as isolation. He was surely justified in saying that Britain had all along been adjusting to her changed status in the world. Thus the Japanese alliance was merely a further step in this natural course of adjustment. If this is true, it was certainly still a departure but only a modest one. On that point, probably Cranborne, Balfour and Lansdowne would all be in agreement.

The alliance, being subject to geographical limitations, was not a full-fledged flight from isolation. If Britain now came to assume new commitments, these commitments were ordinarily confined to the far east. In the event of an outbreak of war, the degree of commitment would probably be less in the case of a Japanese alliance than it would in the case of an alliance with a European power. It was so regarded by the government. The parliamentary opposition had shown at question-time and in debates that they were aware of some of the dangers entrenched in it. But the fact remains that the British people came to accept the new alliance without any great sense of the risk which it entailed. Indeed, the first alliance did not capture the public

---

[1] *British parliamentary debates*, 4th series, vol. 102, 13 February 1902, col. 1294.
[2] Monger, p. 20; Grenville, pp. 324–6.
[3] Some of the other implications in the term 'isolation' have been analysed by Christopher Howard, 'Splendid isolation', *History*, no. 47 (1962), 32–41.

imagination of Britain. This tends to support the view that it was not widely recognized, either in informed or in less-informed circles, that Britain was making a major departure in foreign policy.[1]

[1] This view would not be universally shared. Howard, loc. cit., 40–1, concludes that 'it was recognised that Britain had given up her "fixed policy of not making alliances" whether or not one chose to term that policy "isolation" '. Lord Strang, *Britain in world affairs*, London, 1961, p. 250, contends that it was part of a 'revolutionary turn in our foreign policy'. On the other side, Lord Vansittart, *Mist Procession*, London, 1955, p. 51, speaks of 'such strokes of traditional diplomacy as the Anglo-Japanese treaty'.

PART THREE

War with Russia and the Second Alliance

If the existing [Anglo-Japanese] compact were expanded so as to take effect when any single Power [attacked either of the allies], all direct incentive to Russia to rebuild her fleet would be removed.... Such a modification of the Alliance might conceivably lead to an indefinite abandonment of her aspirations to sea power, which only arose on a large scale in connection with the needs of her Far Eastern policy, as the movements of her fleets for years past have amply testified ....

It is of the essence of the present international situation that the interests of Great Britain and Japan can only be perfectly safeguarded, so long as the Island Powers remain indissolubly united.

Fisher to the cabinet, May–June 1905
Fisher papers, ii, 76–9

R

CHAPTER XII

Japan in Korea and Manchuria

1902–1903

THE Anglo-Japanese alliance affected seapower in the Pacific and altered Japan's status in Korea and Manchuria. The maritime alliance reduced the importance of the naval power which Russia had been building up in east Asia along with her reluctant ally, France. The improvement in Japan's continental position led to increasing tension between her and Russia, which could not be resolved by peaceful means and eventually precipitated an unnecessary war in 1904. Japan's victories in the war were spectacular; but her government foresaw that she might find herself in the postwar world with her resources exhausted and requiring the added assurance of the British alliance. The alliance was therefore revised in August 1905 and extended in scope beyond the limited alliance of 1902.

Before examining the diplomacy of these events, it is necessary to consider some of the consequences of the first alliance which were only gradually worked out. Let us first discuss those who had a hand in them.

INTERNAL AFFAIRS

The governments which concluded the alliance in 1902, both remained in power until the signature of the second alliance. In Britain there was a Conservative ministry and in Japan a non-party ministry under General Katsura throughout the period.

In Britain Conservative rule continued uninterrupted until the end of 1905. Salisbury retired from office in July 1902 and died in the following year. He was succeeded by A. J. Balfour, who had acted as Salisbury's adviser and deputy and was preferred to the leading political figure in the country, Joseph Chamberlain. Chamberlain stayed on for a while but resigned in 1903, when his son, Austen, joined the cabinet as chancellor of the exchequer. The elder Chamberlain, freed from ministerial responsibility, called for a policy of imperial preference, thus dividing the Tory party and in the end wrecking the ministry.

Foreign affairs were still under the charge of Lord Lansdowne who had held office since October 1900. As the years passed, he gained experience and confidence to add to his undoubted industry, shrewdness and capacity for international understanding. By 1905 he gives the impression of being much more assured and less dependent on his Foreign Office secretariat than he was in his early years. His parliamentary under-secretary had been Lord Cranborne. When he went to the House of Lords on Salisbury's death, his place was taken by Lord Percy, who was active and not uninfluential in the negotiation of the second alliance.

Perhaps the greatest influence on policy-making outside the Foreign Office was Balfour, who had under the earlier ministry deputized for Salisbury as foreign secretary on several occasions. Lansdowne referred to him a great deal on larger issues of policy and, as this study will demonstrate, Balfour had a rare capacity for detachment and logical thinking which made his memoranda invaluable. It was due to his far-sightedness that an institution which was to leave its mark on British foreign policy became prominent. In December 1902 the Committee of Imperial Defence was set up on a new basis.[1] By its regular meetings, it went some way towards co-ordinating Britain's strategic thinking with her diplomacy. After a permanent secretariat was set up in 1904 with Sir George Clarke (Lord Sydenham) as secretary, its value was further increased. The work of the C.I.D. has a special bearing on far-eastern policy, which was necessarily bound up with the security of the Indian Empire and Britain's possessions farther east. Since the Japanese alliance was intimately bound up with strategic considerations and with Britain's naval strength, it was natural that its renewal in 1905 could not be considered without consulting the C.I.D. Indeed the shape which the new treaty took was largely suggested by the Committee.

Among the permanent staff at the Foreign Office, there were

---

[1] Detailed studies of the C.I.D. will be found in F. A. Johnson, *Defence by committee*, London, 1960; G. S. Clarke, *My working life*; Monger, chapter 5; J. P. Mackintosh, 'The role of the Committee of Imperial Defence before 1914', *English Historical Review*, no. 304 (1962), 490–503.

significant changes. Sir Thomas Sanderson continued as permanent under-secretary until his retirement in 1906 but was rarely concerned with policy for the far east. Francis Bertie, the head of the Asiatic section during the diplomacy of 1901, was appointed ambassador to Rome in 1903 and later to Paris (1905–18). Charles Hardinge was an influential figure, first as assistant under-secretary (1903–4), and then as ambassador at St Petersburg during the war period. He consistently advocated good relations with Russia; and this had the effect of preventing an exclusive attachment to Japan. F. A. Campbell replaced Bertie as the head of the Asiatic Department but, despite his careful, informed minutes, he does not give the impression of having initiated policy in the same confident way that Bertie did in 1901. In any case, Lansdowne now knew the ropes and required less outside guidance.[1]

Britain was vexed at the prospect of war in the far east. Her interests which were dominated by her large commercial stake in China, were best served by peace, as her statesmen had realized since 1860. Moreover she was reluctant to be implicated in a war which affected her interests as little as did one over Manchuria. The South African war had dragged to a close on 31 May 1902 and left Britain in an exhausted state to face the problems of rehabilitation involved. The army had shown itself in need of modernization, a task to which the war minister immediately turned his hand. The Admiralty also considered naval reorganization to be an urgent necessity. The trouble was that the Treasury insisted that the nation's finances should be restored to a peace footing without delay. In these circumstances, the British government was not anxious to diversify its strength by sending forces to the far east, although it was generally favourable to Japan and hostile to Russia.[2]

In Japan the period from the first to the second alliance was also covered by a single government, that of Count Katsura (as he became in 1902). General Yamagata seems to have acted as a close adviser to him during his terms of office, so much so that Katsura's cabinet came to be known as the 'donchō' (literally 'silk curtain') cabinet because Yamagata was suspected of prompting it from behind an imaginary arras of silk.[3] With this help and a good measure of political good

---

[1] Zara Steiner, 'The last years of the old Foreign Office, 1898–1905', *The Historical Journal*, no. 6 (1963), 73–84.

[2] *History of 'The Times'*, iii, 381–2, Chirol to Morrison, 25 May 1903.

[3] Oka, *Yamagata*, p. 87.

fortune, the Katsura ministry exceeded the most sanguine predictions by continuing in office until December 1905.

Foreign affairs were handled by Baron Komura Jutarō, whose first act on coming to office in September 1901 was to steer through the British alliance. By a rare coincidence, he was also to be responsible as foreign minister for the successor-agreements of 1905 and 1911. In his dealings with Britain, he was assisted by the continued presence there of Viscount Hayashi, who was pro-British and remained a popular figure in London society until his departure in 1906. In framing his country's policy, Komura seems to have been punctilious in consulting Katsura, the cabinet, and at times of crisis the genrō.

Galperin describes the years 1902–3 as a period of political crises in Japan.[1] The Katsura ministry was a non-party one and it was frequently under attack in the Diet from the parties. At the general election in August 1902, the Seiyūkai was returned again as the majority party and decided to oppose a government which did not represent it. It therefore subjected some of the government's budgetary measures to vigorous attack. In the autumn, the Seiyūkai formed a coalition with the Kensei Hontō in opposition to Katsura's scheme for financing the increase in naval building from the land tax. Katsura therefore dissolved the Diet in December. Before the general election on 1 March 1903, Katsura appealed to Itō as one of the genrō to withdraw the opposition of the Seiyūkai of which he was president. He reached agreement with Itō by foregoing the proposed increase in land-tax and arranging for the increase in naval building by raising a loan. At an emergency session held after the general election when the results were similar to those of 1902, Katsura had his naval proposals passed with the general support of the Seiyūkai. They were, however, attacked by the Kensei Hontō and part of the Seiyūkai; and the tension between the government and the parties continued throughout 1903. As war approached, the parties were prepared to submerge their differences in the cause of national unity; and until the coming of peace, political parties were not an important influence on Japan's foreign policy. The British alliance was accepted by government and opposition as the basis of their foreign policies. Whatever problems were posed by the renewal of that alliance were not aggravated by the existence of widespread opposition.

Amid all the uncertainties of domestic affairs, the alliance was a

[1] Galperin, p. 177.

success to which the governments in Britain and Japan could point. Moreover the alliance conferred practical benefits which gradually materialized.

NAVAL DEVELOPMENTS

The diplomatic notes exchanged at the signing of the alliance had provided that the naval forces of the allies should act in concert in peacetime, that mutual facilities should be given for the docking and coaling of warships and that the allies should maintain 'available for concentration in the waters of the Extreme East' naval forces superior to that of any third power. If these provisions were to be translated from the vagueness of treaty language into practice, they had to be discussed by naval experts. To this end a series of high-level naval consultations took place in 1902. Their decisions were among the more practical results of the alliance.

There were none who looked so favourably on the alliance as the British Admiralty and the Japanese Ministry of Marine. But, when their enthusiasm is analysed, it is evident that they welcomed the treaty for mutually incompatible reasons. The Japanese looked to their ally for naval assistance because they wanted to ensure that the strength of British battleships and cruisers in east Asian waters was kept superior to that of Russia. The British, on the other hand, while recognizing that they might have to give Japan naval help, resisted the idea that they must keep a given number of warships in the far east, provided they held them 'available for concentration' there. The Admiralty sought two positive advantages. Selborne, the hard-working First Lord, wrote that the alliance 'will not make it necessary for us to retain as large a fleet on the China Station as we should otherwise have had to do'.[1] The far-eastern ships were required elsewhere as part of the redistribution scheme and during 1902 two cruisers were removed. In addition, it was a relief for Britain that she could use Japanese protected bases, if necessary, for coaling and repairs. Britain was then investigating the cost of expanding the dockyard at Hong Kong and was boggling at the estimates. The use of the Japanese yards was therefore a boon and a saving, both in war and peace.

During the summer of 1902 special naval talks were held. The Japanese government was quick to instruct its admirals to act in

[1] Bridge papers, Selborne to Bridge, 11 February 1902.

concert with the British navy and offer Britain full docking facilities at its ports. To implement this, a preliminary conference was held on 14 May at Japan's main naval dockyard at Yokosuka between Japanese officials and Admiral Sir Cyprian Bridge, commander-in-chief of the China squadron. The major decisions were reserved for a conference in London which was attended by the service members of the Japanese mission visiting Britain for the coronation. On 7 July Rear-Admiral Ijuin and Major-General Fukushima discussed general co-operation with the heads of British military and naval intelligence, Lieutenant-General Nicholson and Rear-Admiral Custance. Since Britain had no thought of giving military assistance, that aspect of the talks may be ignored. In the naval discussions, however, the delegations agreed on the dispositions of the fleets in event of war and on practical arrangements such as the exchange of intelligence. Commander Ballard who was intimately connected with the talks, gives the following account of their results:

The dispositions of the Allied navies in the event of war were worked out to the last detail, and a joint system of manœuvring was prepared whereby an admiral belonging to either service could take command of a mixed force of British and Japanese ships and handle them as one fleet in action. Full arrangements were drawn up for co-ordinating the two Admiralty administrations, including the pooling of war-supplies, the exchange of docking plans and the drafting of secret orders, to be kept in readiness for issue in both Admiralties and revised in consultation from year to year to meet developments and changes in the situation as they arose.[1]

These were emergency arrangements but they were none the less substantial decisions.

The points agreed upon were further elaborated at a meeting in Tokyo between Admiral Bridge and Admiral Yamamoto, the Japanese minister of marine, on 25 November. Perhaps the most important issues settled were that a joint signal book should be printed and that intelligence should be freely exchanged through the British and Japanese naval attachés.[2]

The other issue — the number of battleships which each ally would maintain — was a matter of high policy which had to be decided at cabinet level and was not raised at any of the conferences at which

---

[1] G. A. Ballard, *Influence of the sea on the political history of Japan*, pp. 183–4.

[2] FO *Japan* 574, Admiralty to Foreign Office, 3 January 1903, containing Bridge to Admiralty, 26 November 1902; Bridge papers 15, Kerr to Bridge, 2 January 1903.

admirals were the spokesmen. The object of each ally was to encourage the other to maintain the strength of its naval squadron in east Asia; and each felt some disappointment at the performance of the other.[1] Britain's complaint was that, with the completion of the Japanese shipbuilding programme during 1902, there was no sign of any renewal of building activity. The Japanese government was unable to undertake further construction because of shortage of funds but claimed that it intended to go ahead with the building of battleships, cruisers and three new docks. Down to the Russo-Japanese war, however, no new construction was begun. Britain was afraid that Japan was intending to rely on the strength of the Royal Navy. But the Japanese government was able to make countercharges about Britain's true intentions. On 27 April 1903, Japan's minister of marine pointed out that, while the tonnage of Japanese and Russian naval forces in the far east was being increased, British tonnage there was decreasing.[2] It is, of course, debatable whether the tonnage figure was a reasonable comparison to make; but even on a ship-by-ship basis there was some justification for the complaint. Lansdowne in a carefully worded reply, which was prepared in co-operation with the Admiralty, did not altogether deny the charge. He argued instead that Britain was pre-occupied with the power whose action alone would call Britain into any struggle against Russia, namely France.[3] Whatever the merits of this explanation, it did not really assure Japan that Britain was not proposing a gradual withdrawal of her naval squadron. But, even though the naval results did not fulfil the hopes of the navy ministers on both sides, who appear to have been among the strongest supporters of continuing the alliance, the naval benefits were not few.[4]

FINANCIAL DEVELOPMENTS

The alliance also conferred indirect benefits on Japan which were nowhere provided for in the treaty: among these was the availability of British finance. While the new treaty made little significant difference

[1] Details of accusation and countercharge will be found in A. J. Marder, *The anatomy of British sea power, 1880–1905*, pp. 431–3.

[2] FO *Japan* 568, MacDonald to Lansdowne, 27 April 1903.

[3] FO *Japan* 574, F. A. Campbell to Hayashi, 10 June 1903; FO *Japan* 564, Lansdowne to MacDonald, 10 June 1903.

[4] Just as it is clear that Selborne was a staunch advocate of the alliance, there is evidence that the navy minister, Admiral Yamamoto, was a consistent sponsor of the alliance in Japan. In the Japanese Honours list, published after the alliance, he received promotion to the rank of baron.

to trade, it did ease the flow of British capital to Japan for purposes of national development. In the past, Japan had not made undue use of foreign loans for fear of the consequences which had attended them in China but domestic loans had given disappointing yields. The recognition of Japan's status as a world power under the alliance improved her credit in the money markets; and in London, which was then the leading capital market in the world, it enabled Japanese bankers to negotiate more advantageous loans. In 1902 prominent emissaries like Shibusawa and Matsukata led missions abroad with the avowed object of attracting foreign capitalists to invest in Japan. There was a ready response among British capitalists. In September 1902, the Hong Kong and Shanghai Banking Corporation recommenced loan negotiations just after the Matsukata mission visited London at the time of Edward VII's belated coronation. The necessary arrangements for the flotation of a loan by resale of Japanese 5 per cent war bonds to the face value of ¥50 million were undertaken by Barings on behalf of the Hong Kong Shanghai Bank and the Yokohama Specie Bank.[1] Asked for its views on the loan, the Foreign Office replied that it was a matter of political importance 'that Japan should be able to raise in this country rather than elsewhere, the money which she requires and they hope that she will obtain a loan in London on reasonable terms'. Lansdowne, it continued, had formed a high opinion of the energy and enterprise of the Japanese and was convinced of their desire to introduce sound methods of administration and to establish their credit on a sound basis.[2] Later the Hong Kong Shanghai Bank asked the Treasury for inscription of the bonds at the Bank of England before opening the loan to public subscription on the London market. Though the Treasury was traditionally averse to this procedure, it agreed at the instigation of the Foreign Office because of the political importance of the loan.[3] The British public took up more than had been hoped. In a letter of thanks, Viscount Hayashi, as he had recently become, stated that 'the success of the recent sale of the Japanese bonds was no doubt greatly due to the announcement that the Bank was prepared for its inscription'.[4]

---

[1] The bonds were Japanese government war bonds issued in 1901–2, to the face value of ¥50 million (£5 million) at £98 per ¥1000.

[2] FO *Japan* 560, Bertie to Rothschilds, 22 September 1902.

[3] Balfour papers Add. MSS 49727, Lansdowne to Balfour, 1 October 1902; FO *Japan* 550, Lansdowne to MacDonald, 13 October 1902.

[4] FO *Japan* 558, Hayashi to Lansdowne, 16 October 1902.

The alliance also gave a boost to loans for the private sector in Japan. For railway development, private loans were given, in return for certain relaxations of the property law, to the Kyūshū, Hokuetsu and Hankaku railway companies. There were also examples of municipal loans being floated in Britain in 1902: the 6 per cent bonds of Yokohama municipality were taken up by Samuel Samuel & Co., the Tokyo agents of Rothschilds; the ¥3,500,000 bond issue of the Osaka Harbour Works Board was also undertaken. The greater ease with which these loans were concluded, was a consequence of Japan's improved credit in London. Was this one of the motives behind the alliance or merely a fortuitous result of it?

The Japanese leaders were certainly aware that an alliance might help their country to attract British capital. Komura had put the issue pointedly to the genrō when he commended a British alliance as a means of gaining financial advantages: an agreement with Britain would not only improve Japan's credit in financial circles but, since its development would then accord with Britain's interest, the British people would also gladly meet the financial and economic needs of Japan.[1] It was Komura's argument that financial advantages were one among many which Japan could derive from closer connections with Britain. The problem is to decide what weight the Japanese leaders attached to this aspect. When the financial attractions of the alliance are compared with the political attractions, it becomes clear how secondary the financial factor was. Had it only been money that Japan sought, it might equally well have been obtained from France without political complications. Moreover, between the alliance and the outbreak of the war with Russia, the amount of the loans concluded was comparatively small; there was no sudden surge of foreign borrowing. What the Japanese wanted in the short term was a political alliance, and the political and strategic advantages outweighed the various other fringe-benefits, financial and commercial.[2]

This is not to say that the alliance did not have important financial consequences in the long term. In the past Japan had not been a very attractive place for the foreign investor because of the lack of security for his money. The alliance created an atmosphere of confidence in Japan and improved the security felt by British investors there. This

[1] *Komura gaikōshi*, i, 277–80. Appendix D.
[2] Cf. Kuroha Shigeru, 'Nichi-Ei dōmei no seiritsu to kokka zaisei mondai', *Rekishi kyōiku*, no. 5 (1957), 13–19 and 50–9.

tended to reduce the interest rates charged on loans and overcame some of the reluctance which Japanese leaders still felt over accepting foreign loans for national development. But it was mainly between 1906 and 1913 that Japan took steps to acquire large peacetime loans. Since there was no such urgency in 1902, it seems to be confirmed that the desire for British loans was only a secondary motive behind the alliance.

RESULTS FOR CHINA AND KOREA

Since the agreement contained in its title special reference to China and Korea, it may be worth while to inquire how it affected them. Certainly, in so far as the alliance offered China and Korea protection against Russia, there was no reason why it should not be welcome to them. But there were dangers; and official reactions were varied. The Koreans confined themselves to welcoming the guarantee it gave of their country's independence; the Chinese were non-committal and less than frank. It is important therefore to look for unofficial Chinese reaction. T'ang Shao-i, a Foreign Ministry official close to Yuan Shih-k'ai, the important viceroy of Chihli, told the Peking correspondent of *The Times*, Dr Morrison, that the alliance was 'a humiliation for China who will be put to sleep', by which he presumably meant that China would lose her independence and have to rely for her security on Britain and Japan.[1] But Liang Tun-yen, a member of the Tsungli Yamen, professed to be very pleased. Morrison remarked in his diary that the question that occurred to the Chinese was: 'suppose Russia be driven forcibly out of Manchuria by Japan, a military feat which is regarded as well within Japanese power, will Japan remain in possession of the territory so occupied?'[2] To this extent, the Chinese had a deeper appreciation of Japan's military power than any European government and showed a realistic anticipation of events.

It was a vanquished and abject China that survived the Boxer disturbances. She was subjected by the Peking settlement of September 1901 to a crushing monetary indemnity and was later required to accept a fresh set of commercial treaties with the powers. Britain led the way by concluding the Mackay treaty of September 1902 and was followed by Japan and the other trading nations. Perhaps the greatest effect of all this was the shift in the focus of trouble from China proper to Manchuria after 1900.

[1] Morrison papers 312/62, 23 February 1902.
[2] Morrison papers 312/62, 22 February 1902.

Even as the Anglo-Japanese treaty was being concluded, Manchuria was in the news. The Russians were trying to get China to agree to a convention with the Russo-Chinese Bank, a subsidiary of the Russian Ministry of Finance, granting the bank financial concessions in Manchuria, and a separate convention providing for the evacuation of Russian forces from Manchuria. Negotiations for the first were broken off by the Chinese on account of Japanese and American protests in January and February 1902. At the same time, Prince Ch'ing, who had become the leading Chinese statesman after the death of Li Hung-chang in November, had been trying to secure a reduction in the terms imposed by the second. In this, he was supported by the Japanese and the Americans. As early as 25 January, the Japanese advised Prince Ch'ing to sign the revised Manchurian agreement quickly; and on 1 February the American secretary of state published a circular objecting to continued Russian occupation of Manchuria. Britain, on the other hand, was still advising China in March to delay and to have further amendments made. On 1 April Japan pressed China to sign the agreement without delay. One week later, Russia and China signed a convention providing for the phased withdrawal of Russian troops from various sectors of Manchuria. Evacuation was to be carried out over three six-month periods starting in October 1902; but it was to be conditional on there being no trouble in China. Russia was therefore given time by the convention to safeguard her interests in Manchuria by civil guards rather than armed forces and a 'let-out' clause which would enable her to cancel or postpone her undertakings.[1]

It was said at the time, and has frequently been repeated, that this Manchurian agreement was a triumph for the Anglo-Japanese alliance. The Japanese historian, Kiyozawa, wrote that the Russo-Chinese agreement was 'clearly the result of the pressure of the alliance'. Chang Chung-fu, the author of one of the few monographs in English on the alliance, claimed that the strength of the alliance was shown in the fact that 'only two months after its publication, Russia came to an agreement with China in regard to Manchuria'.[2] These views are largely illusory. There was not a direct relationship between the alliance and this Manchurian convention. It is not true that Russia, from fear of the new alliance, offered China attractive terms which were speedily

<hr>

[1] E. H. Zabriskie, *American-Russian rivalry in the far east, 1895–1914*, Philadelphia, 1946, pp. 78–80.

[2] Kiyozawa, *Gaikōshi*, i, 303; Chang, *Anglo-Japanese alliance*, p. 98.

accepted. Russia's evacuation terms were by no means generous and had been communicated in the previous autumn. Indeed China was being encouraged by the United States and Japan to sign the agreement, even before the alliance was announced. The convention was due to the action of these powers, not the action of Britain, far less the alliance.

Britain and Japan failed signally to work together on the issue of the Manchurian convention. Lansdowne thought that the Japanese had become 'rather easy going' and that, 'after having protested so loudly, we ought not to climb down out of sheer weariness in too great a hurry'.[1] He regretted that Japan was out of line with Britain. After the convention had been signed, Sanderson, the permanent under-secretary, wrote that:

The tendency of the public here is to be more satisfied with the Manchurian Agreement than its contents quite warrant and to look upon it as due mainly to our diplomacy. We are inclined at the F.O. to be much more modest on the subject but I think on the whole it is as favourable as we could have reasonably expected.[2]

Sanderson was frank enough to confess that the outcome had not been due to British diplomacy and hinted that 'the F.O.' was to some extent dissatisfied with its terms. Japan thought differently and acted according to her own insights. This was an early confirmation that the allies would often act separately, even on issues which seemed to be fairly central to the alliance.

The fact was that the interests of Britain and Japan were not at one over Manchuria. While they were both devoted to the Open Door, there was a difference in the degree of their commitment. Britain was interested in expanding her markets throughout China but did not hold out great hopes for sales to Manchuria. Moreover she had recognized Russia's railway rights there in 1899. By contrast, Japan was developing a stake in the country. Admittedly, her immigration into Manchuria was slight: in December 1903, there were only 2806 Japanese nationals resident in the ports who were mainly engaged in a wide variety of occupations as workmen, small merchants and shop-keepers. But the Japanese controlled most of the seaborne trade operating through Newchwang and were worried that they were losing ground to the Russians who had the advantage of controlling the

[1] Lansdowne papers, Lansdowne to MacDonald, 31 March 1902.
[2] Satow papers 7/2, Sanderson to Satow, 11 April 1902.

railway network and most of the productive areas. Since the Japanese were affected by the presence of Russian troops there, theirs was among the strongest voices calling for Russian evacuation.

In this area, Japan had more in common with the United States. Among the major powers they were the only ones who had not compromised with Russia over Manchuria. France was Russia's ally, while Germany had since the Manchurian crisis of 1901 shown herself to be unwilling to challenge the Russians in the far east. On the other hand, the United States was developing commercial and financial interests in Manchuria. With Theodore Roosevelt as president, she was on occasion prepared to take a strong stand, as the protest over the proposed Russo-Chinese banking convention of 1902 has shown. Although Roosevelt was not anxious for close co-operation with any other power, he publicly favoured Japan's efforts to challenge Russia over Manchuria in 1903 and 1904.

Japan's stake in Manchuria was much smaller than in Korea, where she had improved her position since the alliance. The British minister in Seoul, Sir John Jordan, wrote in March 1902 that 'their recent convention with us seems to have perceptibly stiffened their Corean policy, which still, however, proceeds on very cautious lines where there is any risk of a collision with Russia'.[1] The policy of the Japanese was one of political and economic consolidation. They placed their advisers at the Korean court and strengthened their position over the Russians there. In this, they felt that they enjoyed the co-operation of the British minister.[2] But a permanent improvement in Japan's standing in the peninsula depended on economic penetration. Although it was difficult to procure suitable emigrants, the number of Japanese who went to settle in the south-eastern districts, grew rapidly in 1903 to 30,000. Moreover, despite the shortage of capital for development, Japan gradually assumed control of mines, posts and telegraphs. The Japanese-controlled Daiichi Bank was beginning to secure financial control as great as that of a central bank, issuing the only currency notes and making loans to the Korean court. Its chairman, Shibusawa Eiichi, visited London in 1902 and succeeded in raising a loan for the construction of the railway between Fusan and Seoul, which had been held up since the lease was granted in 1898. Late in 1902, the Japanese

---

[1] Jordan papers, 3, Jordan to Bridge, 31 March 1902.
[2] *Meiji hennenshi*, xi, 424. There is no support for this opinion in any Foreign Office documents.

cabinet passed a resolution deploring the fact that Japan which was so close to the continent and had so many vital continental interests, had very little commerce and industry there. The cabinet decided to vote almost two million yen for 1903 towards specified projects in Korea, of which the most important was the building of the Seoul-Fusan railway.[1] Thus, Japanese enterprise in the peninsula was becoming perceptibly more dynamic; and the government was becoming increasingly involved. But Japanese advances in Korea were likely to be anathema to the Russians who had for a decade been building up influence at the court and adding to their interests in the north of the peninsula.

There was a divergence within the Japanese leadership over the attitude to be taken towards Russia. During his visit to St Petersburg in November 1901, Itō had put forward the formula known as Man-Kan Kōkan, literally the 'exchange of Manchuria for Korea'. This formula offered a range of possible courses rather than merely one single course. The basic idea was that peace could best be secured if Japan and Russia reached a compromise: Japan should recognize Russia's superior position in Manchuria on condition that Russia recognized Japan's superior position in Korea, while Japan would give up her claims in Manchuria in return for Russia giving up her claims in Korea. Since 1895 there had been several types of solution for Korea. First, there was the division of the peninsula into Russian and Japanese spheres of influence which was incorporated into the agreements of 1896 and 1898. Then the Russian proposal for Korea's neutralization under international guarantee was turned down by Japan early in 1901. Now that the Man-Kan Kōkan formula had been unofficially proposed, it was a sign of Japan's increasing strength and ambition in the peninsula. In any case Russia was not prepared to make the necessary concessions and the discussion was suspended. For his part, Katsura was not prepared to support Itō's approach to Russia because Japan could not fail to be involved in Russia's activities in Manchuria and could not with propriety ignore them as part of a package deal.[2] But Man-Kan Kōkan continued to be supported by Itō and was still a live issue.

With his hands strengthened by the British alliance, Katsura was

---

[1] *NGB* 35, no. 268.

[2] On Japan's economic progress in Korea, see Conroy, *Japanese seizure of Korea*, ch. IX *passim*.

determined to negotiate with Russia. What course would he choose: Man-Kan Kōkan or the more extreme course of insisting on the entire evacuation of Russian armies from Manchuria, if need be, by force of arms? The weakness of the former was that it was doubtful whether it would offer a long-term solution. It might secure peace for a few years but the Japanese were not likely to be permanently satisfied by exclusion from Manchuria. If they were to offer Russia a free hand there, they would be proposing something which they had little intention of observing because they had ambitions in that territory. Moreover, Japan had by 1903 pushed Russia out of Seoul so that, by adopting the compromise formula, she would be gaining less than she gave. The weakness of the more direct course was that, with Russia as ambitious, as obstinate and as confident as she was in 1903, the gauntlet was likely to be picked up and the result would be war.[1]

[1] See Appendix E for the views of Itō and Katsura.

S

CHAPTER XIII

Japan approaches Russia

April 1903–January 1904

THE east Asian crisis of 1903 was provoked by a gesture of defiance by Russia. In April the tsarist government deliberately refused to withdraw its forces from Manchuria in accordance with its treaty with China. Although it was the end of the second six-month period, the Russians did not evacuate their second quota of troops and kept their occupation armies stationed round Mukden. To give her actions a veneer of legality, Russia informed China on 18 April that seven fresh demands would have to be met before her troops would be withdrawn. These conditions leaked out to the foreign representatives in Peking. Japan speedily warned China against accepting them, thereby asserting an initiative which she was to retain throughout the crisis. On the advice of Japan, Britain and the United States, the Chinese statesmen turned down Russia's demands and asked for her compliance with her treaty obligations.

Russia's action was thought to be associated with the increasing activity of Russian entrepreneurs over the Yalu timber concessions in north Korea and east Manchuria. This caused the Japanese especially grave anxiety. But in the so-called 'new course' adopted by the tsarist government at various conferences between February and August 1903, it was laid down that the Yalu enterprises would be abandoned and that withdrawals from Manchuria would continue provided guarantees were obtained.[1] In fact, the 'new course' was belied by Russian actions in the east so that Russia's every act was viewed with suspicion by the powers.

The Japanese minister in China asked his government to formulate its policy in response to the new situation. On 21 April, four of Japan's leaders discussed this subject at Murinkaku, Yamagata's country house

---

[1] Malozemoff, p. 228.

at Kyoto. The prime minister presented a draft memorandum, recommending a solution based on Man-Kan Kōkan, and proposed that it should be laid before Russia. Itō who had himself advocated this in discussions with Witte and Lamsdorf in 1901, was eager to promote it again. It also met with support from Yamagata and Komura.[1] The steps to be taken were worked out by the cabinet but gave rise to some dissension. Itō and his fellow genrō, Inoue, wanted a less forceful approach to Russia than the cabinet. An imperial conference at which Itō, Yamagata, Ōyama, Matsukata and Inoue represented the genrō, was called on 23 June. The following terms were approved as the basis for Japan's approach to Russia:

1. to preserve the independence and territorial integrity of China and Korea and the principle of equal opportunity for commerce and industry there;
2. Japan and Russia to recognize mutually the rights which they possess at present in Korea and Manchuria respectively and the measures which have to be taken for their protection;
3. Japan and Russia to recognize mutually their right of sending forces when they need to preserve their above-mentioned interests or to repel uprisings in these territories. Troops to be withdrawn immediately after the object of sending them has been achieved. Police needed for railways and telegraphs are not covered by this;
4. Japan possesses the special right to advise and assist Korea to carry out internal reforms.[2]

While paying lip service to the independence of China and Korea, this statement is really only a refined version of Man-Kan Kōkan. The terms were of course intended as the basis for discussion and were accordingly one-sided. The conference, however, agreed that, when Russia had tightened her grip on Manchuria, Japan should take the opportunity to improve her standing in Korea.

The British minister in Tokyo was told that steps would be 'taken without delay to endeavour to induce Russia to fulfil her promises, and to evacuate Manchuria'. What these steps were Komura was unable to say, as no ultimate decision had been reached.[3] Since the Japanese council had already decided on its policy, it must be assumed either

[1] Oka, *Yamagata*, 92.
[2] *NGB* 36/I, no. 1, draft plan for negotiations with Russia, from the cabinet resolution following the imperial council, 23 June 1903.
[3] FO *Japan* 566, MacDonald to Lansdowne, 25 June 1903.

that Komura was as yet doubtful about how his mandate should be handled, or that he could not decide whether Britain should be taken into Japan's confidence. At their next meeting, Komura said that the cabinet had decided to approach Russia directly for an arrangement but did not believe that it was bound by the alliance to consult Britain 'because the arrangement would certainly not jeopardize the interests which the alliance was meant to protect'.[1] Under the alliance the signatories were not supposed to enter into separate agreements with a third power to the prejudice of their joint interests without consulting each other. In claiming that she need not consult Britain, Japan was claiming that her new proposals were not prejudicial to the alliance.

This view presupposed that Japan's approach to Russia was truly motivated by a desire for the independence of Korea and Manchuria. In this Japan may have been indulging in 'make believe'. This is suggested by a conversation which Marquis Itō arranged with MacDonald, where he argued that Manchuria was really no longer a part of China. Why not be realistic? Japan, he suggested, should take Korea; Russia should take Manchuria.[2] He had in mind a division of spoils. Assuming that he was correctly understood, Itō put forward Japanese ambitions more frankly than any government document or statement of the time.

Eventually Japan decided to consult Britain. On 3 July Hayashi read to Lansdowne a detailed memorandum on the Manchurian crisis. He explained that Japan was disposed 'to offer to Russia a solution of the present situation based on the clear definition of those interests [Russia's in Manchuria] as well as Japan's interests in Corea'.[3] Lansdowne replied that he would lay the statement before the cabinet after the visit to London of President Loubet of France had ended. He stated that it was most important that Britain and Japan should arrive at an understanding with the United States on the Manchurian question. The British government was faced with a problem, both in principle and in practice.

The problem was whether Man-Kan Kōkan was inconsistent with the alliance. This is still disputed by historians. The Japanese expert, Professor Imai, states positively that 'contrary to what the Japanese government claimed, the Anglo-Japanese alliance and a Russo-

---

[1] FO *Japan* 566, MacDonald to Lansdowne, 2 July 1903.
[2] FO *Japan* 566, MacDonald to F. A. Campbell, 2 July 1903; *BD*, ii, no. 236.
[3] *NGB* 36/I, no. 2; FO *Japan* 564, Lansdowne to MacDonald, 3 July 1903.

Japanese agreement were not compatible'.[1] Was a Russian agreement based on Man-Kan Kōkan compatible with the professions of faith in the independence of China and Korea contained in the alliance? Man-Kan Kōkan is by its nature a most imprecise term. In so far as the Japanese draft accepted the integrity of Manchuria and Korea, it was not a violation of the alliance. But statements of this kind are unreliable. It was certain that the independence of Korea and of China in Manchuria would be prejudiced when the two powers established their spheres of interest there. In this sense, one principle of the alliance was likely to be superseded.

The Foreign Office saw that it would be affected also in practice. 'If Russia is to be given a free hand in Manchuria as far as Japan is concerned', argued one minute, 'we shall be left to fight the battle [for China's integrity] alone or with only such help as we can get from the United States — a very uncertain quantity'.[2] Lansdowne evidently agreed that a major change of policy had been broached and urged the Japanese to avoid committing themselves until Britain had considered the question. The Japanese agreed but left the British minister with the impression that they had 'quite made up their minds to address the Russian Government direct, and that any representations we may make . . . will not deter them from their resolve'.[3]

On 14 July the British cabinet decided that a separate arrangement between Russia and Japan would indicate a weakening in the good understanding that had prevailed with Japan since 1901 and should be approached by her with caution. Hayashi was told that the British government would 'not criticise in an unfriendly spirit an Arrangement desired by their Ally, and consistent with the interests and Treaty obligations of Great Britain as well as Japan' but was asked that the Russian negotiations 'should not be conducted in a manner which might suggest that the Anglo-Japanese Agreement had been in any way impaired'.[4] Japan agreed to keep Britain informed of the course of negotiations and would have proceeded with the parleys, had it not been for a serious cabinet crisis.

On 1 July Katsura, claiming that his health would not stand up to

---

[1] Imai Shōji, 'Nichi-Ei dōmei kōshō ni okeru Nihon no shuchō', *Kokusai seiji*, 1957 autumn, 136.

[2] FO *Japan* 575, F. A. Campbell to Lansdowne, 2 July 1903.

[3] FO *Japan* 568, Lansdowne to MacDonald, 3 and 5 July 1903; FO *Japan* 566, MacDonald to Lansdowne, 9 July 1903.

[4] FO *Japan* 572, Lansdowne to Hayashi, 16 July 1903.

the important problems which his government was facing, offered his resignation and asked that the genrō should choose the next prime minister from among themselves as they had formerly done. In reality, Katsura was protesting against the undue interference in policy-making of Itō in his joint capacity as genrō and president of the majority Seiyūkai party. The premier retired to his villa at Hayama, leaving Admiral Yamamoto, the navy minister, as acting head of the government. The crisis was only resolved when the emperor, on Yamagata's recommendation, issued a rescript on 6 July commanding Itō to take over the court office of president of the Privy Council. Since this could not be combined with the leadership of a party, he was forced to resign and was thus deprived of one way of putting pressure upon the government. Meanwhile Katsura was commanded by the emperor to continue as prime minister and returned to Tokyo. By this remarkable extra-constitutional device, the cabinet crisis came to an end by mid-July.[1] Itō was no longer able to dominate the Seiyūkai when he passed over the leadership to Prince Saionji; but Saionji was his nominee and the two worked closely together. Moreover Itō still retained his influence with the emperor. As an indication of this, he stipulated, when he reluctantly joined the Privy Council, that Yamagata and Matsukata should be appointed as ordinary members of that body. Such was his influence that this condition was accepted. The British minister observed, not inappositely, that Itō 'was determined that, if he had to undergo an inconvenient process of elevation, his rivals should do the same, but in a humble manner'.[2] The political situation was restored.

RUSSO-JAPANESE NEGOTIATIONS

On 28 July Komura informed Russia that Japan wished to exchange views over their respective interests in the far east. The Russian foreign minister, Count Lamsdorf, agreed to open discussions and received the Japanese note containing the proposed settlement in Manchuria and Korea on 12 August. Since the tsar had just appointed Admiral Alexeyev as his special representative in the east and given him the title of 'Viceroy of the Far Eastern Provinces', he asked that negotiations should take place in the Japanese, rather than the Russian, capital because of its proximity to Port Arthur, the seat of Alexeyev's head-

[1] Oka, *Yamagata*, pp. 92–3; *Rikken Seiyūkai shi*, ii, 283–92.
[2] FO *Japan* 566, MacDonald to Lansdowne, 21 July 1903.

quarters. On 22 September, the Russian minister to Japan was called there for talks and, on his return to Tokyo, presented Russia's counter-proposals. The gist was that Russia would recognize Japan's position in south Korea provided that Korea north of the 39th parallel was recognized as a neutral zone and the coast and ports were permanently unfortified; Manchuria was to be regarded as outside Japan's sphere of interest and no guarantees were given about the evacuation of Russian troops. These terms were not acceptable to Japan as a reasonable compromise. There followed five conferences in Tokyo before the Japanese counterproposals were finally handed over on 30 October. Japan agreed to set up a 50-kilometre neutral zone on both sides of the Korean frontier with Manchuria where troops should not be sent. In Manchuria, Japan was prepared to recognize Russia's commercial rights but wished to have assurances about Japan's existing treaty rights there. The Russians, as if to indicate their unconciliatory reaction, occupied Mukden with 1000 men late in October and drove out the Chinese troops.

Dr Chang had claimed that the British government was 'fully and accurately informed' about the progress of events and gave Japan its complete approval and support.[1] While it is true that it was kept informed, it was not explicitly consulted. It occasionally let its views be known to Japan but it tried to have a moderating effect. Thus, Lansdowne tried to persuade the Japanese who wanted to secure a definite assurance from Russia that it would respect China's sovereignty and territorial integrity in Manchuria, not to insist upon such a clause since Russia was already pledged to it. But Komura, from past experience, would not accept anything less than a precise undertaking; and this became a stumbling-block in the negotiations.[2] On the whole, therefore, it should not be thought that, despite the 'frank exchange of opinions'[3] which took place, Japan permitted Britain to have any say in the negotiations. There is no evidence for believing that Britain induced Japan, by prejudicing her against the Russian terms, to adopt a more extreme position than she otherwise would or coaxed Japan to go to war.

Russia's reply was handed over in Tokyo on 11 December. Russia would not depart from her privileged position in Manchuria and made

[1] Chang, p. 104.
[2] FO *Japan* 568, Lansdowne to MacDonald, 26 October 1903.
[3] Malozemoff, p. 241.

no concession to Korea beyond those given to Japan in 1898. When the Japanese Diet opened its session that day, the political parties attacked the ministry because of its weakness towards Russia. Instead of resigning, the prime minister dissolved the Diet. In the charged atmosphere which this created, the cabinet met with the genrō on 17 December and, under the conciliatory influence of Itō, decided to request the Russians to reconsider their statement and, especially, to give assurances over Manchuria.

The Japanese had difficulty in deciding how serious developments were. Komura told MacDonald on 29 October that Japan did not think there would be any war because his evidence suggested that the Russians were not prepared and would not fight. But there was abundant evidence that other Japanese viewed the situation differently. Japanese businessmen were making approaches to British bankers for substantial loans; they were negotiating the purchase of five steamers; and the N.Y.K. shipping line was negotiating to transfer its fleet of vessels to Jardine Matheson's strength for the duration of the war.[1] However pacific the statements of the government, private interests were seriously troubled and were acting in anticipation of war breaking out. Meanwhile politicians and journalists were criticizing the ministry's failure to check Russia's activities in north-east Asia. Right-wing groups whose programmes included continental expansion, were active and by December things had reached a climax.[2]

It was the government — and the genrō — which served as a brake on this enthusiasm for war. They knew that there were strong arguments for an early war. In June the chief of the general staff had presented a memorial to the throne in which he argued that Japan at present enjoyed some advantages from a strategic point of view but that a few years' delay would place Russia in a superior position.[3] None the less both groups within the genrō did their utmost for peace. In December Yamagata sent the prime minister a letter deploring the possibility of war.[4] But the strongest force working for peace was Itō's group which probably prevented war being declared in December. Itō, because of his known pacifism, had to have his house regularly guarded to prevent hooliganism. But gradually the dilatoriness of Russian diplomacy and its unwillingness to be conciliatory, drove him

---

[1] FO *Japan* 568, MacDonald to Lansdowne, 28 October 1903.
[2] Rōyama, *Seijishi*, pp. 359–60.   [3] *Katō*, i, 507.
[4] Kiyozawa, *Gaikōshi*, i, 315.

to admit that war was the only solution. Recognizing that their decision was momentous, Japanese leaders had taken four months to make it. In a study which is primarily concerned with Japan's relations with Britain, there is no need to undertake a detailed examination of Japanese objectives in going to war, which is a subject of bitter controversy among Japanese scholars. But Japan's motives are so bound up with the position of Korea and of China in Manchuria which are in their turn so vital to the alliance that the subject cannot altogether be neglected. Which was more important in Japan's decision for war, Korea or Manchuria? Some historians hold that the prime object was Manchuria: the Japanese were concerned with revenge against Russia, the recovery of Liaotung and the expansion of their markets. They would justify this view by citing Japan's preoccupation with the various Russo-Chinese agreements over Manchuria. Others hold that Japanese policy was much less expansionist: its objective was to maintain the 'territorial integrity of Korea'.[1] But this phrase is woolly and is open to a kaleidoscopic range of interpretations. At one extreme it could mean her continued independence under the rule of the Korean emperor; at the other it could be taken to mean — and it often was by the Japanese — freedom from interference there by foreign powers apart from Japan.

It is fanciful to pretend that Japan set out with clearly defined objectives. Her written demands did not reveal her ambitions entirely. Most Japanese at the time held that Korea was essential to the defence of Japan. But some were prepared to make war against Russia for benefits they might acquire in Manchuria; and some of these may have been close to the government. But the more influential statesmen, and particularly the genrō, were opposed to undertaking the risks involved. Under their influence, the Japanese government concentrated on its rights in Korea. But the Russians would not restrict their operations to Manchuria and insisted on retaining residual rights in north Korea. In refusing any diminution of their powers, the Russians underestimated the earnestness of the Japanese. Since Japan did not intend

---

[1] Representative of the first group are Shimomura Fujio, 'Nichi-Ro sensō no seikaku', *Kokusai seiji*, 1957 autumn, 137–52 and Imai Shōji, 'Nichi-Ro sensō zengō Manshū zairyū Nihonjin no bumpu jōtai', *Rekishi chiri*, no. 89 (1960), 171–83. The other view which stresses the importance for Japan of the Manchurian market would be found in Furuya Tetsuo, 'Nihon teikoku shugi no seiritsu wo megutte', *Rekishigaku kenkyū*, no 202 (1956), 40–6. A good account of the 'great debate' will be found in Shinobu and Nakayama, *Nichi-Ro sensōshi no kenkyū*, 24–6, and in Conroy, *Japanese seizure of Korea*, ch. IX.

to move far from her initial demands, there was not much scope for compromise. The object for which the Japanese pressed most strongly, was to secure their position in Korea but there may have been deeper motives unstated.

After Russia gave Japan her reply on 3 October, Britain had to consider the possibility that war might emerge. This posed a new problem for Britain. The Japanese had kept Britain generally abreast of their intentions; and, since the act of negotiating with Russia and even the terms were not wholly inconsistent with the alliance, there was no reason why they should not meet with Lansdowne's approval. But the Japanese had made it clear that they intended to approach Russia alone since 'common action forms no part' of their scheme.[1] Now that events were more threatening, it was a moot point whether Britain should take a more active role towards Japan and Russia. Britain was sympathetic towards Japan but wanted to avoid doing anything to encourage the Japanese to go to war over Korea and Manchuria where she was much less hostile to Russia than they were. Britain's relations with Russia had greatly improved during 1903 and a deterioration in the far eastern situation was likely to make the settlement of outstanding disputes more difficult. Towards Russia's ally, France, the British government had already made approaches during the summer 'in order to minimize the chances of future trouble with that country'.[2] But, if war came about, Britain and France might be dragged in under the terms of their respective alliances. If this were to be avoided, it was essential for Britain to pursue negotiations with France and not let relations with Russia deteriorate. In short, the British cabinet often had to reconcile the conflicting objectives of its European and its far eastern diplomacy, to support its ally and to avoid alienating France and Russia.

In the last quarter of 1903, Britain had to take many decisions connected with the possible outbreak of war. There was the problem of preventing the war. Lansdowne knew that an international settlement in which the major powers would take part, would be unacceptable to Japan, who chose to regard the dispute as a local issue. In any

[1] *BD*, ii, no. 238.
[2] Gerald Balfour papers, 36, memorandum by Lansdowne, 10 September 1903.

case, the most important unattached power in east Asia, the United States, was not likely to help. It was doubtful if Britain alone could usefully mediate between Japan and Russia. Another set of problems concerned Britain's neutrality. Would Britain be justified in aiding her ally by selling armaments, offering finance or in other practical ways?

The first problem which presented itself to Britain was the mysterious case of the Chilean warships which precipitated a serious cabinet crisis in Britain. Anticipating an outbreak of war between themselves in 1902, Chile had ordered two battleships to be built in British yards, and Argentina had ordered two first-class armoured cruisers from Genoa. The dispute was resolved without fighting and the ships, which were due for completion early in 1904, were placed on the market for sale under British orders.

Britain wanted to encourage Japan to buy them. As early as February, Lansdowne warned Japan of rumours that Russia was likely to purchase the Chilean battleships; but there was no follow-up through diplomatic channels. On 25 November the position became urgent when Russia made an offer of £1,870,000 to Chile's agents in Britain. Lansdowne managed to postpone the conclusion of the transaction in order to give Japan the chance of outbidding. Japan replied that she had offered £1,600,000 a month earlier and was unwilling to pay the higher sum without consulting the Diet which was due to meet in three days. Komura explained that the only reason why Japan wanted to buy the ships was to prevent the Russians from doing so and that they were not really suitable because their guns would not take Japanese ammunition.

This thrust the responsibility back on Britain where the matter was discussed by the cabinet on 27 November. Inquiries were made in several quarters about the genuineness of the Russian offer. The British minister to Chile cabled that he was satisfied that Russia was bidding for the ships. After a lengthy special sitting, the British cabinet on 30 November agreed to make an offer of £1,875,000 for the two ships.[1] The offer was accepted on 2 December and the vessels joined the Royal Navy as the *Swiftsure* and *Triumph*. Lansdowne, in justifying this drastic action, wrote that the cabinet decided to buy the ships 'with the object of facilitating the execution of our own programme of naval construction and at the same time preventing a

[1] Royal archives R 24/31, Balfour to the king, 27 November 1903; and R 24/40 Balfour to the king, 30 November 1903.

disturbance of the balance of naval power to the disadvantage of our Allies'. Clearly the second was a weightier consideration than the first. 'We desire', he added, 'to strengthen their hands if they are being unduly pressed by Russia, particularly in regard to the abandonment of their treaty rights in Manchuria. On the other hand, we should be sorry if our action were to encourage the war party to make unreasonable demands.'[1] Admittedly this statement was intended to be published in justification of this extraordinary expenditure of public funds. But it reveals a dichotomy in British policy — obstruct Russia without assisting Japan too much — which was to recur in the last months of peace.

On 17 December Hayashi asked whether Britain would permit Japan, which had just dissolved her Diet and was under less financial constraint, to purchase the two Chilean ships. After consulting his colleagues, Lansdowne replied that Britain could not accept the Japanese offer for fear of its being regarded by Russia as evidence of hostility. In any case, the ships could not be delivered until March and, if war had by then started, it would not be possible to let the vessels leave Britain.

The two cruisers built in Italy for the Argentine government were bought by British brokers on behalf of Japan.[2] They sailed from Genoa on 9 January with British officers in a generally Italian crew. They were renamed *Kasuga* and *Nisshin* and, sailing under the Japanese flag, reached Japan on 16 February, just six days after the declaration of war. It seems likely that these vessels were so vital to Japan's naval strength that war was not declared until they reached the China seas. Certainly they played an important part in naval operations during the war.

Japan's motives are not at all clear. Assuming that she knew war was already certain by the end of November, it is surprising that she awakened so late to her needs. The decision to refuse was a many-sided one but probably the real reason was that her financial advisers thought the Chilean price was too high and the alleged Russian offer bogus. The British government which was well placed to know, thought that this was an error of judgment. Certainly the Japanese leaders' argument that they could not reply until they had consulted the Diet in

---

[1] FO *Japan* 567, Lansdowne to MacDonald, 3 December 1903.

[2] The Russians criticized the part which the British government had played through the brokers, Antony Gibbs. *DDF*, 2me serie, iv, no. 173.

session, seems to be shallow; the Diet was likely to be more bellicose than the government and was unlikely to question the provision of funds for such a timely purchase.[1]

Britain's motives in purchasing the Chilean vessels are fairly well documented because it was regarded as a critical issue and involved two cabinet meetings and much high-level correspondence. The claim by Lansdowne that Britain purchased the vessels to build up her naval strength, need not be taken too literally. The navy did not want or need such vessels. At the same time, they were reliable, British-built ships and, considering the tightness of money for naval shipbuilding, were quite cheap. The real motive was to prevent them falling into Russian hands. It was a gesture of sympathy towards the Japanese by the Balfour cabinet. But it has to be remembered that, when the decision was taken, it was not certain that Britain would not herself be involved in a naval war with Russia which would by its nature become world-wide and require all her available strength.[2]

BRITAIN AND NEUTRALITY

At the end of the year Britain had urgently to formulate her policy towards the approaching war. Since the prime minister and most of the ministers were out of London for Christmas, it was not possible to call together the cabinet and its members had to express their opinions in writing. The resulting exchange of letters by Balfour, Lansdowne, Selborne and Austen Chamberlain shows how far they were thinking along different lines and illustrates in a more graphic way than would have been possible if the cabinet had met, how British policy crystallized.

There was no doubt that Britain was behind Japan and against Russia. Lansdowne was disappointed with the unhelpful Russian counterproposals when they came to be known in London on 15 December; but he did not see 'that we can usefully intervene unless we are consulted'. He was quite open in speaking to the Japanese minister of the 'unsatisfactory character of the latest Russian counter-proposals'. None the less he did not rule out external mediation. On

---

[1] There is no satisfactory treatment of the episode in Japanese. *Komura gaikōshi*, i, 365–6, states that Japan was grateful to Britain for forestalling the Russian purchase but does nothing to explain Japan's actions.

[2] Bridge papers 15, Kerr to Bridge, 29 November 1903.

22 December he suggested to his colleagues that Britain should try to extract from the Russians, with the help of France and the United States, some assurances over Manchuria which the Japanese could accept. At the same time 'we should tell the Japanese distinctly that they must be content with the best bargain they can get as to Korea — the Korean clauses, barring that as to the neutral zone, are upon the whole not unsatisfactory'.[1] Balfour, however, replied:

> while I would avoid giving any advice to Japan which would enable her to say hereafter that we had got her into war, I would *not* put pressure upon her of any kind to abate her demands.

Lansdowne's suggestion would offend the sentiments of the Japanese people and 'enable the Japanese Government to transfer their well-deserved unpopularity to us'.[2] Lansdowne was inclined to disagree; he attached more importance to averting war than Balfour did: 'The most promising exit from the present situation would be found in an arrangement under which Russia might enter into an engagement, not with Japan only, but with all the Powers having Treaty rights in Manchuria, to respect those rights in any agreement which she may make with China.' He wanted Britain to 'try its hand as a mediator' and to enlist the help of the United States. Selborne dreaded the consequences of war for Japan and, while he saw great dangers in Britain's acting as sole mediator, he favoured a joint approach with France and the United States. Austen Chamberlain did not like the idea of Britain intervening unasked to cut down Japan's demands or of soliciting American intervention.[3] The members of the 'inner cabinet' were divided over the issue of mediation and decided, following Balfour's view, to take no initiative to prevent war. It was one of the few occasions when Balfour and Lansdowne differed and when the latter was overruled.

By this time there was little doubt in the Foreign Office that Japan was determined to resort to war if the need arose. Although the Russians believed that Japan was not serious about going to war, the British ministers realized that Japan must 'go to war almost at once, before the large Russian reinforcement now in the Mediterranean gets out'.[4]

---

[1] Balfour papers Add. MSS 49728, Lansdowne to Balfour, 22 December 1903.

[2] Cabinet I/4/43, Balfour to Lansdowne, 22 December 1903; Dugdale, *Balfour*, i, 376.

[3] Cabinet I/4/43, memoranda by Selborne and A. Chamberlain, 25 December 1903.

[4] Balfour papers Add. MSS 49728, Selborne to Lansdowne, 21 December 1903.

How did Britain assess Japan's chances in war? One aspect was the prospect of Japan's home islands being invaded. The British ministers were agreed that this was unlikely, if not impossible. The other aspect was Japan's capacity to wage an overseas campaign against Russia. It was thought that, if Japan did not occupy Korea at the start of the war, then Russia would. Balfour could not 'see how, unaided by some other naval power, the Japanese are to land any effective force in Corea or Manchuria, and, if I am right, it appears to me that both diplomatically and strategically they are in a very helpless position'.[1] He referred the problem for discussion by the Defence Committee. Britain's ministers were divided about Japan's capacity. While Balfour was sceptical over Japan, the First Lord of the Admiralty, Selborne, wrote thus to the commander-in-chief in the far east:

Japan is a little the stronger but, when both Russian and Japanese reinforcements now in the Mediterranean have reached the scene of the action, the paper preponderance will have passed to the Russians. It is not, however, paper strength which will decide the day but the personal element, the skill of the Admirals and the shooting of the men.[2]

It is evident from all this that Britain was by no means as confident that Japan would triumph in any war with Russia as some have indicated.[3]

Would Britain become involved in any such war? Balfour considered that she was not bound in law, in equity or in honour to join Japan in a war against Russia single-handed and her policy in the event of hostilities must be dictated solely by a cool calculation of national interests.[4] This statement involves a new awareness about the alliance: that any action arising out of it would always be considered in the light of self-interest. 'If we interpret the Japanese Alliance as one requiring us to help Japan whenever she gets to loggerheads with Russia, it is absurdly one-sided. Japan certainly would not help *us* to prevent Amsterdam falling into the hands of the French, or Holland falling into the hands of the Germans. Nor would she involve herself in any quarrel we might have over the north-west frontier of India.'[5] Of course these last contingencies were expressly ruled out by the first alliance. But Balfour's idea is clear: Japan would apply the criterion of

[1] Balfour papers Add. MSS 49728, Balfour to Lansdowne, 22 December 1903.
[2] Bridge papers 15, Selborne to Bridge, 11 January 1904.
[3] E.g. Chang, *Anglo-Japanese alliance*, p. 105.
[4] Cabinet I/4/39, note by Balfour, 29 December 1903.
[5] Balfour papers Add. MSS 49707, Balfour to Selborne, 29 December 1903.

self-interest before being implicated in action under the alliance; similarly, Britain should try desperately to avoid war over Manchuria and Korea, which were not part of Britain's traditional interests.

On 29 December Hayashi explained to Lansdowne the course of negotiations with Russia and inquired whether Japan might expect support from Britain in the event of war and in what direction. Asked what sort of aid Japan expected, Hayashi mentioned docking and coaling facilities and added unofficially that Britain might help much by observing a 'benevolent neutrality'. All that the alliance required was neutrality; and Lansdowne replied that Britain intended to follow a policy of strict neutrality. The Japanese accepted this with dignity, saying that 'they could neither ask nor expect anything more'.[1] The notion that Britain, either in theory or in practice, offered Japan 'benevolent neutrality' is incorrect and unfounded.[2]

But this did not exhaust the possibilities of Britain being drawn into war. 'If Japan goes to war', Balfour wrote, 'who is going to lay long odds that we are not at loggerheads with Russia within six months?'[3] Thus China or some minor power might join Russia and bring the alliance technically into play. Or the need might arise without the alliance being involved at all. Thus, if the war went badly for Japan, the British public might force the government to intervene on behalf of the Japanese. This is a useful corrective to the view that Britain never seriously imagined that she would have to intervene, except by the action of France.

Early in the New Year, the subject came before the Defence Committee. It was agreed that Britain could neither issue a threat to Russia nor a guarantee to Japan but should take certain precautions in case of involvement; there was the possibility that, if Russia were joined by China, Britain might have to join Japan — but that prospect was fortunately remote.[4] Certain military measures were taken in preparation.

The Japanese were acutely aware of the inadequacy of their financial resources for war. The cabinet foresaw a long war for which the funds would not be available in Japan in anything like the quantity required. Since October the government had been negotiating through Hayashi

---

[1] *NGB* 36/I, no. 51.   [2] Malozemoff, p. 246.

[3] Balfour papers Add. MSS 49720, Balfour to Brodrick, 28 October 1903.

[4] Cabinet 2/1, C.I.D. meeting, 4 January 1904; 4/1/128, memorandum by Balfour, 2 January 1904.

with one of the London financial houses, Samuel Samuels, to see whether it would undertake to raise a large loan. The company was prepared to accept if the British government would guarantee the loan and put out feelers in government circles.[1] Lansdowne consulted his cabinet colleagues, arguing that, if Britain guaranteed the loan, it would 'clinch their friendship for us'. The scheme was rejected by Austen Chamberlain as chancellor of the exchequer.[2] But Lansdowne told the company that, if an application were received from the Japanese government, it would be most earnestly considered.[3] He gave no promise but was more optimistic than the reaction of his colleagues would have justified.

The need for money became more urgent in December. On 24 December the Japanese cabinet decided to ask Britain for a loan. Hayashi was instructed to inquire what sort of help Japan might expect from Britain in event of war and to what extent. Because of Christmas festivities, Hayashi was not immediately able to meet Lansdowne. The foreign secretary received two calls from Sir Marcus Samuel, a director of Samuel Samuels, which operated in Japan as the agent for Rothschilds, and was told that Samuels had been invited by Japan to ask whether the British government would make a loan of £20 million or, failing that, £10 million. Lansdowne held out no hope of providing such assistance. Meanwhile at the meeting between Hayashi and Lansdowne on 29 December, which has already been mentioned, Hayashi, expressing his own opinion, inquired whether Britain might lend the Japanese money. The foreign secretary said that Sir Marcus Samuel had already sounded him but there were serious difficulties in the way of such a transaction.[4]

Meanwhile the Japanese government, deducing that it was unwise to leave private companies to handle such delicate issues, decided to make a direct diplomatic approach. In a message of 31 December, it stated that it 'would feel more secure if the British government could offer financial assistance before the war breaks out'.[5] This was the first official request for financial assistance. If Japan were successful in the war, the Japanese argued, the results of her efforts would be equally

[1] *Komura gaikōshi*, i, 407.
[2] Balfour papers Add. MSS 49728, Lansdowne to Balfour, 28 October 1903.
[3] *Komura gaikōshi*, i, 407.
[4] *BD*, ii, no. 265; *Komura gaikōshi*, i, 408; FO *Japan* 564, Lansdowne to MacDonald, 31 December 1903.
[5] *NGB* 36/I, no. 51.

T

shared by all those with commercial interests in Manchuria. When Hayashi passed over this note on New Year's day, the foreign secretary did not close the door completely but he held out little hope either of giving Japan a loan from government sources or of guaranteeing a private loan.[1] Disappointed at Britain's reaction, Komura instructed Hayashi on 3 January to make a further appeal.

Japan's requests were referred to the chancellor of the exchequer together with various suggestions about how aid could be provided. Austen Chamberlain, who was the mouthpiece for Treasury objections to giving any aid, replied that 'the moment is not opportune for raising any new loans in the London market which, owing to our own large borrowings during the Transvaal war, is overstocked with what are known as "Gilt-edged" securities'; if the government were to guarantee a loan, it would be open to the same objections as increased government borrowings. On 4 January Lansdowne conveyed the gist of this to Hayashi.[2] The minister, however, made a final appeal for 'some private arrangement between the two governments' and a meeting was arranged between him and Austen Chamberlain. The Japanese were again told of Britain's inability to offer financial aid in any form. While Hayashi was not convinced that Britain could not get the money if she really wished to do so, the Japanese cabinet accepted the position and gave up the idea of securing a loan with a British government guarantee.[3] It did not try to float a private loan in Britain or elsewhere until after the war had begun.

Britain's decision was made not only for economic but also for political reasons. Balfour was perfectly frank about his motives:

It would be difficult at any time [to find the £20,000,000] since guaranteeing a War loan to be used against Russia is as near as possible an 'act of war': indeed, morally it *is* an 'act of war'. Apart from this, money market considerations render the transaction practically impossible. And observe: if, by any unfortunate chance, we get dragged in, we shall require every shilling for ourselves.[4]

Britain considered that, if she was not going to intervene to prevent the war, she was not going to the other extreme by providing Japan

---

[1] FO *Japan* 576, Lansdowne to MacDonald, 1 January 1904.

[2] FO *Japan* 585, A. Chamberlain to Lansdowne, 4 January 1904; *Komura gaikōshi*, i, 409.

[3] *BD*, ii, nos. 268 and 269; FO *Japan* 577, MacDonald to Lansdowne, 14 January 1904.

[4] Balfour papers Add. MSS 49728, Balfour to Lansdowne, 31 December 1903; Dugdale, *Balfour*, i, 380.

with the bottomless war-chest which Russia found in Paris. Britain wanted to avoid giving the impression that she was departing from neutrality and offering active encouragement to Japan. Indeed Lansdowne admitted to Hayashi that he was actuated by political as well as financial considerations.[1] The financial grounds for refusal were plausible but it has to be remembered that Britain had offered nearly two million pounds six weeks before for the Chilean warships, though payment was not required straightaway. If money had been required, it could probably have been procured. But the objects in this case were *politically* dangerous.

LAST STAGES OF PEACE

From the end of December, the Japanese speeded up their preparations for war. The cabinet authorized special additional expenditure for the services in time of emergency and the army and navy were brought under a supreme command. At a cabinet meeting on 30 December, the diplomatic policy to be adopted towards China and Korea in the event of war was discussed. There were two alternatives: to get China to oppose Russia alongside Japan; or to get China to remain neutral and keep out of hostilities. The cabinet took the second course for a wide variety of reasons: to prevent the widening of the geographical scope of the war; to avoid interrupting the payment by China of the Boxer indemnity; and to avoid any resurgence of Yellow Peril feelings which might happen if Japan and China united to oppose Russia. By far the biggest risk was from international intervention in the war. The cabinet believed it to be most desirable to confine hostilities to Russia and Japan, otherwise, if China joined in and other powers followed, a world-wide conflagration would result.[2] The Japanese advised the Chinese authorities that, should peace be broken, they should remain neutral while Korea was to be placed under Japanese protection.

On 6 January the Russian minister passed over his country's fresh proposals to Komura. The Japanese cabinet discussed them and later Itō at an imperial council withdrew his objections to war with Russia. The council resolved that 'Russia had made no adequate concession over Korea but had even refused to enter into negotiations of any sort over Manchuria, while at the same time trying to build up its military

[1] FO *Japan* 576, Lansdowne to MacDonald, 6 January 1904.
[2] *NGB* 36/I, no. 50.

resources and tightening its grip'.[1] Japan decided to send Russia an ultimatum, though she did at least allow some time for reconsideration by Russia and for intervention by the powers if they so wished. Japan consented to this delay in her own interest because the navy minister claimed that naval preparations were incomplete. Yet it was fairly clear that only a climb-down by Russia would prevent the outbreak of war.

Although direct negotiations had reached a deadlock, there might still be a place for good offices to be offered to the two contestants. When offers were made, the Japanese did not welcome them because they considered these problems to be confined to Russia and Japan and that Russia was trying to build up an alliance of European powers against Japan as in 1895. Komura issued an official statement of policy on mediation: Japan would not agree to mediation at this juncture since Russia, in seeking or accepting good offices, did so only 'for the purpose of gaining time in order to strengthen and consolidate her position in the Far East without any desire to come to a complete and permanent understanding on the present question'. Any offer of mediation had to be made in the face of this explicit statement.[2]

On 13 January, the French foreign minister announced that he was willing to mediate but Japan refused.[3] Delcassé hinted to Britain a week later that the war could be stopped if Britain would bring pressure to bear on Japan. But Lansdowne replied that it was impossible to press Japan to modify demands, several of which seemed to be reasonable. Late in January, Lansdowne turned down the suggestion that the king should try to impress the tsar with the gravity of the situation on the ground that the Japanese had 'on no less than four occasions expressed their decided objection to mediation'. When the foreign secretary inquired whether Britain could help in finding a solution, the Japanese did not take him up.[4] Despite further approaches from France, the British government announced in parliament that Britain did not intend to put pressure upon Japan, which did not want mediation.

Japan received no reply to her final demands which were sent on 13 January. The situation was discussed at a cabinet meeting on 3 February with five genrō present and at an imperial council on the following day. On 6 February Japan broke off diplomatic relations

---

[1] *NGB* 37/I, no. 44, imperial council resolution, 12 January 1904.
[2] FO *Japan* 576, Lansdowne to MacDonald, 5 January 1904.
[3] *DDF*, 2me serie, iv, nos. 181, 185–7.
[4] FO *Japan* 576, Lansdowne to MacDonald, 29 January 1904.

which, she thought, entitled her naval squadrons to attack Russian warships in Port Arthur two days later. On 10 February the imperial rescript declaring war was issued.[1] A last-minute skirmish for peace was unsuccessful: on 7 February the Russian ambassador in London unofficially asked Lansdowne to help to resolve the Manchurian question but, although Lansdowne put the proposal to Hayashi, it was not done with great enthusiasm.[2]

Britain's policy towards Japan in these months has been subjected to certain serious criticisms.[3] The charges are: that Britain had it within her power to prevent the war but failed to take advantage of her opportunities; and that, on the contrary, she 'egged on' Japan to go to war while she was herself taking steps to avoid becoming involved. On the first criticism, it is true that Britain failed to take advantage of her opportunity for keeping the peace. But it is doubtful whether mediation in the strict diplomatic sense was ever possible in the Russo-Japanese dispute. Britain did not even offer her 'good offices' because Japan was absolutely opposed to intervention. She took the line that she would assist only if desired to do so by Japan and the Japanese leaders never asked Britain for such help. The second criticism was heard in 1904 and has frequently been repeated since. Thus, Cecil Spring Rice of the British embassy in Russia, trying to explain why Japan dared to fight, concluded that 'she was egged on by England and America'.[4] This view can be supported by some evidence. There is the oft-quoted statement by Balfour that 'even if we assume Russia to get the best of [the war], we can by no means assume that she will come out of the fight stronger than she went in'.[5] Therefore, a war, in which Britain was not implicated but which exhausted Russia, would be of great benefit to Britain. But as has been shown, the Balfour ministry took pains to avoid giving Japan any encouragement. Indeed, the head of the far-eastern department at the Foreign Office, despite his otherwise scrupulous vocabulary, noted as early as November that it was Britain's policy to say nothing 'that could be taken as "egging on" Japan to fight'.[6] All that is known of Britain's actions in these

---

[1] *NGB* 37/I, no. 40.
[2] FO *Japan* 576, Lansdowne to MacDonald, 7 February 1904.
[3] E.g. E. Brandenburg, *From Bismarck to the world war* (English translation by Annie E. Adams), London, 1927, pp. 199–200.
[4] Satow papers 9/15, Spring Rice to Satow, 24 March 1904.
[5] Cabinet I/4/39, memorandum by Balfour, 29 December 1903.
[6] FO *Japan* 568, F. A. Campbell to Lansdowne, 23 November 1903.

months supports this statement. The most effective way, in which Britain could have incited Japan to war, would have been to give promises of direct or indirect support. But the British government took care to give Japan long notice of the fact that it was determined to observe *strict* neutrality and not to offer any financial assistance. Japan could have been under no misapprehension that Britain would willingly be drawn in except as provided in the alliance itself.

Meanwhile Britain continued to negotiate with both partners in the Franco-Russian alliance. The agreements with France were signed after the war had begun.[1] Lansdowne also tried to benefit from Russia's eagerness not to fall out with Britain when war was in the offing. In November the Russian ambassador told Lansdowne that his government felt that steps should be taken to remove all sources of misunderstanding and he was to return to the Russian capital early in 1904 to report progress.[2] The Foreign Office worked out for discussion with Russia some 'heads of agreement'. When these were circulated to the cabinet on 1 January, Lansdowne was not very optimistic: he confined himself to the comment that it was 'difficult to refuse [the ambassador] some indication of our views'.[3] Instructive as they are as an indication of British policy, they were not used because of the onset of war. None the less some steps had been taken towards a settlement of differences over Afghanistan, Tibet and Persia; and a rapprochement might have been speedily reached had not war supervened in the far east, when British opinion became generally pro-Japanese.[4]

The negotiations, which led to the outbreak of war, are singularly detached from the Anglo-Japanese alliance. Japan's overture to Russia in August was not made under the alliance, although Britain had been informed of Japan's intentions. Japan's later decision for war was taken without prior consultation with Britain. It sprang from national causes which would have existed regardless of the alliance. There is not much evidence to suggest that these negotiations were the natural outcome of the alliance or that the Russo-Japanese war was the 'alliance in action'. Indeed these negotiations demonstrated only too clearly how limited a thing the alliance of 1902 was.

[1] See below, pp. 286–7. [2] *BD*, ii, no. 258.

[3] Gerald Balfour papers 41, note by Lansdowne for the cabinet, 'Proposed Agreement with Russia', 1 January 1904.

[4] Balfour papers Add. MSS 49728, Balfour to Lansdowne, 21 and 31 December 1903; Malozemoff, p. 242.

CHAPTER XIV

The Russo–Japanese War

February 1904–August 1905

IT IS NOT the purpose of this chapter to deal with the Russo-Japanese war in all its complexities nor even with the complex web of Anglo-Japanese relations during the war period. It concentrates on two areas, where the alliance was at issue. How did Britain interpret her neutrality in giving financial or military aid to Japan? How far did Britain assist in bringing the war to an end? It would appear that she tried to act wherever possible in Japan's interest though she observed neutrality and was not consulted by Japan about her conduct of the war.

BRITAIN'S NEUTRALITY

The British government left no doubt that it intended to maintain a strict neutrality. Early in February when Japan announced that negotiations were being broken off, Britain deliberately confirmed that she would fulfil her obligations under the alliance and try to prevent other powers from joining in the hostilities.[1] Japan, for her part, made it plain that she had no intention of invoking Britain's assistance as an ally unless special circumstances arose. Unlike her action in the Sino-Japanese war, Britain did not try by her mediation to restore peace after the war had begun. The British leaders realized that Japan was determined to be guided by her own interests in resolving the dispute with Russia and was not likely to be swayed by an appeal in the name of the alliance.

A declaration of neutrality did not necessarily imply that Britain might not become involved in the struggle in defence of her own interests. Just as Japan was in 1914 to declare war on Germany to suit

---

[1] FO *Japan* 585, Lansdowne to Hayashi, 6 February 1904.

herself rather than to fulfil the provisions of the British alliance, Britain might have found herself in 1904 placed in circumstances where it was necessary to enter the war. Some of these hypothetical circumstances such as the case of the Russian Black Sea fleet forcing the Dardanelles to go to the Pacific, were examined by the Committee of Imperial Defence, at the beginning of the war.[1] The unpredictable nature of the war meant that Britain had to keep her services in a state of reasonable preparedness for the duration of the emergency.

The Japanese were uncertain about Britain's true feelings towards their country at the outbreak of the war. Perhaps they had resented Britain's refusal to give financial assistance in January. They wanted to convince their ally of the righteousness of their cause and to demonstrate that the Japanese government had been forced to take up arms in self-defence. The government considered that it was necessary to prevent the growth of misunderstanding among the British people. It was evidently afraid of disaffection fomented among the people by the press, rather than of opposition from the government itself.

The Japanese leaders decided to remedy this by sending a special unofficial ambassador to Britain for the period of the war. It selected a distinguished person for the task by sending Baron Suematsu Kenchō. Suematsu had taken the Law Tripos at Cambridge in 1885, had served in the Japanese legation in London and was pro-British. He was a prominent member of the Seiyūkai party and had been home minister in Itō's cabinet of 1900–1. He was therefore a person of influence, ranking as high as Hayashi himself. To prevent misunderstandings, his instructions laid down that, whereas Hayashi would deal with the government, Suematsu would deal with liaison matters which could not appropriately be dealt with through official channels. One of his tasks would be to 'manipulate the British press'.[2] The other prominent emissary sent overseas at this time for political duties was Baron Kaneko Kentarō, who was posted to the United States and was later to play an important part at the time of the Portsmouth Peace conference. This indicates that the Japanese government was aiming to improve

---

[1] Cabinet 4/1/15B, memorandum by Balfour, 28 January 1904. The Committee of Imperial Defence which only acquired a permanent secretariat from 1904 onwards, showed its value during the early stages of the Russo-Japanese war by examining Britain's military problems systematically.

[2] *NGB* 37/38, Nichi-Ro sensō v, nos. 441 and 459. No. 441 which contains the government's version of the instructions is translated in Appendix F, while Suematsu's version is given in no. 459. Also Suematsu Kenchō, *The risen sun*.

relations with friendly countries, rather than with countries which were potentially hostile.

Suematsu was the son-in-law of Itō, who was partially responsible for his being sent and wrote to Lansdowne commending his mission. Itō recalled their meeting at Bowood, the foreign secretary's estate, early in 1902 and repeated his remark at that time that:

it was necessary for the maintenance of peace in the Orient to create a more solid and durable understanding between the two countries most interested in its [the?] affairs of Corea and Northern China and that a solid and durable understanding was possible only on the basis of Russia's cordial recognition of our actual paramount interests in Corea. . . . The high-handed policy of [the] Russian Government of late has obliged us to begin to think seriously of our future safety . . . I need only assure you that we have tried our best for the maintenance of peace, and that we had failed.[1]

It is rare indeed to find a letter from Itō written in English. It is interesting for its account of his late conversion to the need for breaking off negotiations with Russia and for embarking on war. There is also the underlying implication that it was necessary to justify Japan's decision to declare war because of some deep-rooted suspicion on Britain's part. If this is so, it was hardly necessary for the Balfour ministry did not doubt Japan's motives, although it was anxious to avoid undue commitment in the struggle.

Suematsu's immediate objective was to convince the British people through the press of the righteousness of Japan's cause and to persuade them that Japan had only taken up arms in self-defence. He was given elaborate instructions whose primary object was to prevent an anti-Japanese union of European countries, thus

The so-called doctrine of the Yellow Peril readily moves the hearts of western peoples and is nowadays popular on the continent. If we do not combat this doctrine with all our power, there is a danger that European countries will actually join together against us. By attacking the Yellow Peril doctrine in all quarters, we shall prevent the combined interference of various European powers.[2]

While the Japanese were doubtful about Britain's true attitude, they were also afraid that Germany, the home of the Yellow Peril doctrine,

---

[1] Lansdowne papers, Itō to Lansdowne, 9 February 1904.
[2] *NGB* 37/38, Nichi-Ro sensō v, no. 459. Evidently the kaiser, with his addiction to the notion of the Yellow Peril, was suspected of enlisting support for the Russian cause and working up feeling against Japan among European powers.

might combine with France to assist Russia. Thus Suematsu directed his articles not only at the British press but also at continental newspapers and periodicals.

Suematsu never doubted that Britain would remain neutral. In fact Britain's position of neutrality was strongly aided by the conclusion of the agreement with France on 8 April. The treaties dealt with Egypt, Morocco, Newfoundland, Madagascar, Siam and the New Hebrides and, according to Lansdowne, formed part of a comprehensive scheme for 'the improvement of the international relations of two great countries'.[1] To the Japanese they became known as the 'Anglo-French agreements regarding colonies'; to Europeans they were commonly but inaccurately known as the Entente Cordiale. The treaty contained no reference to the current war. Yet, in so far as it removed causes of tension between Britain and France, it made both countries even less keen to take part in the war and thus had the effect of keeping the ring for the contestants.

Japan was not consulted beforehand about these conventions as she might have expected under the 1902 treaty. There was no obligation on Britain to consult Japan in advance, since the new conventions did not apply to the far east. But Britain was joining the ally of Japan's wartime enemy; and some sort of advance intimation would have been desirable. The gist of the transaction was passed over on 9 April just after signature but before the treaties were published.[2] Suematsu shortly after his arrival in London in March, had reported that rumours were circulating about an Anglo-French agreement, which he welcomed because Japan's intention of limiting the war would gain strength thereby.[3] Apart from this, Japanese comment on the entente is rare; and this may only reveal that the Japanese government did not feel itself to be adversely affected thereby.

Did Britain conclude the agreements with a view to safeguarding herself against the entry of France into the Russo-Japanese war? There is some evidence to support this view. At the cabinet meeting on 11 December, Lansdowne had been authorized to tell the French ambassador that a war between Russia and Japan might draw Britain in and

France might find it difficult to keep out in face of her treaty obligations. It was impossible to contemplate anything at once so horrible and so absurd

---

[1] Balfour papers Add. MSS 49728, Lansdowne to Balfour, 7 April 1904.
[2] *NGB* 37/II, nos. 1260–5.   [3] *NGB* 37/38, Nichi-Ro sensō v, no. 442.

as a general war brought on by Russia's impracticable attitude in Manchuria.[1]

This desire to keep out of the far-eastern war was unquestionably one factor behind the conclusion of the entente[2] but it may not have been the major cause. Thus, when Lansdowne initially proposed an approach to France, he made no reference to eastern problems and wrote only of Britain's unsatisfactory international position 'in view of our present relations with Germany as well as Russia'.[3] Admittedly there is the coincidence that Lansdowne's early discussions with Cambon and Delcassé corresponded roughly with Japan's overtures to Russia in July and August. But it should not be assumed that war became a certainty until December. So it can scarcely be said that the Anglo-French talks were sparked off by the prospect of involvement in a far eastern war. Nor can it be argued that their progress was greatly accelerated by the coming of war. It took about six weeks from the start of the war before the conventions — or what Lansdowne called the 'Newfoundland-Egypt-Morocco labyrinth'[4] — were finally concluded.

Not all historians would agree that Britain was as anxious to remain neutral as this recital would suggest. Galperin, the Soviet historian, argues that Japan could not have gone to war without the help of Britain and, though this is less relevant to the present study, the United States; that both gave financial help which enabled Japan to buy armaments, build up her fleet and proceed with her expansion; and that Britain, in her capacity as Japan's ally, gave her every encouragement to make war. He would thus deny Britain's claim that she was maintaining strict neutrality.[5] Galperin, however, is hardly justified in blaming the British government for complicity in raising loans for Japan when these were raised from the commercial capital market which was international and free from state control.

The Japanese cabinet decided to send to London Takahashi Korekiyo, the deputy chairman of the Bank of Japan, as special representative responsible for financial negotiations. On 17 February

---

[1] Royal archives R 24/46, Balfour to the king, 11 December 1903.

[2] Among those who hold that the far-eastern crisis was the main cause of the agreements are A. J. P. Taylor, *The struggle for mastery in Europe*, p. 417; Monger, p. 128; and E. W. Edwards, 'The Japanese Alliance and the Anglo-French Agreement of 1904', *History*, no. 42 (1957), 19–27.

[3] Gerald Balfour papers 36, memorandum by Lansdowne, 10 September 1903.

[4] Balfour papers Add. MSS 49728, Lansdowne to Balfour, 7 April 1904.

[5] Galperin, pp. 216–37, 'British aid to Japan during the war'.

it resolved to float a loan on the London money market. Three months later, Takahashi reached an arrangement with a London syndicate, consisting of Parrs Bank and the Hong Kong Shanghai Bank, and a New York syndicate, consisting of Kuhn Loeb and the National City Bank, to raise a loan of £10 million sterling at 6 per cent interest. The terms of the loan caused much indignation and disappointment in Japan but the cabinet realized that the terms were as good as a borrower at war could obtain.[1] In November, Takahashi signed the contract for a second loan of £12 million at 6 per cent with an Anglo-American syndicate as before. Just after the battle of Mukden in March 1905, a further loan was arranged between the Yokohama Specie Bank and the Anglo-American syndicate for £30 million at 4½ per cent. This larger amount proved inadequate for the continuing demands of war, however, and Takahashi negotiated the fourth loan in New York in July. But the German bankers, supported by their government, tried to break the monopoly of loan operations. Japan proposed that syndicates in the three centres should each undertake a loan amounting to £10 million. When the German banks were admitted, the British banks declined. But Takahashi informed London significantly that he would go ahead without them, dividing the loan between Berlin and New York. The British banks came to heel and the fourth loan, in which the three powers shared, was concluded in July.[2]

The British government was careful to avoid offering any active assistance in raising these loans, which it treated as a purely commercial transaction. Lansdowne wrote that 'we could take no official cognizance of the matter, and we must be able to say that we had not been in any way concerned in it'.[3] It was one of the canons of the Treasury that it should intervene as little as possible in this kind of transaction and this seems to have been observed. The loans could not be regarded as a breach of neutrality. Yet Galperin is right when he argues that the war could not have lasted long without British finance. A Japanese

---

[1] Takahashi Korekiyo, *Jiden*, Tokyo, 1936, p. 659; C. Adler, *Jacob C. Schiff, his life and letters*, i, 214–15; *Komura gaikōshi*, i, 409–14.

[2] Japan's foreign loans concluded during the war

First £10 million	May 1904	6%	93.5	U.K., U.S.A.
Second £12 million	November 1904	6%	90·5	U.K., U.S.A.
Third £30 million	April 1905	4½%	90	U.K., U.S.A.
Fourth £30 million	July 1905	4½%	90	U.K., U.S.A., Germany

Prepared from FO 371/85, MacDonald to Lansdowne, 25 November 1905; Shinobu, pp. 331–41.

[3] Balfour papers Add. MSS 49728, Lansdowne to J. S. Sandars, 21 February 1904.

authority has estimated that about one-half of Japan's war expenditure was derived from these four loans and that by far the largest share came from Japan's ally, Britain.[1] But even if this was aid to a belligerent, it was not British government aid.

THE RUSSIAN FLEET

The major danger for Japanese sea power was that the Russian fleet would be augmented from Europe. The Russian Black Sea fleet might be moved through the Dardanelles. Britain reassured Japan by warning Russia and Turkey that she would regard any such move as a grave violation of treaty engagements. In the outcome, the Black Sea fleet did not pass the straits but ships of the volunteer fleet, carrying stores under the mercantile flag, did. As a result of Japanese protests, Britain urged Turkey and Russia to ensure that only merchantmen should pass the Dardanelles.[2]

The progress of the Baltic fleet which set off for the far east on 16 October, was in a different category. The British government decided that it would refuse to grant coaling facilities to these ships since they came clearly within the definition of belligerent vessels and, according to the interpretation of its legal advisers, could not be supplied by neutrals. On the other hand, Britain realized that nothing could be done to prevent the ships making for the far east.

On the evening of 21–22 October took place the Dogger Bank incident. On entering the North Sea, the Baltic fleet encountered some trawling vessels of the Hull fishing fleet in the Dogger Bank area. Mistakenly thinking that there were among them Japanese torpedo-boats about which they had received intelligence information, the Russians opened fire, sank one ship and damaged others, causing several deaths. They continued on their way without pausing to pick up the British survivors and sent no wireless report of the incident. Since it was foreseen that this would set off a series of acts of defiance

---

[1] Shinobu, pp. 352–3; Galperin, pp. 218–19; Kuroha Shigeru, 'Nichi-Ei dōmei no seiritsu to kokka zaisei mondai', *Rekishi kyōiku*, no. 5 (1957), 59.

[2] *BD*, ii, no. 285. Britain decided that it could not 'permit any ship now in the Black sea to take part in warlike operations' but there is no sign that this was ever passed over to Russia as a warning. *BD*, iv, pp. 41–60. At Britain's request Turkey refused to allow vessels of the Russian Black Sea fleet through the Straits. This did not completely resolve the case of the Russian volunteer fleet, some vessels of which were allowed to pass the Straits on certain conditions.

by the Russian fleet, there was a popular outcry to make war against Russia. Balfour decided that, unless Russia gave satisfactory assurances, the British navy would be told to prevent the Russian fleet from proceeding to the east. The Channel fleet, reinforced by six battleships, armoured cruisers and all available destroyers, assembled at Gibraltar.[1]

The Russian emperor promptly expressed his regret for the incident and promised financial reparations on a liberal scale. It was jointly agreed that the case be referred to an international court of inquiry under the Hague Convention. To this end, Russia detained at Vigo in Spain the vessels present when the incident took place although she accepted the version of the admiral that the incident had been an attack on Japanese torpedo-boats. But when Balfour spoke at Southampton on 28 October, he was able to announce that Russia had just accepted certain conditions which Britain had imposed. The cabinet on that day decided not to mobilize the fleet.

Then started the second phase of the crisis. After the Russian admiral disembarked at Vigo the officers required at the inquiry, Russia held that there was no reason why the squadron should remain there any longer. Britain tried to have the squadron detained until the inquiry was at least under way and wanted to be satisfied that the officers disembarked were really responsible and not too subordinate. Britain made further stipulations but these were not accepted. The Mediterranean fleet which was shadowing the Russians, was soon called off. Admiral Fisher who was close to Balfour during the crisis, wrote that 'it has nearly been war again. *Very near indeed*'.[2]

How near did Britain come to war? Despite naval and public opinion which would have favoured a battle, the British government had no wish for a show-down with Russia. Yet Lansdowne wrote that it looked to him on 27 October 'as if the betting was about even as between peace and war' and Austen Chamberlain shared this view as can be seen from his remark that 'we have been much nearer war than the public knows'.[3] Thus there was a distinct possibility that Britain might have gone to war with Russia in support of her own interests, not because of alliance obligations. Not that the Japanese tried to induce Britain to enter the war over the incident. But they would have

[1] *BD*, iv, pp. 5–40.

[2] Marder, *Fear God and Dread Nought*, ii, 47. Fisher to his wife, 1 November 1904.

[3] Hardinge papers 7, Lansdowne to Hardinge, 29 October 1904; papers of Mary Chamberlain, deposited in the University Library, Birmingham, Austen to Mary Chamberlain, 11 November 1904.

been happier if Britain had insisted on the detention of the squadron at Vigo. They were, as MacDonald reported, disappointed that Britain did not insist upon the admiral not going on with the fleet.[1]

Since the Russians had not been allowed the use of British ports en route to the east, they had to call on others, especially the French and the Germans, for fuel and supplies. In those months Britain received from Japan a succession of protests about (what was diplomatically called) the hospitality shown by the French to the Russian fleet in Madagascar. Lansdowne urged France not to permit the Russians to stay on for long but the French found it difficult in practice to dislodge the ships. Balfour was genuinely worried in December that 'the Japanese will enter into an angry diplomatic quarrel [with France] which may end in something worse'.[2] But nothing happened; and the fleet moved on eastward. After passing Singapore, the Baltic fleet dropped anchor in Kamranh Bay in Indochina on 13 April and used it as a rendezvous. Komura had on several occasions obtained assurances of strict neutrality from Delcassé. On 20 April he demanded that France should fulfil her undertakings by expelling the Russian vessels. While Delcassé protested his innocence, he tried to persuade Russia to remove the vessels.[3] Naturally Komura appealed to France's new partner, Britain, for her good offices. The Japanese hinted that, while it was their earnest desire to continue to localize the war, this might not be possible for long.[4] Britain, which could only interpret this as a threat that Japan was thinking of declaring war on France, had some anxious moments. Lansdowne urged the French, albeit with discretion and reserve, to order the Russians away from their ports and cautioned the Japanese against any extension of hostilities: 'it would be most unfortunate that a serious complication should arise from such a cause'. Eventually on 12 May, the French government informed Tokyo that it had instructed the authorities in Indochina that every effort should be made to get the Russian fleet to leave their waters.[5]

At the same time that Japan was appealing to Britain, the British government had worries of its own. It was of course quite possible

[1] FO *Japan* 579, MacDonald to Campbell, 11 November 1904.
[2] Balfour papers Add. MSS 49729, Balfour (Whittinghame) to Lansdowne, 31 December 1904.
[3] *DDF*, 2me série, vi, nos. 309–10, 326; *Komura gaikōshi*, i, 405–6.
[4] FO *Japan* 595, MacDonald to Lansdowne, 20 April 1905; *NGB* 37/38, Nichi-Ro sensō, i, nos. 468–79.
[5] *DDF*, 2me série, vi, nos. 396, 399, 424; *Komura gaikōshi*, i, 406.

that Britain could have been involved in the war, quite apart from the provisions of the alliance. Such a circumstance arose when the Russian fleet was off Indochina. The Admiralty sent the commander-in-chief, China Station, a message marked 'very secret indeed' that:

There is a possibility of Russian Fleet attacking you unawares, though possibility very remote, yet information received must not be ignored.[1]

It went on to say that the government did not wish ships to move up from Singapore in order to avoid any further risk of meeting the Russian fleet at sea. Again nothing happened. Doubtless the scare was based upon unreliable information. But the incident shows how the British thought they might easily be implicated in the war, even at a fairly late date, and how this might have occurred independently of the alliance.

Britain had stated that she would maintain an attitude of strict neutrality during the war. But 'strict neutrality' is capable of widely differing interpretations. The French gave it an enlarged reading and turned a blind eye to many Russian moves in their territories. Many other neutrals, including Germany, did likewise. Though Britain was unquestionably sympathetic to Japan, she was fairly scrupulous in her interpretation of her obligations as a neutral. It might have been expected from her position as Japan's ally and from her pre-war attitude over the Chilean battleships, that she would have interpreted her duty in wartime more in favour of Japan. Apart from supplying Japan with finance to wage the war, which the British government took to fall entirely within the sphere of private enterprise, she seems to have held the balance during the war years fairly evenly between Japan and Russia. This gave the Japanese some grounds for dissatisfaction. Thus Lord Percy wrote to the prime minister:

I am personally very doubtful about *popular* sentiment in Japan towards this country. The Japanese Cabinet, of course, knew the motive of the purchase of the Chilian ships and why we could not prevent the coaling of the Baltic fleet. But competent observers have doubts whether the Japanese public regard our conduct in the same light.[2]

Britain may have given the impression of being more a neutral and less an ally.

[1] Papers of Admiral Sir Gerard Noel, commander-in-chief, China station, 1905–6, deposited in the National Maritime Museum, Greenwich, Admiralty to Noel (Singapore), 20 April 1905.
[2] Balfour papers Add. MSS 49747, Percy to Balfour, 13 January 1905.

MOVES FOR MEDIATION

It might be argued that the true test of Britain's neutrality would be the extent to which she tried to bring a costly and seemingly unnecessary war to an end. What role could Britain take in any mediation for peace? Britain was Japan's ally and was not especially friendly to Russia. It was unrealistic to expect that she could take the part of a prime mover in such a mediation. Nor could France. It had to be the role for a neutral power; and the only acceptable one was the United States. Elected in November 1904 as its president, Theodore Roosevelt was keen to take on these tasks and marked out a secondary function for Britain: by using her friendship with Japan, she could get her to keep her peace terms moderate. Britain was by no means prepared to accept this role and has been criticized for wanting the war to continue.

As victories accumulated, thoughts naturally turned to peace. In the long winter campaign, Japanese armies occupied Liaoyang (4 September), Port Arthur (1 January) and finally the Manchu capital, Mukden itself (9 March). While the war at sea could not be decided until the Baltic fleet was defeated, the capture of Mukden gave Japan a victory which might lead the way to peace-making. Moreover, the battle impressed the Japanese military leaders with the enormous effort which would be involved in bringing the Russians to their knees. Russia was beginning to benefit from her rail communications: with fresh men and resources transported from European Russia, she was not hampered as much as her heavy losses would suggest. By contrast, the Japanese commanders were aware of a shortage of men and munitions which was irremediable and were in favour of peace feelers. Yamagata as chief of the general staff suggested this in a letter to the prime minister; Ōyama and Kodama, the responsible commanders in the field, wholeheartedly agreed; and Terauchi, the war minister, was also insistent on the need for ending the war.[1]

The Japanese cabinet had laid down several aspects of its views on peace. In June 1904 Japanese diplomats in Europe had been informed that Japan would not accept *either* an international congress to settle the peace *or* the intervention of third parties in reaching a settlement.[2] Komura wanted to avoid, on the one hand, anything like the Peking conference of 1900 and, on the other, the intervention of an 'honest broker', a power which would use its mediatory function to its own

---

[1] Oka, *Yamagata*, p. 95; Shinobu, p. 424.   [2] *Komura gaikōshi*, ii, 27.

advantage. Komura wanted Russia to sue for peace. But there was little likelihood of this, for the Russians were as obstinate about making peace as they had been over the original negotiations. Their leaders were divided into war and peace parties. The latter made frequent informal overtures for mediation to end the war; the former among whom the tsar was more often to be found, refused to *intercede* for peace. Since this was a basic Japanese requirement, there was not much hope of a solution unless the major powers mediated.

The fall of Port Arthur and the uprisings in Russia which culminated in the massacre of Black Sunday seemed to create an atmosphere suitable for mediation. In an exchange of messages in the last week of January, Lansdowne encouraged Roosevelt to mediate if an opening were to present itself, adding that Britain would do its 'best to secure from Japan a favourable reception of the President's proposals'.[1] But the Japanese were still unwilling. The possibility of mediation continued to be discussed intermittently in February without either of the belligerents seriously calling for peace. After the battle of Mukden on 10 March, Roosevelt offered his services, claiming that the Japanese had asked for mediation. The British government announced that they would 'second his efforts to the best of their ability, although they would, of course, be unable to bring pressure to bear on Japan with a view to her abating demands which are considered reasonable'.[2] However politely it was phrased, this statement showed the limits beyond which Britain was not prepared to go on encouraging American mediation. The British government was trying to encourage Roosevelt, who was since his re-election ready to pursue positive policies, to take an interest in the peace settlement in order to achieve an Anglo-American rapprochement in east Asia. But there were times, as in this instance, when America had to be warned of Britain's responsibilities towards Japan.

That an Anglo-American rapprochement was not merely a casual whim can be seen from the private writings of the British prime minister. At the beginning of the war, Balfour had expressed the hope that, if Russia annexed Manchuria as the price of victory, the Americans would join Britain in going to war to defend the integrity of China.[3] This gloomy prophecy was of course disproved by Japan's unexpected

---

[1] FO *United States* 2581, Lansdowne to Durand, 25 January 1905.
[2] FO *United States* 2581, Lansdowne to Durand, 16 March 1905.
[3] Lansdowne papers, Balfour to Lansdowne, 11 February 1905.

success in the war; but it shows that Balfour was not satisfied that much could be achieved by the armed strength of Britain and Japan alone. In January 1905 he repeated the same idea in slightly different form. The British diplomat, Spring Rice, had been invited by Theodore Roosevelt to visit the United States to renew their friendship and to discuss their countries' policies unofficially. Balfour prepared a draft letter for Spring Rice to serve as a brief and an answer to Roosevelt's invitation. He wrote:

If Russia, in the later steps of the war, were to be so successful as to bring Japan to her knees, the victor might extort what terms he pleased, and the Anglo-Japanese Treaty would provide no remedy. This contingency is not thought probable either here or in America. But on the Continent it is commonly regarded as certain, and in my judgment it might be worth while for the United States and Britain to consider what terms they would regard as inimical to their interests, and how they can best prevent Russia indemnifying herself for the moral and material cost of the war by appropriating a large slice of Chinese territory.

Balfour was angling for an Anglo-American treaty to prevent Russian aggression in China; 'together we are too strong for any combination of Powers to fight us'.[1] In the end the letter was not sent because it broke established Foreign Office custom; but it is likely that it was in substance communicated to Roosevelt on Spring Rice's arrival late in January. The overture, however, had only a partial success in that Roosevelt, while he repeated on several occasions his desire that the two countries should stand together on far eastern issues, insisted that there should be no formal agreement.[2]

Moreover, there came a time when Roosevelt, in offering mediation, seemed to Britain to be acting in his own interest rather than furthering the ends of her ally, Japan. Thus, on 24 March the president asked to be confidentially informed of Japan's conditions for peace; but the Japanese deliberately avoided giving a clear reply. It appeared that Roosevelt had made up his mind that peace must be concluded, even though the time might be premature for Japan to secure the most advantageous terms. It was at this stage that Britain ceased to second Roosevelt's efforts at mediation, even though she did not discontinue the general co-operation which existed between them. It was not until 21 April that the Japanese cabinet formulated its conditions for peace

[1] Dugdale, *Balfour*, i, 386–8.
[2] Lansdowne papers, Durand to Lansdowne, 30 January 1905.

and disclosed them to Roosevelt and Lansdowne. Finally on 1 June after the successful outcome of the naval battle of the Japan Sea was known, Japan took the initiative to ask Roosevelt for his good offices — not mediation — to bring the two belligerents together.[1] This she did secretly and without informing Britain. Thus, when Roosevelt did succeed in bringing both sides to agree to discuss peace, the British government assumed that it was the result of an American initiative and gave it no active support.

Britain was bitterly criticized in June and July by Roosevelt for her lack of co-operation in the cause of peace.[2] This stems from a misconception of British policy. Britain was opposed to encouraging America to force on Japan a solution not of her own choosing. There is no evidence of any official advice being given by Britain to the Japanese about the peace settlement. Japan had to act for herself and independently. To this extent there was a lack of co-operation with Roosevelt. The editors of the *British Documents on the Origins of the War* devote a section to 'the British contribution to the mediation of President Roosevelt'.[3] From this, it might appear that Britain, because of her special position under the alliance, played a large part in bringing the two sides together. This was not so. Britain took the view that undue interference by the powers in the final stages of the war was undesirable. In this, Lansdowne may have been influenced by the shrewd remark of MacDonald that:

the moment when we can be of the greatest use to [the Japanese] will be during the peace negotiations. If we stick to them then, and prevent other nations interfering, as they will most certainly try to do, and as they have done before, I think we shall continue to have a say in matters Far Eastern.[4]

If this is accepted, it would appear that Britain contented herself with a passive role in the peace-making because she felt that the less interference by outside powers the better for Japan. But how far was this merely self-interest? It is possible to argue — and difficult to disprove — that Britain thought her true interests would be better served by the war continuing until Russia was fully exhausted. Certainly Britain's anxieties over India could be relieved in this way. Be this as it may,

---

[1] *NGB* 37/38, Nichi-Ro sensō v, no. 207.

[2] Morison (ed.), *Letters of Theodore Roosevelt*, v, no. 3671; H. F. Beale, *Theodore Roosevelt and the rise of America to world power*, p. 303.

[3] *BD*, iv, p. xii and 64–107.

[4] Lansdowne papers, MacDonald to Lansdowne, 2 February 1905.

there were abundant reasons why Lansdowne did not actively support Roosevelt in his role as peace-maker.

Balfour's hopes for Anglo-American co-operation in east Asia which had been associated with Roosevelt's offers of mediation, petered out because they seemed to run counter to the other prong of Britain's far eastern policy, the alliance with Japan. Britain's failure to obtain any definite pledge of United States' support in maintaining the integrity of China, made it all the more necessary that the Japanese alliance should be strengthened. It is against this background that the revision of the alliance which took place during these same months, must be considered.

CHAPTER XV

The Alliance under Review

January–May 1905

JAPAN'S success in the Russo-Japanese war had shown that the status as a world power which she had acquired in 1902 by the British alliance was not unjustified. By force of arms, she had confirmed the title that she had formerly gained through diplomacy. During the war months the alliance had been reduced to a shadow as Britain tried to reconcile her anomalous position as Japan's ally and as a strict neutral; while she sympathized with the Japanese, she abstained from assisting their operations. But it was still a vital instrument and continued to draw the two powers together. Because of the rapid transformation wrought in the far east by Japan's victories, the original alliance was no longer wholly relevant and required to be adjusted. It is the object of the remainder of this study to consider how the alliance was modified to meet these changed circumstances. We shall begin, therefore, by examining the first stage in this process, namely, the exchanges which took place during a period of extreme tension, while the powerful Baltic fleet was moving east and north towards an engagement with the Japanese.

Katsura and his foreign minister, Komura, had been responsible for concluding the initial alliance in 1902. The alliance still remained the centrepiece of their diplomatic and defence policy. They were also anxious to continue it for the prestige which they would gain for, although the political scene was tranquil compared to prewar days, it was likely that political opposition would spring up as soon as peace was restored. There was every reason to believe that a renewal of the alliance would be acceptable to the people at large, although there were many in Japan who felt that Britain had not supported her as effectively as she might over, for example, the coaling and anchoring of the Baltic fleet.

In Britain, the renewal of the alliance had to be a secondary aspect of policy. In the prolonged party crisis over Imperial Preference, which the Balfour ministry was facing, British interests in the far east became marginal. The alliance, which was central to Japanese thinking, was by no means so vital to Britain. Yet it would be wrong to discount it completely. A successful foreign policy was one of the factors which held the tired and divided ministry together. The French treaty and the Japanese alliance became important rallying cries at Conservative meetings in the pre-election period in 1905.

The renewal of the alliance in 1905 was to some extent an issue above party. Within the Unionist party, it was supported both by the protectionists and the free traders. It was also welcomed by the Liberal supporters who had accepted the conclusion of the 1902 treaty. The Liberal Imperialists, and especially Sir Edward Grey, favoured it. It was unlikely that the 'Gladstonian Liberals', the 'Little Englanders', were so much in favour, but for the moment they held their peace. The alliance was not a serious point of criticism on the part of the opposition or the press.

RUMOURS OF THE RENEWAL

Although the 1902 treaty was not due to expire until 1907, there were veiled signs that some thought was being given to its renewal in Tokyo and London. In December 1904, the British minister in Tokyo reported that in talks with Katsura and Komura, both said that 'if Japan was successful in war, she would seek for a closer alliance with England'.[1] Quite independently it was being discussed in Britain. Lord Percy, the parliamentary under-secretary to the Foreign Office since 1903, who was responsible for speaking on foreign affairs in the House of Commons, used his friendship with the prime minister to suggest that Britain should present the Garter to the emperor of Japan and make the Japanese minister an ambassador and that Britain should now offer to renew the alliance for another period of five years. He had already mentioned the second course to Lansdowne who thought it 'worth considering'. Percy continued:

As I feel doubtful of the prolonged existence of the present Government I hope you won't mind my suggesting it to you. A press agitation is going on all over the Continent for the purpose of presenting this country as only waiting for an opportunity (when the present term of the Agreement expires

[1] Hardinge papers 7, MacDonald to Hardinge, 23 December 1904.

and when a Liberal Government favourable to an Anglo-Russian Entente is in power) to back out of the Japanese connection. Why not at once put a stop to such a campaign by taking time by the forelock and binding ourselves for another five years? We shall have the whole country behind us. And we shall frustrate possible Continental intrigues. We might at the same time invite America to join.[1]

Balfour replied that it would not be feasible to honour the emperor and increase the status of the embassy while hostilities continued. This part of the proposal was not pursued meantime.

On the renewal of the alliance, Balfour asked: 'If we renew before the natural period for renewal arrives, can there be any other inference from it than that we do not trust our successors!' It would commit the Liberal party, if they came to office. Turning to the overtures which had been made by the American ambassador, he added: 'If, indeed, we could bring in the Americans, that would be a new arrangement, and, as part of it, an extension of the Japanese Treaty would clearly be legitimate. Much, however, as I desire a Treaty with America, the difficulties — not on our side, but on theirs — are obviously immense'.[2] The American overture did not afford an opportunity to bring in Japan. But Lansdowne thought that, even without the Americans, Britain should offer Japan '*now* an extension of the Anglo-Japanese agreement for another term of 5 years', although the cabinet would have to be consulted.[3] Percy then raised what was to be a fundamental issue:

the nature of the terms upon which Japan would make peace would depend necessarily on whether she can or cannot count on the continuance of the English alliance. She cannot know this unless we either renew the Alliance now or give a binding pledge that we will not exercise the option of withdrawing when the time comes.[4]

Japan had not yet announced her peace terms and might be encouraged to put the question to Britain about her attitude. Since one of Britain's objects in arranging the renewal would be to facilitate the peace, the Liberals could not legitimately take exception to it. Britain decided not to take the initiative but to wait for an expression of Japanese views.

[1] Balfour papers Add. MSS 49747, Percy to Balfour, 13 January 1905.
[2] Balfour papers Add. MSS 49747, Balfour to Percy, 15 January 1905; the American approach is dealt with in *BD*, iv, no. 61.
[3] Balfour papers Add. MSS 49729, Lansdowne to Balfour, 16 January 1905.
[4] Balfour papers Add. MSS 49747, Percy to Balfour, 18 January 1905.

This came at a dinner given by the Japanese foreign minister on 12 February to celebrate the third anniversary of the alliance. In the presence of a large number of Japanese political leaders and the British community in Tokyo, Komura proposed the health of King Edward VII and, according to MacDonald's account, added the hope that the alliance 'would continue to grow in strength and solidity'. MacDonald also reported that Katsura had, in conversation with him, expressed the wish 'that the alliance might be extended for a further and longer period and that its provisions might be given a larger and wider scope'. MacDonald added that if Britain wished 'to enter into negotiations for an extension for a further period or a widening of the scope of the alliance or both, Japan would be found more than willing to acquiesce'.[1] But who was to take the initiative? MacDonald wrote that it might be advisable to let them 'fire first'. But the Japanese were not so keen as he thought.

When MacDonald's telegram arrived, Lansdowne replied cordially enough and remained non-committal. But he set on foot inquiries and, in doing so, may have been influenced by the Japanese victory at Mukden on 10 March when there was widespread talk of the need for peace. By 16 March, he was able to write to Washington that the Japanese might wish to ascertain, in connection with the peace negotiations, what prospects there were of a renewal of the alliance and the president might like to know that, 'were such a proposal made to us, it would be favourably considered'.[2] Perhaps the stratagem was to encourage the loquacious Americans to act as Britain's mouthpiece with the Japanese. Lansdowne was doubtless confirmed in this view when he received by sea on 23 March MacDonald's account of Komura's and Katsura's remarks. At the same time, *The Times* printed reports from its correspondent in Tokyo that three influential Tokyo papers, *Jiji Shimpō, Tokyo Asahi* and *Tokyo Keizai Zasshi*, had published articles which favoured the renewal of the alliance and the extension of its scope. A former foreign minister, Katō Takaaki, had also written in *Nichinichi Shimbun*, of which he was the manager, to the same effect.[3]

Lansdowne brought the subject before the cabinet for the first time

---

[1] FO *Japan* 673, MacDonald to Lansdowne, dispatch no. 39, 15 February 1905.
[2] FO *United States* 2581, Lansdowne to Durand, 16 March 1905.
[3] *NGB* 38/I, no. 77, p. 74; *Katō*, i, 533–4; FO *Japan* 673, MacDonald to Lansdowne, dispatch no. 40, 15 February 1905.

on 23 March. Balfour, in his report to the king, illustrated the alternatives open to Britain:

Ought we to start *pourparlers now* with respect to its renewal? If it is to be renewed, ought it to be on the old terms, or ought these to be extended and varied? If so in what direction? One suggestion well worth weighing was to turn the alliance into one offensive and defensive in favour of the *status quo* in the Far East. The effect of this would be to oblige us to aid Japan if Russia attempted, after the peace, to encroach upon Japanese rights; and Japan would be equally bound to assist us in defending the position of Afghanistan and India. These are but rough ideas, which, even if acceptable in principle to the contracting parties, will require the most careful thinking out in detail.[1]

On the authority of the cabinet, Lansdowne sounded Hayashi on the following day about his ideas and the speech which Komura had made. In his own account of the conversation, Lansdowne said that, while he could not regard the statements of Komura as an overture, he felt justified in asking for an expression of Japan's intentions. Hayashi, who was evidently without instructions, replied that he did not doubt that Japan would desire a renewal of the alliance. Lansdowne then assured him that, without anticipating the moment when renewal would arise, Britain would entertain favourably the idea of continuing the alliance for another term of years. This was the same message which had been imparted in Washington earlier in March. Hayashi's report specified three alternatives which Lansdowne offered: renew for a single year then stop; renew for a fixed period; or extend the scope beyond the present treaty. Lansdowne asked what the Japanese press meant by the alliance being given a larger and wider scope. Hayashi could not reply and referred the conversation to Tokyo, mentioning that an extension of the alliance's scope was desired by powerful groups in Britain and might suit Japan's interest quite well.[2]

Komura, however, denied that he had spoken in favour of a wider scope for the alliance: the most he had said at the dinner was that he hoped that, in the interests of the two countries and the world, the alliance would continue in future and grow in strength. Hayashi replied that it was this last aspect which had impressed the British government.[3] Komura warned Hayashi to take care in his conversations with

[1] Royal archives R 26/3, Balfour to the king, 23 March 1905.
[2] FO *Japan* 673, Lansdowne to MacDonald, 24 March 1905; *NGB* 38/I, no. 1.
[3] *NGB* 38/I, nos. 2 and 3.

Lansdowne not to commit the Japanese government to extend the scope of the alliance and even accused him of having encouraged this idea. In some indignation Hayashi replied that he had not committed his government in any way.[1] His disclaimer was accepted.

Meanwhile, in a House of Commons debate on the army estimates on 29 March, Claude Lowther, the Conservative member for Cumberland, urged on the government 'the renewal on a stronger basis of our alliance with Japan, because he saw in it the only possible means by which we could secure retrenchment and efficiency with safety to the Empire'. The relevant part of his argument ran as follows:

Our extended Indian frontier had become as vulnerable as the frontier of any European Power. . . . Russia had just completed the Transcaspian Railway at enormous expense. . . . During the last twelve months, she had completed a second great trunk line from Orenburg to Tashkend. . . . With two lines of railway completed she would, in the event of hostilities, be able to plant on our frontier an army of considerably over 500,000. . . . How, then, were we [sic] to obtain an Army efficient for the defence of our Indian frontier, which, inadequately guarded, was a direct incentive to any nation envious of our rich Indian possessions? Apart from conscription, a system which would never be tolerated in this country, because it was wholly alien to the British character, there was only one solution. . . . In another year our treaty with Japan would lapse. He urged not only that we should renew it, but that we should make it of such a character that in the event of either country's Asiatic possessions being attacked they should mutually help each other — Great Britain with her Fleet — Japan with her army. . . . Great Britain would be relieved of the upkeep of an [Indian] Army, which if brought to the huge standard of efficiency demanded by the new conditions would become an intolerable burden to the British taxpayer. . . . Even if peace were happily concluded, Japan could not ignore the fact that Russia's enormous resources enabled her to build three ships where she could build one, and to build or buy three times as quickly. . . . Not only could our Fleet guarantee her immunity from this menace, but behind its shadow she would reap the full fruits of her sacrifices and enjoy that recuperation which alone could save her from financial exhaustion.[2]

Though the essential idea of extending the alliance to India had been discussed by the cabinet on 23 March, Lowther's formulation of the case and the publicity given to it were important for the germination of the idea.

[1] *NGB* 38/I, nos. 4, 5 and 6.
[2] *British parliamentary debates*, 4th series, vol. 143, cols. 1559–62.

The Japanese government agreed to enter upon the exchange of views, leaving the duration and scope of the alliance to be discussed later. Hayashi was disappointed at Japan's reply. He suggested to his government that, after the end of the war, Russia would inevitably plan a war of revenge, that it would be to Japan's advantage to provide for this by concluding an extended alliance and that it was desirable to undertake discussions as soon as possible because the days of the Balfour cabinet were numbered and because, if there were any leakage, European powers like Germany and France might take steps to prevent the new alliance.[1]

On 6 April, Suematsu Kenchō, whose role as special emissary to Europe during the war was described previously, informed his government that 'in view of the general political atmosphere in Europe it is desirable to advance steps towards the consolidation of the Anglo-Japanese treaty with all expedition'.[2] He had earlier reported conversations with Sir Edward Carson and Gerald Balfour, two members of Balfour's ministry, who assured him that the cabinet wanted to renew the alliance. This view may have had an influence not only on the government but on the genrō. It appears that Suematsu was worried by the possible interference of European powers in the Russo-Japanese struggle and the anti-Japanese attitude of Germany which, taken together, held out the possibility of a renewed Dreibund.

Up to this point both governments had avoided expressing their intentions openly and clearly. During April and May both sides were left to consider their needs and formulate their demands.

FIRST NEGOTIATIONS

At its meeting on 8 April, the Japanese cabinet agreed that its interests would be best served by the continuation of the alliance on the same lines as 1902. It felt that the treaty did not require any change except for an adjustment to meet changed circumstances in Korea after the war. At that same cabinet, Japan decided to assume protective rights in Korea and decisions were taken to bring political into line with military

[1] *Komura gaikōshi*, ii, 163–4.
[2] *NGB* 38/I, nos. 8 and 9; *NGB* 37/38, Nichi-Ro sensō, v, no. 455. See above, pp. 284–6.

strategy. It was therefore necessary for this Korean stipulation to be included in the new alliance and for Britain's approval to be obtained. The foreign minister was authorized to undertake an exchange of views with the British government.[1] Shortly afterwards, the cabinet laid down the terms for the peace settlement with Russia, on the same lines as its other decisions. These three issues — Korea, Russia and the British alliance — were inextricably entangled in Japanese thinking.

On 16 April, Komura sent Hayashi two telegrams, the first containing a statement of the cabinet's objectives, the second a draft for an amended treaty. The most significant clause laid down that it might be necessary for Japan to take steps to preserve her special political interests in Korea. The provision for Korean independence which had been inserted in the 1902 treaty, was to be dropped; and all the safeguards which Britain had included to ensure that she was not associated with any acquisition of Korean territory, were omitted. The Japanese also asked that the duration of the new treaty be fixed at seven years *from the present date* and suggested that the sooner they came to an agreement the better.[2] This was the first indication that what was being discussed was a renewal of the treaty in 1905 rather than an undertaking to renew in 1907 at the time of its expiry. The Japanese remained as opposed to its extension beyond the far east as they had been in 1901.

On 19 April, Hayashi discussed his government's instructions with the foreign secretary, who confirmed that Britain would be glad to renew the alliance. But he could only reply after consultation with the cabinet which was about to break up for the Easter recess. Hayashi did not pass over the Japanese terms until 10 May. He justified this to Komura by saying that, since it contained an indication of future strategy in Korea, it was advisable to avoid a leakage and unwise to present it yet to the Balfour government which might go out of office during the summer.[3]

In Britain, the problem had been referred to the Committee of Imperial Defence which discussed it on 12 April, at the meeting where the needs of the Indian frontier came up for discussion. The study of the alliance by the army and navy produced a number of important

---

[1] *NGB* 38/I, nos. 10 and 250, cabinet resolutions, 8 April 1905.
[2] *NGB* 38/I, no. 13.
[3] FO *Japan* 673, Lansdowne to MacDonald, 19 April 1905; *NGB* 38/I, no. 13.

memoranda. On 10 April, Sir George Clarke as secretary of the C.I.D., prepared one which drew the conclusion that a *mere renewal* would not be of any real benefit to Britain. He thought that 'any arrangement under which a portion of the Japanese army might be rendered available to reinforce us on the Indian frontier would be a direct gain'.[1] This seems to be the first official mention of this important proposal. Clarke's view was reinforced by a memorandum to the Board of Admiralty by Captain C. L. Ottley, director of naval intelligence. He favoured the renewal of the alliance, modified so as to prevent Russian aggression into 'the whole of the Empire of Japan and of all British possessions in Asia north of the Equator'. He proposed that Japan be asked to supply, in event of the Indian frontier being threatened by Russia, 'a large contingent of (say) 150,000 troops . . . which could arrive in India, by a *safer route*, in as many *weeks* as a numerically equal army from home would take months'.[2] Taken together, these memoranda seem to have convinced the C.I.D. of the wisdom of including an Indian clause in the revised alliance.

When the alliance was informally discussed by the C.I.D. on 12 April, many new issues were raised about extending the scope of the treaty. It was essential, they thought, that 'provisions should be so framed as neither to constitute a menace, in reality or in appearance, to the position and interests of friendly Powers, such as France and the United States, nor to be regarded as an Anglo-Japanese alliance against Europe'. Further, the scope might be extended so as to make it operative if either party was attacked by a third power. As a safeguard against war being started by the action of a 'semi-barbarous power' without proper caution, 'the Treaty might be made operative in the case of Persia, China and Afghanistan only when they were acting in alliance with either of the Contracting Parties'. Finally, 'if we bind ourselves to place the services of our navy at the disposal of Japan in such an eventuality, we should naturally expect her to make a reciprocal promise as regards her army, which should be made available for the defence of India against external aggression'. Considerable attention was devoted in the drafting to these three points. For the present the alliance was referred to the War Office, the Admiralty and the India Office for study. It was above all necessary to obtain Indian views on

[1] Cabinet 17/54, memorandum by Clarke, 10 April 1905.
[2] Cabinet 17/67, memorandum by Ottley, prepared for Admiralty on 8 April and subsequently amended.

whether there was scope for Japanese troops to co-operate with British Indian troops. Meanwhile the Admiralty came out strongly in favour of renewing the alliance on an extended basis.[1]

Lansdowne informed the cabinet on 3 May that the British idea of extending the scope of the alliance had been explicitly rejected by the Japanese. Discussing what steps should next be taken, the cabinet decided that 'although an extension of the treaty such as would guarantee Japan against attack by a single Power, and would ensure Japanese assistance if India were threatened, might be highly advantageous to both Powers, it was not our business to sue for it *in forma pauperis*'.[2] It was agreed to let the matter lie until the Japanese altered their views. Lansdowne met Hayashi but was unable to supply a statement of British views.

The Japanese cabinet now claimed that it was keen to proceed with the renewal of the alliance as it 'would serve as an indication to other Powers of the course of action' which Japan was likely to pursue. Komura tried to impress MacDonald on several occasions with the need for haste.[3] Evidently the Japanese wanted to ensure that the discussions were not interrupted by the Balfour ministry's resignation. At a further meeting with Lansdowne on 10 May, Hayashi passed over the form of the agreement which Japan would be willing to accept. But the more Japan called for haste, the more Britain became aware that the alliance could be renewed on the British, and not the attenuated Japanese, terms.[4]

Inquiries were continuing in Britain. Clarke in a further memorandum advised the government against accepting Japan's proposals for a simple renewal of the existing treaty. In return for the naval protection which Britain would afford, Japan should undertake to supply (say) 150,000 troops for the defence of the Indian frontier.[5] Lansdowne was also advised by Charles Hardinge, who was on leave from St Petersburg, that an agreement with Japan could lead to Britain's coming to terms with Russia after the war. What weight

---

[1] Cabinet 2/1, minutes of 70th meeting, C.I.D., 12 April 1905; *Fisher papers*, ii, 75.

[2] Royal archives, R 26/14, Balfour to the king, 3 May 1905.

[3] FO *Japan* 673, MacDonald to Lansdowne, 5 May 1905.

[4] FO *Japan* 673, Lansdowne to MacDonald, 10 May 1905; there are no published Japanese documents on this subject between 19 April and 17 May.

[5] Papers of Lord Sydenham (Sir George Clarke), deposited in the Manuscripts room, British Museum, Add. MSS 50836, note by Clarke, 'Future relations of Great Britain and Japan', 4 May 1905.

Lansdowne gave to Hardinge's recommendation is difficult to tell; but Hardinge was certainly influential in court circles.[1]

On 16 May the British cabinet again discussed the alliance and concluded:

we, though firmly adhering to the policy of renewal, see some difficulty in renewing at a period so far anterior to the natural expiry of the existing treaty. If the treaty was to be extended in *scope*, this would supply a sufficient reason for immediate action. If, on the other hand, the Japanese Government desire an extension *in time*, without any alteration of *substance*, there seem to be strong reasons against immediate action and few reasons in its favour.

Britain had finally decided to hold out for the expanded terms. Yet Lansdowne was to make it clear to Japan '*before* the issue of the coming naval battle is known, that whatever its event we are wedded to the principle of the alliance' since it would be altogether unworthy of the British government to give the impression that they were mere 'waiters on fortune', only prepared to assist the successful.[2] This is a reminder that Britain's decision was taken in the light of the steady progress of the Russian squadron towards Japanese waters. While many people in Britain foresaw a Japanese victory, there were also many who had grave doubts. Balfour speculated on whether the Russian odyssey might not end in a maritime reverse for the Japanese. On 28 April, Admiral Fisher wrote that the Admiralty had 'made a very careful scrutiny of possibilities this morning, and I regret to say the result is to the disadvantage of the Japanese'.[3] Thus Britain confirmed her intention to renew the alliance without any real certainty of victory for Japan.

On 17 May Lansdowne passed over the cabinet's assurance and repeated to Hayashi the now familiar argument that it would be easier to justify the premature renewal of the alliance if its terms were revised and its scope enlarged. He was more explicit about Britain's wishes: 'the parties might undertake to assist one another in the event of either of them being unprovokedly attacked, whether a third Power had previously intervened or not, and . . . in return for the promise that Great Britain would place the whole of her naval resources at the disposal of Japan, in the event of Japan being attacked by a *single Power*, Japan might on her side undertake to assist Great Britain, by

[1] Hardinge, *Old diplomacy*, p. 115.
[2] Royal archives R 26/22, Balfour to the king, 16 May 1905.
[3] Marder, *Fear God and Dread Nought*, ii, nos. 18 and 20.

land as well as by sea, within certain geographical limits'.[1] This was to convert the existing defensive alliance into an offensive-defensive one and to confer added security on Japan. Lansdowne went on to say that Russia, faced by this declaration of Anglo-Japanese co-operation in the far east, 'would almost certainly turn her attention to other parts of the Asiatic continent, with the result that Britain would be more seriously threatened than at present upon the Indian frontier and at other points'. Lansdowne was asking for some compensating advantage in India in return for the additional naval liability which she would thus assume.

JAPAN ACCEPTS IN PRINCIPLE

In order to influence his government over these new British terms, Hayashi sent a special telegram, putting the 'extended alliance' in the setting of the European political scene. He advocated a strengthening of the alliance not only to prevent a Russian war of revenge for many years but also for the following three reasons:

1. Japan could obtain the sympathy and assistance of practically all the powers (United States, Italy and France) at the peace conference;
2. Japan could neutralise the schemes which were being devised by the Russians and French at present to form a European union to oppose Japan under the banner of the Yellow Peril;
3. relations between the Japanese and Anglo-Saxon peoples (British and Americans) would improve and objections to Japanese labourers on racial grounds in British colonies and in America might be withdrawn.

Hayashi concluded that it was to Japan's advantage to enlarge the alliance on the basis suggested by Lansdowne. Komura replied that his views would be duly considered.[2]

As at the corresponding point in the negotiations in 1901, Komura wrote for the Japanese cabinet a lengthy memorandum, containing a reasoned argument in favour of accepting in essence the British proposal. He believed that it was necessary to revise the agreement quickly 'while *Britain's confidence remains unaltered* and its cabinet does not go out of office'. He stressed the usefulness of the alliance on the new basis, the protection it would afford against Russian revenge and

---

[1] Fo *Japan* 673, Lansdowne to MacDonald, 17 May 1905 [my italics]; *NGB* 38/I, no. 15; *Komura gaikōshi*, ii, 165.
[2] *NGB* 38/I, nos. 16 and 17; *Komura gaikōshi*, ii, 166 (Appendix G).

x

the co-operation it would guarantee to Japan in the event of her isolation after the war. His memorandum contains some evidence that Hayashi's recommendations had had some effect.[1] Councils were held to discuss this and other important business on 23 and 24 May. The cabinet, and subsequently the genrō and the chiefs of staff, decided to accept the British proposals, altering the present treaty to an offensive-defensive alliance and agreeing to extend the scope to cover India and countries to the east. Komura informed MacDonald that the resolution was passed without a single dissentient voice.[2]

On 26 May Hayashi met Lansdowne to pass over Japan's reply. While the Japanese claimed that it was not a draft treaty, the reply was drawn up in that form, containing 6 articles and 3 separate articles of which the latter were to be kept secret. The objects of the allies were defined as peace and the protection of their interests. Clauses which extended the scope of the agreement to apply to India and to cover an offensive-defensive alliance, were included. It was to remain valid for ten years from the date of signature. But the Japanese introduced two new clauses dealing with Korea:

Article IV. The right of Japan to take such measures as she may deem right and necessary in order to safeguard her special political, military and economical interests in Corea is fully recognised by Great Britain.
Special Separate Article III. In case Japan finds it necessary to establish [a] protectorate over Corea in order to check [the] aggressive action of any third Power and to prevent complications in connection with [the] foreign relations of Corea, Great Britain engages to support the action of Japan.

These clauses were to be Japan's price for agreeing to Britain's wishes on the other points. Lansdowne promised to give them his early consideration.[3]

Why did the Japanese make these considerable concessions? There is some evidence in Komura's memorandum, in which he urged his colleagues to concentrate on long-term, rather than short-term, interests. Japan wanted long-term protection against Russia from

---

[1] *Komura gaikōshi*, ii, 167–9 (Appendix H). My italics.
[2] FO *Japan* 673, MacDonald to Lansdowne, 25 May 1905. In an undated memorandum probably written in April/May, Itō speculated about Japan's postwar position. The powers, he thought, were holding their hands until the results of the Russian naval expedition were known. As for the alliance, its continuation was being discussed. But in Britain the cabinet seemed to be ripe for a change; and it was difficult to foretell the future pattern of events there. *Itō hiroku*, i, 285–7.
[3] *NGB* 38/I, no. 20; FO *Japan* 673, Lansdowne to MacDonald, 26 and 27 May 1905.

Britain, who in turn was entitled to demand her price. Japan was thinking of the peace-making and beyond. But was she thinking of the naval battle ahead also? There is nothing in Komura's memorandum to suggest this. But there is the obvious haste with which these decisions were taken before the battle on a subject which, seemingly, could have been kept over until after the result was known. It is not that the Japanese had doubts about the result of the battle though they did not foresee the scale of their victory.[1] It appears that the Japanese wanted to accept Britain's conditions and to notify their own before the naval victory began to affect the issues.

Britain's decision to back the Japanese cause was allowed to leak out. At a Conservative rally on 1 June, Lansdowne denied that there had been any question of a withdrawal from the alliance; 'the only practical question will be whether it shall be renewed in its present form or whether we should not seek for some means of strengthening and consolidating it'.[2] The foreign secretary did not disclose that negotiations were already in progress but he was frank in admitting Britain's intentions. His object was partly to indicate Britain's confidence in Japan and partly to justify the Balfour ministry in staying on in office until this important project was accomplished.[3] Unlike 1902, when Lansdowne had kept the negotiations a closely guarded secret, they were in 1905 publicly discussed in advance. This was politically possible in Britain because the Liberal party, mindful of the possibility that, on attaining office, they would have to work the alliance, generally spoke in favour of it. Thus, in a speech on 31 May, Sir Edward Grey said that no one doubted that the obligation of maintaining the Japanese alliance under the present trying conditions was as keenly felt by the Liberals as by the Conservatives.[4]

What progress had been made over the alliance before the battle of the Japan Sea? It had been accepted that the renewal would take place in 1905 and not in 1907. This was not such a premature renewal as it might appear: if either signatory had wished to cancel the first alliance, it was required to notify its intention in January 1906 so that it would in any case have had to consider its policy in 1905. Japan wanted a

---

[1] Katsura in a speech on 22 May 1905 said that 'the end is still unfortunately far off'. *Japan Daily Mail*, 24 May 1905.

[2] *The Times*, 2 June 1905.

[3] *British parliamentary debates*, 4th series, vol. 151, speech by Sir Charles Dilke, 3 August 1905, cols. 111–14.

[4] *The Times*, 1 June 1905.

simple renewal of the 1902 treaty for a prolonged period while Britain wanted an expansion of it. With Britain occupying the stronger bargaining position the latter view prevailed. By 26 May the Japanese had (in Balfour's words) 'somewhat unexpectedly accepted our view' that the alliance should be extended. Their reply was by no means a *carte blanche* acceptance of Britain's wishes: it only approved the basic principle of extension and details still had to be worked out. It was not until the first British draft on 10 June that these extensions were generally defined and even then only from the British point of view. Indeed the alliance was held up by differences over these extensions rather than by opposition to its renewal.

The extensions contemplated were of two kinds: covering the nature of the alliance and its geographical scope. These extensions which made the alliance of 1905 more complicated than its predecessor, involved considerable examination of the issues in both countries. It is therefore convenient to pause at this stage in the narrative to analyse the changes sought and ask why they were thought to be desirable.

ENLARGEMENT IN SCOPE

The British prime minister wrote that his country's object was that 'the Treaty should be renewed on new lines, and with a much extended scope'.[1] By 'new lines', he meant that either party to the new alliance would be required to go to the aid of the other if it were attacked by any third power. This considerably strengthened the obligation laid down in the 1902 alliance where one signatory was only liable to assist the other when it was attacked by more than one power. The new alliance would continue to be aimed at Russia and be designed to prevent her from attacking Japanese or British interests. But why was the nature of the alliance changed? It was primarily a British proposal and can be traced through various stages, first in the cabinet deliberations of 23 March when Balfour toyed with this idea in dilettante fashion and later at the C.I.D. meeting on 12 April. In preparation for the second, two memoranda were prepared. Sir George Clarke, the secretary of the Committee of Imperial Defence, argued that in the new alliance the contracting powers should 'bind themselves to resist by force any attempted aggression against the territory in question'. In

---

[1] Cabinet 1/5/28, memorandum by Balfour for the cabinet, 27 May 1905; reprinted with postscript, 1 June.

an Admiralty memorandum, the director of naval intelligence recommended that it would be eminently desirable from the naval point of view 'if the existing compact were expanded so as to take effect when any single Power [attacked either of the signatories]'. Neither of these memoranda explains clearly the reasons for the change. Ottley suggests that it would have naval advantages for Britain:

> Russia might build a fleet against Japan alone, but she could not reasonably hope to outrival Japan and Great Britain combined, and such a modification of the Alliance might conceivably lead to an indefinite abandonment of her aspirations to sea power. . . . In that case Great Britain would be freed from the perpetual menace which the expansion of the Russian fleet has constituted.[1]

Apart from this ground which was too shallow to persuade the cabinet, the historian is left to his own speculations. It is plausible to suggest that since France was now a partner with Britain in an entente, it was unwise for Britain to regard her as a possible abettor of Russia. This is one reason for treating Russia alone as the potential aggressor in the second alliance. It is also arguable that this extension was offered as a bait to Japan to accept the expansion of the new treaty to cover India and served no good purpose for Britain.[2] Certainly there is no documentary evidence that the implications of this change were adequately worked out in London.

When Komura received the British proposal, he recognized that it represented a change from a defensive to an offensive-defensive alliance (Kōshu dōmei). Yet he recommended the acceptance of this important alteration on the ground that Japan would after the war have to increase her army to prepare for a war of revenge with Russia; 'but if Japan concludes a "Kōshu dōmei" with Britain and builds up its armaments to the same extent as Russia's in the far east, there should be no occasion for Russia to contemplate revenge and we should thereby help to maintain peace'.[3] In short, Komura thought that the alliance, so amended, would give the allies such a preponderance in an emergency that it would deter Russia from waging war on either party. This point was also recognized by Lansdowne who declared in a speech that this change 'would not only prevent the spread of the

---

[1] Cabinet 17/54, memorandum by Clarke, 10 April 1905; Cabinet 17/67, memorandum by Ottley, 9 May 1905.
[2] Monger, p. 193.
[3] NGB 38/I, no. 18 (Appendix D).

conflagration but prevent a conflagration from taking place at all'.[1] Unlike the 1902 treaty, the new alliance was intended to have a deterrent effect.

But there were risks as well as advantages in this: the powers would be bound to one another much more closely than in the existing alliance; one power might have to assist the other in some action which was not wholly defensive and was more or less acquisitive. Thus Balfour told the cabinet that he was afraid that Britain might be drawn into Siberian border disputes in order to satisfy Japan's ambitions. And the Japanese were similarly worried that they might be enveigled into some punitive expedition on the Indian frontier which would do them little credit. Much of the negotiation which took place in June and July was intended to limit these risks.

Balfour also wrote of the 'much extended scope' which Britain desired to give the new alliance. By this he meant primarily its extension to India. Both powers eventually approved of this arrangement for the benefits which they gained from it: Britain in India, Japan in Korea. The problem for the negotiators was to equalize these benefits. This was complicated because, as Balfour explained:

Both we and Japan have interests outside the frontiers of our respective dominions, which it is as important to safeguard as the frontiers themselves. An attack on Corea would rightly be regarded by the Japanese, and an attack on Afghanistan would rightly be regarded by us, as in no essential sense to be distinguished from an attack on Japan and on India respectively.[2]

It is necessary to consider why and how the two powers sought to safeguard these interests by the new treaty.

EXTENSION TO INDIA

The problem of Indian defence was to maintain the security of its frontiers against possible attack by Russia. Britain, it was argued, had not the manpower or the money adequately to defend the frontiers adjoining the independent countries of Afghanistan, Tibet and Persia, especially eastern Persia and Sistan. Anglo-Russian rivalry had been serious since the turn of the century and there had been a series of crises involving these territories. There was the risk that, after defeat in east Asia, Russia might intensify her efforts on India's frontiers.

[1] *The Times*, 2 June 1905.
[2] Cabinet 1/5/28, memorandum by Balfour, 27 May 1905.

Not all military men viewed this situation with equal alarm. Thus Sir George Clarke wrote it off as a popular scare:

As few people study history, and as the panic [with?] Russian schemes — real or alleged — has persisted with greater or less severity for more than a hundred years, we must not expect that the British public will feel more secure in regard to the safety of the Indian frontier than before the present war.[1]

Yet he and Balfour felt that this was a practical problem which could not be neglected.

For the time being, the most serious trouble-spot was Afghanistan.[2] The new Amir, Habibullah, cast off British suzerainty, refusing in 1901 to draw the grant which Britain had traditionally paid to his country and disdaining the use of British troops to defend its frontiers. The Dane mission was sent to Kabul in December 1904 and, after a deadlock, the treaty of alliance was renewed on 21 March 1905. Under this, Britain pledged herself to defend Afghan frontiers against Russia — a promise which Britain as a naval power with a small army was hardly capable of fulfilling. The newly established Committee of Imperial Defence frequently discussed the defence of India and was well aware of Britain's difficulty in meeting her obligations in Afghanistan.[3] All the more so as the Russians had completed the Orenburg-Tashkent railway in October 1904 and could bring troops in great numbers to within 400 miles of Kabul.

Another trouble-spot in central Asia was Sistan (Seistan), a province of eastern Persia with frontiers adjoining Afghanistan and British India. This was a time in Persia when there were disturbances which made central government difficult and when the country seemed to be ripe to fall into the lap of Russia. The British government, under strong pressure from the viceroy of India, was determined to maintain its sphere of influence in southern Persia. So far as defending its position in the Persian gulf was concerned, this was a naval problem and did not present undue difficulties. Sistan was different: the government of India insisted that it was essential for the defence of its north-west frontier; the difficulty was that it could only be defended by

[1] Cabinet 17/54, memorandum by Clarke, 10 April 1905.
[2] For further reading, see D. P. Singhal, *India and Afghanistan, 1876–1907*, Brisbane, 1963, and W. Habberton, *Anglo-Russian relations concerning Afghanistan, 1876–1907*, Urbana, 1937.
[3] Cabinet 6/1, 6/2 and 6/3 contain C.I.D. memoranda about Indian defence.

landpower which was much more of a problem for Britain than for Russia. The British government had laid down that it could never allow Russian predominance in Sistan[1] and had sent a mission under Colonel MacMahon in 1903 to define the frontiers. Despite their conciliatory attitude towards Britain late in 1903, the Russians were not prepared to entertain Britain's claims in Sistan. During the war, the situation continued to be a source of anxiety. In 1905, Lord Kitchener reported 'that there were moves in Seistan which looked as if a forward adventurous policy were in the ascendant; and that guns and strong reinforcements had been sent to the eastern frontier of Bokhara'. Under her alliance with England, Kitchener continued, 'Japan need not move a finger to support England in Central Asia, so long as the assailant was a single power'.[2] There seems to be a suggestion here that Kitchener would have welcomed some sort of Japanese military aid against a single adversary. Sistan was only the symbol of a widespread distrust of Russia's intentions in central Asia.

The capacity of the British Indian armies to deal with this situation was in doubt. The responsibility rested with Lord Kitchener, the hero of the hour in South Africa who had gone to India as commander-in-chief in November 1902. After a year's inquiry, he reported that the condition of the Indian army was not satisfactory and put forward a scheme for reorganizing the army in 9 divisions. Apart from his more familiar recommendation for the abolition of Dual Control, which has obscured his other proposals, Kitchener made significant estimates of the manpower required in the event of war with Russia on the north-west frontier: India would require reinforcements from Britain for the first year of such a campaign of 158,700 men.[3] This pushed the responsibility back on to Britain who could only offer him 100,000. Kitchener's proposals could not be turned down for fear of his resignation but his figures were thought to be very suspect. How could he place five British divisions in Kabul so far from the railhead with the limited transport facilities available? How could he supply and feed such a force in an unproductive country like Afghanistan? Quite apart from these doubts, the Balfour cabinet was suffering from headaches

[1] *BD*, iv, no. 182, Lansdowne to Spring Rice, 25 November 1903.
[2] *Letters of Spring Rice*, i, 460.
[3] Cabinet 6/2/58D, Kitchener's redistribution scheme for the Indian army, 27 October 1903, circulated to C.I.D., January 1904.

over the reorganization of the British army. The effect of various schemes put forward since the Boer war had been to keep the army short of manpower and this led to a 'deficiency in long-service troops available for Indian and colonial drafts'. The urgency of providing some means by which the Indian garrison could be kept up to strength, wrote Austen Chamberlain, 'has overwhelmed all other army questions'.[1] This would not have mattered if there had been little prospect of Russia making trouble on the north-west frontier. But incidents like the Dogger Bank crisis which might have mushroomed into full-scale war, drew attention to the danger of Russia making mischief on the Indian frontier.[2]

The question was aired at the decisive meeting of the Defence Committee on 12 April when the Japanese alliance was also discussed. Balfour told the meeting that the constant increases which had been made in the Indian government's demands for reinforcements, placed considerable difficulty in the way of army reform at home. Finally, the committee agreed that the supply of reinforcements might be fixed at some 150,000. Needless to say, such an arrangement would leave Britain's small peacetime army heavily depleted. It was natural therefore that, by the sheer juxtaposition of the two subjects, the proposal to obtain military aid for India from the victorious Japanese army should be raised.[3]

How could the alliance be used to resolve the problems created by Indian defence? In return for a guarantee of British naval support to Japan, the Japanese should be asked for troops to be sent to India. Whether they would ever be required was debatable; but they would have an important deterrent influence. 'The fact that a large Japanese contingent would be supplied in the event of our Indian frontier being threatened would amply suffice to put an end to Russian projects in that direction — if they exist'.[4] An appropriate amendment to the new agreement offered a way out of this dilemma. On balance, the evidence suggests that this solution was hatched by the C.I.D. secretariat in London and supported by Balfour. Clarke and Ottley even suggested that Japan should be asked to promise 150,000 men,

---

[1] Austen Chamberlain papers, 43, memorandum by Austen Chamberlain, 6 February 1905.
[2] Dugdale, *Balfour*, i, 406, Balfour to Curzon, 3 November 1904.
[3] Balfour addressed the House of Commons on 11 May 1905 on this subject, *The Times*, 12 May 1905; *British parliamentary debates*, vol. 146, cols. 62–84.
[4] Sydenham papers Add. MSS 50836, note by Clarke, 4 May 1905.

the same figure that was estimated to be needed for Indian reinforcements. It was then adopted by the government; but no figure was mentioned to Japan.

But did the British Indian administrators want this? One observer states that 'the Indian military authorities are believed to be in favour of receiving such assistance'.[1] But what of the civil authorities? Lansdowne wrote that the secretary for India must have consulted the government of India[2] but, if this was done, it cannot be traced. There is no evidence that Kitchener sponsored such a project and it is unlikely that Curzon would have dreamt of soliciting Japanese aid.

While the subject was being mulled over by the cabinet, the war minister, Arnold-Forster, submitted a statement of his views. These were important because the second alliance was to be a military alliance rather than a naval one. Moreover the defence of India presented problems which were primarily military and only secondarily naval. Arnold-Forster hoped that 'the question of the extension [of the alliance] to Seistan and Persia will not be insisted upon. Whatever the nature of the Alliance, the actual interests and temper of the two nations at the time when it is invoked will be the dominant factors. . . . It is the existence of the treaty, the common policy which it will involve, and the consultations which it will bring about which are of importance, not the exact limits of the territory to which the agreement is supposed to apply'. He further urged that it should be made clear from the start 'that we shall expect Japanese military assistance to be *an addition to* and not *a substitute for* our own Army in India'. Otherwise Britain ran the danger of a reduction of armaments and preparations which could be brought about quickly but could only be slowly repaired. 'The Japanese Alliance', he argued, 'will be of value while it lasts, but if, when it comes to an end, we are found with reduced establishments and diminished power of striking, our position will be much worse than it is now.'[3] There is evidence that these views, which were eminently sensible, had their effect on the British draft. Arnold-Forster was not a popular or influential member of the ministry but on this occasion he had logic on his side. Hitherto the military view had been expressed by the C.I.D. rather than the War Office and the

[1] FO *Japan 673*, Major-General Grierson to Sanderson, 16 June 1905. This paragraph is unfortunately omitted from the text as printed in *BD*, iv, no. 127.

[2] Minute by Lansdowne on 54 above, 17 June 1905.

[3] Gerald Balfour papers, 40, memorandum by Arnold-Forster, 2 June 1905.

General Staff. Arnold-Forster had redressed the balance for the War Office.

Now it was the turn of the generals who thought it necessary to challenge the whole policy fundamentally. In a letter purporting to set out the views of the army General Staff, it was argued that it would not be prudent to place too much reliance on Japan coming to Britain's aid in India in any war to defend her special interests there; a power would only fulfil the military obligations which a treaty imposed, if the acts which it bound itself to perform were acts which its own interests required to be done; Britain could not rely on Japan's interest in Afghanistan and Persia carrying sufficient weight to induce Japan to assist Britain in India. Moreover, the General Staff argued that Japan would not dare to send troops to the other side of the Asiatic continent until she felt quite sure that any war which broke out, would not spread to her own possessions; in any future war, it was still likely that Russia would threaten Japan's standing in Korea and Manchuria and that Japan would be so fully committed that she would not be able to send forces to the Indian frontier.[1] Lansdowne rightly described this as an 'extremely important expression of opinion' which he asked to be printed for the cabinet. Though its views were over-ruled, its basic argument was valid.

The British government had also to decide on the extent of military assistance to expect in India. On the one hand, the opponents of the Japanese alliance in 1902 had complained that it was one-sided and conferred greater benefits on Japan than on Britain. In 1905 it was determined that a proper balance would be struck within the treaty. If Japan wanted special rights in Korea to be recognized, Britain should have her rights in India recognized in such a way as to secure some military assistance. On the other hand, it would be unwise to ask Japan for too much armed assistance. Balfour wrote of the 'real danger that, if a Radical Government came into power, they would reduce our Army below the limits of safety; and this danger will be greatly augmented if they think they can rely on an unlimited supply of men from Japan'.[2] For this reason and that put forward by Arnold-Forster, Japan's assistance in the defence of India would have to bear a fixed relation to the efforts which Britain herself would make to send adequate forces to that front. Since no figure was ever mentioned to

[1] FO *Japan* 673, Grierson to Sanderson, 16 June 1905, paragraph 8.
[2] Dugdale, *Balfour*, i, 390.

Japan at an official level, the whole issue was to some extent hypothetical. But the fact that domestic politics in Britain crept into these calculations is significant.

EXTENSION TO KOREA

Japan accepted the British proposal to extend the scope of the treaty to India on a strict *quid pro quo* basis. Britain's demands were only to be granted in return for her recognition of Japan's position in Korea. Komura stated bluntly that:

as a Japanese protectorate of Corea after the war was absolutely essential to the future peace of Japan the Japanese Government had considered what *quid pro quo* they could offer to Great Britain in order to induce her to acquiesce in such a protectorate and to nullify the declarations respecting the independence of Corea contained in [the] preamble and article I of [the] existing agreement.[1]

It was for this reason that Japan accepted, albeit reluctantly, the extension to India which had been suggested by Britain and rejected by Japan during the negotiations in 1901.[2]

Japan was working towards a change of policy in Korea. In the first month of the war, when Japanese forces entered the peninsula, Japan concluded a treaty which gave her wide powers to protect Korea but still recognized Korean independence and the rule of the Korean king. She was still acting within the legal framework erected by the alliance of 1902. But Japan's status changed when her armies occupied the country and she was able to advise and control the government. In May, the Korean government was asked to reject all treaties concluded with Russia and abolish Russian political privileges.[3]

In Tokyo the government was elaborating a programme for Korea. On 30 May 1904 two memoranda were placed before the genrō, the first laying down that Japan must obtain full rights of protection, both politically and militarily, and must plan the progressive development of Japan's economic interests there, the second that Japan should secure control of defence, foreign affairs and finance and take over communications and signalling installations. These were approved by the

---

[1] FO *Japan* 673, MacDonald to Lansdowne, 8 July 1905.
[2] *Komura gaikōshi*, ii, 169.
[3] *NGB* 37/I, nos. 375-6 and 450-1.

genrō and later obtained the imperial consent on 11 June. Some of these new ideas were worked out in a short treaty of three articles, signed in Seoul on 22 August, whose essence was that Japan took over Korea's foreign policy. In finance and foreign affairs, the Koreans would follow the recommendations of an adviser who would be a Japanese nominee.[1]

But what of the postwar settlement? The cabinet of 8 April 1905 which agreed to the renewal of the British alliance, also agreed to establish a protectorate over Korea by imposing upon her a treaty of protection. Japan's problem was not to impose this settlement on Korea, where it was already a *fait accompli*, but to convince Britain and the United States who were regarded by some as Korea's protectors. Japan's object was to secure a renewal of the alliance which would specify Britain's recognition of her changed status in Korea; and since this was something which Britain would only reluctantly concede, it would require some worth-while concession from Japan.[2]

Although the Japanese were unaware of it, Britain had, from January 1905 at least, admitted that Korea might have to forfeit her independent status and that a protectorate under Japan seemed to be preferable to a corrupt Korean court, rife with Russian intrigue. This was the tenour of the views of Britain's professional advisers in the area.[3] When the Japanese announced their intentions, Britain shed few tears over the loss of Korean independence and raised no objections. Balfour wrote privately that:

We have throughout [the negotiations] accepted such a reversal [of policy towards Korea] as inevitable and not only do we admit that it is indispensable from the Japanese point of view but we see no reason why we should not welcome it.[4]

In this, Britain was acting with the agreement of the United States.

These basic changes in the structure of the alliance had been agreed in principle by both sides. Its extended obligations were accepted without dispute. This was not unnatural for Japan as she was placed in May although it is not so easy to understand Britain's desire for a tighter and more exacting treaty. Over India and Korea, the two powers were prepared to make a *bargain* but this did not mean that there would not be many disagreements over details in the formulation

[1] *NGB* 37/I, nos. 390 and 414.   [2] *NGB* 38/I, no. 19.
[3] MacDonald and Jordan shared this view and urged it in private correspondence with London. Cf. *BD*, iv, no. 135.
[4] Balfour papers Add. MSS 49729, Balfour to Lansdowne, 23 August 1905.

of these clauses. Indeed these were the major issues which took up most of the negotiations in June and July.

Part of this 'bargain' — the sacrifice of Korean independence — has come in for criticism from historians. The complaint made is that the Japanese at this time gave up acknowledging Korea's territorial integrity, however ambiguous this concept was, and moved towards a policy of territorial expansion in the peninsula, while Britain accepted this change and tacitly supported Japanese ambitions there. Thus the alliance was transformed from an essentially benevolent instrument designed to maintain the *status quo* into something which condoned expansion.[1] There is some substance in this view. In 1905, if not earlier, both Japan and Britain 'wrote off' an independent Korea on the ground that she had had the opportunity to turn herself into a modernized, independent state but had failed to introduce effective reforms. Since Korea in her weakness seemed to be a ready victim for Russia, the Japanese felt entitled to intervene more conspicuously. The merits of this issue cannot be assessed here. What can be said is that for Britain to revise the alliance in such a way as to omit any reference to Korean independence, was tantamount to giving her assent to Japanese intervention in that country. It is not unlikely that Japan would have gone ahead with her plans, even without British support. Nevertheless, the second alliance, even at this drafting stage, was not an alliance of the *status quo*; it was devised to sanction political changes in east Asia.

[1] Chang, *Anglo-Japanese alliance*, pp. 204–5. Also Conroy, *Japanese Seizure of Korea* and Chong-sik Lee, *The politics of Korean nationalism*, Berkeley, 1963.

CHAPTER XVI

The Bargain Clinched

June–September 1905

'BY THE GRACE of Heaven and with the help of the Gods, our combined fleet fought the second and third Russian squadrons in the Sea of Japan on 27–28 May and succeeded in nearly annihilating them.'[1] So ran the official report of Admiral Tōgō on his resounding naval victory which was to be a vital turning-point in Japanese history.

Was it equally vital in the history of the second alliance? The approach of the Russian fleet had cast a shadow over the earlier negotiations with Britain. One of Britain's motives in offering a renewal was to give the Japanese an inkling of her moral support and encouragement for the battle. The Japanese, who could not foresee that the battle would be such an overwhelming victory for them and feared that there might be not one but a series of naval actions, agreed to Britain's terms on 24 May before the battle took place. The cabinet's action was a token of uncertainty about Japan's future security. But the decisions taken before the naval battle when Japan was bargaining at a slight disadvantage, could not be reversed when it became known that victory had been hers.

This is not to say that the naval victory was without its effect on the remainder of the negotiations. Even if the decisions already reached could not be altered, it is possible to detect a tougher attitude in Japan's bargaining after the battle. The Japanese government was still eager to go ahead with the treaty because it felt that victors were not invariably popular and were often confronted by suspicion and jealousy. It still wanted to obtain an assurance that it would not be left in isolation. But it was not prepared to accept what it considered to be Britain's unreasonable attempt to involve Japan beyond the north-west frontier of India. As a result, there was a good deal of hard bargaining,

---

[1] *Meiji hennenshi*, xii, 437. Tōgō's report was published on 15 June 1905.

although the conclusion of the treaty never seems to have been in doubt, as it had been in 1902.

On the basis of the Japanese draft of 26 May, a British counter-draft was circulated to the cabinet and to those like Sir George Clarke who were specially invited to study it.[1] Revised versions of the proposed treaty were discussed at several cabinet meetings, until a satisfactory redraft was approved by them on 9 June. Balfour explained to the king Britain's difficulty in meeting her military obligations: she could not send her military forces to assist Japan in the far east. This meant that Britain had instead to promise to offer Japan naval assistance, in order to induce her to help Britain by sending troops to India. Balfour, who was probably the member of the cabinet most keen to obtain this Japanese support, ended his report by stating that he was sanguine that a satisfactory agreement might be come to.[2]

The British re-draft was handed to Hayashi on 10 June. Many of the clauses were non-controversial and passed through into the final treaty without change. Some terms of the British draft which were later to be hotly disputed, need to be reproduced *in extenso* as the text then stood:

Article III
The right of Japan to take such measures as she may deem right and necessary in order to safeguard her special political, military and economical interests in Corea is fully recognized by Great Britain, provided always that such measures do not infringe the principle of equal opportunities for the commerce and industries of all nations.

Article IV
Japan, on the other hand, equally recognizes the special interests of Great Britain in the regions adjacent to the Indian frontier and her right to take such measures as she may deem proper and necessary in order to safeguard these interests.

Note A
After the conclusion of the present war, each of the Contracting Parties will endeavour to maintain at all times available for concentration in the waters of the Far East a naval force superior in strength to that of any European Power in those seas.

---

[1] Clarke, *My working life*, pp. 181–2.   [2] Dugdale, *Balfour*, i, 389–90.

Note B
It is agreed that Japan will, in the event of war, provide and maintain a force
which shall be equal to the force of British troops from time to time in India
up to a limit of   ,000.

It may be convenient to consider first the secret note which was
designed to set out the military-naval obligations on both sides. Note A
contained a peacetime naval obligation substantially the same as in the
secret notes attached to the 1902 treaty. In the battle of the Japan Sea,
the Russian far-eastern squadron was destroyed; and the next strongest
naval force in the far east became that of the United States with three
battleships. Britain had no intention of outrivalling the American fleet
in the Pacific and prescribed in her draft that the obligation would
relate only to European powers. The Japanese still wanted even this
attenuated guarantee. On the other side of the balance sheet, they did
not favour the obligation to send thousands of troops to India (Note
B). They omitted it deliberately from their counterdraft of 23 June
and turned down Britain's suggestion for a less specific provision.
But these were see-saw provisions: the naval obligation balanced the
military obligation. When Japan refused to undertake in advance to
send a given number of troops to India, Britain was only too glad to
withdraw the naval clause. By mutual agreement, the proposed secret
notes were discarded on 14 July and a new article was substituted
whereby military and naval talks would be arranged by military experts
'who will from time to time consult one another fully and freely upon
all questions of mutual interest',[1] thus removing in effect the commitment on either side.

This left the other see-saw provisions dealing with mutual support
and assistance in Korea and India. Komura complained that Britain
was proposing 'to extend further the geographical limits of the
alliance'; Japan was prepared to include Afghanistan as well as all
native and protected states within British India; but regions adjacent
to the Indian frontier might be taken to apply to Sistan, Tibet and
even Persia. If Japan were to admit that these were covered by the
treaty, she would be committing herself in regions where she had no
connections; Britain's interests there were quite marginal to her own
security and were different from Japan's interests in Korea which were

---

[1] FO *Japan* 673, Lansdowne to MacDonald, 14 July 1905.

Y

vital. He saw no alternative but to omit an enormous obligation of this kind from the next Japanese draft.[1]

Over Korea, Komura was generally content with the intention behind the British draft. But he redrafted the clause to specify Japan's right to take measures of guidance, control and protection in Korea. This made clear officially for the first time the Japanese intention to convert Korea into a Japanese protectorate. Britain generally conceded this important point in her counterdraft of 1 July.[2]

KATSURA AS NEGOTIATOR

Meanwhile a change took place in the Japanese negotiators. Komura was nominated to the unenviable office of chief delegate to the Peace Conference, which Itō and Katsura had declined.[3] Komura's duties as foreign minister were taken over by Katsura, who combined them with those of the prime minister from 3 July and therefore became responsible for the final stage of the British negotiations. The effect was small, though it may have slowed down the conclusion of the agreement. Katsura had always been an active coadjutor of Komura in foreign relations but the British negotiations became only one among many matters to which he now had to give his attention. Further, Komura was consulted on aspects of the alliance while he was at Portsmouth, New Hampshire, where the conference was ultimately held. A more serious delaying factor may have been the absence from Japan of Denison, the American-born adviser to the foreign ministry, who had special responsibilities for English drafts. He had gone to the United States as a member of Komura's entourage. It may be for these reasons that in the later negotiations Japan does not give the impression of having the same sure touch.

It was Katsura who replied on 6 July to the standing British draft. He again urged Japan's claims to a protectorate over Korea and refused in unequivocal language Britain's wide demands beyond the Indian frontier. Why should there be an Indian clause at all? His reply stated that Japan 'has no treaty connections with countries bordering on the Indian frontier [and] does not expect to be asked to say that it recognises Britain's right to take the measures which it deems necessary

---

[1] FO *Japan* 673, MacDonald to Lansdowne, 13 June 1905; *Komura gaikōshi*, 174–5.
[2] *Komura gaikōshi*, ii, 174.   [3] *Komura gaikōshi*, ii, 16–17.

in order to protect its interests in these territories'. The only region beyond the frontier to whose inclusion he would agree, was Afghanistan. According to a new piece of evidence which emerges from the Japanese published documents, Hayashi thought this reply rather unconciliatory and, before following his instructions, he asked Katsura to reconsider the Indian clause. Katsura replied that Japan was 'prepared to consider as perfectly legitimate within the meaning of Article II all measures which the British Government may see fit to take in regions in the proximity to the Indian frontier, provided those measures are found necessary for safeguarding their territorial rights in India itself'. By this Katsura meant that Japan would undertake to support Britain on the Indian frontier under the general alliance provisions without this being explicitly stated in a special 'Indian clause'. Hayashi informed Lansdowne of this on 14 July, too late to be discussed at the cabinet meeting on 11 July.[1]

It was at that meeting that the cabinet discussed the prickly topic of Korea. MacDonald had taken the initiative to suggest to his government that, whether Britain agreed to a Japanese protectorate in Korea or not, it would come about; hence Britain's consent counted for little and she would be well advised to close with such an offer as Japan was willing to give over the Indian frontier. In this, MacDonald misapprehended the cabinet's difficulty: it had no desire to prevent Japan from obtaining a protectorate over Korea but was afraid that the 'rights which existing treaties conferred on *other* Powers ... were likely to be interfered with by the proposed Protectorate'.[2] Lansdowne was told to make inquiries about those treaties, 'lest we should unexpectedly find ourselves in the position of having to join Japan in a conflict with some third Power — say the U.S.A. — due to the desire of the latter to defend rights which it had already secured by treaty with Korea'. The main problem was to define 'treaty rights'. If they implied the right of other powers to construct railways and telegraphs, Japan was not prepared to agree since they would only make her protectorate illusory. The British cabinet discussed the issue again on 19 July and decided not to accept 'a treaty obligation to assist Japan in any quarrel arising out of existing treaty arrangements between Korea and other countries'.[3] Lansdowne was instructed to obtain some guarantee

---

[1] *NGB* 38/I, nos. 34–7.
[2] Royal archives R 26/49, Balfour to the king, 11 July 1905
[3] Royal archives R 26/52, Balfour to the king, 19 July 1905.

against such a contingency. He saw Hayashi later in the day and passed over a draft note asking Japan for an undertaking, which need not form part of the treaty, that the article on Korea did not contemplate the adoption of any measures in violation of established treaty rights and that Japan did not consider herself entitled to call upon Britain to come to her assistance in support of such measures.[1] Britain's object was not necessarily to prohibit Japan from violating 'established treaty rights' but to ensure that it was not 'dragged into any quarrel which those rights might occasion'.[2] Over Korea, Britain was concerned about the effect of the alliance on her relations with the United States.

The issues which were holding up the signature, had now been narrowed down to India and Korea. Since there was some measure of agreement on both topics, only a formula was lacking.

Reluctant though she was, Japan raised no formal objection to the principle that she might be called upon as an ally to send forces to India. This was recognized as part of the *quid pro quo*; and Japan stood to gain from the corresponding benefits which she would gain in Korea. In practice, Japan had doubts that troops would be available, at any rate in the thousands that Britain seemed to expect. The Japanese minister for war, General Terauchi, discussed this with the British minister on 13 July. He hoped that the articles laying down the numbers of military and naval forces to be maintained would be struck out. In particular, he thought it would be a waste of strength for Japan to maintain in her home-islands for service in India a force which was not less than 'the force of British troops in India'.[3] Accepting the views of Terauchi and of his naval colleague, Britain agreed to waive any precise commitment about the number of troops to be sent.

This left only the general obligation imposed on Japan to assist British interests in India. The Japanese government did not object to this but held that it was already implicit in the agreement and did not require to be mentioned in a separate clause. Katsura therefore suggested that it was superfluous for Japan to recognize Britain's interests in India as part of the treaty. But Lansdowne argued that such a clause was essential if the treaty was to be accepted in parliament which would not tolerate a one-sided agreement. It was only as a gesture to an ally

---

[1] FO *Japan* 673, Lansdowne to MacDonald, 19 July 1905.
[2] FO *Japan* 673, Balfour to Lansdowne, 19 July 1905.
[3] FO *Japan* 673, MacDonald to Lansdowne, 14 July 1905.

that Katsura agreed to this article. On 8 August a formula was found which prevented Japan's aid being used for the extension of British territories.

Turning to Korea, the Japanese held that it was derogatory to them to have to guarantee in the proposed note those treaty rights which would be respected as a matter of course. Britain was thinking not so much of her own treaty rights, about which she already had satisfactory assurances, as of America's. Britain found it desirable to inform the United States of the forthcoming alliance and to explain her particular difficulty. The American president, Theodore Roosevelt, was at the time suspicious that Britain favoured a continuation of the Russo-Japanese struggle and was not prepared to co-operate with his attempts at mediation.[1] To prevent further suspicion, the British ambassador, Sir Mortimer Durand, explained to Roosevelt at Oyster Bay on 3 August about the alliance and assured him that Britain could 'not be compelled to go to war say with the United States in event of a violation of established Treaty rights'.[2] Durand read over the Korean article to him carefully twice and was told that it 'merely expressed in greater detail what he had himself told the Japanese'.[3]

Everything that Britain gleaned led to the impression that Roosevelt was prepared to accept the demise of Korea. Roosevelt, who had virtually taken over the control of foreign affairs since John Hay's death on 1 July, told Durand of Taft's interview with Katsura in Tokyo on 27 July. Taft had stated that 'the establishment by Japanese troops of a suzerainty over Korea to the extent of requiring that Korea enter into no foreign treaties without the consent of Japan, was the logical result of the present war'. Roosevelt completely confirmed Taft's statement; and Katsura was so informed on 7 August.[4] Lansdowne had also broached the Korean question in London to F. B. Loomis, Roosevelt's assistant secretary of state, and Senator Lodge and 'found them both strongly in favour of giving Japan a free hand there'. None of them sounded the note of alarm as to the possibility of 'inordinate Japanese predominance in Eastern Asia'. So Roosevelt was

---

[1] *Letters of Spring Rice*, i, 474, Roosevelt to Spring Rice, 16 June 1905: 'I earnestly hope that your people . . . will not permit any feeling that they would like to see both combatants exhausted to prevent them doing all they can to bring about peace.'

[2] FO *Japan* 673, Lansdowne to Durand, 29 July 1905; Lansdowne papers, Durand to Lansdowne, 4 August 1905.

[3] Lansdowne papers, Durand to Lansdowne, 10 August 1905.

[4] *NGB* 38/I, no. 193. Also *NGB* 38/I, nos. 189–92.

as much prepared to forego Korea as was Britain and was not unduly worried about her treaty rights.[1]

Roosevelt also informed Durand that Katsura had, in conversation with Taft, suggested that America should join the Anglo-Japanese alliance.[2] According to the 'Taft-Katsura conversation', Katsura recommended a 'good understanding between the three governments of Japan, United States and Great Britain' in the far east. Katsura realized that, because of the constitution, it was difficult for America to enter into a formal alliance but suggested 'some good understanding or an alliance in practice, if not in name'.[3] Taft told the Japanese prime minister that this was impossible and Roosevelt, in relating the story to Durand, did not hold out any hope that any active identification of the United States with the alliance was possible.

To remove Britain's anxieties, the Japanese government gave the undertaking that it would not disregard the treaty rights of other powers in Korea and that it recognized the binding force of Korea's existing treaties. In the Japanese view,

even the establishment of a Protectorate would not *ipso facto* terminate [the] Treaties of other Powers with Corea, and if any changes become necessary in regard to those Treaty rights, such changes will have to be made only after direct negotiations with the Powers concerned.[4]

Britain could not unreasonably conclude that there was not much likelihood of her being tied to Japan in a quarrel with the United States over treaty rights in Korea. She therefore accepted the Japanese contention that a formal exchange of notes would not be necessary. This Korean episode illustrates the fact that Britain was indifferent to the cause of Korean independence and that her main concern in the second alliance, as in the third alliance of 1911, was so to devise the treaty as to avoid coming into conflict with the United States. It also draws attention to the degree to which Katsura was anxious to win Roosevelt's goodwill.

THE ALLIANCE SIGNED

The last stage of the negotiations was held up for a while by an

[1] FO *Japan* 673, Lansdowne to Durand, 29 July 1905; *Katsura-den*, ii, 316–17.
[2] Lansdowne papers, Durand to Lansdowne, 4 August 1905.
[3] T. Dennett, *Roosevelt and the Russo-Japanese war*, London, 1925, pp. 112–14. This part of the text is not found in *NGB* 38/I, no. 193.
[4] *BD*, iv, no. 148.

unforeseen incident. On 20 July the Balfour ministry was defeated in a division in the House of Commons by 199 votes to 196 on an amendment moved in the Committee on the Irish Estimates. Hearing this, Katsura asked Hayashi whether it was better to pursue the negotiations while the Balfour cabinet was in office or to leave the question undecided, taking it up with the same cabinet after the crisis had passed or, in the event of a change of ministry, with its successors. Balfour cleared the air by announcing in the House of Commons on 24 July that, since the government party still had a majority, he did not propose to resign or to dissolve the House, which would continue in session until 11 August. The Japanese minister, therefore, advised his home government to conclude the treaty with the present government before the closing of parliament and pointed out that, even if the Balfour cabinet did resign, a Liberal ministry would have some difficulty in deviating from past principles and would probably accept the alliance.[1]

Katsura was uncertain of his own judgment on the British draft and decided on 26 July to consult Komura, to whom all recent telegrams were now sent. Komura replied in a lengthy telegram, criticizing several aspects of that draft. Katsura got Hayashi to raise Komura's criticisms with Lansdowne on 3 August.[2] This incident shows that it would be incorrect to imagine that Komura was without influence on the shape of the second alliance, because of his absence at the peace conference.

The agreement was now ready for signature. In a memorial to the throne, Katsura reported the course of negotiations since the initial decision at the cabinet meeting on 24 May and obtained authority for Hayashi to sign and seal the new agreement. On Saturday, 12 August, at 10.30 a.m., the second Anglo-Japanese treaty was signed by Hayashi and Lansdowne at the foreign secretary's residence in London.[3] It was a treaty of eight articles with no secret clauses or diplomatic notes. It bound the two powers for ten years and imposed on them a measure of co-operation in disputes arising in the far east, in India and in countries east of it. The text read as follows:

The Governments of Great Britain and Japan, being desirous of replacing the Agreement concluded between them on the 30th January 1902, by fresh

[1] *NGB* 38/I, nos. 40–2.   [2] *NGB* 38/I, nos. 43, 45 and 48.
[3] *NGB* 38/I, nos. 57–60.

stipulations, have agreed upon the following Articles, which have for their object:

(a) The consolidation and maintenance of general peace in the regions of Eastern Asia and India;

(b) The preservation of the common interests of all Powers in China by insuring the independence and integrity of the Chinese Empire and the principle of equal opportunities for the commerce and industry of all nations in China;

(c) The maintenance of the territorial rights of the High Contracting Parties in the regions of Eastern Asia and of India, and the defence of their special interests in the said regions:

Article I

It is agreed that whenever, in the opinion of either Great Britain or Japan, any of the rights and interests referred to in the preamble of this Agreement are in jeopardy, the two Governments will communicate with one another fully and frankly, and consider in common the measures which should be taken to safeguard those menaced rights or interests.

Article II

If, by reason of an unprovoked attack or aggressive action, whenever arising, on the part of any other Power or Powers, either Contracting Party should be involved in war in defence of its territorial rights or special interests mentioned in the preamble of this Agreement, the other Contracting Party will at once come to the assistance of its ally, and will conduct war in common, and make peace in mutual agreement with it.

Article III

Japan possessing paramount political, military and economic interests in Corea, Great Britain recognizes the right of Japan to take such measures of guidance, control and protection in Corea as she may deem proper and necessary to safeguard and advance those interests, provided always that such measures are not contrary to the principle of equal opportunities for the commerce and industry of all nations.

Article IV

Great Britain having a special interest in all that concerns the security of the Indian frontier, Japan recognizes her right to take such measures in the proximity of that frontier as she may find necessary for safeguarding her Indian possessions.

Article V

The High Contracting Parties agree that neither of them will, without consulting the other, enter into separate arrangements with another Power to the prejudice of the objects described in the preamble of this Agreement.

Article VI

As regards the present war between Japan and Russia, Great Britain will continue to maintain strict neutrality unless some other Power or Powers should join in hostilities against Japan, in which case Great Britain will come to the assistance of Japan and will conduct the war in common, and make peace in mutual agreement with Japan.

Article VII

The conditions under which armed assistance shall be afforded by either Power to the other in the circumstances mentioned in the present Agreement and the means by which such assistance is to be made available, will be arranged by the military and naval authorities of the Contracting Parties who will from time to time consult one another fully and freely upon all questions of mutual interest.

Article VIII

The present Agreement shall, subject to the provisions of Article VI, come into effect immediately after the date of its signature, and remain in force for ten years from that date.

As Hayashi reminded his government in a lengthy report on the negotiations, which remains one of the major sources on the Japanese side,[1] the discussions on the new treaty had lasted almost six months. Most of that time was spent in finding formulae which would safeguard the interests of the signatories in Korea and India without committing either too far and would give the impression of equality between the two signatories. Sometimes it was unpleasant for one ally to countersign the others' demands; but that was an inevitable part of the bargain. There was not the fundamental doubt about the wisdom of an alliance as such, which had been the main obstacle to the 1902 alliance.

It has been the custom to speak of the 1905 treaty as the 'renewal' of the 1902 agreement. As some writers have pointed out, the new treaty 'was no mere renewal of the terms of the alliance of 1902'.[2] Indeed, it was in many ways a new and dissimilar treaty. The clauses which

---

[1] *NGB* 38/I, no. 77, Hayashi to Katsura, 2 October 1905.
[2] *Annual Register for 1905*, p. 396.

resemble those of 1902 are the insignificant ones; the significant clauses — those relating to India and Korea — are quite new. It might be claimed that the alliance treaty of 1905 was not a renewal but in effect a separate and distinct treaty. The Japanese speak of it as the second alliance (dai-ni-kai Nichi-Ei dōmei) or as a revision of the first (kaisei dōmei). It would be preferable if the Anglo-Saxon world could follow this terminology rather than describing it as a 'renewal' of the 1902 alliance.[1]

The 1905 alliance was primarily an official alliance, springing from government initiative rather than devised in response to public opinion. On the Japanese side, its main sponsors were Katsura and Komura. Hayashi was still a major influence on his government and on the British. But policy was made in Tokyo and Hayashi was mainly a persuasive intermediary. At the Tokyo end, there was not the opposition by the genrō that had been generated by Itō and Inoue in 1901. Indeed there was comparatively little consultation with the genrō. Presumably the reason is that the alliance was no longer controversial. Until the start of the Russian war, Itō was still persuaded of the need for some settlement with Russia but he then came round to admitting the value of the alliance which was revised without the delaying tactics with which he had complicated the earlier negotiations. This illustrates a major difference between 1901 and 1905. The first alliance was a major element in a new policy; but the second alliance was an almost unobjectionable element in an established policy. In 1901 it was for the Japanese cabinet the focus of all foreign policy decisions; in 1905, one among many vital decisions to be made.

In Britain also, it was an official alliance, negotiated in London less secretively than in 1901 but with many of the same features present. Two new factors were brought to bear upon it. First, the newly constructed Committee of Imperial Defence and its secretary, Sir George Clarke, decided to use the Japanese alliance as part of the scheme of imperial defence. The danger of Russia in Asia was assessed as rationally as possible and the alliance was modified, rather over-subtly, to meet it. Thus, a wider range of considerations — defensive as well as diplomatic — were taken into account in 1905.

Second, Balfour as prime minister and chairman of the Defence Committee encouraged the conclusion of an expanded alliance, despite

[1] Cf. Galperin, p. 243. 'Britain appeared in 1902 as the initiator of one type of alliance and in 1905 of quite another.'

his doubts in 1901. He probably played a larger part in shaping the second alliance than Salisbury played in shaping the first. At a dinner given by the Junior Constitutional Club to celebrate the conclusion of the 1905 alliance, Lansdowne waived the tributes directed to himself and declared that 'there had been no prime minister who had given a closer and more unremitting attention to foreign affairs than Mr Balfour'.[1] There is every reason to believe that Balfour did play a large part in shaping foreign policy and also that there was a remarkable harmony and co-operation between himself and Lansdowne. Sir George Clarke has left it as his judgment that 'if the secret history of the last few years is ever written, it will be found that Lord Lansdowne's successes were largely due to Mr Balfour'.[2] But this is too disparaging of Lansdowne's own contribution. He was by nature a cautious diplomatist and was careful in 1905, as in 1901, to consult the prime minister and cabinet frequently over his moves. Yet, despite this tendency to back his views by wider consultation, Lansdowne had a special genius for foreign policy and played the major part in bringing into being the second alliance.[3]

PUBLICATION DEFERRED

It had always been intended that the Anglo-Japanese treaty of 1905, like that of 1902, would be published. While the treaty did not have to be ratified, it had to be placed before the legislatures of both countries and thus before the public. This had its effect upon the nature of the negotiations themselves in so far as pains had to be taken to find a formula for the controversial clauses which would be acceptable to the public.

The publication of the treaty has to be seen against the backcloth of the Portsmouth peace conference, which was exploring ways of ending the Russo-Japanese war. The conference held its first formal session on 10 August; and its last session opened on 26 August. On 1 September a protocol concerning an armistice was signed; and four

---

[1] *Annual Register for 1905*, p. 228.

[2] Sydenham papers Add. MSS 50832, Clarke to Chirol, 7 January 1906.

[3] Cf. Dugdale, *Balfour*, ii, 292–3. 'You can't expect the Prime Minister *not* to interfere with Foreign Office business. It's only when you get a combination of two men who see absolutely eye to eye and work in perfect harmony that you can avoid it. Lansdowne and myself were one of the rare cases.'

days later the treaty of peace itself. Thus the Portsmouth conference opened just before the second alliance was signed on 12 August. It was not unlikely that, if the alliance were published straight away, it would prejudge some of the issues involved and be regarded by Russia as an insult which would bring the peace talks to nought. Such a move might act to Japan's detriment in that her demands at the conference might be turned down on the ground that her postwar security had already been assured by the alliance.

During the early stages of the alliance negotiations, it was implicit in the Japanese attitude that the new alliance should be published while the war still continued. But this proved impossible because of the protracted negotiations, and unnecessary because of the decisiveness of the Russian defeat in the battle of the Japan Sea. As the peace conference drew near, Japan became less certain what effect publication would have on negotiations with Russia. On the one hand, Katsura wrote that 'since one of the reasons for the present British cabinet staying in office seems to be the conclusion of the Anglo-Japanese agreement, it is unlikely that it would accept any postponement of its publication'.[1] On the other hand, Komura urged from the United States that it was a matter of guesswork how the peace conference would progress and whether it would ultimately be successful. 'If there were any prospect of some peace settlement', he continued, 'it would certainly be better to postpone the publication of the British treaty which would only interfere with the course of negotiations. If, on the other hand, it becomes clear that the talks will ultimately be unfruitful, the publication of the alliance would probably be harmless and of some advantage to us.'[2] In Komura's view, it was wisest to leave the date of publication undecided until the negotiations at Portsmouth got under way. This policy was adopted in Tokyo and transmitted to London.

Quite independently of this, publication was discussed by the British cabinet on 3 August. Balfour reported to the king that he would have preferred to lay the treaty on the table of the House of Commons before prorogation, which was due to take place on 11 August. But this course was 'perilous in view of the impending peace negotiations. . . . It is not easy to calculate what effect the announcement of this new treaty would have on Russian susceptibilities. It might produce a condition of

---

[1] *NGB* 38/I, no. 51. *Komura gaikōshi*, ii, 180.
[2] *NGB* 38/I, no. 53. *Komura gaikōshi*, ii, 181.

irritation very unfavourable to an amicable arrangement — though the possession *in secret* of an assurance that they could count upon our fleet might make the Japanese moderate in their demands'.[1] The cabinet resolved on these grounds that no announcement should be made until the negotiation at Portsmouth was concluded. Lansdowne informed Hayashi that publication at present would be improper and indefensible.[2] It is also conceivable, he added, that if the agreement were to be revealed, any failure of the peace negotiations would be blamed on Britain. Thus, rather against Japan's expectations, the British government did not press for early publication. It had decided against an autumn election and felt that it still had a few months of life.

It can therefore be said that the influence of the alliance on the Portsmouth conference was slight. Its existence was of course known to the Japanese and to Roosevelt. Although the treaty leaked out in the London papers in the last week of August,[3] it is doubtful whether it influenced the Russian position unduly. Certainly Britain did not try during the conference to make use of the alliance by offering Japan advice.

The question of publication was not significantly discussed again until the armistice was signed on 1 September and there was a prospect of the peace treaty being concluded, as it ultimately was four days later. There were no longer the same grounds for withholding publication and Britain proposed that the announcement should be made within a week. While Katsura was considering this, he received the views of Komura. Komura's argument was that, although the details of the alliance were still not widely known, it was a public secret that it had been signed. He thought it desirable not to publish it until the Russians ratified the peace treaty, which was not likely until October. The Japanese adopted this policy and Hayashi was told to persuade Lansdowne. Britain reluctantly deferred to Japan's wishes and agreed

---

[1] Lansdowne papers, Balfour to the king, 3 August 1905.

[2] FO *Japan* 673, Lansdowne to MacDonald, 3 August 1905.

[3] The leakage was not the British government's doing; it was thought to have been the result of over-zealousness on the part of Hayashi. This destroys the validity of the deductions made by Dennett, *Roosevelt and the Russo-Japanese war*, pp. 257–8, where he concluded that the publication of the second alliance on 25 August was a reply by the Foreign Office to an appeal which Roosevelt had directed to Durand on 18 August. 'In this way the British Government rendered substantial though exclusively indirect support to the President.' The leakage was unintentional and was not an attempt by Britain to curry favour with Roosevelt.

on 12 September to postpone the announcement for a fortnight on the understanding that it would then be further discussed.[1]

The Foreign Office regarded Japan's request for a postponement as 'very tiresome'. Lansdowne was already engaged in communicating the treaty privately to a number of foreign governments in advance of publication, a practice which had been followed in 1902. This could only be done with safety if the 'date of communication' was not long before the 'date of publication'. On the assumption that the treaty would shortly be published, Britain had already passed it over to Russia and France. It was therefore with some irritation that Britain agreed to hold up publication.

On 2 September, the British ambassador in Russia, Hardinge, who was doubtless influenced by the meeting of the Russian and German emperors which had taken place at Björkö on 24 July, asked whether he might pass over the new agreement with an assurance of its un-aggressive and purely defensive intent.[2] Hardinge had just received from the Russian foreign minister, Count Lamsdorf, a note expressing his hope for 'a loyal and sincere *rapprochement* of our countries' and for 'an understanding for their reciprocal good' — an invitation, as it seemed, to take up again the negotiation for an Anglo-Russian entente which had only been interrupted by the outbreak of war. Lansdowne, who was in Ireland for the summer recess, set about preparing a reassuring dispatch which, after approval by Balfour, was sent on to Hardinge on 6 September and handed to Lamsdorf next day. The dispatch assured Russia that it was only in the case of an unprovoked attack on one of the allies by another power, and when that ally was defending its territorial rights and special interests from aggressive action, that the alliance would come into force. Moreover the treaty merely affirmed the arrangements regarding Korea which had been readily conceded by Russia at Portsmouth.[3]

In an accompanying letter to Hardinge, Lansdowne set out his attitude more informally and less defensively. He hoped that moderate Russian opinion would be reassured. The new agreement, he argued, was from the force of circumstances aimed at Russia more than at any other power, but that was inevitable:

---

[1] *NGB* 38/I, nos. 62, 64 and 65; FO *Japan* 672, Lansdowne to MacDonald, 12 September 1905.

[2] FO *Japan* 672, Hardinge to Lansdowne, 2 September 1905.

[3] *BD*, iv, nos. 166, 170.

All measures of precaution, whether they take the shape of military and naval precautions or, as in this case, of Alliances, must be directed against somebody, and no country has, it seems to me, the right to take offence because another country raises the wall of its back garden high enough to prevent an over-adventurous neighbour or that neighbour's unruly or overzealous agents from attempting to climb over it.

Finally Lansdowne gave the assurance that Britain desired to live on neighbourly terms with Russia.[1] This showed that the Conservative government had not given up the idea of pursuing the Russian rapprochement.

An assurance in similar form was sent to the British ambassador in Paris and was passed over to the new foreign minister, Rouvier, on 8 September.[2] In the case of France which was not an enemy of Japan, it would have been a courtesy on Britain's part to have given Japan notice of it in case she wished to associate herself with the communication. When the Japanese heard of it, they also gave France advance notice through their minister in Paris on 22 September.[3] Thus the partners in the Franco-Russian entente became aware of the new alliance. Would they accept the assurances as a conciliatory gesture or would they join as they had done in 1902, in a declaration of independent action, if not of defiance? Times had changed. France was by 1905 Britain's partner in the entente and the moderates in Russia were keen to win back British support. The advance communications were received with remarkable goodwill.

The next approach was to Germany. To prevent the spread of the idea that the new alliance was likely to harm German interests in the far east, which was supposed to be current among German officials, Japan communicated the treaty to Germany with appropriate assurances about her objects. Britain made a similar approach at the same time.[4]

More important than these was the approach to the United States. At Oyster Bay on 3 August, Durand had passed over the Korean clause to Theodore Roosevelt. Should the text of the treaty be given to the president, who was using his good offices to bring Russia and Japan to a settlement? Lansdowne expressed his doubts:

I am most anxious to show the President that we trust him completely, but can we be sure that the secret would be kept? I must leave it to your

---

[1] Hardinge papers 7, Lansdowne (Derreen) to Hardinge, 4 September 1905.
[2] *BD*, iv, nos. 171 and 172 (a).   [3] *NGB* 38/I, no. 71.
[4] *NGB* 38/I, nos. 69 and 72; *BD*, iv, nos. 177-8.

discretion to decide whether you can safely impart this important intelligence to him for his personal information only and under pledge of absolute secrecy.[1]

Evidently Sir Mortimer did not fancy asking Roosevelt for a pledge of secrecy — and understandably so. In the last week of August, the news of the alliance leaked out to the world press. On 5 September Durand wrote to Roosevelt that the treaty had been signed. He added that Britain felt that, by promptly concluding the agreement and thereby relieving Japan of all apprehension of vindictive action on the part of Russia, she would enable Japan to moderate her demands.[2] It is not without significance that Roosevelt was not informed until the peace of Portsmouth had been concluded. Admittedly there was a lack of liaison between Lansdowne and Durand; but there is evidence that Lansdowne felt that if it were divulged too soon, Roosevelt would use the fact to talk Japan into reducing her terms further — a form of intervention which Britain wanted to prevent.[3] Whatever Britain's fears, Roosevelt replied cordially that he had no doubt that the treaty was a powerful factor in inducing Japan to be wise and reasonable as to her peace terms. Komura probably informed Roosevelt at their meeting on 9 September.

Communication of the second alliance which was (as Komura described it) a 'public secret',[4] was more of a courtesy than anything else. Although the motives differed in each case, it had the common object of reassuring friendly powers and disarming the opposition of hostile ones. Britain was particularly anxious to maintain her cordiality with the United States and not to alienate Russia. Japan saw fit to communicate it to Germany, France, the United States and China. Yet this incident reveals the state of British and Japanese fortunes in the far east, for, while the allies did not meet with hostile reactions, they knew that they were surrounded by jealousy and suspicion.

PUBLICATION AND REACTION

On 10 September, Japan had asked for a further deferment of publication by 50 days on the ground that the war party, which had gained

---

[1] FO *Japan* 672, Lansdowne to Durand, 16 August 1905.

[2] Dennett, *Roosevelt and the Russo-Japanese war*, p. 258 footnote.

[3] FO *Japan* 672, Lansdowne to Durand, 10 September 1905. 'It was more convenient that, while negotiations were proceeding, the fact of signature having taken place should remain undisclosed.'

[4] *NGB* 38/I, no. 64; *Komura gaikōshi*, ii, 181.

ascendancy in Russia, was opposed to the ratification of the Portsmouth treaty and, if the alliance was published, it would increase the resistance. This may not have been Japan's true motive. Britain did not think so for her information suggested that there was no 'desire on the part of the Russian Government or the War Party to prevent ratification'.[1] None the less she agreed, as we have seen, to defer publication for a fortnight.[2]

It is more likely that the Katsura ministry was afraid of the anti-government campaign which was starting in Japan. It had a foretaste on 5 September when riots by the anti-peace movement took place in Tokyo at Hibiya Park as soon as the terms of the Russian peace were known. All sections of the press called upon the government to resign over the humiliating peace and begged the emperor to refuse to ratify the treaty. Press censorship was introduced and martial law declared in Tokyo. But the fury of the campaign was likely to be directed against the ratification of the treaty. It was evidently decided that the announcement of the Anglo-Japanese treaty would be used as a means of reconciling Japanese public opinion to the Portsmouth settlement. It was hoped that this, together with the visit to Japan of part of the British China squadron, could be so timed as to help towards the safe return of Komura from Portsmouth and the ratification of the treaty. This cannot be proved: there is no admission of this kind by any of the ministers or any Japanese document to support it. Yet it seems to have been widely assumed by contemporaries: the British minister was convinced that publication had been delayed to 'synchronise with the coming of the fleet and the return of Komura'.[3]

On 24 September Katsura informed Britain that, according to up-to-date information, the immediate announcement of the alliance would not affect Russia's ratification of the peace treaty and suggested that it should be published simultaneously in London and Tokyo on 27 September.[4] This was agreed. Since parliament was not in session in either country, it only required to be publicly announced.

In Japan it was announced by the premier after he had reported to the Privy Council and was published in the official gazette of 27 September without explanation. The press was generally favourable

[1] FO *Japan* 672, MacDonald to Lansdowne, 21 September 1905. *NGB* 37/38, Nichi-Ro sensō v, no. 284, states the case for Japan.
[2] FO *Japan* 672, Hayashi to Barrington, 10 September 1905; *NGB* 38/I, no. 67.
[3] Hardinge papers 7, MacDonald to Hardinge, 25 October 1905.
[4] *NGB* 38/I, no. 73.

Z

but was without the exultation with which it had greeted the alliance of 1902. Criticisms were few and reasoned. Thus, the *Nippon*, the nationalist newspaper, suggested that it might have the effect of drawing Russia and Germany together. The coverage was much smaller than in 1902, probably because it was only one among many vital national issues and the press was much taken up with the opposition to the peace treaty. Nor were there many public functions in celebration of the new alliance. Such ceremonies of mutual congratulation as there were, were reserved for the visit of the British naval squadron to Yokohama which began on 12 October. During its stay there were many parties and dinners; and the squadron celebrated the centenary of the battle of Trafalgar. The Japanese wrote with grave appreciation of the Confucian precept which Nelson had then adopted in his message to the fleet: England expects every man to do his duty.

The publication of the alliance was used by the Japanese government for purposes of domestic policy. With Britain more or less a consenting party, the publication had been postponed so as to improve the acceptability to Japanese public opinion of the unpopular settlement with Russia. To that extent, it succeeded: the Portsmouth treaty was ratified and published on 16 October and ratifications were exchanged with Russia on 25 November without the anticipated difficulty. Where it failed was that it did not overcome the widespread dissatisfaction with the government's foreign policy which eventually drove the Katsura ministry from office in January 1906. This was not a reflection upon the revised alliance: it only showed that this one success was not sufficient to remove the prejudice among politicians and the press against its foreign policy in general. When the alliance was signed on 12 August, parliament in Britain had only just ended; and since it was generally understood that an alliance was about to be signed, much of the debate on Foreign Office supply on 3 August, was in anticipation devoted to the new alliance. Two at least of the speeches — those by Sir Charles Dilke and George Harwood, M.P. for Bolton — contained trenchant criticisms. Harwood in particular foreshadowed many of the complaints which were to be made about the alliance in years to come.[1]

---

[1] Sir Charles Dilke, earlier an advocate of the alliance, had turned fiercely against it. Morrison papers 312/65, 9 March 1905.

Harwood made the following points: 'While the Government were making the new treaty ostensibly with the same Power with which we made the first treaty, it was really quite a different Power . . . and would have to be treated on different principles. . . .

When the treaty was published as a parliamentary paper on 26 September along with a reassuring dispatch from Lansdowne, comment was confined to public speeches. With the election in the offing, the Unionists used the alliance as one of the planks of their platform. The Liberals, on the other hand, foreseeing that, if they came to power, they would be forced to work the new treaty, were prepared to welcome it. Sir Edward Grey, speaking in London on 20 October, commended the extended alliance, as Asquith had earlier done. John Morley, who might have been expected to attack it, said at Arbroath on 23 October that he had misgivings but welcomed the treaty because it would facilitate an understanding with Russia. Dr Monger quotes from the private correspondence of the Liberal leaders at this time and concludes justifiably that they were 'indifferent, or even hostile' to the alliance.[1] The only way in which this evidence can be squared with their public professions is to conclude that even those who had private reservations thought it tactical to approve the alliance publicly. This policy probably paid dividends because Grey, when he took over as foreign secretary in December, was able to assure Japan that he would maintain all the engagements entered into by his predecessor.[2] When the alliance was first taken up in the debate on the king's speech on 19 February 1906, the government spokesman, Lord Ripon, stated that 'we accept that Treaty in the spirit in which we believe it was made, and it is our firm intention to carry out strictly and readily the obligations it imposes on us'.[3] Whatever their inner reluctance, the Liberals had officially committed themselves to the Japanese connection.

Press reaction in Britain was similarly affected by the party struggle and the prospect of the Liberals coming to power. The Conservative newspapers like *The Times*, the *Birmingham Post* and the *Glasgow Herald*, together with periodicals like the *Spectator* and the *National Review*, welcomed it cordially. On the whole, comment, even from papers which had the reputation of being Liberal or pro-Russian,

Any treaty we made with Japan ought carefully to exclude the possibility or supposition that they could be brought into relationship with our Indian Empire. . . . In making a treaty with the Japanese we were making a treaty with a people who were more or less an enigma to us.' *British parliamentary debates*, 4th series, vol. 151, cols. 161–5.

[1] Monger, p. 286.
[2] FO *Japan* 594, Grey to MacDonald, 14 December 1905.
[3] *British parliamentary debates*, 4th series, vol. 152, House of Lords, 19 February 1906, col. 32.

was restrained for the alliance had come to be regarded as part of the accepted order. The *Monthly Review*, for example, ran two parallel articles, one praising and one criticizing, the revised alliance.[1] The hostile article by 'Coloniensis' dwelt on the theme that the alliance was an example of Britain's decadence: 'the appearance of Japanese troops in the Hooghly is more likely to break than consolidate the British Empire'.[2] While there were criticisms of this sort, it would be a travesty of the facts to represent the second alliance as something which gave rise to much excitement or opposition in Britain.

[1] 'Coloniensis', 'The seamy side of the alliance', *Monthly Review*, no. 21/2 (1905), 1–10; and E. J. Solano, 'The world-influence of Britain and Japan', *Monthly Review*, no. 21/2 (1905), 11–37. Another critical viewpoint is expressed by 'Pro patria', 'England's decadence, the Anglo-Japanese treaty', *Contemporary Review*, no. 88 (1905), 703–7.

[2] 'Coloniensis', loc. cit., 10.

CHAPTER XVII

Results of the Second Alliance

1905–1907

IT IS NEVER easy for the historian to determine what were the precise results of a treaty. This is especially true in the present case when it is difficult to differentiate between the results of the second alliance and those of the Russo-Japanese war. Indeed, it is impossible to distinguish between them. None the less, making allowances for this, it is necessary to attempt some assessment of the political and military consequences of the alliance of 1905.

POLITICAL RESULTS FOR BRITAIN AND JAPAN

In Britain, the government which was responsible for concluding the alliance, did not remain in office long after its publication. Balfour had been in political difficulties since he became prime minister in 1902. The division between the protectionist and free trade wings of the Conservative party was all the more serious because a general election would have to be called in 1906 under the Septennial Act and Joseph Chamberlain was asking for a declaration of policy on imperial preference which Balfour was trying to avoid giving. In the last stages of the parliament which ended in August 1905, the government lost a division, conceded by-elections to the opposition and faced public controversy over India, which later culminated in Curzon's resignation as viceroy in September. The alliance was a factor in these events. One of the pleas put forward by Balfour for staying in office so long, was the need to conclude the revised alliance; and insubstantial as it seems as a justification he may genuinely have believed it.[1] When it was concluded, the alliance was acclaimed — along with the French entente

[1] Balfour papers Add. MSS 49774, Balfour to Joseph Chamberlain, 2 November 1905. 'Dissolution either in June or in August would have been very undesirable in view of the Japanese Treaty.'

— as one of the two pillars of the successful foreign policy of which the ministry boasted. But this was not enough to bridge the deep divisions within the party. At its conference in November, Chamberlain won the vote in favour of his tariff policy; and Balfour announced the resignation of his ministry on 4 December. The Liberal party, which had long been split, was meanwhile able to heal its wounds enough to offer a spirited opposition. When Balfour resigned, it formed a cabinet under Sir Henry Campbell-Bannerman, held a general election and was returned with a substantial majority.

Before they left office, the Conservatives decided to honour the Japanese in several ways: the raising of the British legation in Tokyo to an embassy and the conferment upon the Japanese emperor of the Order of the Garter. Both were long-standing projects which had been discussed since 1902. Britain asked Japan on 26 October 1905 whether she approved of raising the status of the British legation in Tokyo with immediate effect. This was readily accepted by the Japanese who offered to reciprocate by converting their London legation to an embassy.[1] The existing incumbents, Viscount Hayashi and Sir Claude MacDonald, were in due course raised to the rank of ambassador. France, Germany, Italy and the United States were among those who followed Britain's example. This was a symbol of international recognition for Japan's status as a first-class power which was won as much by her victory in the war as by the alliance.[2]

Associated with this was Lansdowne's desire to confer upon the Japanese emperor the Order of the Garter. Hitherto Edward VII had resisted the idea on the ground that the Garter could not be given to non-Christian sovereigns. In 1903, however, the Garter was conferred upon the Shah of Persia for political reasons which forced the cabinet virtually to overrule the king. Had it not been for Britain's neutral status in the war, it might have been granted to the Japanese emperor in January 1905. As it happened, it was the new alliance which persuaded the government to insist upon the offer in October. The king appointed Prince Arthur of Connaught to lead an eminent Garter mission which conferred the decoration on the emperor in Tokyo on 20 February 1906. In accordance with the mystique of the Order, the emperor was required to return thanks by sending a full-scale mission to Britain, as he did in 1907 under the leadership of a prince of the blood, Prince Fushimi.

[1] *NGB* 38/II, nos. 930–1.   [2] *Komura gaikōshi*, ii, chapter VIII, section 10.

Apparently realizing the value which the Japanese set on decorations, Britain presented them with great liberality. The Order of the Bath was conferred on Katsura and the Order of St Michael and St George on Komura for services in connection with the alliance. Moreover Admiral Tōgō and two generals were given the Order of Merit.

The change in the balance of power in the far east forced Britain to consider the position of her lease of Weihaiwei. In the region where the balance had most changed, Korea, Manchuria and north China, Britain was not vitally interested, except for Weihaiwei. In 1898 she had taken a lease on the island and mainland territory 'for so long a period as Port Arthur shall remain in the occupation of Russia'. By the peace settlement, Port Arthur was handed back to China by the Russians and transferred to Japan. Germany, however, retained a foothold in north China at the naval base of Kiaochow. Would Britain return Weihaiwei to China? British opinion was deeply divided. The services — the army, the navy and the Imperial Defence Committee — were in favour of abandoning Weihaiwei, because the harbours of Japan, including Port Arthur, would be available to Britain in an emergency.[1] The Foreign Office, acting on the advice of its representatives in the far east, the Colonial Office, and commercial opinion were strongly in favour of retaining it. Lansdowne commented:

The fall of Port Arthur leaves the Russian lease still in existence, and the Russians will probably say that they intend to retake the place. Agreements of this kind ought not to be construed as if they were documents drawn up in Lincoln's Inn.[2]

After some inconclusive talk at the Defence Committee, the Balfour ministry passed the matter unresolved to its successors. Grey as the new foreign secretary was not initially convinced of the case for retaining Weihaiwei, but he eventually minuted that 'the conclusive argument for the retention of Wei Hai Wei for the present appears to me to be the strong feeling of the Japanese'.[3] Japan, which might now have regarded Britain's presence there as an intrusion, continued to press Britain to stay on; and decisive talks were held in November 1906 when Grey informed the ambassador that 'the alliance was made subsequent to the lease of Wei Hai Wei and it was the British desire

[1] Sydenham papers Add. MSS 50836, Clarke to Balfour, 7 October 1905.
[2] Satow papers 7/3, Lansdowne to Satow, 14 September 1904.
[3] *BD*, iv, no. 107.

to avoid any steps which might in the least impair their ability to fulfil the obligations of the alliance'.[1] So Britain continued with her lease of Weihaiwei.

This incident is significant for two things: first, it shows that the Liberals were ready to honour the alliance and to comply with awkward requests made by Japan; second, it shows that Japan kept up pressure to ensure that Britain remained fully committed in north China.

The Katsura ministry met the same fate as the Conservative ministry in Britain at the end of 1905. After the outbreak of war, active opposition against the cabinet disappeared. But, with the approach of peace, vocal groups demanded terms which could not have been enforced in Japan's state of exhaustion. When the terms of the Portsmouth settlement were announced, they were fanatically attacked. The ministry allowed the undoubted gains of the settlement to be ignored and failed to win the press over to its side. This turned a huge tide of disappointment and hostility against the ministry, which, having no party support in the Diet, had no resources of strength.[2]

In Japan, even more than in Britain, the alliance was expected to be a factor in the political scene. It was hoped that the treaty would be acknowledged as a success, if not a triumph, for the ministry. Moreover its publication had been so timed as to coincide with the announcement of the terms of the Portsmouth treaty. In the end, however, the alliance proved to be less of a sop to Japanese opinion than the ministry had hoped.

Having seen this reaction, the Katsura ministry decided to clear up its outstanding affairs and resign. In a methodical way, it secured the ratification of the Russo-Japanese treaty (15 October); it sent Komura to conclude a treaty with China over Manchuria (December); and it completed a treaty with Korea to establish a protectorate there (17 November). With these aspects of the peace settlement fulfilled, Katsura tendered his resignation late in December, recommending as his successor Prince Saionji. By this procedure, Katsura left no doubt that the alliance would continue as the first string of Japan's foreign policy.

The alliance did have a bearing on Japan's domestic affairs. It was of course not striking in its commercial effects and did not give rise to an increase in trade which cannot be accounted for in other ways. As Grey wrote, the alliance did not include commercial matters.[3] But

---

[1] *NGB* 39/II, no. 1312.   [2] Shinobu, *Nichi-Ro sensōshi no kenkyū*, pp. 418–45.
[3] FO 371/87, Grey to Bertie, 23 November 1906.

one immediate advantage which followed closely upon the revision of the alliance was that Japan secured funds in Britain.[1] With the coming of peace, Japan's need for foreign help was great as she had been deprived of the expected indemnity. In November 1905, the Japanese financial commissioner, Takahashi, concluded a 4 per cent sterling loan for £25 million in London, New York, Berlin and Paris for the redemption of internal loans. It was the successor of the Japanese government's first sterling loan at 4 per cent which had been concluded in 1899. The amount was ultimately raised jointly by a British consortium and the Paris house of Rothschilds. It is not unreasonable to conclude that the support which the loan received among British subscribers was due to the feeling of security created by the revised alliance. But financial support was not automatic. In 1906, while the Tokyo and Yokohama city authorities were able to raise municipal loans in Britain for specific projects, the central government found the London money market unwilling to raise a further national loan. It was felt that British investors were put off partly by the fear that the Japanese government was borrowing beyond its capacity for repayment and partly by the anxiety caused by the legislation which was passed in 1906 for the nationalization of Japan's railway trunk lines. When therefore a redemption loan of £23 million was raised in London and Paris in March 1907, it could only be secured at 5 per cent. If the Japanese obtained less than they expected in the aftermath of the Russo-Japanese war, they none the less gained substantially from Britain's friendship through these sterling loans.[2]

Japan also had financial needs in her new sphere of influence in south Manchuria. She relied upon foreign investment in the South Manchurian Railway Company, which was set up in 1906 as a semi-government enterprise to act as the spearhead for Japanese commercial development on the Asian continent. Between 1907 and 1909, the company successfully issued bonds for £6 million at 5 per cent on the London money market under the guarantee of the Japanese government.

This action of the British bankers was not without its anomalies because foreign merchants in the far east were already complaining about the monopolistic attitude of the Japanese — and especially the

---

[1] *Komura gaikōshi*, ii, 184.

[2] For information on loans, *Gaisai kankei shiryō* ['Materials on foreign loans'], 2 vols., Ministry of Finance, Tokyo, 1932.

South Manchurian Railway Company — in their new leased territory of Liaotung. The Japanese made it clear by promoting emigration and by the continued presence of their armed forces that they intended to proceed actively with the development of this territory. By their control of the railways and of the ports, the Japanese were in a strong position to dominate the commerce of all Manchuria. The foreign mercantile community claimed that, despite her professed belief in the Open Door, Japan intended to regard Manchurian trade as her own preserve. The cordial assurances which the American and British governments received in answer to their protests in Tokyo, bore little relation to the treatment which their nationals suffered on the spot. A formal appeal, asking for the principle of the Open Door to be observed at Manchurian ports, was made to the Tokyo authorities by Britain in March 1906, and was fully supported by the United States.[1] It was referred to a joint meeting of cabinet and genrō, thus indicating that it was impossible for the cabinet alone to reconcile this dispute between the differing attitudes of civilians and military over Manchuria. As a result, the port of Dairen was reopened to foreign trade in September 1906.[2] But this did not silence the British merchants. In the working out of the peace settlement, many Britons became disillusioned over Japan's observance of the Open Door doctrines to which she had subscribed in the alliance treaty.[3]

More directly affected by the alliance was Korea, where Britain had recognized Japan's right to take the necessary measures of guidance, control and protection.[4] The Japanese leaders were worried that the powers would object when Japan tried to convert what had been emergency measures to meet the war situation into a permanent policy of protection. The government's first step was to announce in September 1905 that it 'had no alternative but to assume the charge of the external relations' of Korea. In reply, Lansdowne made it plain that Britain was entirely favourable to the development of Japanese influence in Korea and that Japan was not likely to encounter any

[1] *NGB* 39/I, nos. 158 and 161; *Katō*, i, 582-5.
[2] *NGB* 39/I, no. 192, resolutions of the joint meeting of cabinet and genrō, 22 May 1906.
[3] Morrison papers 312/68, 6 July 1906, when Morrison was on a visit to Manchurian ports to investigate anti-Japanese feeling there.
[4] Jordan papers, FO 350/3, Jordan to Campbell, 3 October 1905. The Korean government expressed its disappointment with the terms of the new alliance and was worried with the consequences of Japanese control over the customs.

difficulties from Britain in giving effect to her policy.[1] When Japan received a similar assurance from the United States, she had neutralized the opposition of the powers likely to be most sympathetic to Korea. After Komura returned from Portsmouth on 16 October, he took steps to put into effect the protectorate which was Japan's next objective in Korea. On 27 October, the cabinet, recognizing that the British alliance and the Russo-Japanese treaty clearly laid down that Korea must inevitably come under the tutelage of Japan, authorized the approach to the Korean government.[2] Marquis Itō was appointed as special ambassador to persuade the Korean emperor of the need for these measures and Japan was able, though not without some coercion, to conclude a treaty with Korea whereby Japan should be represented by a resident-general 'who shall reside at Seoul primarily for the purpose of taking charge of and directing matters relating to diplomatic affairs' and 'shall have the right of private and personal audience' of the Korean emperor.[3] Itō himself was appointed as the first resident-general with supreme power over foreign affairs. He was content with a policy of gradualism and aimed at the progressive coalition of Japan and Korea rather than the annexation which the other groups were already advocating. The Korean emperor, however, in an attempt to win international support for his cause, sent a delegation of his own to the Hague Peace Conference of 1907. It was not admitted to membership but succeeded in gravely embarrassing the Japanese. Japan forced the abdication of the emperor and then secured the agreement of the Koreans to a fresh treaty in July 1907 whereby the Japanese resident-general received additional powers.

Korea's future might have been affected by the alliance, had Britain chosen to interfere. But Britain's inclination was to shrug her shoulders at Korea's permanent loss of independence. Itō himself likened Japan's position in Korea to Britain's in Egypt and alleged that he was aspiring to become a great proconsul in the British style like Lord Cromer.[4] The protectorate of 1905 had practical implications for Britain, which had to withdraw her legation from Korea and merge its staff in her diplomatic organization for Japan. There were two Britons who stood

---

[1] *Komura gaikōshi*, ii, 261; FO *Japan* 590, Lansdowne to MacDonald, 26 September 1905.
[2] *Komura gaikōshi*, ii, 261–2; *NGB* 38/I, no. 259.
[3] *NGB* 38/I, nos. 264–9. For general aspects, Conroy, pp. 334 ff.
[4] FO *Japan* 593, MacDonald to Lansdowne, 1 November 1905; *Itō-den*, iii, 710–1.

in the way of the Japanese protectorate. One was the financial adviser to the Korean emperor, John McLeavy Brown, who had formerly belonged to the Chinese Maritime Customs Service. On the eve of signing the second alliance, the Japanese tried to arrange with Lansdowne for Brown's retirement. The British government was asked to smooth the path of his release by arranging for his inclusion in the next Honours List but, claiming rightly that Brown was not its employee, it declined to do so. The Japanese proceeded to negotiate directly with Brown who left Korea on 30 November.[1] Another *cause célèbre* was that of Bethel, the editor of the English-language *Korea Daily News*, whose critical articles were a thorn in the flesh of the Japanese authorities. The paper was suppressed by the British consular court on the complaint of the Japanese, then Bethel himself was expelled in 1908.[2] Thus, on two occasions, Britain had not interfered with the fulfilment of Japanese plans by standing up for her own nationals.

This did not mean that Britain was prepared to condone Japan's annexation of Korea straightaway. The government view was that, while in the last resort it would not object to annexation, it hoped that Japan would be content with the protectorate. Lansdowne had written of his desire that Japan would 'not force the pace too much'[3] and Grey probably shared that view. There were some grounds for confidence. Sir John Jordan speculated from Seoul that Japan's loss of indemnity and consequent shortage of capital was likely to militate against any rapid improvement of her position in Korea.[4] But, whereas Britain might have wielded some influence, she preferred to leave matters to take their own course.

Britain was committed in general terms to supporting Japan's policy in Korea and south Manchuria, but not to the exact form which that policy took. Indeed there were many aspects which Britain disliked. None the less, to the world at large the alliance was an encouragement to the Japanese to entrench themselves in these territories. Britain's attitude was a narrowly commercial one: she would not criticize these actions, provided the Open Door was maintained and the trading position of her nationals was safeguarded.

---

[1] *NGB* 38/I, nos. 798–810; Morrison papers 312/66, 18 January 1906.
[2] *NGB* 38/I, nos. 825–30.
[3] FO *Japan* 600, minute by Lansdowne, 4 November 1905.
[4] Jordan papers, FO 350/3, Jordan to Campbell, 3 October 1905.

MILITARY-NAVAL ASPECTS

Was there evidence of greater military-naval co-operation arising out of the second alliance? In the first draft of the alliance, the Japanese had inserted a clause binding each signatory to keep its naval force superior in strength to that of any third power. Immediately afterwards, the Russian squadron was destroyed; and Britain's battleships were withdrawn from the far east. This left the American fleet as the naval power next strongest to Japan in the Pacific. Japan's landslide victory also affected the naval balance throughout the world. Whereas Britain had since 1900 feared a hostile combination of the Russian, French and German fleets, the Admiralty was able by the end of 1905 to claim that it disposed 'of a force of battleships considerably *superior* to the combined battleship strength of these three powers'.[1] This was achieved by the transfer of five British battleships from the China station to reinforce the Channel fleet. This was only possible under the alliance: so long as Japan remained Britain's ally, Britain could afford to leave the naval defence of her far-eastern interests to Japan. The First Lord wrote in 1906: 'Japan is our ally and her Navy is an element in our strength on the seas for ten years to come.'[2] Thus, even although there were no naval provisions in the 1905 alliance, Britain reaped a rich harvest. During the drafting, Britain had made clear that she would not risk a collision with the U.S. fleet and could only agree to maintain superiority over European fleets. It was ultimately agreed that no precise naval clause should be inserted and that any naval arrangements, together with the military provisions, should be worked out by their naval and military authorities who would meet from time to time. Thus, the secret notes, which had been signed along with the alliance of 1902, form no part of the 1905 alliance. Japan did not want to be too precise over her expectation of naval help in case Britain was similarly precise about the number of troops which she required for service in India.

But the meetings of military and naval authorities proved none too easy to arrange. Attempts were made. The initiative seems to have lain

---

[1] The papers of Lord Cawdor, deposited in the Naval Library, Ministry of Defence, memorandum by Cawdor, 16 November 1905. For an assessment of the naval position, see *Fisher papers*, ii, 79–84, 'Balance of naval power in the far east'.

[2] The papers of Lord Tweedmouth, deposited in the Naval Library, Ministry of Defence, vol. 1, memorandum by Tweedmouth, 'The question of further naval economies', 1906.

with Britain where both the army and navy lost no time in raising the matter. Their proposals came up for discussion at three successive meetings of the Defence Committee early in 1906. But it did not prove immediately possible to fix a venue. Britain was bound to entrust the naval negotiations to Admiral Sir John Fisher whose duties did not permit him to go to Japan, while Japan's generals were so preoccupied with the postwar reorganization of the army that they found it impossible to send representatives to London. It was undesirable to split the military and naval aspects so there was no alternative but to delay the conference. It was not until February 1907 in fact that a practical proposal emerged. The Japanese suggested that Admiral Yamamoto and General Nishi who would accompany Prince Fushimi on his mission of thanks for bestowing the Garter on the Japanese emperor, should undertake the necessary talks in London.[1] Britain cordially agreed. The fact that the military-naval talks could be delayed for almost two years after the signing of the alliance, indicates that its military aspects had lost much of their urgency.

The main strategic proposals in the second treaty — and these implicit rather than explicit — had been military rather than naval. They laid down that Britain should in certain eventualities obtain Japan's assistance in the defence of its Indian frontiers. The Committee of Imperial Defence considered Britain's stand at its meeting on 15 February 1906. The new viceroy, Lord Minto, had advised after consultation with Kitchener that it would not be advisable in case of hostilities 'to employ Japanese troops in or through India. We are not, however, prepared to say this might never be advisable'. The new secretary of state for India, John Morley, added that the government of India was not prepared to lend troops to co-operate with the Japanese outside India.[2] The General Staff argued that Japan could in the event of trouble best play her part by undertaking a vigorous offensive against Russia in the far east. It recommended that:

we should not ask Japan to send troops to India, first, because the number of men that could be employed across the north-west frontier is limited by the means of transport and supply; and secondly because to ask for assistance to ward off attack by a single adversary would not be consistent with either our dignity or self-respect. Such a request on our part would, in fact, be interpreted and not without reason as a clear proof of our national decadence,

[1] See above, p. 346.
[2] FO 371/85, minutes of C.I.D. meetings, 1 and 15 February 1906.

and would be highly detrimental, if not absolutely fatal, to our prestige throughout the Asiatic continent.[1]

On the basis of these views, the meeting concluded that Japan should not be asked to send troops to co-operate in a campaign on the north-west frontier and further that the proposal for furnishing a contingent of horse artillery and cavalry for service with the Japanese in the far east should be abandoned.[2]

What was the explanation for this apparent volte-face? The Indian commitment had largely been the brain-child of Balfour and Sir George Clarke. But within a year this demand had been jettisoned by the Committee of Imperial Defence. It would not be unreasonable to suggest that when the Balfour ministry resigned, his idea was rejected by the Liberals. But this does not fit the facts: the idea was not thrown out by the Liberals but by a committee of advisers on military matters and, less forcibly, by the new administration in India.[3]

While the General Staff remained, as before, adamant in its hostility, Kitchener's thinking had subtly changed. Hitherto Kitchener had been obsessed by the difficulty of supplying nine divisions for the Afghan frontier. In November 1905, however, he realized that this would similarly be a serious obstacle to the active employment of a Japanese contingent.[4] Still he was not unhappy about the general prospect of Japanese assistance:

With 8 divisions as reinforcements and the Japanese alliance, we may I think sit down and work for efficiency and economy in the army without any fear of Russian aggression in the near future.[5]

The conclusion is inescapable that these schemes for Indian defence were devised as a brainwave without enough consultation and without enough consideration of the ultimate tactical problems involved. It is possible to argue that Japan was asked to share in the defence of India purely in order to give the new treaty an appearance of equality. But, while this was one factor which weighed with the British leaders, it

[1] Cabinet 4/1/68B, memorandum by the General Staff, 4 November 1905.
[2] FO 371/85, minutes of C.I.D. meeting, 15 February 1906.
[3] Lord Roberts at the Oxford Union on 16 November 1905 said that it would be 'a fatal blow to British prestige if India ever regarded her defence as dependent upon the strength of Japan'.
[4] WO 106.48 G3.12, observations by Lord Kitchener on C.I.D. paper 68B of 12 August 1905. Probably written in November but not circulated.
[5] Sydenham papers Add. MSS 50835, Kitchener to Clarke, 25 January 1906.

must be admitted that they were also influenced by strategic considerations which were tactically unrealistic. In view of the outcome, it is strange that such pains were taken to talk the Japanese into accepting this obligation initially.

Britain's attitude was still far from settled. The matter came before the Defence Committee early in 1907 when the conference with the Japanese was just a few months ahead. The General Staff bemoaned the fact that Britain would 'enter the Conference with rather a negative programme as regards the possibilities of military cooperation'.[1] At the Defence Committee meeting on 25 April, R. B. Haldane as secretary for war expressed the view that the authorities in India had been premature in rejecting the idea that Japanese troops should be employed in India and that the subject should be discussed at the coming conference. It was decided that no request for co-operation should be made to the Japanese but the possibility of Japanese help should not be excluded from discussion. It should be ascertained, the minute added, whether the Japanese were prepared to render direct military assistance and whether they would prefer to act from the side of Persia. But this point was not treated as a formal British demand nor was it communicated to the Japanese in the memorandum of points for discussion.[2]

The Japanese might well have chuckled that Britain for internal reasons had seen fit to omit any precise reference to obligations in India which their military men were most anxious to avoid. Among the elaborate written instructions which the Japanese delegates were given, General Nishi received a brief from the chief of the General Staff,[3] warning him to avoid as far as possible any commitment whereby Japan should be required to send troops to the Indian front or Britain to send them to the Manchurian front. Nishi was further instructed to try to obtain from Britain the transports needed for a Japanese expeditionary force. It is noteworthy that in Japan's strategic thinking Russia was still identified as the major enemy rather than (say) the United States or Germany. This may be due to General Yamagata's plan for imperial defence which was adopted in October 1906. Under it Japan's main defence obligations were those prescribed in the British alliance and were thus still directed against Russia.[4] Even though

[1] WO 106.48 G3.10, memorandum by the General Staff, 14 March 1907.
[2] Cabinet 2/2/1, minutes of 97th C.I.D. meeting, 25 April 1907; *NGB* 40/I, no. 31.
[3] *NGB* 40/I, no. 34, General Nishi to General Terauchi, 9 June 1907, appendix.
[4] A. Ōyama, 'Teikoku kokubō hōshin an' ('Draft plan for imperial defence'), *Kokusai seiji*, no. 3 (1961), 170–7.

Japan was then negotiating an agreement with Russia, her main strategic concern was with Russia and the Manchurian frontier.

Unlike Admiral Fisher, whose instructions (if indeed he agreed to accept any) have not been traced, Admiral Yamamoto was given precise and detailed instructions. He was to say that Japan hoped 'that the British navy which is not only the greatest navy in the world but also in every way the most advanced navy, will agree to assist the navy of its ally, Japan, by its advice on every aspect of naval education and research'.[1] Britain was merely to be asked at what strength her naval power would be kept and how her ships would be distributed; she was not to be asked to maintain her naval forces in the far east at a prescribed level. This was a turning-point in Japan's naval attitude since the alliance was first conceived: Japan now regarded herself as navally self-sufficient and no longer appealed to Britain for support in ships.

The secret military talks began on 29 May. The major conclusion reached was that in any war with Russia, 'each of the Allied Powers by operating as far as circumstances admit in their respective theatres of war upon the Indian frontier and in the Far East should thereby seek to create a diversion on behalf of its ally'. Several subsidiary arrangements were reached over secondment of staff, cypher, cables, etc. The Japanese asked for British help in what was for them primarily a military problem: the supply of 412,000 tons of shipping suitable for transporting Japanese forces to Manchuria in the event of war. In Britain this was regarded as a responsibility for the Admiralty, which would not commit itself to assist with transports. The Japanese reported jubilantly that 'apart from the transport ships the military arrangements have almost all been decided in accordance with our proposals'.[2] But on the whole the decisions were not of great significance.

The naval discussions between Yamamoto and Fisher were held on 29–30 May. While a report of 13 clauses was issued, it was largely generalized and unspecific. Britain made no commitment about keeping her naval forces at a given strength in the far east: 'Britain could best guard the allied interest by destroying the ships of an enemy as they issued from their European bases.'[3] This was certainly far from the intention of the signatories in 1905.

---

[1] *NGB* 40/I, no. 28, appendix 3, Saitō to Yamamoto, February 1907.
[2] *NGB* 40/I, no. 32.   [3] *NGB* 40/I, no. 33.

In an interview with the Japanese ambassador on 4 June, Sir Edward Grey said that he wanted to overcome the hitch which had taken place over the transports. Under pressure from the Foreign Office, the Admiralty became more co-operative and undertook to charter the tonnage which the Japanese wanted in any given emergency. An agreement on this basis was signed and Nishi cabled home that the arrangement for transports had also been made in accordance with Japan's wishes.[1]

These military-naval talks were the fulfilment of the Anglo-Japanese treaty of 1905. But the results, which they achieved, were of a minor order. When the allied military experts came to examine the 1905 formula, they found that it was no longer relevant to 1907. Balfour had said of the 1905 treaty that it was 'a defensive alliance, not against any two Powers, but against any single Power, which attacks either us or Japan in the East: so that Japan can depend upon *our* Fleet for defending Korea, etc. and we can depend upon *her* Army to aid us on the North-West frontier if the security of India is imperilled in that quarter'.[2] Neither of these forms of assistance was any longer reliable. The Admiralty under Fisher wanted to confine its ships to European waters as far as possible and could not be relied on to help in defending Korea, while Britain's leaders were not agreed on the desirability of using Japanese assistance against Russia on India's frontiers in spite of the hard bargaining it had entailed in 1905. Moreover Japan made it plain that, instead of sending troops to India, her first duty would be to fight Russia by creating a diversion on the frontiers of Manchuria.

INTERNATIONAL CONSEQUENCES

Another reason why these talks lacked major significance was that the international situation in east Asia was undergoing fundamental changes. After the Japanese had dealt with the more urgent problems of postwar reconstruction and some of the large tasks associated with the administration of Korea and Manchuria, they proceeded to consider the reorientation of their foreign policy. In 1906, Japan's foreign policy came under the control of Hayashi Tadasu who seems to have approached Japan's problems in the spirit of Lansdowne's policy which he had witnessed at close quarters in London: he set out to conclude clearing-up agreements with powers with which Japan had disputes.

[1] *NGB* 40/I, no. 34, pp. 45–6.
[2] Balfour papers Add. MSS 49747, Balfour to Cooper, 11 September 1905.

In particular, he wanted to obtain the greatest possible measure of agreement among the powers for Japan's major steps in Korea and Manchuria. As we have seen, the most important step pending was to conclude a fresh agreement with Korea giving the Japanese resident-general increased powers. Although this did not come to a head until the 'Hague demonstration' of July 1907, it had been in contemplation for some time. It was primarily in order to obtain from France and Russia their approval for this more intensive protectorate that the Japanese were anxious to make approaches to them.[1]

France, the ally of Russia and partner of Britain, was quite ready for a rapprochement with Japan. In March 1907, the Paris money market, which had not been able to take part in the wartime Japanese borrowing, raised a loan for Japan of 300,000,000 francs as part of the sterling loan then being negotiated; and the French government thought it appropriate to combine it with negotiations for a political understanding. The agreement, which was signed in Paris on 10 June, contained a declaration granting Japan most-favoured-nation treatment in French Indochina and an 'arrangement' declaring that Japan and France had a special interest in seeing peace and order maintained in regions of the Chinese Empire adjoining territory where they had sovereignty and engaging to support one another to assure peace and security there. This was amplified by a secret exchange of notes which laid down that these regions of China were deemed to include Fukien in the neighbourhood of Formosa. In effect, therefore, the two powers recognized each other's rights: Japan's spheres of influence in Korea, Manchuria and Fukien; and France's in Indochina and south China.[2]

More important and fundamental was the Russo-Japanese agreement. It might be thought that it would have been impossible to reach any agreement so soon after the bitterness of the war. But, in fact, both sides came to realize the potential advantages. Russia, sealed off in the far east as a result of defeat, gave up the tactics, which she had used since 1894, of dominating the Chinese court in order to extract

[1] Good accounts are given in *Hayashi memoirs*, chapters VI and VII; E. B. Price, *The Russo-Japanese Treaties of 1907–16*, Baltimore, 1933, pp. 26–38; E. W. Edwards, 'The Far Eastern Agreements of 1907', *Journal of Modern History*, no. 26 (1954), 340–55; Kajima Morinosuke, *Nihon gaikō no shiteki kōsatsu*, pp. 219–31. But there is abundant new material in *NGB* 40/I which has not been used by any of these. Britain and the United States were deemed to have given their approval to Japan's actions in Korea already.

[2] *NGB* 40/I, nos. 84–5 and 88.

concessions. Instead she saw that she would have to depend for any-thing which she gained in future on a compromise settlement with Japan. Although many Russians were opposed to this course, Izvolskii who became foreign minister in May 1906, opened negotiations at the end of that year. On the Japanese side, Hayashi was eager to negotiate. He had the support not only of the civilians — the cabinet and genrō — but also of the military who thought it was the only solution for Manchuria. Negotiations were not completed earlier because of the difficulty of getting the two powers to recognize each other's rights: Japan's freedom of action in Korea and Russia's in outer Mongolia. The treaty was finally signed on 30 July 1907, following on two lesser agreements dealing with railways and fisheries. The open agreement did not advance the position much beyond the Portsmouth treaty; the secret agreement laid down their spheres in Manchuria, Japan in the south, Russia in the north, and provided for the mutual recognition of Japan's new status in Korea and Russia's special interests in outer Mongolia, which were further defined in an exchange of notes.[1]

This treaty depended to some extent upon the encouragement of the French and British governments. The French government en-couraged Izvolskii to direct his attention to Europe rather than to Asia and put pressure on the Japanese to be moderate by withholding its assent to the Japanese loan until they reduced their demands on Russia.[2] The British government was also kept informed during the negotiations and received the full text and secret notes after its com-pletion. It encouraged Japan to persevere with the negotiations. Grey told the Japanese ambassador in March that a Russo-Japanese agree-ment would only reinforce the Anglo-Japanese alliance and would be valuable for Britain's negotiations with Russia which were already in train. While the British government was very satisfied, it would be an exaggeration to say that British pressure was exerted on Japan: it was at most encouragement.[3]

The Russo-Japanese agreement was only a partial settlement of differences. There would continue to be disputes between these powers in east Asia but it was a turning point in Japan's policy which had its effects on the British alliance. The military provisions of the 1905 treaty had been designed to cater for a hypothetical war of revenge by

[1] *NGB* 40/I, no. 182; Price, pp. 107–8, does not give the exchange of notes.
[2] *NGB* 40/II, nos. 816–17.   [3] Edwards, loc. cit., 344.

Russia against Japan. By the time of the military conferences in May 1907, it was already clear that there was no longer any prospect of such a war. The agreement also foreshadowed a new alignment in east Asia which would run parallel with the British alliance. Japan had taken the first steps towards building up a two-tiered system: a maritime alliance with Britain and a continental and landward alliance with Russia which was not achieved until 1916. For the present all that emerged was that Japan could entrench herself in south Manchuria without the prospect of Russian opposition.

British opinion became increasingly suspicious of Germany after the Moroccan crisis of 1905 and the Algeciras conference. While the new Liberal government tried to patch up its differences with Germany, the mainstream of its policy was directed towards strengthening the entente with France which would reinforce its position in Europe and reaching an agreement with Russia which would resolve its imperial worries. Negotiations with Russia which had been started by the Conservatives in 1903, were taken up with energy by Lamsdorf and his successor, Izvolskii, after the war. A convention was concluded in 1907 covering Persia, Afghanistan and Tibet. Russia acknowledged that Afghanistan was 'outside the Russian sphere of influence'; Persia was divided into spheres of influence and Sistan, which had been a subject much discussed during the negotiation of the Japanese alliance, was allotted to the British sphere. The Russians had in effect disabused Britain of any anxieties she had that they would perpetrate further expansionist adventures on India's frontiers after 1905. To that extent, Japan's undertaking to furnish military aid there was no longer necessary.[1]

The far east was outside the purview of the Anglo-Russian treaty but it had been mentioned during the negotiations. Russia had asked whether Britain would give undertakings over outer Mongolia as a *quid pro quo* for concessions offered elsewhere. Grey was naturally reluctant and asked Komura, now the Japanese ambassador in London, whether Japan had been similarly approached. Komura replied that no mention had been made of Mongolia in the Russo-Japanese talks. He was not in possession of the full facts about the St Petersburg negotiations and may not have been aware that Mongolia was a major issue.[2]

---

[1] The most recent treatment is in Monger, chapter 11, especially pp. 292–5.

[2] *BD*, iv, p. 284; *NGB* 40/I, nos. 111–12 in which Komura makes no mention of this point.

At any rate, the Foreign Office tried to devise some formula but, by the beginning of May, Izvolskii had decided, much to Britain's relief, that there was no need for a Mongolian clause in the British agreement.

These agreements had a bearing on the alliance. They were primarily clearing-up arrangements of a detailed nature; but the fact that agreements had been brought about at all was probably more significant than the minutiae of their terms. Now that both allies had signed treaties with Russia which had been the focus of hostility under the alliances of 1902 and 1905, the direction of the alliance itself was bound to be changed. In effect, Japan had become identified with the Triple Entente in Europe; and, in so far as that was anti-German, the alliance too would in the long term tend to become anti-German, both in Europe and east Asia. Thus the alliance which was due to last till 1915, was by 1907 already showing that it needed redefinition, if not further revision. The treaty of 1905 catered for a situation which was quickly outgrown after the war.

Did this mean that the alliance had become weaker? When tensions with Russia had been relaxed, some of the driving force behind the alliance was certainly lost. The Japanese leaders were seriously alarmed at the change in Britain's outlook towards the end of 1907. On 6 November, Itō as resident-general in Korea sent the foreign minister a long memorandum on the 'attitude of Britain, Germany and America towards Japan'.[1] Itō argued that, with the conclusion of the Russian entente, the British government evidently thought that the main source of trouble for many years past had been removed and that the Japanese alliance was no longer so important. If Japan was to avoid being isolated, she must take care of the interests of the other powers in China. Hayashi shared some of Itō's despondency. In referring the matter to the cabinet, Hayashi expressed the view that the good feeling of the British public which had been very favourable to Japan during the war, was gradually being lost, because of the actions of Japanese in Manchuria; but there was no reason to believe that the British government would at this stage forego the alliance, whose objects were by no means limited to relations with Russia. The strategy of Japanese foreign policy, he argued, should be to avoid isolation by making the British alliance its vital instrument. Moreover, Hayashi readily supported Itō's contention that Britain was being alienated by Japan's commercial aggressiveness and urged the need

[1] *NGB* 40/III, no. 2199, Itō to Hayashi, 6 November 1907.

for observing the principles of the Open Door.[1] It will be observed that the Japanese were not conscious that they were less dependent upon the alliance, although Britain unquestionably was.

What was the true state of British feeling towards Japan? Those ministers like Morley who had never favoured the second alliance, were becoming confirmed in their dislike of it.[2] But it is certain that Grey continued to support the alliance consistently and that the majority of the Liberal cabinet did not change their attitude decisively. The Japanese decided to probe the British attitude: Hayashi told MacDonald of his fear that Britain was becoming unfriendly to the alliance. When he was thus accosted by Hayashi, MacDonald was able to quote a telegram which he had just received from Grey expressing Britain's hope that the goodwill and friendship which had resulted from the alliance would continue undiminished. He assured Hayashi that he was mistaken in thinking that any feeling hostile to the alliance existed within the government.[3] The real difference was that there was no longer the same consensus in the cabinet or the country which had existed earlier. The Japanese anxieties were greatly exaggerated but contained a grain of truth. Despite all the forthright protestations by Grey,[4] it has to be admitted that the Japanese alliance had declined in importance. In Britain, the period when the far east was front-page news had ended with the war. After the Russian agreement had lessened the anxieties over British India and the Persian Gulf, it was possible, and indeed essential, for the ministry to concentrate on European affairs.

Apart from the new alignments in Europe, the alliance was influenced by the attitude of the United States. Since the Russo-Japanese war when Roosevelt had been pro-Japanese, American opinion had veered against Japan over immigration and the Open

[1] NGB 40/III, no. 2200, Hayashi to the cabinet, 29 November 1907.

[2] Cf. Grey papers, MacDonald to Grey, 19 February 1908. '[last summer Mr Morley] mentioned to me doubts about the Alliance for he was afraid the Japanese would draw us by its means into a policy of adventure. I illustrated to him then, by the Kamranh Bay incident, when [they could have drawn us into the row] but they never mentioned the word alliance'. Also Sydenham papers, Add. MSS 50836, note by Clarke on Anglo-Japanese treaty of 1905, 15 December 1906. Clarke prepared the note for Morley and argued that the treaty gave Britain 'considerable advantages and moderate liabilities'.

[3] FO 371/472, MacDonald to Grey, 31 January 1908.

[4] BD, viii, no. 349, Grey to MacDonald, 1 February 1908. 'We regard the new arrangements with Russia made by ourselves and by Japan as making the objects of the Anglo-Japanese Alliance more secure, but not as diminishing the importance of those objects or making the co-operation of Japan with us to maintain them less desirable.'

Door in Manchuria. In particular it began to resent the alliance whose success in military terms ultimately depended on expanding Japan's naval power. The United States which was left as the second Pacific naval power after Britain's withdrawal in 1905, was uncomfortable at the encouragement which Britain gave to Japanese naval building. It was no coincidence that in November 1907, the U.S. fleet set off to stage a naval demonstration in the Pacific. As the United States aired her objections openly, the British government preferred to weaken the alliance rather than forfeit the goodwill which she was trying to build up with that power. In this direction also, the alliance of 1905 had within two years lost much of its force.

Conclusion

1907 may seem to be an odd date at which to end this study. But two events of that year did bring one phase of the alliance towards a close: the military-naval talks and the agreements between the two allies and Russia.

The military-naval talks tied up the loose ends of the 1905 alliance but also exposed some of its shortcomings and out of dateness. Japan approached these talks unwilling to help in the defence of India, while Britain was just as unwilling to offer the naval co-operation that Japan expected. As it happened, neither of the powers was anxious to make an issue of its demands so that a compromise settlement was reached in each case. Since, however, the effectiveness of an alliance depends on policies of practical co-operation being worked out, the unsatisfactory outcome of this conference was in itself a reflection on the alliance.

One month after the military-naval talks, the allies signed agreements with Russia who had hitherto been regarded as the main enemy contemplated by the alliance. This naturally reduced its value further. Japan's treaty led her to co-operate in certain ventures in Manchuria with Russia. Britain's treaty certainly had the effect of lessening, if it did not entirely remove, the long-standing anxieties felt about Russia's activities in central Asia. Thus, the alliance could no longer be looked at as an instrument of anti-Russian policies.

1907 also marked a turning-point in the relationship between the powers in the far east. As we have seen in this study, the far east became in 1895 a focus of attention for European powers which were ambitious for territorial gains and were stimulated by their intense jealousy for one another. By 1907 when Russia had given up the thought of a war of revenge, the powers had given up their territorial appetites in east Asia. Not that they lost interest in China; they continued to be commercially active there. But they were content to leave the military-naval ascendancy in the far east to the Japanese, while they concentrated in Europe. At this juncture it is not inappropriate to break the story of the alliance.

This leads us to consider, by way of conclusion, the strength and durability of the influences in Japan and Britain which brought about these alliances. In discussing this subject previously, we concluded that it was in both countries predominantly a 'secretariat alliance', that is, it was negotiated more or less secretly by the foreign ministries on both sides without consulting mercantile, political, or indeed any other form of non-official, opinion. It is true that, in the narrow activity of negotiating these alliances, those outside official circles took little part. But the Anglo-Japanese alliance, like any other alliance, grew out of a community of interest and feeling between the two powers; and this could not be built up unless there were those outside official ranks who were prepared to agitate for it and publicize it. In seeking for influences on the alliance, we should look for groups who created a climate of opinion suitable for the acceptance of the alliance and who justified it after its creation.

In Japan, it is possible to identify certain groups which were consistently anti-Russian and consequently alliance-minded. These included the military leaders. It is not the view taken in this study that there existed a 'military party' or a unanimous military line on policy issues. At the same time, even in the 1900s the army leaders were able to influence policy. As professional groups the army and navy had traditionally recognized Russia as Japan's natural enemy. There were times when Yamagata as the outstanding military leader, favoured a settlement with Russia; but from April 1901 his attitude changed; he favoured the alliance and carried Katsura with him. Even service rivalries did not affect the solidarity of this group which, whether army or navy, was anti-Russian and favoured an alliance with Britain. Perhaps some of their influence penetrated to the anti-Russian societies. Of these the most prominent was the *Kokumin Dōmeikai* which opposed a conciliatory diplomacy towards Russia because it favoured the establishment of Japan's power in Korea and China. As a means to this end the *Dōmeikai* supported friendship with Britain. In April 1902, shortly after the alliance was signed and the Manchurian situation improved, the *Dōmeikai* was dissolved on the grounds that its objects had been achieved. Another group, very necessary for the success of the British alliance, were the pro-British newspapers in Tokyo. In the

1890s and 1900s prominent editors or managers like Fukuzawa Yukichi or Katō Takaaki encouraged editorial policy of this kind by sponsoring articles in favour of the alliance in the *Jiji Shimpō* and the *Nichinichi Shimbun*. It was in this capacity that Katō played a part in the 1902 alliance and was again influential behind the scenes in 1905.

Influential as these groups were in appealing to public opinion, they had little effect in bringing about the alliance which was primarily a government alliance. In Tokyo, the policy of a British alliance appears to have been followed with single-minded devotion by foreign minister Komura from his appointment in September 1901 onwards. It may be that it had already been accepted by prime minister Katsura as one of his objectives and remained so until 1905. Of course, there was the difference between the first and second alliances that there was no repetition of the opposition on the part of Itō and Inoue in 1901. Until the start of the Russo-Japanese war, Itō still favoured concessions to Russia; thereafter he could not claim that there was any alternative to the policy of the British alliance. Thus, the alliance of 1905 did not have to be snatched in the teeth of influential opposition.

In Japan as in Britain, the attitude of the Foreign Ministry was important. Those who had special experience as ministers in London — Aoki, Katō, Hayashi — all took office later as foreign ministers and were able to ensure good relations with Britain. In the achievement of the alliance, a special place must be given to Hayashi Tadasu who was minister in London from 1900 to 1906. His was not a policy-making role, for he was a man under instructions, but the role of a persuasive intermediary in negotiations which took place almost wholly in London. In his *Memoirs*, he has left a testament which bears witness to his abiding enthusiasm for the alliance and has shown how he kept the alliance before the attention of his government. Moreover, below ministerial level, the Foreign Ministry secretariat, with a few notable exceptions, was anti-Russian.[1]

In Britain, the forces behind the alliance were roughly the same: it was a government alliance; there were outside agencies working towards an alliance but without great influence; and there were splits within the policy-forming groups.

[1] The majority of Foreign Ministry officials were anti-Russian. The exceptions were Nishi, Kurino and Motono who tended to favour good relations with Russia and France. In 1901 the departmental heads like Ishii and Yamaza were by training and experience deeply suspicious of Russia.

Voices in favour of an alliance had been raised in Britain for many years. But any prospect of an alliance being brought about was a late development; and the influence which persons outside the government exerted in this direction was very slight. It was argued by Hayashi that the way for the alliance had been prepared by such publicists as Valentine Chirol and Dr G. E. Morrison of the London *Times* and by Sir Edwin Arnold of the *Daily Telegraph*.[1] They doubtless had their say in favour of a possible alliance and were helpful in creating by their books and articles an atmosphere conducive to it. But the audience was narrow. Certainly the British cabinet was not convinced in February 1902 that the publicists had succeeded in fostering the idea of an alliance in the press and feared that its announcement would be badly received. On the whole, it was received quietly and favourably, but this does not seem to have been because of the previous publicity.

Chirol was different from the others mentioned, for he could claim to have had some influence with the government. Sir Valentine Chirol, foreign editor of *The Times*, was a friend of Japan and a frequent visitor there. He was unquestionably an expert on foreign affairs and had access to the foreign secretary and to senior officials at the Foreign Office.[2] Theodore Roosevelt who invited him to the United States in 1905, welcomed him as the godfather of the first alliance; and Chirol was widely regarded as having had some responsibility for it.[3] What is less well known is his influence in Japan. There is evidence that *The Times*' correspondent there, Brinkley, passed on to Itō Hirobumi letters which he received from Chirol about current problems.[4] Being convinced of the need for Japan's friendship, he placed the weight of *The Times*' influence behind efforts to secure it until his retirement in 1911.

Another influence on British foreign policy was the monarchy. Edward VII, who succeeded to the throne in January 1901, was a well-meaning but inconsistent dabbler in foreign affairs. His official biographer has left it on record that the king disliked the idea of an alliance with a yellow race, though he later yielded any personal

---

[1] *Hayashi memoirs*, pp. 110–13.

[2] Morrison papers 312/65, 14 and 29 September 1905; *The Holstein papers*, iv, nos. 786–9 and 793.

[3] Chirol, *Fifty years in a changing world*, pp. 208–9.

[4] Cf. *NGB* 40/III, no. 2199.

prejudice against such an alliance.[1] This sentiment, if it is a true representation of the king's view, was not shared by the government and it cannot therefore be construed as of any particular political significance. Moreover it was the understanding of the Japanese that the king's true sentiments were as expressed to Sir Claude MacDonald in July 1901 and as reported by him to Hayashi.[2] Accordingly, the king was thought to favour the alliance and the Japanese government was not unduly disturbed. In 1905, the king tried by his cordiality to the representative of the Japanese royal family, Prince Arisugawa, to pave the way for the revision of the alliance. In general, however, he had not as much interest in far eastern affairs as he showed in European politics.

In Britain as in Japan, the alliance was in conception and execution, the work of officials guided by strategic and political considerations. These strategic objectives were primarily naval in the first alliance and primarily military in the second. In 1902 the Admiralty wished to concentrate Britain's fleet in European waters and could only do this by entrusting its defence in the east to Japan. The Treasury encouraged this by insisting upon thrift on the part of the services and a return to peacetime budgeting. In 1905, under the influence of the Defence Committee, thinking had turned to the task of defending the Indian frontier without making large-scale increases in Britain's standing army. The solution adopted, which was largely the work of Balfour and Sir George Clarke, was that Japanese assistance should be sought to meet the deficiency.[3]

Now that many private archives have become available, it is possible to state more accurately than before the attitude of government circles. It is possible to analyse the attitudes taken by members of the cabinet and Foreign Office and in some cases to detect differences of opinion. What was previously known of the cabinet's views from fragments of

---

[1] I have not been able to confirm Lee's allegation from the Royal Archives. Lee, *King Edward VII*, ii, pp. 140–2. Also Magnus, *King Edward the seventh*, pp. 276–97 and Monger, p. 263 ff.

[2] See above pp. 145–7.

[3] Marder, *From Dread Nought to Scapa Flow*, i, pp. 26 and 234–5, states that Sir John Fisher described the alliance as 'the very worst thing that England ever did for herself'. His attitude must have changed in accordance with his mercurial temperament because there are cases where he argued in favour of it, e.g. *Fisher papers*, ii, 70–8.

Curzon as viceroy of India does not seem to have been consulted over the alliance in 1901 or 1905. He described the first alliance as 'a cleverly timed and statesmanlike coup', Royal archives W 1/18, Curzon to the king, 24 February 1902.

the ministers' writings often proves to be unreliable when compared with a wider range of material. Thus, the common idea that Salisbury was bitterly opposed to the first alliance must be revised. He may have been doubtful of the value of an alliance with Germany in 1901 but not the Japanese alliance, to which he was a party. Similarly, there is no great evidence that Joseph Chamberlain was a great advocate of the Japanese alliance from as early as 1898.[1] He was not opposed but neither was he favourable; his attitude was helpful but lukewarm. He was so engrossed with colonial problems connected with the South African war that his interest in the alliance was secondary. Once the alliance was in force, however, he was its defender. Austen Chamberlain, who carried on the family view after his father's retirement, was one of those most favourable to Japan in 1905. That it was possible for attitudes to change is shown by the case of Balfour. After his strong memorandum of December 1901, in which he aired his doubts about the proposed alliance, he seems to have been won over to the first alliance. By 1905 he was the initiator and advocate of the second alliance. Lansdowne was, however, the constant supporter of the Japanese connection. While his colleagues may have been doubtful, he followed this course as part of his policy of limited agreements. The greatest characteristic of Lansdowne's personality and of his policy was his caution: for him the Japanese alliance was never a rash, unpremeditated move; it was calculated and deliberate.[2]

At the secretariat level, the person who stands out most clearly as the initiator of the alliance is Francis Bertie. He shared with Lansdowne the task of framing the treaty of 1902 and was, above all others in Japan and Britain, responsible for the shape which it ultimately took. This does not mean that there was not some disagreement between them or within the Foreign Office. Lansdowne kept his policy sensitive to the views of his cabinet colleagues who were preoccupied in 1901 with the possibility of obtaining an understanding with Germany and were inclined to invite Germany to be associated with the Japanese alliance. Bertie, however, warned against any entanglement with Germany and was the leading spokesman of the anti-German group in

[1] Garvin, *Life of Joseph Chamberlain*, iii, 248–50, and Pratt, *War and politics in China*, p. 138, have argued that Chamberlain was the real author of the alliance. While Chamberlain regarded Japan with favour as a developing country, he cannot claim to be the sponsor of the alliance.
[2] Steiner, 'Last years of the old Foreign Office', *Historical Journal*, no. 6 (1963), p. 73. In my view, this article underestimates Lansdowne's considerable diplomatic abilities.

the Foreign Office.[1] In particular, he argued strongly against Germany's association with the Japanese alliance and was gratified when it did not eventually materialize. This does not imply that the choice open to Britain in 1901 was between an alliance with Germany and one with Japan or that, if the first fell through, the second would take its place. It has been the view taken in this study that the two lines of policy were not regarded by the British government as alternatives: they were looked at in separate regional compartments and the Japanese approach was taken up independently of the German approach. If there was any alternative to the Japanese approach open to Britain in 1901, it was some sort of understanding with Russia, such as was unsuccessfully tried in October.

What part was played by the British minister in Tokyo in the deliberations? MacDonald openly admitted that his government had not consulted him from start to finish of the 1905 negotiations; and there is every reason to accept this at its face value.[2] But he did claim to have played a large role in July 1901 when he visited Britain. Jordan, who was a close colleague of MacDonald and was in London at the time, states categorically that he took part in the negotiations for the alliance.[3] There is plenty of evidence to suggest that these July discussions were useful in bringing Britain round to the idea of an alliance with Japan, though they preceded the negotiations by some months. At all events, it was only while MacDonald was in London that he exercised direct influence on the shape of the alliance. This confirms the general conclusion of this study that the alliance in 1902 and 1905 originated in London and was mainly negotiated there. The British government did not owe much to advice from Tokyo or to parleys which took place there.

Hitherto the agreements of 1902 and 1905 have been treated separately. It is now necessary to consider them together as part of a long-term alliance system. They possess some of the features which one would expect to find in an alliance. Britain and Japan shared certain common interests which developed more obviously after 1895 when the powers began to intervene actively in the far east. The serious

---

[1] Steiner, loc. cit., pp. 69–70.
[2] Hardinge papers, 7, MacDonald to Hardinge, 19 July 1905.
[3] Sir John Jordan, 'Sir Claude MacDonald', *Dictionary of National Biography*, 1912–21.

crisis over Manchuria in 1901 persuaded some statesmen that it was desirable for these common interests to be defined in a treaty and for some provision to be made to defend them jointly. In 1902, therefore, they concluded a treaty, limited in time, in geographical scope and in the obligations which it imposed. Within these limitations, it was successful and profitable for both parties. As might have been expected, it was extended both in time and area when the opportunity presented itself in 1905.

The common interests, which were codified in the alliance, included the maintenance of the balance of power in the far east and the preservation of the territorial integrity of China. Britain and Japan claimed to be defending the *status quo* and found themselves increasingly opposed to the nation that seemed to be threatening the balance of power in east Asia, Russia. Both the allies had material interests in dispute with Russia, Japan in Korea, Britain in north China and on the Indian frontier. Though there was this underlying hostility, both powers were anxious to patch up with Russia some settlement of differences. But, even when Japan was putting out feelers to Russia in 1901 and 1903, it was recognized that there was an inevitable clash of interests between them and that any settlement was likely to be temporary. Britain too was not unwilling to come to an arrangement with Russia or France wherever in the world their interests were opposed; but it could not be said that there was any real break in hostility between Britain and Russia in Asia until 1907. Besides the situation was always changing. Indeed after 1905 it was Japan who was more likely to alter the balance of power in the far east than Russia and, when this took place, something of the common interest, written into the Anglo-Japanese alliance, was lost. The second alliance was no longer an alliance of the *status quo*.

The other common interest was of a different kind. The preservation of the territorial integrity of China was a principle and did not affect the allies' material interests. It may be criticized on the ground that it was included in the treaty for propaganda purposes and was not a genuine belief of the two allies. Certainly when their material interests conflicted with an ideological statement of this kind, the latter was very soon dropped. Thus the independence of Korea, which had been solemnly recognized in the 1902 treaty, was dropped in 1905 when it conflicted with Japan's ambitions. In general, it may be accepted that for the duration of the present study, the independence and integrity of China were things to which the allies found it proper and convenient to subscribe. But the professed belief in the integrity of China and the Open Door doctrine associated with it lost much of its validity when Japan took over the lease of the Liaotung peninsula in 1905. In other words, here too the common interests of the allies were changing and declining.

The alliance also served specifically national interests. In the long term, there is little doubt that it enabled Britain to add to her own power the naval power of Japan and thereby to defend her commercial stake in China. It can be argued that it also performed the negative function of preventing Japan from going over to the Russian camp in 1901; but this study has tried to show that, even if this had been achieved, it was bound to be a temporary solution and that British statesmen were fully aware of this. On Japan the alliance conferred status, recognition of her aspirations in the far east and the co-operation of the largest naval power in the world. It saved her from isolation.

In view of the emphasis given in the sub-title of this study to co-operation between the 'two Island Empires', it is necessary to assess the naval benefits of the alliance. In 1902 the diplomatic notes exchanged were vague and the naval conferences produced no very spectacular results. But naval co-operation should not be discounted as a factor in the Russo-Japanese war. Even though Britain was under no obligation to be involved in a war confined to Russia and Japan, the Japanese could rely on British naval support in the event of an attempt being made to invade their shores. The alliance of 1905 was rather similar. There was no specific reference to naval co-operation; and in any case Britain had withdrawn her battleships from far eastern waters. But, as Balfour pointed out, Japan could still count on the British fleet[1] in time of trouble, even though the 1905 treaty made no mention of it. Thus, one should not underrate the extent of potential naval co-operation on account of the guarded language of the treaties concerned.

In order to limit her own commitments, there was a tendency for Britain to encourage Japan's naval building programmes. It may be that British policy on this point was blind and short-sighted. If it was blind in the long term, it suited Britain's interests well in the short term. The maintenance of Britain's profitable commerce with China now ultimately depended on the protection afforded by Japanese naval power. Moreover, the focus of British attention was gradually returning

[1] Lansdowne papers, Balfour to the king, 3 August 1905.

to Europe and she had to devote the resources available for naval building to meeting her defence needs there.

Such were the overall practical benefits of the alliance. It is possible to argue that the benefits were small compared to the obligations imposed on the parties. This is true in the sense that the alliance imposed far-reaching obligations on the powers to go to war; but it must be remembered that the obligations never materialized; there is no case of the alliance being invoked to drag either ally into war.[1]

The agreements served a military purpose as one would expect from an alliance. But one should not read back the predominantly military character of a present-day alliance into those of 1902 and 1905. Indeed one of the debated points is how far the Anglo-Japanese alliance was offensive in character. It is common for Japanese historians to describe it by the phrases 'defensive' (bōshu) or 'offensive and defensive' (kōshu). The three authors of monographs on the alliance have placed the treaties of 1902 and 1905 within the category of 'offensive and defensive'. This is open to doubt. Since there is no scientific way of classifying the treaties by analysing their terms, these descriptions are purely subjective and have no precise meaning. Such phrases reflect either the apologetics of contemporaries or the hindsight of later writers. Few responsible statesmen will admit that an alliance into which their country has entered, is offensive. Thus Balfour wrote of the 1905 alliance, which is often regarded as offensive-defensive, as being 'purely defensive'.[2] It is of course open to historians to make a judgment about these treaties but all too often they merely import prejudices of their own. Thus Dr Chang has described as offensive and defensive the first alliance which is widely spoken of as being defensive.[3] Clearly these phrases should be treated with great suspicion and not be regarded as accurate measuring-rods. Another difficulty is that the terminology adopted depends upon the national standpoint of the user. Thus, however innocuous and defensive the two alliances may appear to those in Britain and Japan, it is understandable that those in Russia should regard them as menacing and offensive.

It seems best, therefore, to ignore these categories and try to evaluate the alliance by asking how far the two treaties can be described as warlike or provocative, despite their professions to the contrary. Much

---

[1] In 1914 Japan did not enter the war specifically under the obligations of the alliance.
[2] Cabinet 1/5/28, memorandum by Balfour, 27 May 1905.
[3] Chang, p. 96.

depends on how provocative Japan's actions towards Russia were after the conclusion of the 1902 alliance. It has been the argument of this study that, by choosing an agreement with Britain, Japan did not exclude the possibility of a later agreement being concluded with Russia and that this was admitted by the British statesmen. To argue that Japan, by opting for a British alliance, showed her preference for a warlike solution of her differences with Russia, seems to be false. The alternatives open to Japan in practice were: a British alliance, which was on offer, and an agreement with Russia for which feelers had been put out without eliciting any definite response. Thus the British alliance was not an unexpected or illogical choice; it did not necessarily have militaristic overtones. On the contrary, it was the understanding between the signatories that Japan would not be prevented by the alliance from approaching Russia for some settlement of outstanding differences. Right down to the outbreak of war, it would have been possible for Japan to reach an agreement with Russia. But when the alliance came up for consideration in 1905, there was no real alternative available to Japan and, at Britain's insistence, a more far-reaching alliance was concluded.[1] With the return of peace, an agreement with Russia again became feasible; and the fact that it was achieved in 1907 was largely because there was not a necessary contradiction between it and the British alliance. Those who write of Japan's foreign policy in this period as one of *mutually exclusive alternatives* are labouring under a misunderstanding. Japan certainly had choices open to her; and the conclusion of the British alliances in 1902 and 1905 did not close the door to peaceful negotiation with the Russians. To this extent the alliance cannot be condemned as being aggressive in intention.

It is the first alliance which is blamed for not being primarily defensive; and it cannot be denied that it had military and naval implications. But there was a significant distinction between them: the military obligations came into force only in case of emergency, whereas the naval obligations came into force with the signing and were to be applied in peacetime. They were however intended to save both powers from increased naval and military expenditure on the far

---

[1] Galperin, p. 243, describes the alliance after 1905 as having the typical form of a warlike alliance and rightly contends that the second alliance was more serious than the first. At the same time, it must be recognized that the chance of hostilities taking place after Russia's defeat and her treaties with Britain and Japan was in practice much smaller.

east. It would be wrong, therefore, to argue that the alliance had purely diplomatic sanctions; it had also military sanctions.

But were these military sanctions likely to precipitate a war? The question turns on the extent to which confidence is placed on the expressed intentions of the two powers. After the South African war, Britain certainly did not want to be involved in a far eastern war.[1] But did she, as Galperin argues,[2] want to involve Japan in war with Russia, while ensuring that she remained outside such a conflict herself? There is no evidence to suggest this. And what of Japan's attitude? The ministry was told by the army that, if war was to be made on Russia, it should be made quickly. It might therefore be expected that Japan would not have delayed too long after the signature of the alliance. Instead, the ministry waited until April 1903, when Russia refused to withdraw from Manchuria. Even then it acted slowly and negotiated deliberately. It acted as a drag on an aroused public opinion. The alliance offered the Japanese increased support in an emergency but did not precipitate them into action. It certainly improved Japan's bargaining position in time of peace but it did not push her into war.

One is led to the conclusion that the Russo-Japanese war started on account of the failure of negotiations, not as a result of the British alliance. Japan's overtures might have succeeded if the Witte-Lamsdorf group had retained power at the tsarist court. But new groups which came into the emperor's favour in 1903 were much less conciliatory. The historian, Chang, is probably right to say: 'It lay with Russia to decide whether the Anglo-Japanese Agreement was to secure general peace in Asia.'[3] To that extent the alliance was not in itself a guarantee of peace; it left the decision in the hands of the unstable Russian regime. For these reasons, it seems to be unjust to condemn the first alliance for being aggressive, offensive or warlike.

From the standpoint of British history, the subject of this study might be said to be an historical by-way, which intersects many major highways, while remaining itself always secondary. Certainly the Japanese treaty was for Britain merely one of many world-wide interests and, down to Japan's success in the war with Russia, an instrument whose significance was recognized only by the few. But,

---

[1] *The history of 'The Times'*, iii, pp. 381–2.
[2] Galperin, p. 243.   [3] Chang, p. 92.

for the Japanese, the treaty was their only significant link with the outside world, the only thing which saved Japan from isolation in a world which was afflicted by suspicions based on fear of the Yellow Peril. It also played an indirect part in solving Japan's domestic problems. Under the shadow of the alliance, Japan was able to devote her energies to attaining the high industrial and commercial objectives which she had set herself. Britain's direct help in this process was only on a minor scale but during the alliance period Japanese goods succeeded in finding markets farther and farther afield. For Japan, therefore, it was in a real sense an important highway.

The foundations had been laid of the alliance which lasted until the Washington conference and continued to be an important factor in the diplomacy of the far east throughout that period. Whatever the limitations of the alliance, Britain and Japan benefited from being partners in a durable combination at a time when the other powers there were unable to act together. But alliances are never static; and the Anglo-Japanese alliance was always changing its character. In many ways its fortunes declined after the Russo-Japanese war.

The alliance reached its highest point in the period from 1902 until 1905. Thereafter, many of the common interests, which had bound together the allies under the first agreement, were gradually lost. Moreover the alliance began to attract opposition from a new direction: the United States did not like the growth of the Japanese navy nor Japan's continental expansion in Korea and Manchuria, which were not expressly provided for in the terms of the alliance but were none the less carried out under its shadow. Britain had already shown herself to be attentive to American views of the alliance in 1905 and became increasingly sensitive to them in the future. Again the enemy envisaged by the alliance became less and less clear after 1907: up to that year it had been understood between the two parties to be Russia, although this had not been specifically stated in the treaty itself. When this focus was lost, something of the heart of the treaty was lost also. Indeed it is the need to deal with Russian expansion in Asia, which linked the British and Japanese governments in a common concern between 1895 and 1907 and gives this study a unity of its own.

APPENDIX

TRANSLATED DOCUMENTS

This appendix contains translations of the most important documents from the Japanese side on the Anglo-Japanese alliances of 1902 and 1905. They have been selected to illustrate especially the motives underlying Japanese government policy and the alternatives open to the Japanese ministers in reaching decisions.

A. Japan's Policy after the Boxer Disturbances

After the legations at Peking had been relieved by foreign armies, it was commonly believed that these troops would proceed to the partition of China. In an attempt to discourage the idea that Japanese troops should be moved into Korea, prime minister Yamagata Aritomo prepared a long memorandum on 20 August 1900, which was brought to the notice of the foreign minister and other cabinet colleagues. Only a brief extract containing the gist of his argument is given.

Nihon gaikō bunsho, 33/III, no. 2370

While the Boxer disturbances have still not been cleared up, the powers have all openly testified that they will maintain the *status quo* in China and will not partition it. Yet although they try to disclaim their ambitions, Russia has quickly built up its forces and naval strength in Manchuria, Britain in the Yangtse and Germany and France likewise. Italy and Belgium despite their smaller interests have nevertheless sent troops. All give abundant evidence of lurking evil intentions. . . .

How should Japan deal with this situation? Japan's concern with China lies in trade, not in aggression, lies in preserving the *status quo*, not in dividing the country. Previously we asked China for the non-alienation of Fukien province, our intention being to keep up with the other powers and to preserve peace in east Asia. At present we should try to fulfil this object and should add Chekiang province to our sphere of influence in Fukien. In this way we can in future build up special strength in China opposite Taiwan; in time of peace it will serve as a base for our trade and industry inside China; in time of emergency we can hold in our grasp the 'throat of the far east' and guard against any intrusions by an enemy. . . .

Those who nowadays discuss our policy in east Asia, all say: Korea is only separated from our outlying island-possession, Tsushima, by a mere girdle of water and is really closely connected with us; if Korea were to fall under occupation by someone else, our people could no longer sleep undisturbed; we must use this golden opportunity to occupy Korea and put a stop to Russia's southward movements in advance. This argument is certainly to the point. If Korea passes into someone else's possession, it would be a serious menace to the safety of our country. So Korea cannot be allowed to fall into the hands of others. At the time of the Russo-Japanese agreement [1898], we sought to lay down spheres of influence with this very object. But, now that all the powers are discussing the joint action to be taken over China, they would not agree to our submitting for discussion by the powers a proposal which has no direct relevance for current problems. Even if Britain privately agreed to it and the United States raised no objections, Russia, Germany and France would join together and oppose it. In event of war, would Britain still help us with her military forces? If we could not rely for sure on Britain allying with us, we would be forced to fight alone against a threefold enemy.

If we are so determined to take Korea, I wonder whether this is the best time. The proverb runs: 'a man who chases two rabbits, can catch neither'. Now that all the powers are working together and 'hunting' in China, we should first chase a rabbit in the south and, after capturing it, it would not be too late to chase another in the north. The fact that we previously returned the Liaotung peninsula, threw away Weihaiwei and then concluded a treaty with Russia, was due to our regarding our national strength as inadequate in the light of the east Asian situation and adopting a national policy of 'defending in the north and advancing in the south'. To complete the operations at our 'southern gate' and develop our commerce and industry, it is vital to obtain a foothold in Fukien and Chekiang. Moreover the situation is favourable for this and the time is ripe.

B. THE IDEA OF AN EASTERN ALLIANCE

After the project for an alliance between Germany, Britain and Japan had been mooted by Eckardstein and Hayashi in London in April 1901, Yamagata who was in retirement but was still active in politics as a genrō or Elder Statesman, prepared a memorandum entitled 'Tōyō dōmei ron' [the idea of an eastern alliance]. It was written on 24 April 1901 and presented to prime minister Itō Hirobumi. Since Itō's cabinet fell shortly after, it was not immediately influential. But his successor, Katsura, was Yamagata's nominee and was probably much affected by it.

Kōshaku Yamagata Aritomo den, III, 494–6

When we reflect carefully on the situation, although the disturbances in north China have ceased, the peace treaty with China has not yet been signed and the powers are no longer firmly united. Though the secret agreement between Russia and China [over Manchuria] has been nipped in the bud by the protests of Japan and other powers, Russia has for a long time been penetrating into Manchuria and the building of the Chinese Eastern Railway and the development of Port Arthur and Dairen all indicate that it is intent on permanent occupation. From now on, it will use every opportunity to expand its sphere of influence and seize the rest of Manchuria. In China, the social order has already broken down; the economic foundations have collapsed; and the country only survives in an effete state. Even if the powers plan to bolster up China for a while in order to uphold the balance of power, it cannot hold together for long, because externally Russia is pressing and internally riots are continually occurring. The 'slicing of the melon' in China is part of its destiny and cannot be averted by human effort. Although its partition is inevitable, China has a history of several thousand years and is a country of 18 provinces and 400,000,000 people; it cannot be destroyed in an instant. The powers seek to maintain the integrity of China not only because they wish to keep the balance but also because they know that they would gain few advantages and suffer great losses from any other policy. We should decide beforehand on a policy to deal with China's predicament and plan both to keep the peace in east Asia and to ensure our own security.

The triple alliance which the German chargé d'affaires in London has recently mentioned to minister Hayashi privately, seems on examination to be something which has been carefully thought out between Germany and Britain. German industry and commerce have recently expanded considerably and are seeking markets urgently. In seeking markets, there is nowhere like China. There Germany hopes for a gradual change in the situation in her favour by preserving peace in east Asia, gaining commercial profits, acquiring railway and mining rights and occupying areas of strategic importance; and she considers it wise to align herself with Britain, even although it antagonizes Russia for a time. On the other hand, Britain has colonies in every part of the globe and is already having difficulty in maintaining them. It has at present no thought of obtaining new territory in China. Having for long been isolated among the powers, it has come to the stage of realizing that it is important to cultivate friendly powers and has secretly exchanged views with Germany. Why should it not accept them? This is what previously brought about the Anglo-German agreement; this is what has given rise to the present plan for an alliance.

Relations between Japan and Russia have not yet suffered a major upset but sooner or later a serious collision is inevitable. If Russia uses violence and invades our rightful spheres, we must be prepared to confront her decisively. But, if we are to avoid a collision and prevent war beforehand, we must secure the help of other powers to arrest Russia's southward advance.

The fact that an alliance is now mooted is of immense advantage to us. We should seek Britain's views and devise with her a treaty of alliance in consultation with Germany. Among its clauses we should stipulate our freedom of action in Korea, even though we do not know how far it would be admitted. In any case, we cannot go beyond the Russo-Japanese agreement [1898] while it lasts. The best thing for us would be if, by keeping Korea outside the present alliance and making an agreement of some sort with Russia later on, we could get recognition for Japan's freedom of action there. In negotiating the alliance, it would be well for this point to be borne in mind. It should be provided that, when one party to the alliance is engaged in fighting with another power and a third power assists the enemy, the remaining signatory to the alliance should intervene, though it is not clear how far it should be involved in the war. This also requires to be settled beforehand. If the alliance is achieved, we can preserve peace in east Asia, build up our trade, stimulate our industry and revive the economy. At a convenient opportunity later, it should not be very difficult to establish spheres of influence in Fukien and Chekiang. Our objective meantime should simply be to conclude this alliance quickly. If we lose this golden opportunity, we shall only have ourselves to blame.

c. Katsura Favours Negotiations with Britain

General Katsura, who came to office as prime minister in June 1901, was favourable towards a British alliance. It was not until Lansdowne spoke to Hayashi on 31 July that the issue was discussed as a practical proposition by the cabinet and genrō. Katsura gives his version of the consultations which took place and of the choices open to Japan in this memorandum which cannot be precisely dated but was written at the time.

Kōshaku Katsura Tarō den, I, 1055-6

In accordance with the emperor's instructions, the draft of Japan's reply [to Lansdowne's suggestions] was passed on to the genrō and their opinion taken without anyone raising any objections. Among them, some like Marquis Itō thought that for Britain to propose such a thing must ultimately be a sign that its national strength was failing. While there was no scope for Britain to extend its power in the far east because of the [south] African war, Russia, taking advantage of Britain's preoccupations, was using it as an opportunity to expand its own power there. This was certainly the reason for Britain's approach to us. But, as we are in any case bound to act against Russia, it would be wise to take advantage of Britain's statement and comply with its request.

Since the war with China, there have been in Japan two separate views: to make friends with Russia or to make friends with Britain. The pro-Russian group are those who think in terms of 'temporary peace': ultimately if the Russians decide to fulfil their ambitions, it will be very difficult for us to stand up to them and we could not match Russia's strength. A national problem of this kind has arisen several times since the Meiji Restoration; and each time we have had difficulty in dealing with the situation. One cannot say in retrospect that the pro-Russian view is unreasonable. But, in my opinion, Russia's policy will not stop with the occupation of Manchuria: if Manchuria comes into its clutches, it will inevitably extend into Korea and will not end until there is no room left for us. If that be the case, it would only be a short-term remedy for us now to make friends with Russia and we would be forced to let Russia proceed as it likes. This could never be the national policy of our Empire and I could never agree to it. On the other hand, if Russia wishes to be friendly to us, even if only on a temporary basis, there is no reason for us to turn it down. But it must be borne in mind that, since it would only be temporary, there is bound to be a clash in the end.

As against this, Britain can by its interests remain on good terms with us: it is not a country with territorial ambitions and, with its power extending almost all over the world, it can unquestionably be assumed that its territorial ambitions are not likely to lead to a conflict with us. The essence of Britain's policy is to get us to resist Russian expansion into the far east. This is especially so at a time when she has her hands full with the disturbances in South Africa.

For these reasons, we decided that it would be best to follow up Britain's request. The cabinet and genrō were also in favour. On 4 August Marquis Itō visited me at my country mansion at Hayama and had a long talk with me. I decided that we should make adequate counter-demands from Britain and drew up the draft reply accordingly. In his conversation with me, Itō questioned whether Britain would open negotiations on the basis of our demands. But, even if Britain would not agree to our demands, we would be none the worse. Itō appeared to think that it would be difficult for Britain to accept our conditions. I returned to Tokyo and consulted Yamagata. I then discussed with the acting foreign minister, Sone, and had instructions sent to our minister in London.

D. KOMURA PLEADS FOR AN ALLIANCE WITH BRITAIN

In order to convince the various genrō of the wisdom of the cabinet's decision in favour of an alliance with Britain, Komura arranged for a memorandum to be prepared setting out the arguments. This was drawn up under special instructions from Komura by Yamaza, the head of the Political Affairs Department of the Foreign Ministry. It was presented to the genrō at their meeting on 7 December 1901 and served its purpose in convincing them. It gives the historian the best available statement of Japanese foreign policy at the time.

Komura gaikōshi, I, 277–80

China and Korea have a very close connection with Japan. Korea, in particular, cannot ever be forgotten since its fate is a matter of life and death for us. Despite several negotiations we have had with Russia over Korea in the past, she has established a frontier with Korea and is always opposed to our wishes because of her Manchurian enterprises. The Japanese government regrets that for this reason a satisfactory solution of the Korean question has still not been reached.

Russia has established itself increasingly in Manchuria and, even supposing it was now to withdraw its forces, it still possesses railways and has the right to retain its troops there on the pretext of defending them. So, if we leave matters to be settled by present-day conventions, there is no doubt that Manchuria will revert to *de facto* occupation by Russia; and if Manchuria becomes the property of Russia, Korea itself cannot remain independent. Thus it is now urgently necessary for Japan to do something quickly about it.

When we consider the present situation in the light of past history, it seems unlikely that we can get Russia to resolve the Korean question as we would like, simply by diplomatic discussions. There are only two methods of achieving this. One is to show our determination not to shrink from war as a means of accomplishing our aims. The other is to link up with a third power and thereby get Russia to accept our wishes. But we must always avoid hostilities with Russia as far as possible; and moreover we do not have good grounds for making a last-ditch stand, since Russia's demands over Manchuria have lately become much milder. I therefore believe that there is no better policy than the second alternative, namely to link up with another power such as Britain and use our combined strength to get Russia to meet our demands.

If we were able to conclude an agreement with Russia by purely diplomatic means and thus increase the friendship between us, the merits and demerits of this approach could be assessed as follows:

1. *It would preserve peace in the east but it would be purely temporary.*
An agreement with Russia could maintain peace temporarily in the east but Russia with its aggressive principles could not ultimately be satisfied with this. Since Russia expects to bring the whole of China progressively under its control, an agreement with Russia would not succeed in guaranteeing the maintenance of peace for any length of time.

2. *The economic advantages would be small.*
Japan can obtain substantial benefits from using the Manchurian and Trans-Siberian Railways even today without any agreement with Russia. But I cannot seriously consider these territories as places with good prospects for

trade until their population increases greatly and conditions there improve. Such a period is still far off.

3. *It would destroy the sympathy of the Chinese and thereby seriously injure Japan's interests.*

Recently Chinese of all classes have come to view this country with affection and confidence. This is really an opportunity which must be taken; and our countrymen must not be lacking in enterprise in China, whether it be in commerce, in industry or in advice on general or military education. In these circumstances, it is most important to retain the warm sympathy of the Chinese people at every level as it is today. If we were to make an agreement with Russia, that current of goodwill would immediately change.

4. *We would require to maintain parity with Britain's naval power.*

An agreement of this kind between Japan and Russia would confer only slight economic benefits and moreover the result of befriending Russia and antagonizing Britain would be that our naval strength would always have to be kept in parity with Britain.

As against these points, there would be the following advantages in concluding an agreement with Britain:

1. *It could ensure a fairly permanent peace in the east.*

Britain does not wish to increase its territorial responsibilities in the east: it wants to preserve the *status quo* and especially to improve its trade. Thus the result of reaching an agreement with Britain could be to limit Russia's ambitions and keep peace in the east on a relatively permanent basis.

2. *Japan can be consistent with its principles without fear of being criticized by the powers.*

The essence of an Anglo-Japanese agreement is peaceful and defensive, its direct objectives being the preservation of China and Korea and the open door for commerce in China. There is not the slightest fear that this would incur the displeasure of the powers; and it corresponds with the principles to which this country has often publicly adhered.

3. *It will advance the standing of our country in China.*

By concluding an agreement with Britain, our country will be even more trusted by China. This will enable us more easily to carry out our intentions, including the expansion of our interests there.

4. *It will help in solving the Korean problem.*

As we mentioned above, there is no means of getting Russia to agree to a solution of the Korean question in accordance with our wishes unless we link ourselves with a third power and force Russia to accept our wishes. If we link ourselves with Britain as the most suitable third power, this will greatly strengthen our hand in solving the Korean question.

5. *It will bring financial benefits.*

The result of an agreement with Britain would be to improve our credit in commercial circles throughout the world. In addition, since our national development would not conflict with the interests of Britain which would be our partner in the treaty, the British people would be pleased to accord Japan financial and economic facilities. The benefits which our government and people would receive, would be large.

6. *Commercial benefits would not be small.*
British colonies extend to the five continents. The benefits which Japan could gain from emigration and trade in these colonies if relations between Britain and Japan became more friendly, would far exceed those to be derived from Manchuria and Siberia.

7. *It would be easier to maintain parity of naval power with Russia.*
Naval parity with Russia would be far easier to maintain than to keep a naval force always superior to that of Britain.

In view of these arguments, it seems to be beyond dispute that an agreement with Britain would be much more to Japan's advantage than an agreement with Russia.

Finally the powers in Europe are at present protecting and extending their interests by some sort of entente diplomacy, whether it be the triple alliance or the dual alliance, and it would not be wise for Japan to remain in isolation. We may deduce that even a country like Britain which has built up a national tradition of non-alignment over many years, has now come round to seeking an understanding with someone else. For these reasons, I believe it would undoubtedly be the best policy for Japan now to conclude a treaty with her. Since there are grounds for believing that Britain has already passed her zenith and will to some extent tend to decline, it would be best to fix a time-limit for any British treaty.

E. THE ITŌ-KATSURA DEBATE

One obstacle to the understanding of the first Anglo-Japanese alliance is associated with Itō's journey to Russia and his presentation there of a draft Russo-Japanese agreement. Since the standpoint adopted by Itō and Katsura is often misunderstood, it is desirable to include some of the telegrams which they exchanged, even though the number is of necessity limited. On 6 December Itō cabled from Berlin that he had gained the impression in St Petersburg that the Russians desired to reach a fresh understanding with Japan but that this would become impossible after the conclusion of the British alliance. In the parallel telegram that follows, he criticizes the terms of the Japanese cabinet's proposed reply to Britain which had been sent to him for comment.

Itō Hirobumi Hiroku, no. 35, Itō to Katsura, 6 December 1901
I present for your information some observations about the draft agreement

with Britain. It seems to be stated in the preamble that the 'status quo' is one of its aims; but I would point out that the 'status quo' as defined in the existing Russo-Japanese treaty is, as far as we are concerned, so unworkable that we want it changed.

In speaking of 'China', do you refer to the Chinese Empire in its totality or to China proper? Considering that the interpretation of Manchuria's position may crop up at any moment, would it not be wise to prescribe more clearly how far the application of the treaty extends? . . .

The so-called obligation in Additional Article 1 to co-operate in naval activity is doubtless most necessary in wartime; but in peacetime, it might, on the contrary, frequently be the cause of much inconvenience to Japan. Not to mention that both powers could if they so desired co-operate in future, without being bound by a restraining agreement. . . . When other powers get to hear of the alliance, some of them will endeavour to pool their resources and increase their naval strength in the far east. Such a result is almost certain and must be taken into account beforehand. Thus the question will automatically arise as to whether our economic resources can cover the great increase in expenditure needed or not. Moreover this clause will certainly be a barrier to other countries entering the alliance later on.

In general I would ask you to consider each clause carefully in the light of our possible future agreement with Russia and Germany's future attitude. I request you to present this telegram to the emperor.

Itō Hirobumi Hiroku, no. 45, Katsura to Itō, 13 December 1901
I have received your two telegrams from Berlin which were presented to the emperor. He noted your arguments and, after examining the cabinet's decision and the result of the genrō meeting, communicated to you by Count Inoue, concluded that in our present position he would not permit further delay on our part and decided that we must now negotiate with the British government.

About your comments on the draft, my opinions are as follows: You say that the use of the term 'status quo' in the preamble will have the disadvantage of circumscribing our future activities in Korea. I do not think it is quite so objectionable since our intention of defending our interests there, is explicitly stated in Additional Article 3, which was inserted as a sort of exception to the terms of the preamble.

The word 'China' as used in the preamble is to be read as 'Chinese Empire' and therefore implies the whole territory of Imperial China. . . . The object of our so-called 'combined action in time of peace' in Additional Article 1, is to prepare the way for both navies to work together in wartime and is no more than a natural precaution. We at present afford such facilities as coaling and repair to warships of all treaty powers. There is no reason why any inconvenience need arise.

If Japan wants to preserve peace in east Asia, it must always have adequate armament. The need for increasing our naval power proportionally to other countries has been accepted without demur and is not affected by whether an alliance is concluded or not. It is, of course, essential for us to consider shifts in the international situation and Japan's economic circumstances when proceeding with a programme of naval expansion.

Katsura further informed Itō that the genrō had concluded that since 'it was not yet possible to predict whether a Russo-Japanese alliance [sic] could be achieved' it would be best to conclude an agreement with Britain. This prompted the further exchange of telegrams.

Itō Hirobumi Hiroku, no. 48, Itō to Katsura, 13 December 1901

1. There is a grave misunderstanding between us. I never intended to set up a Russo-Japanese alliance. Between 'agreement' and 'alliance', there is a vast difference. I believe that, even though we conclude the conditional alliance of defensive character with Britain, on which you have already embarked, there would still be room for us simultaneously to come to terms with Russia over Korea. As I suggested before, we must reserve the right to take independent action to reach an agreement with Russia over the Korean problem, even though it inevitably involves considerable concessions in Manchuria.

2. The conclusion of an Anglo-Japanese alliance would probably destroy the sympathy towards us of several continental governments. In this way, the negotiation of an agreement between Russia and Japan would become increasingly difficult. I would therefore ask you to use delaying tactics to put off the clinching of the alliance as long as possible; or, if no such opportunity arises, at least to keep it secret. Despite the fact that in various British newspapers — especially *The Times* — certain statements have regrettably leaked out about the rapprochement between Britain and Japan, I should entreat you to keep this treaty secret. Among continental powers, Britain is obviously losing prestige and sympathy. Remember that there is no guarantee that a friendlier association with Britain at this time will not have an adverse effect on our national standing.

3. You seem to be worrying about Japan's possible isolation. But, considering the status and renown which present-day Japan has gained in European diplomatic circles, isolation need not be a drawback for us, if all the while we retain close ties with various countries who wish to have contact with us.

Itō Hirobumi Hiroku, no. 58, Katsura to Itō, 21 December 1901

I want to express my heartfelt thanks for your skilful attempt to bring about an agreement with Russia superior to that which we have at present. I am fully in sympathy with your aspirations and shall strive to assist your labour of mediation. But, on the other hand, I must remind your Excellency that, since the crisis in Manchuria developed [early 1901], we have by our policy given guarantees to various foreign powers that we will assume responsibilities which cannot be neglected if Japanese honour is to be respected in the world. This policy began under your cabinet and I have faithfully continued it, because I also consider it to be the wisest policy. . . . If Japan were to make a treaty with Russia in order to obtain Russian concessions in Korea, Japan could only do so by concluding an agreement which was inconsistent with its former attitude over Manchuria. This would destroy its prestige, forfeit China's confidence and deprive it of the goodwill of those countries which loyally follow the principles for which Japan has stood in the past. . . . The Russians have asked that their position in Manchuria might be equivalent to Japan's in Korea; but our current policy would not permit us to accept such a basis. . . . You very well know that I am not opposed to coming to an understanding with Russia but, in my view, that must be reconciled with the obligations which Japan owes to others. . . .

F. BARON SUEMATSU'S MISSION TO BRITAIN

When the Russo-Japanese war broke out, the Japanese leaders were afraid that Britain's sympathies were not entirely with Japan and sent a special emissary, Suematsu Kenchō, to London for the duration. Suematsu who was the son-in-law of Itō and a prominent member of the Seiyūkai, spent his time influencing politicians and the press. This document is an extract from the dispatch sent by the Japanese foreign minister explaining the purpose of the mission and containing the instructions given to Suematsu. It illustrates in a graphic way that the Japanese were not completely confident.

Nihon gaikō bunsho, 37/38, Nichi-Ro sensō v, no. 441, Komura to Hayashi, 23 February 1904

Since the war with Russia is vital to us, it is absolutely essential for us not only to succeed in military operations but also to use every available diplomatic means to create favourable circumstances for us. That is to say, while you are devoting every effort to this task in the foreground, it is most important that we should also be active in the background. By manipulating the British press, we must persuasively explain the righteousness of our cause and help to defend our interests by showing that the Japanese government was obliged to take up arms in self-defence and that Yellow Peril principles are unreasonable, etc. We consider that it is necessary in this way to prevent the growth of misunderstandings among the British people and to deepen their sympathy towards Japan.

The other day we entrusted Suematsu Kenchō with this task and arranged for him to visit Britain. We would suggest that it is necessary for Suematsu generally to co-operate with you and for your actions to be in complete accord if his duties are to be accomplished.

Instructions given to Suematsu

1. We must convince the British that our government employed every means of compromise with the Russian government and that war became inevitable on account of Russia's actions.

2. Since Yellow Peril feelings lie concealed in the thinking of Europeans and Americans and Russia is stirring them up everywhere, we must prevent a further outbreak.

3. One of the important reasons why the Japanese government advised the Chinese government to remain strictly neutral, was to prevent a fresh wave of Yellow Peril feeling. We must make clear how the Japanese government has made every effort to restrict the sphere of hostilities and not to disturb peace and trade generally.

4. The fact that the Japanese government is striving for the education of the Chinese is cited as one of the strongest pieces of evidence by those who stir up Yellow Peril feeling. It is essential for peace in the east to educate the Chinese and make them a civilized people. Not only does this add to the security of our country; but it is even more valuable for other countries which have interests in the far east. We must make it generally understood that military education is intended to serve the same purposes, enabling China to maintain order by itself and thus making it possible to achieve peace in the far east.

5. Since we earnestly desire to promote even closer relations with Britain, you should endeavour to bring this about.* We would welcome occasional reports giving your opinion on this.

6. We have telegraphed to Minister Hayashi a detailed account of the Russo-Japanese negotiations and will telegraph to him everything that takes place from now on. You should get to know about this. You should send your telegrams at the expense of the legation through Minister Hayashi.

7. Since collaboration with Minister Hayashi is imperative, you should act after consultation with him.

G. HAYASHI RECOMMENDS THE SECOND ALLIANCE

Since Hayashi's *Secret Memoirs* do not cover the alliance of 1905, his stand-point on it and his role in its negotiation is little known. In this report to his

---

* Suematsu also provides a version of these instructions which is generally on the above lines. On this item, it is more detailed: 'London should be used as the focal point for your activities and the Anglo-Japanese alliance should be strengthened.' He inserts an additional instruction not to be found elsewhere: 'It may be necessary to send a special adviser on finance. Try to pave the way for a foreign loan.' *NGB* 37/38, Nichi-Ro sensō v, no. 459.

government, which was written at a crucial stage in discussions by the Japanese cabinet, Hayashi pleads for the *extension* of the alliance for reasons of international diplomacy.

Nihon gaikō bunsho, 38/I, no. 16, Hayashi to Komura, 20 May 1905

After studying the European political situation closely, I venture to express my views on the continuance of the Anglo-Japanese alliance though I fear that it may seem very presumptuous.

No relationship among the great powers exceeds in friendship that which now exists between Britain and the United States. Russia's policy has 'cooled' the goodwill of France and the Franco-Russian alliance is no longer based on mutual sympathy and common political interests. As a result, the Anglo-French understanding has gradually grown in goodwill; and Italy has naturally shown sympathy for the Anglo-French entente. Germany is now almost isolated and, if it acts in the future as it has done in the past, it will find itself in even greater isolation. Spain and Austria do not count for much.

If, in this situation, Japan enters into a close alliance with Britain, it will be able to obtain the support of a strong group, consisting of Britain, the United States, France and Italy, and the resulting benefits could be very large. In that event, there would be no need for Japan to fear a war of revenge on Russia's part sometime in the future. Moreover there would be the following advantages:

1. Japan will receive assistance from practically all the powers at the time of the peace talks which will end the present war;
2. Japan can certainly defeat the wicked schemes which are at present being prepared by Russians and Germans to form a European coalition against Japan, inspired by Yellow Peril feelings;
3. the sympathy which will grow up between the Japanese and the Anglo-Saxons [i.e. Britons and Americans] as a result of the alliance may gradually discourage the British dominions and the United States from excluding Japanese labourers because they are of different race. If these racial questions are allowed to persist as at present, they will lead to serious complications in the future.

The only conceivable collisions of interest between Japan on the one hand and Britain and the United States on the other would result from peaceful commercial competition and would have nothing to do with the alliance at all. I cannot think of any disadvantages which would spring from strengthening the alliance.

For these reasons I conclude that the strengthening of the alliance on the basis suggested by Lord Lansdowne the other day, will be to Japan's benefit from any point of view and earnestly hope that the Imperial government will accept his lordship's proposals.

H. Japanese Cabinet Approves the Second Alliance

This memorandum 'regarding the strengthening and extension of the British alliance' was prepared by Baron Komura for the Japanese cabinet meeting on 24 May 1905. Following Japanese practice, it was adopted as a cabinet resolution and later approved by the emperor. It shows the influence of Hayashi's views (document G) and was written before Japan's victory in the battle of the Japan Sea was known.

Komura gaikōshi, II, 167–9

Although Russia's plans for the far east have been destroyed at the roots as a result of the present war, the Russians have not given up their cherished ambitions at all and it is inevitable that they will plan a comeback. Hence Japan too must with all vigilance make preparations accordingly. Even if our country concludes a peace settlement on satisfactory terms, it will take several years for Japan to accomplish its postwar plans. During this period we must take steps to ensure our security. As one method of attaining this object, it was earlier decided [i.e. by the cabinet on 8 April] to renew the Anglo-Japanese agreement, the idea being that the treaty would not be changed in character and the scope of its application but only that its duration would be prolonged. But when we inquired the views of the British government, it wanted to go further. It wished not only to extend the scope of the treaty but also to change its character by altering it from a defensive to an offensive-defensive alliance.

This constitutes an extremely important change but, after thinking deeply over the future course of Japan's affairs, we conclude that our best policy would be to alter the present treaty to an offensive-defensive alliance. Our reasons are:

1. That an offensive-defensive alliance is far more useful than the present treaty for safeguarding peace in the future, does not need elaboration. The British government is certainly not a trouble-maker and is committed to the maintenance of peace so that the views of both countries are at one on this point.

2. Since Russia will significantly increase its armaments in the far east with the object of taking revenge some day, we must increase our precautionary measures against this if we are to ensure peace in the future. As a result of the present war, it is not immediately possible to attain that object. Nevertheless, if Japan concludes an offensive-defensive alliance with Britain and builds up its armaments to the same extent as Russia's in the far east, there should be no occasion for Russia to contemplate revenge and we could thereby help to maintain peace.

3. By reason of the present war, the true merit of our country has come to be recognized by the powers. We must remember that, while it has commanded

admiration, thoughts of suspicion and fear also exist in the background. Such thoughts will gradually increase as our national strength develops after the war; and there is the danger that Japan may find itself isolated. However, by signing an offensive-defensive alliance with Britain, we should be able to prevent that misfortune and avoid other forms of ostracism.

An offensive-defensive alliance with Britain would thus be beneficial to Japan.

[There follows an outline of the new treaty as conceived by Japan].

The present is a favourable opportunity for concluding an agreement which should not be missed. Japan has acquired a dominant position through its succession of victories in battle and Britain is convinced that final victory will go to Japan. Since it has clearly indicated its desires on the lines we have described above, we believe that it is very necessary that we amend the alliance quickly, while Britain's confidence remains unaltered and its cabinet does not go out of office.

BIBLIOGRAPHICAL NOTE[1]

A. L. Galperin, the leading Soviet historian of the Anglo-Japanese alliance, wrote in 1947 that the alliance

has received inadequate and even inaccurate treatment in bourgeois literature. In Britain, as far as we know, not one monograph has appeared on this subject. In Japan, there is only one apart from the work of Muto Chozo dealing with the early period of Anglo-Japanese relations.[2]

Galperin's charge is valid: monographs on the alliance are few and, what is even more surprising, such as there are have not been written in Britain or Japan. Since Galperin made his complaint, the situation has largely remained unchanged and studies of the subject in 'bourgeois literature' have been few. In this note, the literature on the subject, first in European languages and then in Japanese, will be reviewed.

Two studies of the alliance were written before it came to an end in 1923: Justus Hashagen, *England und Japan seit Schimonoseki* (Essen, 1915) and A. L. P. Dennis, *The Anglo-Japanese alliance* (Berkeley, 1923 and 1934). Both works are necessarily dated. Professor Dennis was asked to prepare his monograph by the Carnegie Peace Foundation for the meetings of the Washington conference. The book, which is an indictment of the alliance as an example of pre-1914 entente diplomacy, was not published until after the conference.

Studies of the alliance have naturally been dependent on the source materials available at any given time. The earliest of these was *The secret memoirs of Count Tadasu Hayashi, G.C.V.O.*, edited by A. M. Pooley (London, 1915). These 'memoirs' purported to be translated extracts from a history of Japanese diplomacy from 1871 to 1908 which Hayashi intended to write but left uncompleted. They came into Pooley's hands in 1913 and

---

[1] Full details of the books mentioned and the translations of their titles will be found in the Bibliography.

[2] Galperin, *Anglo-yaponskii soiuz, 1902–21*, p. 8. The Japanese reference is to Mutō Chōzō, *Nichi-Ei kōtsūshi no kenkyū* (Tokyo, 1937), which only deals with the relationship between Britain and Japan down to 1868. The other Japanese work, to which he refers, is Shinobu Jumpei, *Nidai gaikō no shinsō* (Tokyo, 1928) which he wrongly attributes to Shinobu Seizaburō.

were translated into English and smuggled to London for publication. They contained the disclosure that Itō had in 1901 offered Russia an agreement, while the Tokyo government were negotiating with Britain; and the Japanese Foreign Ministry suppressed publication of the story in Japanese. But Pooley, with the knowledge of the British Foreign Office, went ahead with the publication in London. Although the Japanese government considered that the disclosures were discreditable, they were in fact common knowledge in the far east among persons concerned with foreign affairs.[1] It is now possible to compare Pooley's version of the negotiations for the first alliance with Hayashi's own report to his government, written in London on 6 May 1902 and entitled 'Nichi-Ei dōmei teiketsu shimatsu' ('Circumstances of the conclusion of the Anglo-Japanese alliance').[2] While there is a recognizable relationship between the two, there are great discrepancies which suggest that his official report had either been substantially edited for publication by Hayashi or mistranslated into English. These discrepancies destroy some of the confidence which has been placed in the *Hayashi Memoirs*.[3]

A further range of materials became available with the publication of the German and British documents on pre-1914 diplomacy. The volumes of *Die grosse Politik* and *British documents on the origins of the war, 1898–1914*, which were relevant to the alliances of 1902 and 1905, had been published by 1930. The first four volumes of the *British documents*, taken together with the *Blue books*, contain considerable information on the far eastern situation from 1898 to 1907. They contain sections on the first and second alliances and on Russian policy in the far east. None the less affairs in the far east were only of marginal interest in the events leading up to the first Great War; and it was not to be expected that the editors of the series would in their selection emphasize far eastern, as much as European, affairs. The archives, which have now been opened, have much new light to throw on the alliance.

These documents were exploited in studies by Drs Chang, Minrath and Cramer. Chang Chung-fu, *The Anglo-Japanese alliance* (Baltimore, 1931), is a brief account of the alliance from its origins in the Sino-Japanese war to its ending at the Washington conference. It is a sound piece of work, which gives special emphasis to the impact of the alliance on Korea and China. The two German studies — Paul Minrath, *Das Englisch-Japanische Bündnis von 1902* (Stuttgart, 1933) and Anneliese Crämer, *Die Beziehungen zwischen England und Japan von 1894 bis 1902* (Zeulenroda, 1935) — deal only with the antecedents of the first alliance. Minrath's work, which is the

---

[1] E.g. J. O. P. Bland, *Recent events and present policies in China*, 293.

[2] *NGB* 35, no. 24.

[3] W. L. Langer, *Diplomacy of imperialism*, p. ix, wrote of 'the complete reliability of our best Japanese source', the *Hayashi Memoirs*. J. A. S. Grenville, *Lord Salisbury and foreign policy*, p. 391, states that they 'have stood the test of time extraordinarily well'.

more substantial of the two, treats the alliance, as its sub-title — Die Grundlegung der Entente-Politik im Fernen Osten — suggests, as part of the alignment of the powers in Europe and the far east. Both seem to exaggerate the extent to which European considerations weighed with the two powers in entering into the alliance.

Other studies made use of selected Japanese materials. Professor Langer in his *Diplomacy of imperialism* links the alliance to European diplomacy or, at any rate, to European alignments in Asia. The book covers a much broader field than the alliance, since it treats the whole range of imperialist ventures from 1890 to 1902, but it devotes the final forty pages to the alliance. It is based on a formidable set of sources which include parts of the writings of the Japanese statesmen, Katō Takaaki and Itō Hirobumi. Many of Langer's conclusions still hold good. Another writer to make extensive use of the biography of Katō was C. N. Spinks, 'The background of the Anglo-Japanese alliance', *Pacific Historical Review*, no. 8 (1939), 317–40. This is a valuable study of relations between the two countries from 1894 to 1901 but it stops short of the alliance negotiations.

Between 1922 and 1938, many important documents on tsarist diplomacy in the far east were issued in publications such as *Krasnyi Arkhiv*. These threw important light on the alliance which can only be understood in the context of Russia's actions there. These documents have stimulated Soviet historians to write a good deal about the far east in this period. The findings of the leading authority on the alliance, Galperin, are spread over several monographs. His most important book, *Anglo-yaponskii soiuz, 1902–21*, offers the most comprehensive treatment of the subject, using a wide range of sources in Japanese, German, French and English, as well as new material drawn from the archives of the Russian Ministry of Foreign Affairs. He presents the alliance as leading inexorably to the war with Russia. His article 'Iz istorii anglo-yaponskikh otnoshenie, 1902–5', *Uchenie zapiski Tikhookeanskovo Instituta*, no. 1 (1947), 85–222, is in essentials an extract from his larger study. A detailed study of the second alliance and the diplomacy of the Russo-Japanese war may be found in 'Diplomaticheskaya podgotovka Portsmutskoi mirnoi konferentsii yapono-anglo-amerikanskim blokom', *Istoricheskie Zapiski*, no. 50 (1955), 169–223. The only other Soviet writer who need be mentioned is B. A. Romanov, the author of two general studies, *Rossiya v Manchzhurii* and *Ocherki diplomaticheskoi istorii russko-yaponskoi voiny, 1895–1907*. He is also the author of a study on the origins of the alliance under the title 'Proiskhozhdenie anglo-yaponskovo dogovora 1902', *Istoricheskie Zapiski*, no. 10 (1941), 40–65.

The archives of the British Foreign Office on the alliance are open for research under the operation of the fifty-year rule; and a large number of collections of private papers of statesmen who took part in the making of the alliance have become available for study. Making use of these, several studies of foreign policy which touch on the Anglo-Japanese alliance have been published by Zara Steiner, G. W. Monger and J. A. S. Grenville. Dr Monger deals with the first and second alliances, while Miss Steiner and Dr Grenville deal exclusively with the first alliance. These studies, while they cover the alliance only incidentally, render all former accounts of British policy out of date.

It may seem strange to separate the studies in Japanese from those in European languages but this is not unjustified. While Japanese sources have in some cases been translated and used by foreign scholars, the findings of Japanese monographs have generally been ignored in foreign studies. Partly this was because Japanese studies of the alliance were few. Indeed, until the postwar period, Japanese diplomatic historians were frustrated by lack of materials and the riskiness of their subject-matter which might lead to their work being banned. For this reason, prewar diplomatic studies tended to be cautious and to avoid generalization. They were inclined to be more concerned with the actions of foreign powers in the far east than with the motivations of Japanese policy itself. In the postwar period the former limitations have been removed and there have appeared many substantial studies of the period from 1894 to 1905. In the main, these tend to concentrate on the nature of the wars with China and Russia and on the associated problems of Korea and Manchuria. Some of these have shown a sincere and conscientious preoccupation with the causes of these wars, the nature of Japanese imperialism and the growth of Japanese capital expansion. There have also been studies which have made a thoroughgoing examination of Japanese policy in terms of the objects of the government, the methods of decision-making and the influence of individual statesmen and groups on policy-making.

A number of books were published at the time of the first alliance. Such are Hirata Chikao, *Nichi-Ei dōmei to sekai no yoron* (Tokyo, 1902) and Takahashi Tetsutarō, *Nichi-Ei dōmei no eikyō: Taiheiyō ron* (Tokyo, 1902). These are journalistic works which indicate Japan's surprise and exhilaration at the new alliance but contribute little to the story of its negotiation.

The next landmark was the publication of an account of the 1901 negotiation and Itō's mission to Russia by the *Jiji Shimpō* newspaper in July 1913. This was confirmed by the biography of Katsura by Tokutomi Iichirō (Tokyo, 1917). It was a decade before some attempt was made to state Itō's side of the case with the publication of *Itō Hirobumi hiroku*, edited by Hiratsuka Atsushi (2 vols., Tokyo, 1928–30). This consists of a selection of Itō's notes with comment by contemporaries who were associated with the events described. In an appendix to vol. I, there is a collection of telegrams received and sent by Itō while he was touring Europe in 1901–2 and memoranda written during that period under the title 'The Anglo-Japanese alliance and the Russo-Japanese entente' ('Nichi-Ei dōmei to Nichi-Ro kyōshō'). This is an indispensable source for the first alliance. The volume also contains an article by Kurino Shinichirō, which alleges the complicity of Katsura in Itō's activities. The accuracy of the telegrams is not in question but the interpretation of Itō's trip is still a matter of dispute. Another useful eyewitness account is by Ishii Kikujirō, head of the communications department of the Foreign Ministry, in his *Gaikō Yoroku* (Tokyo, 1928).

Then emerged a number of specialized studies of note. Tachi Sakutarō, *Nichi-Ei dōmei teiketsu ni kansuru Yoroppa kyōkoku no gaikō* (Tokyo, 1926), is primarily based on the German published documents and concentrates on the part played by Germany in the negotiation of the first alliance. Shinobu Jumpei, *Nidai gaikō no shinsō* (Tokyo, 1928), deals with the choice which Japan had in 1901 to align herself with Britain or Russia and makes use of the extensive knowledge of the archives of the Japanese foreign ministry which Shinobu had gained during his period as a diplomat. There were also articles by Eguchi, Tokinoya and Tsuboi.

More of the background came to be filled in with the publication of the biographies of Yamagata Aritomo (1933), Inoue Kaoru (1933–4), Katō Takaaki (1934) and Itō Hirobumi (1943). Most of the biographies contain copious extracts from contemporary letters and memoranda which the statesmen continued to keep in their private possession.

With the end of the war, the archives of the Japanese Foreign Ministry were extensively microfilmed under the auspices of the United States government. The microfilm was indexed for the Library of Congress in C. H. Uyehara, *Checklist of archives in the Japanese Ministry of Foreign Affairs, Tokyo, Japan, 1868–1945* (Washington, 1954). This made available some new material on the alliance and related subjects; the portions most relevant were PVM 6 dealing with the alliances of 1902 and 1905 and the military-naval talks of 1907. These archives have also been published in the volumes of *Nihon gaikō bunsho*. This is a series of volumes containing documents from the archives of the Foreign Ministry. The documents are arranged topically within each volume; each year's documents are published separately. These volumes contain dispatches, telegrams, correspondence between ministries and a number of vital cabinet resolutions but do not include secretarial memoranda and ministerial minutes. When the printed volumes are compared with the Library of Congress microfilm, the selection by the editors seems to be fair and comprehensive.

The volume of *Nihon gaikō bunsho* for 1902, which was issued in 1957, contained three valuable memoranda. These are 'Nichi-Ei dōmei teiketsu shimatsu', an account of the London end of the alliance negotiations written by Baron Hayashi on 6 May 1902 (29 pages) with an annexure attacking Itō's conduct written on 31 January 1902 (3 pages) and an account from the Tokyo end by Ishii Kikujirō, written in January 1903 and taken from the Matsumoto archive (30 pages). The volume on the second alliance (38/I) contains a similar report by minister Hayashi on the negotiations which took place at the London end. It was written on 2 October 1905 and is entitled 'Nichi-Ei dōmei shin-kyōyaku teiketsu shimatsu' ('Circumstances of the conclusion of the new Anglo-Japanese alliance', 22 pages). This document fills an important gap in that the second alliance is not mentioned in *Hayashi's Memoirs.*

Two further publications give accounts of the alliance from a personal angle. *Komura gaikōshi* (2 vols., Tokyo, 1953) may best be described as an official diplomatic biography because it was compiled by the Foreign Ministry on the basis of an earlier unpublished biography by Shinobu Jumpei and lays special emphasis on his public life as foreign minister. It is indispensable for a study of this period because it makes abundant use of the archives of the ministry and it meets a definite need in that Komura was the only Meiji statesman to be without a major biography. The second consists of fragments from 'Katsura Tarō jiden', *Meiji Shiryō*, no. 7 (1961) and no. 11 (1962). The three sections of the uncompleted autobiography of General Katsura, which are there printed, cover the period from Itō's third cabinet of 1898 to the start of the Russo-Japanese war. While parts had previously been used by Tokutomi in his biographies of Katsura and Yamagata, it is particularly useful to have a full account of the alliance negotiations of 1901 from Katsura himself.

In 1957, Kajima Morinosuke published his comprehensive study, *Nichi-Ei gaikōshi*, which deals with the relations between Britain and Japan from Will Adams to the Washington conference but devotes 150 pages to the subject-matter of this study. It is reliable and authoritative, being based on an official publication, *Nichi-Ei gaikōshi* (2 vols., Tokyo, 1937), which was circulated privately by the Japanese Foreign Ministry. As a Foreign Ministry official, Professor Kajima had been responsible for compiling these volumes and obtained permission to incorporate some of the original material in his own historical work. It is primarily a narrative account and is fairly guarded in its judgments, avoiding most of the controversial domestic issues.

Much of the recent scholarly work on this subject has been published not in monographs but in periodical articles, especially in the issues of *Kokusai Seiji* devoted to 'Nihon gaikōshi kenkyū' ('Study of Japan's diplomatic history'). In a number of studies, Professor Imai Shōji has been concerned to throw light on the motives underlying Japanese policy. Another writer, Shigemitsu Osamu, in an article contributed to *Kindai Nihon gaikōshi no kenkyū*, deals with the alliance of 1902 from a European standpoint: as a departure from Britain's isolation, as the offshoot of the Open Door policy and the successor to a possible Anglo-German alliance. Kuroha Shigeru has analysed the alliance in a number of papers dealing with the international and financial aspects of the first alliance.

A set of essays by various scholars associated with Nagoya University, has been edited by Shinobu Seizaburō and Nakayama Jiichi under the title *Nichi-Ro sensōshi no kenkyū* (Tokyo, 1959). Although it concentrates on the war, much of the book is concerned with Korea and Manchuria and is therefore useful for a study of the alliance. It also contains essays on the first and second alliance and a valuable bibliography on Japanese foreign policy from 1895 to 1905.

SELECT BIBLIOGRAPHY

I. MANUSCRIPT MATERIAL

A. OFFICIAL RECORDS

Public Record Office, London

Foreign Office, General Correspondence, *Japan* (FO 46). In accordance with the rearrangement of Foreign Office filing, the files for Japan after 1906 were merged in the series FO 371.

Foreign Office, Embassy and consular archives, *Japan, Correspondence* (FO 228), consisting of bound correspondence maintained by the legation in Tokyo.

Foreign Office, General Correspondence, *China* (FO 17). Diplomatic correspondence relating to Korea was until 1906 maintained as part of the China series; thereafter it became part of the Japan files.

Foreign Office files for other countries, War Office and Admiralty records were consulted as required.

Cabinet Office, Miscellaneous records (*Cabinet* 1). These contain the miscellaneous printed papers which were circulated to members of the cabinet for information and decision. Minutes were not kept for cabinet meetings until 1916 and the only record of decisions taken can be found in the prime minister's reports to the Crown, see the remarks on the Royal Archives and the Salisbury papers (below).

Papers of the Committee of Imperial Defence (*Cabinet* 2–20), consisting of the minutes of C.I.D. meetings and of subcommittee meetings and miscellaneous memoranda circulated to its members.

Microfilm

Archives of the Japanese Ministry of Foreign Affairs. As indexed in C. H. Uyehara, *Checklist of archives in the Japanese Ministry of Foreign Affairs, Tokyo, Japan, 1868–1945* (Washington, 1954). Especially the reels dealing with Anglo-Japanese relations (PVM 6).

Archives of the Japanese Army and Navy Ministries. As indexed in John Young, *Checklist of microfilm reproductions of selected archives of the*

Japanese army, navy and other government agencies, 1868–1945 (Washington, D.C., 1959). Especially the reels on the Sino-Japanese war, the Boxer Uprising and the Russo-Japanese war.

B. PRIVATE PAPERS

Foreign Office Library, London[1]

Henry, fifth Marquis of Lansdowne, secretary of state for foreign affairs, 1900–5. These papers consist of Lansdowne's private correspondence during his period at the Foreign Office, grouped according to country. The volumes on Japan and China contain much unpublished material.

Sir Edward Grey (Viscount Grey of Fallodon), under-secretary of state for foreign affairs (1892–5), secretary of state for foreign affairs (1905–16). These papers consist of Grey's private correspondence during his two periods at the Foreign Office but are disappointing for China and Japan.

Also Sir Thomas (Lord) Sanderson, permanent under-secretary, Foreign Office, 1894–1906; Sir Francis Bertie, head of the Asiatic Section, Foreign Office, 1894–1903; and Sir Frank Lascelles, ambassador to Germany, 1895–1908.

Manuscripts room, British Museum, London

Arthur James, Lord Balfour, first lord of the treasury, 1895–1902, and prime minister, 1902–5 (Additional Manuscripts 49683–962). These papers include voluminous correspondence with cabinet colleagues. As prime minister, Balfour kept in close touch with foreign affairs and his exchanges with Lansdowne are detailed and illuminating.

Also St John Brodrick (Lord Midleton), secretary of state for India, 1903–5 (Additional Manuscripts 50072–77); H. O. Arnold-Forster, secretary of state for war, 1903–5 (Additional Manuscripts 50275–357); and Sir George Clarke (Lord Sydenham), secretary, Committee of Imperial Defence, 1903–7 (Additional Manuscripts 50831–5).

Public Record Office, London

Sir Ernest Mason Satow, minister to Japan, 1895–1900, and to China, 1900–6 (PRO 30/33). These papers include not only Satow's letter-books containing copies of his outgoing private letters but also incoming private letters from London and British representatives overseas. As a distinguished Japanese linguist who had spent much of his career in Japan, Satow was a shrewd commentator on the situation there, all the more so since his relations with the Japanese leaders were close. He was in Peking for the duration of

---

[1] These papers have recently been transferred to the Public Record Office, London.

the first Anglo-Japanese alliance and the Russo-Japanese war and was naturally much involved in these events and received many illuminating letters.

Sir John Newell Jordan, consul-general at Seoul, 1896–1901, and minister to Korea, 1901–6 (FO 350). These contain Jordan's unofficial letters from 1901 onwards, a period when the affairs of Korea were becoming increasingly critical.

Gerald W. Balfour, president, Board of Trade, 1900–5, president, Local Government Board, 1905 (PRO 30/60). These papers include cabinet papers and a fairly complete set of Foreign Office confidential print, collected during his period as a member of the cabinet.

Also Horatio Herbert, Lord Kitchener, commander-in-chief in India, 1902–9 (PRO 30/57); Major-General Sir John Charles Ardagh, Director of Military Intelligence, War Office, 1896–1901 (PRO 30/40).

Royal Archives, Windsor

Queen Victoria and King Edward VII. These papers are valuable not only for the correspondence of the monarchs and their secretaries but also for the accounts of cabinet meetings which the prime minister had the duty to submit.

University Library, Birmingham

Joseph Chamberlain, secretary of state for the colonies, 1895–1903, and of Austen Chamberlain, chancellor of the exchequer, 1903–5. The papers of the former have little new light to throw; those of the latter are useful for fresh insights on Britain's attitude to the Russo-Japanese war.

University Library, Cambridge

Charles, Lord Hardinge of Penshurst, secretary to the embassy, St Petersburg, 1898–1903, and ambassador to Russia, 1904–6. Vols. 3–8 cover the period of this study. Hardinge had special knowledge of Russian problems and, since Britain's policy towards Japan was closely connected with Russian activities in east Asia, his correspondence contains much that is of incidental interest.

The Library, Christ Church, Oxford

Robert, third Marquis of Salisbury, prime minister, 1895–1902. These papers include his reports to the Crown on cabinet meetings. While they are full of interest about the making of British foreign policy, they contain relatively little on the far east.

Mitchell Library, Sydney, New South Wales

Dr George Ernest Morrison, *The Times'* correspondent in Peking, 1897–1912. While this collection contains a great deal of Morrison's correspondence, it is most valuable for the detailed diaries which he kept of his conversations in China, Korea and Japan and on his trips to Europe. While Morrison was never a policy-maker, he was a well-informed observer of the far eastern scene with pro-Chinese sympathies which were unusual among Europeans of his time. Since his opinions appear to have carried some weight at the Foreign Office, his papers are an invaluable source.

National Maritime Museum, Greenwich

Admiral Sir Cyprian A. G. Bridge, commander-in-chief, China, 1901–4, and Admiral Sir Gerard H. U. Noel, commander-in-chief, China, 1904–6. Since naval factors were important in influencing Britain in favour of the alliance, these collections — and especially the Bridge papers — are invaluable for the communications from the Admiralty which they contain.

The Naval Library, Ministry of Defence, London

Three first lords of the admiralty, Lord Selborne, 1900–5, Lord Cawdor, 1905, Lord Tweedmouth, 1905–8, left bound volumes of papers, consisting of printed Admiralty memoranda, mainly on shipbuilding and the distribution of the fleet.

II. PRINTED MATERIAL

A. DOCUMENTS

British documents on the origins of the war, 1898–1914, edited by G. P. Gooch and H. W. V. Temperley, London, 1926–38. Especially vols. I–IV.

British parliamentary papers, vol. XCI (1901), 'Correspondence respecting the disturbances in China' (Cd 436) and 'Further correspondence respecting the disturbances in China' (Cd 589 and Cd 675).

British parliamentary debates:

Kemp, P. K. (ed.), *The papers of Admiral Sir John Fisher*, 2 vols., London, 1960–4.

Marder, A. J. (ed.), *Fear God and Dread Nought: the correspondence of Admiral of the Fleet Lord Fisher of Kilverstone*, 3 vols., London, 1952–9.

Documents diplomatiques français, Paris, 1930–59. Especially first series, tomes XI–XVI and second series, tomes I–VII.

Die grosse Politik der europäischen Kabinette, 1871–1914, edited by J. Lepsius, A. Mendelssohn-Bartholdy and F. Thimme, Berlin, 1922–7. Especially vols. XV, XVI and XVII.

The Holstein papers, edited by M. H. Fisher and N. Rich, 4 vols., London, 1955–63. Especially vols. III and IV.

Krasnyi Arkhiv, Moscow, 1923–38. Especially no. 14 (1926), 1–49, 'Boxer rebellion'; no. 19 (1926), 53–63, 'British policy in India and Indo-Russian relations, 1897–1905'; no. 52 (1932), 34–124, 'First steps in Russian imperialism in the far east: 1888–1903'; no. 63 (1934), 3–54, 'On the eve of the Russo-Japanese war, December 1900–January 1902'.

Morison, E. E. (ed.), *The Letters of Theodore Roosevelt*, 8 vols., Cambridge, Mass., 1951–4. Especially vols. III and IV.

Nihon gaikō bunsho ('Japanese diplomatic documents'), Research Division, Ministry of Foreign Affairs, Tokyo. Volumes consulted were from Vol. 25 (1952) containing correspondence for 1892 to vol. 40/III (1960) containing correspondence for 1907.

Nihon gaikō bunsho: jōyaku kaisei kankei ('Japanese diplomatic documents relating to treaty revision'), 4 vols., Tokyo, 1948–50.

Nihon gaikō bunsho: bekkan hokushin jihen ('Supplementary volumes on the Boxer disturbances'), 3 vols., Tokyo, 1955–6.

Nihon gaikō bunsho: bekkan Nichi-Ro sensō ('Supplementary volumes on the Russo-Japanese war'), 5 vols., Tokyo, 1958–60.

Nihon gaikō nempyō narabi ni shuyō bunsho ('Chronology of Japanese foreign affairs together with important documents'), Ministry of Foreign Affairs, 2 vols., Tokyo, 1955.

Nichi-Bei gaikōshi ('History of American-Japanese relations'), Ministry of Foreign Affairs, Tokyo, 1939.

Nichi-Ei gaikōshi ('History of Anglo-Japanese relations'), 2 vols., Ministry of Foreign Affairs, Tokyo, 1938.

Nichi-Ro gaikōshi ('History of Russo-Japanese relations'), 2 vols., Ministry of Foreign Affairs, Tokyo, 1944.

Naikaku seidō 70-nen shi ('70 years of the cabinet system'), Prime Minister's Office, Tokyo, 1955.

Gaisai kankei shiryō ('Materials connected with foreign loans'), 2 vols., Ministry of Finance, Tokyo, 1932. Vol. I deals with central government loans; vol. II with municipal loans and those contracted by companies with government guarantee.

Itō Hirobumi hiroku ('Private writings of Itō Hirobumi'), edited by Hiratsuka Atsushi, 2 vols., Tokyo, 1928–30.

Itō Hirobumi hisho ruisan ('Collection of private writings of Itō Hirobumi'), edited by Hiratsuka Atsushi, 27 vols., Tokyo, 1934–6. In this multi-volume series, there are three volumes containing Itō's miscellaneous writings on foreign affairs.

Nihon kokusei jiten ('Dictionary of Japanese politics'), 12 vols., Tokyo, 1954–7. Relevant to this study were vols. 4–8.

Nikkan gaikō shiryō shūsei ('Collection of materials on Korean-Japanese relations'), edited by Kamikawa Hikomatsu and Kim Ching Myong, 8 vols. in course of publication, Tokyo, 1962– .

Shimbun shūsei Meiji hennen shi ('The annals of the Meiji period compiled from newspapers'), edited by Nakayama Yasumasa, 15 vols., Tokyo, 1934–6. Especially, vols. IX–XIII.

B. SECONDARY WORKS

European language works

AKITA, G., 'Ito, Yamagata and Katsura: the changing of the guards, 1901', *Papers of the Hong Kong International Conference on Asian History*, no. 12.

ALLEN, B. M., *Sir Ernest Satow: a memoir*, London, 1933.

ARNOLD, (SIR) EDWIN, *Japonica: Essays on Japan*, London, 1892.

ASAKAWA KANICHI, *The Russo-Japanese conflict: its causes and issues*, Cambridge, Mass., 1904.

BALLARD, G. A., *The influence of the sea on the political history of Japan*, London, 1921.

BEACH, VICTORIA A. HICKS, *Life of Michael Hicks Beach, Earl St Aldwyn*, 2 vols., London, 1932.

BEALE, H. K., *Theodore Roosevelt and the rise of America to world power*, Baltimore, 1956.

BLAND, J. O. P., *Recent events and present policies in China*, London, 1912.

BRIDGE, C. A. G., *Some recollections*, London, 1918.

BRINKLEY, F., and (BARON) KIKUCHI DAIROKU, *History of the Japanese people*, London, 1910.

BERESFORD, (LORD) CHARLES, *The break-up of China*, London, 1899.

CAMPBELL, C. S., *Special business interests and the Open Door policy*, Newhaven, 1951.

CAMPBELL, C. S., *Anglo-American understanding, 1898–1903*, Baltimore, 1957.

CHANG CHUNG-FU, *The Anglo-Japanese alliance*, Baltimore, 1931.

CH'EN, JEROME, *Yuan Shih-k'ai, 1859–1916*, London, 1960.

CHIROL, (SIR) VALENTINE, *The far eastern question*, London, 1896.

DD

CHIROL, (SIR) VALENTINE, *Fifty years in a changing world*, London, 1927.

CLARKE, G. S. (LORD SYDENHAM), *My working life*, London, 1929.

CONROY, F. H., *The Japanese seizure of Korea, 1868–1910*, Philadelphia, 1960.

CRÄMER, ANNELIESE, *Die Beziehungen zwischen England und Japan von 1894 bis 1902*, Zeulenroda, 1935.

CURZON, G. N. (LORD), *Problems of the far east*, London, 1894.

DAWSON, R. MACG. (ed.), *Mackenzie King*, vol. I, 1874–1923, London, 1958.

DENNIS, A. L. P., *The Anglo-Japanese alliance*, Berkeley, 1923 and 1934.

DUGDALE, BLANCHE E. C., *Arthur James Balfour*, 2 vols., London, 1936.

ECKARDSTEIN, H. VON, *Lebenserinnerungen und politische Denkwürdigkeiten*, 2 vols., Leipzig, 1919–20. Translated as *Ten years at the court of St James, 1895–1905* (edited by G. Young), London, 1921.

EDWARDS, E. W., 'The far eastern agreements of 1907', *Journal of Modern History*, no. 26 (1954), 340–55.

EDWARDS, E. W., 'The Japanese alliance and the Anglo-French agreement of 1904', *History*, no. 42 (1957), 19–27.

GALPERIN, A. L., *Anglo-yaponskii soiuz, 1902–21.* Moscow, 1947.

GALPERIN, A. L., 'Iz istorii anglo-yaponskikh otnoshenii, 1902–5', *Uchenie zapiski Tikho-okeanskovo Instituta*, no. 1 (1947), 85–222.

GALPERIN, A. L., 'Diplomaticheskaya podgotovka Portsmutskoi mirnoi konferentsii yapono-anglo-amerikanskim blokom', *Istoricheskie Zapiski*, no. 50 (1955), 169–223.

GARVIN, J. L., *Life of Joseph Chamberlain*, 4 vols., London, 1934–51. Especially vol. IV (1901–3), written by Julian Amery.

GOUDSWAARD, J. M., *Some aspects of the end of Britain's 'Splendid Isolation', 1898–1904*, Rotterdam, 1952.

GRENVILLE, J. A. S., 'Lansdowne's abortive project of 12 March 1901 for a secret agreement with Germany', *Bulletin of the Institute of Historical Research*, no. 27 (1954), 201–13.

GRENVILLE, J. A. S., *Lord Salisbury and foreign policy: the close of the nineteenth century*, London, 1964.

GREY, E. (Viscount Grey of Fallodon), *Twenty-five years, 1892–1916*, 2 vols., London, 1925.

GWYNN, S. (ed.), *The letters and friendships of Sir Cecil Spring Rice*, 2 vols., London, 1929.

GRISCOM, L. C., *Diplomatically speaking*, London, 1941.

HARDINGE, C. (LORD), *Old diplomacy*, London, 1952.

HARGREAVES, J. D., 'Lord Salisbury, British isolation and the Yangtse valley, June–September 1900', *Bulletin of the Institute of Historical Research*, no. 30 (1957), 62–75.

HASHAGEN, J., *England und Japan seit Schimonoseki*, Essen, 1915.

HOHLER, T., *Diplomatic petrel*, London, 1942.

HOWARD, C., 'Splendid isolation', *History*, no. 47 (1962), 32–41.

JANSEN, M. B., *The Japanese and Sun Yat-sen*, Cambridge, Mass., 1954.

JONES, F. C., *Extra-territoriality in Japan, 1853–99*, Newhaven, 1931.

KAWAI KAZUO, 'Anglo-German rivalry in the Yangtse region, 1895–1902', *Pacific Historical Review*, no. 8 (1939), 413–33.

KELLY, J. S., *A forgotten conference: the negotiations at Peking, 1900–1*, Geneva, 1962.

KENNEDY, A. L., *Salisbury, 1830–1903: portrait of a statesman*, London, 1953.

KENNEDY, M. D., *Some aspects of Japan and her defence forces*, London and Kobe, 1928.

KIERNAN, E. V. G., *British diplomacy in China, 1880–5*, London, 1939.

KLESTADT, E., 'Some notes on the Sino-Japanese conflict, 1894–5: Tokyo's Decision for War', *Kokusai seiji*, autumn 1957, 1–6.

LANGER, W. L., *The diplomacy of imperialism, 1890–1902*, New York, 1951.

LEE, CHONG-SIK, *The politics of Korean nationalism*, Berkeley, 1963.

LEE, (SIR) SIDNEY, *King Edward VII*, 2 vols., London, 1925–7.

LUNG CHANG, *La Chine á l'aube du XXe siècle, les relations diplomatiques de la Chine avec les puissances, 1894–1904*, Paris, 1962.

MACCORDOCK, R. S., *British far eastern policy, 1894–1900*, New York, 1931.

MACDONALD, (SIR) C. M., 'The Japanese detachment during the defence of the Peking legations, June–August 1900', *Trans. Proc. Japan Society (London)*, no. 12 (1913–14), 1–20.

MAGNUS, (SIR) PHILIP, *Kitchener: portrait of an imperialist*, London, 1958.

MAGNUS, (SIR) PHILIP, *King Edward the seventh*, London, 1964.

(COUNTESS OF) MALMESBURY, *Life of Sir John Ardagh*, London, 1909.

MALOZEMOFF, A., *Russian far eastern policy, 1881–1904*, Berkeley, 1958.

MARDER, A. J., *The anatomy of British sea power: a history of British naval policy in the pre-Dreadnought era, 1880–1905*, London, 1940.

MARDER, A. J., *From the Dreadnought to Scapa Flow, the Royal Navy in the Fisher era, 1904–19*, vol. I, *The road to war, 1904–14*, London, 1961.

MINRATH, P., *Das englisch-japanische Bündnis von 1902*, Stuttgart, 1933.

MONGER, G. W., 'The end of isolation: Britain, Germany and Japan, 1900–2', *Transactions of the Royal Historical Society* (fifth series), no. 13 (1963), 103–21.

MONGER, G. W., *The end of isolation: British foreign policy, 1900–7*, London, 1963.

NISH, I. H., 'Japan's indecision during the Boxer disturbances', *Journal of Asian Studies*, no. 20 (1961), 449–61.

NISH, I. H., 'Australia and the Anglo-Japanese alliance, 1901–1911', *Australian Journal of Politics and History*, no. 9 (1963), 201–12.

NISH, I. H., 'Japan reverses the unequal treaties: the Anglo-Japanese Commercial Treaty of 1894', *Papers of the Hong Kong International Conference on Asian History*, no. 20.

NISH, I. H., 'Korea, focus of Russo-Japanese diplomacy, 1898–1903', *Asian Studies*, vol. II/7.

NORMAN, (SIR) HENRY, *The real Japan*, London, 1892.

NORMAN, (SIR) HENRY, *Peoples and politics of the far east*, London, 1900.

PELCOVITS, N. A., *Old China hands and the Foreign Office*, London, 1948.

PENSON, (DAME) LILLIAN M., 'Principles and methods of Lord Salisbury's foreign policy', *Cambridge Historical Journal*, no. 5 (1935), 87–107.

PENSON, (DAME) LILLIAN M., 'The new course in British foreign policy, 1892–1902', *Transactions of the Royal Historical Society* (fourth series), no. 25 (1943), 121–39.

PENSON, (DAME) LILLIAN M., *Foreign affairs under the third Marquess of Salisbury*, London, 1962.

PIGGOTT, F. S. G., *Broken threads*, Aldershot, 1950.

POOLEY, A. M. (ed.), *The secret memoirs of Count Tadasu Hayashi, G.C.V.O.*, London, 1915.

RANSOME, S., *Japan in transition*, London, 1899.

ROMANOV, B. A., *Rossiya v Manchzhurii*, Leningrad, 1928. Translated by Susan W. Jones as *Russia in Manchuria, 1892–1906*, Ann Arbor, 1952.

ROMANOV, B. A., 'Proiskhozhdenie anglo-yaponskovo dogovora 1902 g', *Istoricheskie Zapiski*, no. 10 (1941), 40–65.

ROMANOV, B. A., *Ocherki diplomaticheskoi istorii russko-yaponskoi voiny*, *1895–1907*, Moscow, Leningrad, 1955.

(LORD) RONALDSHAY, *Life of Curzon*, 3 vols., London, 1929.

SANIEL, JOSEFA M., *Japan and the Philippines*, *1868–98*, Quezon, 1962.

SIEBOLD, A. VON, *Japan's accession to the comity of nations*, London, 1901.

SPINKS, C. N., 'The background of the Anglo-Japanese alliance', *Pacific Historical Review*, no. 8 (1939), 317–40.

STEAD, A. (ed.), *Japan by the Japanese*, London, 1904.

STEINER, ZARA, 'Great Britain and the creation of the Anglo-Japanese alliance', *Journal of Modern History*, no. 31 (1959), 27–36.

STEINER, ZARA, 'Last years of the old Foreign Office, 1898–1905', *The Historical Journal*, no. 6 (1963), 59–90.

SUEMATSU KENCHŌ, *The risen sun*, London, 1905.

SUN, E-TU ZEN, 'Lease of Weihaiwei', *Pacific Historical Review*, no. 19 (1950), 277–83.

SUN, E-TU ZEN, *Chinese railways and British interests*, *1898–1911*, New York, 1954.

SYKES, (SIR) PERCY, *Sir Mortimer Durand*, London, 1926.

TAKEUCHI TATSUJI, *War and diplomacy in the Japanese Empire*, London, 1936.

TAN, C. C., *The Boxer catastrophe*, New York, 1955.

History of 'The Times', vol. III, 'The Twentieth Century Test, 1884–1912', London, 1947.

TREAT, P. J., *Diplomatic relations between the United States and Japan*, *1895–1905*, Stanford, 1938.

VARG, P. A., 'Foreign policy of Japan and the Boxer Revolt', *Pacific Historical Review*, no. 15 (1946), 279–85.

VARG, P. A., *Open Door diplomat: life of W. W. Rockhill*, Urbana, 1952.

WALDERSEE, A. VON, *Denkwürdigkeiten*, 3 vols., Stuttgart, 1923. Edited by F. Whyte, and translated as *A Field-marshal's memoirs*, London, 1924.

WALTON, (SIR) JOSEPH, *China and the present crisis*, London, 1900.

WHITE, J. A., *The diplomacy of the Russo-Japanese war*, Princeton, 1964.

WRIGHT, S. F., *Hart and the Chinese customs*, Belfast, 1950.

Japanese language works

EGUCHI BOKURŌ, '1901-nen no Ei-Doku dōmei mondai' ('The Anglo-German alliance project of 1901'), *Shigaku zasshi*, no. 44 (1933), 1529–70.

EGUCHI BOKURŌ, with TAKAHASHI KŌHACHIRŌ and HAYASHI KENTARŌ, *Kokusai kankei no shiteki bunseki* ('Historical analysis of international relations'), Tokyo, 1949.

EGUCHI BOKURŌ, *Teikoku shugi to minzoku* ('Imperialism and race'), Tokyo, 1957.

FURUYA TETSUO, 'Nihon teikoku shugi no seiritsu wo megutte' ('About the development of Japanese imperialism'), *Rekishigaku kenkyū*, no. 202 (1956), 40–6.

Gaikōshi oyobi kokusai seiji no sho mondai, being studies in diplomatic history presented to Professor Hanabusa, Tokyo, 1962.

Gendai Nihon bummeishi ('Cultural history of modern Japan'), 18 vols., Tokyo, 1941–5. Especially the following volumes:
  Watanabe Ikujirō, *Ippanshi* ('General history')
  Rōyama Masamichi, *Seijishi* ('Political history')
  Kiyozawa Kiyoshi, *Gaikōshi* ('Diplomatic history')
  Itō Masanori, *Kokubōshi* ('Defence history')

HARA TANEYUKI, 'Taisenzen ni okeru Nichi-Doku kankei no issokumen — Nichi-Ei dōmei no kakudo yori mitaru' ('One aspect of German-Japanese relations before the war viewed from the standpoint of the Anglo-Japanese alliance'), *Tōzai kōshō shiron* ('Studies on the history of east-west relations'), 2 vols., Tokyo, 1939, vol. II, 1207–42.

HIRATA CHIKAO, *Nichi-Ei dōmei to sekai no yoron* ('The Anglo-Japanese alliance and world opinion'), Tokyo, 1902.

HIRATSUKA ATSUSHI, *Shishaku Kurino Shinichirō den*, Tokyo, 1942.

IMAI SHŌJI, 'Dai-ikkai Nichi-Ei dōmei kyōyaku: Nichi-Ei dōmei to Chosen mondai' ('The first Anglo-Japanese alliance and Korea'), *Rekishi kyōiku*, no. 5 (1957), 56–67.

IMAI SHŌJI, 'Nichi-Ei dōmei kōshō ni okeru Nihon no shuchō' ('Japan's case during the negotiations for the Anglo-Japanese alliance'), *Kokusai seiji*, autumn 1957, 119–36.

IMAI SHŌJI, 'Nichi-Ro sensō zengo Manshū zairyū Nihonjin no bumpu jōtai' ('Distribution of Japanese residents in Manchuria about the time of the Russo-Japanese war'), *Rekishi chiri*, no. 89 (1960), 171–83.

ISHII KIKUJIRŌ, *Gaikō yoroku*, Tokyo, 1928. Translated by F. C. Langdon as *Diplomatic commentaries*, Baltimore, 1928.

ITŌ MASANORI, *Katō Takaaki*, 2 vols., Tokyo, 1934.

KAJIMA MORINOSUKE, *Nichi-Ei gaikōshi* ('History of Anglo-Japanese diplomacy'), Tokyo, 1957.

KAJIMA MORINOSUKE, *Nichi-Bei gaikōshi* ('History of American-Japanese diplomacy'), Tokyo, 1958.

KAJIMA MORINOSUKE, *Nihon gaikō seisaku no shiteki kōsatsu* ('Historical reflections on Japan's foreign policy'), Tokyo, 1958.

KANEKO KENTARŌ, *Itō Hirobumi den*, 3 vols., Tokyo, 1943.

KATSURA TARŌ, 'Jiden' ('Autobiographical fragments'), *Meiji shiryō*, no. 7 (1961) and no. 11 (1962).

Komura gaikōshi ('History of Komura's foreign policy'), 2 vols., Tokyo, 1953.

KUROHA SHIGERU, '1902-nen ni okeru Nichi-Ei dōmei no seiritsu dōki ni tsuite' ('Regarding the motives for concluding the Anglo-Japanese alliance in 1902'), *Bunka*, no. 16/3 (1948), 23–43.

KUROHA SHIGERU, 'Nichi-Ei dōmei seiritsu ni kansuru ichi-dammen' ('One aspect of the conclusion of the Anglo-Japanese alliance'), *Nihon rekishi*, no. 74 (1954), 30–9.

KUROHA SHIGERU, 'Nichi-Ei dōmei no seiritsu to kokka zaisei mondai' ('The Anglo-Japanese alliance and Japanese finances'), *Rekishi kyōiku*, no. 5 (1957), 13–19 and 50–60.

KUROHA SHIGERU, 'Nichi-Ei dōmei shisō no hatsugen to sono tenkai katei' ('The principles of the Anglo-Japanese alliance and the course of their development'), *Nihon rekishi*, no. 119 (1958), 13–24.

MAEJIMA SHŌZŌ, 'Nisshin Nichi-Ro sensō ni okeru tai-Kan seisaku' ('Policies towards Korea between the wars against China and Russia'), *Kokusai seiji*, 1961/III, 71–86.

MUTŌ CHŌZŌ, *Nichi-Ei kōtsūshi no kenkyū* ('History of Anglo-Japanese relations'), Tokyo, 1937. Translated as *A short history of Anglo-Japanese relations*, Tokyo, 1936.

MUTSU HIROKICHI, *Hakushaku Mutsu Munemitsu Ikō* ('Posthumous works of Count Mutsu'), Tokyo, 1929.

NAKAYAMA JIICHI, *Nichi-Ro sensō igo: Higashi Ajia wo meguru teikoku shugi no kokusai kankei* ('After the Russo-Japanese war: imperialism in international relations affecting east Asia'), Osaka, 1957.

ŌHATA TOKUJIRŌ, 'Nihon gaikōshi kenkyū no kindai hōkō' ('Current trends in the study of Japanese diplomatic history'), *Kokusai seiji*, 1959/III, 138–48.

ŌHATA TOKUJIRŌ, 'Nichi-Ro kaisen gaikō' ('Diplomacy at the start of the Russo-Japanese war'), *Kokusai seiji*, 1961/III, 102–18.

OKA YOSHITAKE, 'Nisshin sensō to tōji ni okeru taigai ishiki' ('Japanese foreign attitudes at the time of the Sino-Japanese war'), *Kokka gakkai zasshi*, no. 68 (1954–5), 101–29 and 223–54.

OKA YOSHITAKE, *Yamagata Aritomo*, Tokyo, 1958.

OKA YOSHITAKE, *Kindai Nihon no seijika* ('Statesmen of new Japan'), Tokyo, 1960.

Rikken Seiyūkai shi ('History of the Seiyū party'), edited by Kobayashi Yūgō, 4 vols., Tokyo, 1924–6.

Segai Inoue-kō den, 5 vols., Tokyo, 1933–4.

SHIGEMITSU OSAMU, 'Nichi-Ei dōmei' ('Anglo-Japanese alliance') in *Kindai Nihon gaikōshi no kenkyū*, being studies presented to Professor Kamikawa, pp. 175–230, Tokyo, 1956.

SHINOBU JUMPEI, *Meiji hiwa: nidai gaikō no shinsō* ('Meiji revelations: the truth about two major diplomatic events'), Tokyo, 1928.

SHINOBU SEIZABURŌ and NAKAYAMA JIICHI, *Nichi-Ro sensōshi no kenkyū* ('Studies in the history of the Russo-Japanese war'), Tokyo, 1959.

SHINOBU SEIZABURŌ, *Meiji seijishi* ('Meiji political history'), Tokyo, 1950.

SHINOBU SEIZABURŌ, *Nihon no gaikō* ('Japan's diplomacy'), Tokyo, 1961.

TABOHASHI KIYOSHI, *Nisshin seneki gaikōshi no kenkyū* ('Studies in the diplomatic history of the Sino-Japanese war'), Tokyo, 1951.

TACHI SAKUTARŌ, *Nichi-Ei dōmei teiketsu ni kansuru Yoroppa kyōkoku no gaikō* ('The diplomacy of the European powers over the conclusion of the Anglo-Japanese alliance'), Tokyo, 1926.

TAKAHASHI KOREKIYO, *Takahashi Korekiyo jiden* ('Autobiography of Takahashi Korekiyo'), Tokyo, 1936.

TAKAHASHI TETSUTARŌ, *Nichi-Ei dōmei no eikyō: Taiheiyō ron* ('The influence of the Anglo-Japanese alliance: the Pacific question'), Tokyo, 1902.

Tanaka Giichi denki ('Biography of General Tanaka'), 2 vols., Tokyo, 1958.

TOKINOYA TSUNESABURŌ, 'Dai-ikkai Nichi-Ei dōmei no seiritsu to Doitsu teikoku' ('Germany and the conclusion of the first Anglo-Japanese Alliance') in *Tōzai kōshō shiron*, vol. II, 1147–207.

TOKUTOMI IICHIRŌ, *Kōshaku Katsura Tarō den*, 2 vols., Tokyo, 1917.

TOKUTOMI IICHIRŌ, *Kōshaku Yamagata Aritomo den*, 3 vols., Tokyo, 1933.

TSURUMI YŪSUKE, *Gotō Shimpei*, 4 vols., Tokyo, 1937.

Tōzai kōshō shiron ('Studies on the history of east-west relations'), 2 vols., Tokyo, 1939.

TSUBOI KUMAZŌ, 'Dai ni-kai Nihon Igirisu dōmei seiritsu no shimatsu' ('The conclusion of the second Anglo-Japanese alliance'), *Shigaku zasshi*, no. 40 (1929), 1189–201.

YAMAGUCHI KAZUYUKI, 'Kenseitō naikaku no seiritsu to kyokutō jōsei' ('The setting up of the Kensei party and the far-eastern situation'), *Kokusai seiji*, no. 3 (1961), 87–101.

YAMAMOTO SHIGERU, *Jōyaku kaiseishi* ('History of treaty revision'), Tokyo, 1943.

YANO JINICHI, *Manshū kindaishi* ('History of modern Manchuria'), Tokyo, 1941.

YANO JINICHI, *Nisshin ekigo Shina gaikōshi* ('China's diplomatic history after the Sino-Japanese war'), Tokyo, 1949.

INDEX

Afghanistan, 302, 314–15, 325, 361
Alexeyev, Admiral E. I., 111, 266
Anglo-French agreements (1904), 240, 282, 286–7
Anglo-German agreement on China (1900), 104–11
Anglo-German alliance project, 124–6
Anglo-German loan to China (1898), 51
Anglo-Japanese alliance, general, 1–2, 7, 11, 18–19, 37; first alliance (1902), 211–12, 216–26; naval aspects, 213–14, 251–3; second alliance (1905), 331, 335–44; military-naval aspects, 325, 353–8, 373–4; assessment, Ch. XI *passim*, 282, 366, 371–4
Anglo-Japanese commercial treaty (1894), 10
Anglo-Japanese trade, 8
Anglo-Russian agreement (1899), 74–5; (1907), 361
Anglo - Russian rapprochement (1897–8), 51; (1901), 179–81
Aoki Shūzō, Viscount, 11, 18, 37, 69–71, 78, 82, 85, 87, 100–1, 367
Argentinian warships, 272
Arisugawa, Prince, 369
Arnold, Sir Edwin, 12, 368
Arnold-Forster, Hugh O., 318–19
Arthur, Prince of Connaught, 346
Asahi Shimbun, 226, 301
Asquith, Herbert H., 343
Australia and Japanese immigration, 76, 309

Balfour, Arthur J., as deputy prime minister, 39, 43, 65, 86, 102–4, 131; and 1898 crisis, 51, 55–6; and first alliance, 182–3, 204–6, 224, 240, 243; as prime minister, 247–8, 331, 345–6; and Russo-Japanese war, 273–8, 281, 290–1; and second alliance, 295, 297, 299–302, 307–8, 312–19, 324, 335–8, 355, 358, 369–70, 373–4
Balfour, Gerald W., 304
Ballard, Commander George A., 252
Bank of England, 254
Baring Brothers, 254
Battle of Japan Sea (1905), 296, 311, 323, 325, 336
Beach, *see* Hicks Beach
Beresford, Lord Charles, Admiral, 12, 76
Bertie, Sir Francis L., biog., 153–4, 249; and China crisis (1901), 115 n. 1, 137–40, 143–5, 148–9; and first alliance, 153–7, 177–8, 180, 187, 370–1
Bethel, E. T., 352
Board of Trade, 32
Boer war, *see* South African war
Boxer disturbances, Ch. IV *passim*
Bridge, Sir Cyprian A. G. Admiral, 252
Brinkley, Frank, 12, 368
Britain, and far east, 6, 9–10; China squadron to Japan, 341–2; financial problems in China, 176–7; General staff, 319, 354–6

414

British documents on the origins of the war, 296
Brodrick, W. St John (Viscount Midleton), 86, 103, 176, 182
Brown, Sir John McLeavy, 352
Bülow, Bernhard Prince von, 120–2, 125, 220, 232

Cambon, Paul, 287
Campbell, Sir Francis A., 249, 281
Campbell-Bannerman, Sir Henry, 224, 346
Canada and Japanese immigration, 76, 309
Carson, Sir Edward, 304
Chamberlain, Sir Austen, 248, 273–4, 277–8, 290, 317, 370
Chamberlain, Joseph, as colonial secretary, 39, 56–7, 103, 131, 220, 247–8, 345–6; and talks with Katō, 63–6; and first alliance, 92–3, 104, 208, 226, 242, 370
Chang Chih-t'ung, viceroy of Hankow, 82, 142
Chang Chung-fu, 236, 257, 267, 374, 376
Chilean warships, 270–3
China, 14–15, 67–8; war with Japan, Ch. I *passim*; Boxer disturbances, Ch. IV *passim*; Peking conference (1901), 134–42; and alliance, 256, 373; *see also* Fukien, Kiaochow, Port Arthur, Weihaiwei
Chinda Sutemi, 192
Ch'ing, Prince, 257
Chirol, Sir Valentine, 12, 368
Churchill, Arthur G., Colonel, 93
Clarke, Sir George (Lord Sydenham), 248, 306–7, 312, 315, 317, 324, 334–5, 355, 369
'Coloniensis', 344
Committee of Imperial Defence, 248, 275–6, 284, 305–6, 312–13, 315, 317–18, 334, 347, 354–6, 369
Cranborne, Lord (4th Marquess of Salisbury), 103, 108, 223–4, 228, 242, 248

Cromer, 1st Earl of, 351
Curzon, George N. (1st Baron), 12, 39, 56–7, 71, 318, 369 n. 3, 345
Custance, Sir Reginald N., Admiral, 252

Daiichi Bank, 259
Daily Mail, London, 150
Dane, Sir Louis, 315
Delcassé, Théophile, 186, 238, 280, 287, 291
Denison, Henry W., 3, 172, 194, 326
Dennis, A. L. P., 236
Devonshire, Duke of, 60, 131
Dilke, Sir Charles, 12, 342
Dogger Bank incident, 289–90, 317
Dreibund, *see* Three-power intervention
Durand, Sir Mortimer, 329–30, 339–40

Eckardstein, Hermann Freiherr von, 124–34, 139, 150, 153, 220, 232
Edward VII, King, 220–1, 254, 280, 346, 368–9

Fisher, Sir John, Admiral, 290, 308, 354, 357–8, 369 n. 3
France, 6, 26–30, 84, 270
Franco-Japanese agreement (1907), 359
Franco-Russian alliance, 36
Franco-Russian declaration (1902), 238
Fukien, 59, 70–1, 92–3, 100, 120, 359
Fukushima Yasumasa, General, 84, 252
Fukuzawa Yukichi, 13, 37–8, 367
Furuya Tetsuo, 94, 235
Fushimi, Prince, 346, 354

Galperin, A. L., 132, 236, 250, 287–8, 375 n. 1, 376
Garter, Order of, 346, 354
Genrō (Elder Statesmen), 4–5, 188, 192–6, 266–8, 280, 320

Germany, in east Asia, 16, 26–30, 49–50, 84, 89, 145, 147; and first alliance, 133, 204, 207, 219–22, 231–2, 370–1

Glasgow Herald, 226, 343

Goschen, George J., 56–7, 103–4

Grey, Sir Edward, as foreign under-secretary, 11, 31, 33, 37; and alliance, 224, 299, 311, 343, 348, 358, 360, 363; as foreign secretary, 144, 347, 352, 361

Habibullah, Amir of Afghanistan, 315

Hague Peace Conference (1907), 351

Haldane, Richard B., 356

Hamilton, Lord George, 182

Harcourt, Sir William, 224

Hardinge, Sir Charles, 189–90, 249, 307, 338

Hart, Sir Robert, 54–5

Harwood, George, 342

Hatzfeldt, Paul Count von, 105, 124

Hay, John, 75–6, 92

Hayashi Tadasu, Count, biog., 127–8, 14, 51, 79, 250, 346; as deputy foreign minister, 29, 38; as minister to London, 112–16, 127–34, 138–41, 146–9, 153, 155–7, 159–61, 173, 177, 182; and first alliance, 185–91, 195–6, 204–7, 211–16, 221, 228, 230; and Russo-Japanese war, 254, 264, 272, 276–9, 284; and second alliance, 302–5, 307, 309–10, 324, 327–8, 331–4, 337; as foreign minister, 358–60, 362–3, 367–8

Hibiya Park riots, 341

Hicks Beach, Sir Michael (Lord St Aldwyn), 51, 56, 104, 175–6, 184, 208

Hippisley, Alfred E., 75

Holstein, Friedrich von, 125, 129, 150, 232

Hong Kong and Shanghai Banking Corporation, 54, 254, 288

Ijuin Gorō, Admiral, 252

Imai Shōji, 264

India, 296; and first alliance, 176, 205–6, 208; defence of, 302–3, 306–7; and second alliance, 314–20, 321, 327–8, 354–5, 365, 369, 333–4

Inoue Kaoru, Marquis, as Elder Statesman, 13, 42, 53, 111, 164, 168, 197, 263; and alliance, 128, 158, 193–5, 213, 219, 334, 367

Ishii Kikujirō, Viscount, 172, 202

Italy in China, 70

Itō Hirobumi, Marquis, biog., 13, 48, 250, 266, 285, 326; general approach, 165–70; as prime minister (1892–6), 23, 25, 29, 35, 45–7; as prime minister (1897–8), 48, 50–1, 55, 61, 66; and China (1898–1901), 82, 84, 86–7; as prime minister (1900–1), 100–2, 107–11, 118, 128, 150; and visit to Europe (1901–2), 150–2, 169–70, 173, Ch. IX *passim*; and first alliance, 126, 128, 130, 158–9, 219–20, 225, 237, 375–9; and Russia, 239, 260, 263–4, 268, 279; and second alliance, 334, 362, 367–8; as ambassador to Korea, 351–2

Iwasaki Yanosuke, Baron, 150

Izvolskii, A. P., 110–11, 112, 119, 170–1, 239, 360–2

James of Hereford, Lord, 208

Japan: Emperor, *see* Meiji emperor; army and navy in politics, 4–5, 8; foreign ministry, 2–3; loans from Britain (1899), 77; (1902), 253–6; (1903–4), 276–9; (1904), 287–9; (1905–7), 349; naval expansion, 250, 373–4

Jardine Matheson & Co., 268

Jiji Shimpō, 13, 38, 226–7, 301, 367

Jordan, Sir John N., 259, 352, 371

Kaiser, *see* Wilhelm

Kajima Morinosuke, 25, 26 n. 1, 41

Kaneko Kentarō, Baron, 284

K'ang Yu-wei, 68

Katō Takaaki, Count, biog., 37, 14, 171; as minister to London, 30, 33, 44, 50, 56, 58, 78–9; and talks with Chamberlain, 63–6; as foreign minister (1900–1), 101–2, 107–11, 121–2, 137, 162; and Manchurian crisis (1901), 112–14, 116–20; and first alliance, 126–7, 140, 172, 225; and second alliance, 301, 367

Katsura Tarō, General Marquis, biog., 164–5; general approach, 165–70, 239, 260; as war minister (1898–1901), 72, 82, 101; as prime minister (1901–5), 131, 152, 164, 247, 249–50, 265, 347–8; and first alliance, 158, 173, 185–8, 192–7, 199–200, 204, 208, 224, 227, 230, 366; and second alliance, 298–9, 301, 326–30, 331, 334, 336–7, 341, 367

Kawamura Kazuo, 82

Ketteler, Klemens Baron von, 84

Khitrovo, M., 27

Kiaochow, 49–50

Kimberley, 1st Earl of, 23–4, 29–31, 33, 37–9

Kitchener of Khartoum, Field-Marshal Lord, 316, 318, 354–5

Kiyozawa Kiyoshi, 257

Kodama Gentarō, General, 100, 173, 293

Kokumin Dōmeikai, 109–11, 120, 171, 366

Kokumin Shimbun, 38, 225, 227

Komura Jutarō, Marquis, biog., 142, 170–4, 347, 361; as diplomat, 44, 60, 126; as foreign minister (1901–5), 185–9, 238–9, 250, 351; and first alliance, 192–3, 196, 212, 219, 255; and Russo-Japanese war, 263–4, 266–8, 271, 278, 279–80, 291, 293–4; and second alliance, 298, 299, 301–2, 305, 309–11, 313, 320, 325–6, 331, 334, 336, 340, 367

Korea, 16–17, 42–5, 109–11; and first alliance, 212, 215, 233, 256, 259–60; and second alliance, 310, 320–2, 325, 328–9, 333–4; and Japanese protectorate, 350–2, 358–9; *see also* Man-Kan Kōkan

Korea Daily News, 352

Korean-Japanese treaty, (1904) 320; (1905) 348

Kowshing, merchantman, 24

Kuhn Loeb, 288

Kurino Shinichirō, 168–9, 200, 237–9

Kuropatkin, A. N., 198

Lamsdorf, Count V. N., 111–13, 117–19, 197–9, 238–9, 263, 266, 338, 361, 376

Langer, W. L., 163, 234, 239

Lansdowne, 5th Marquess of, biog., 103, 56; as foreign secretary, 104, 125–7, 177–80, 248–9, 258; and Manchurian crisis, 112–17, 120–2; and Peking conference, 136–40; and first alliance, 128, 131–4, 143, 153–6, 157–62, 174, 181–91, 196, Ch. X *passim*, 226, 228–32, 235–6, 240–3, 254; and Russo-Japanese war, 264, 267, 270–4, 276–7, 278–81, 285–6, 287–8, 290–1, 294, 296; and second alliance, 301–3, 307–11, 313, Ch. XVI *passim*, 340, 343, 346, 350, 352, 370

Lascelles, Sir Frank, 127, 221

Li Hung-chang, 27–9, 41, 52

Liaotung territory, 29, 33–4

Liang Tun-yen, 256

Liu K'un-yi, viceroy of Nanking, 142

Lobanov-Rostovski, Prince A. B., 41, 44

Lodge, Senator Henry Cabot, 329

Loomis, Francis B., 329

Loubet, President Émile, 186, 264

Lowther, Claude, 303

MacDonald, Sir Claude M., biog., 146; as minister to China, 56–7, 83, 91; as minister to Japan, 79, 133; and visit to Britain (1901), 143–9, 152–3, 155, 158, 160–1; and first alliance

MacDonald, Sir Claude M. *cont.*
189, 194, 204, 222; and Russo-Japanese war, 263–4, 266, 268, 291, 296; and second alliance, 299–301, 307, 310, 327, 341, 371; as ambassador to Japan, 2, 346, 363
Mackay treaty, 256
MacMahon, Sir Arthur H., Colonel, 316
Manchester Guardian, 226
Manchuria, 111–16, 179–81; Russo-Chinese agreement on, 257–8; and alliance, 264–5; *see also* Man-Kan Kōkan
Man-Kan Kōkan, 57, 59–60, 260–1, 263–5
Masampo incident, 72–4
Matsui Keishirō, 188–9, 193
Matsukata Masayoshi, Count, 47–9, 158, 193, 195, 254, 263, 266
Meiji emperor, 2, 3–4, 185–9, 192, 224, 266, 331, 346
Metternich, Paul Count von, 207, 220–1
Minto, 4th Earl of, 354
Miura Gorō, General, 42
Monger, G. W., 343
Mongolia, 360–2
Monthly Review, 344
Morley, John, 343, 354, 363
Morrison, Dr George Ernest, 12, 14 n. 2, 128, 256, 368
Mühlberg, Otto von, 114, 116
Mutsu Munemitsu, Count, 10, 13, 23–5, 27, 29–30, 33, 35, 37, 43–5
Mutsuhito, emperor of Japan, *see* Meiji emperor

National City Bank of New York, 288
National Review, 343
Nichinichi Shimbun, 38, 301, 367
Nicholas II, Russian emperor, 197, 290, 338
Nicholson, Sir William G., General, 252
Nippon, 227, 342
Nishi Kanjirō, General, 354, 356, 358

Nishi Tokujirō, 48, 50–1, 56, 58–60, 65, 71–2, 78
Norman, Henry, 224
Novoye Vremya, 151, 163
N.Y.K. line, 268

O'Conor, Sir Nicholas R., 51
Oka Yoshitake, 165
Ōkuma Shigenobu, Count, 18, 47–8, 66–9, 164
Open Door, 105, 350, 352, 363–4
Osaka Harbour Works Board, 255
Ottley, Captain Charles L., 306, 313, 317
Ōyama Iwao, General, 119, 158, 263, 293

Parkes, Sir Harry, 10
Parrs Bank, 288
Peking Conference, 136–40, 160
Peking Protocol, 256
Percy, Earl of, 248, 299–300
Persia, 180, 314, 325, 346, 356, 361
Philippines, 67
Port Arthur, 50–3
Port Hamilton incident, 17–18, 234
Portsmouth Peace Conference, 326, 335–8
Portsmouth treaty, 341–2, 348

Rice, Sir Cecil Spring, 281, 295
Richthofen, Baron Oswald von, 114
Ripon, 1st Marquess of, 343
Ritchie, Charles T., 208
Rockhill, William W., 75
Roosevelt, President Theodore, and Russia, 259, 293, 294–7; and second alliance, 12, 301, 329–30, 337, 339–40, 363, 368
Rosebery, 5th Earl of, 23, 26, 224
Rosen, Roman, 58–60, 267
Rouvier, Maurice, 339
Russia, in east Asia, 10, 15–17, 26–30, 41–5, 50–3; in China, Chs. IV and V *passim*; navy in far east, 93, 174–5, 289–92; negotiations with Britain, (1901) 179–81; (1904) 282;

Russia, *cont.*
negotiations with Japan, (1901) 195–201; (1902–3) 239, Ch. XIII *passim*
Russian emperor, *see* Nicholas II
Russo-Chinese alliance (1896), 41
Russo-Chinese treaty (1902), 262
Russo-Chinese Bank, 257
Russo-Japanese Agreement, (1896) 44; (1898) 59–60; (1907) 360
Russo-Japanese war, Chs. XIII and XIV *passim*, 376; Britain's neutrality in, 273–9, 283, 292, 298; and peace moves, 293–7

Saigō Tsugumichi, Marquis, 119, 158, 193–4
Saionji Kimmochi, Prince, 35, 101, 130, 164, 266, 348
Salisbury, 3rd Marquess of, biog., 102–3, 247; as foreign secretary (1895–1900), 39, 43–4, 48, 63, 65, 234, 243; on policy to Japan, 39–41; on 1898 crisis, 49, 50, 51–2, 56; on Boxer disturbances, 81, 83, 84, 104–6; as prime minister (1900–2), 113–16, 131, 134, 176, 204; and alliance, 145–6, 148, 178, 208–11, 370
Samuel, Sir Marcus, 277
Samuel Samuel & Co., 255, 277
Sanderson, Sir Thomas H., 126, 223, 240, 249, 258
Satow, Sir Ernest M., 38–9, 40, 43, 53, 61, 70, 78–9, 142, 144–5, 146
Scotsman, 226
Selborne, 2nd Earl of, biog., 103; and far eastern naval policy, 174–8, 181; and first alliance, 208, 213–14, 251; and Russo-Japanese war, 273–5
Seoul–Fusan railway, 259–60
Seymour, Sir Edward H., Admiral, 83, 86
Shanghai, 25
Shibusawa Eiichi, 72, 254, 259
Shimonoseki Peace Conference, 27–8
Shimonoseki treaty, 30–4
Sino-Japanese war, Ch. I *passim*

Sino-Japanese treaty (1905), 348
Sistan, 314–16, 325, 361
Smith, Erasmus P., 3
Sone Arasuke, Viscount, 132, 158, 170
South African war, 63, 81, 175–6, 249
South Manchurian railway, 100, 349–50
Spanish-American war, 67
Spectator, 226, 343
Spencer, 5th Earl of, 224
Spring Rice, *see* Rice
Stübel, Dr Oskar W., 135
Suematsu Kenchō, Viscount, 13 n. 2, 284–6, 304
Sugiyama Akira, 83

Taft, William H., 329–30
Taft-Katsura conversation, 330
Takahashi Korekiyo, 287–8, 349
Takahira Kogorō, Baron, 69, 152
T'ang Shao-yi, 256
Terauchi Masatake, General, 87–8, 293, 328
The Times, 226, 301, 343, 368
Three-power intervention, 26–7, 29–35, 49, 219
Tibet, 314, 325, 361
Tōa Dōbunkai, 74
Tōgō Heihachirō, Admiral Marquis, 8, 323, 347
Tokutomi Iichirō, 169, 226
Tōyama Mitsuru, 109
Treaty revision, 76
Triple entente (1907), 362
Triplice, *see* Three-power intervention
Tsar, *see* Nicholas II
Tsingtao, *see* Kiaochow
Tsuzuki Keiroku, 69, 168, 186, 197
Tweedmouth, 2nd Baron, 353

Uchida Yasuya, Count, 192
United States, 16, 67; and first alliance, 222; and Manchuria, 259, 264–5; and Russo-Japanese war, 293–7; and second alliance, 300, 321, 328–30, 339–40, 363–4; and growing hostility to Japan, 350, 353, 377

Victoria, Queen, 48

Waeber-Komura agreement (1895), 44
Waldersee, General Alfred Count von, 89
Walton, Joseph, 224
Washington Conference, (1921–2), 1–2, 377
Watanabe Kunitake, Viscount, 150
Weihaiwei, 53–7, 347–8
Whitehead, James B., 84, 86
Wilhelm II, emperor of Germany, 46, 89, 104, 124, 127, 221, 338
Witte, S. I., 151, 152, 180, 197–200, 263, 376

Yalu enterprises, 262
Yamagata Aritomo, Marquis, biog., 166, 44–5, 239, 249; policy memoranda (1890), 18; (1900), 93–5; (1901), 130–1; (1906), 356; as prime minister, 69, 72, 100–1; and Boxer disturbances, 82–3, 84, 86, 119; and Itō's visit to Russia (1901), 164, 168–9; and alliance, 130–1, 158, 193, 366; and Russo-Japanese war, 262–3, 266, 268, 293
Yamagata-Lobanov agreement, 44
Yamaguchi Motoomi, General, 89
Yamamoto Gombei, Admiral, biog., 101, 167, 266, 280; and alliance, 173, 213; and naval discussions (1902), 252–3; (1907), 354, 357
Yanaga Chitoshi, 191
Yellow Peril, 285, 309, 377
Yokohama municipality, 255
Yokohama Specie Bank, 254, 288
Yuan Shih-k'ai, 16, 256